Living the urban periphery

Manchester University Press

Living the urban periphery

Infrastructure, everyday life and economic change in African city-regions

Paula Meth, Sarah Charlton, Tom Goodfellow and Alison Todes

with Divine Asafo, Sibongile Buthelezi,
Yohana Eyob, Jennifer Houghton,
Zhengli Huang, Meseret Kassahun Desta,
Tatenda Mukwedeya
and Metadel Sileshi Belihu

MANCHESTER UNIVERSITY PRESS

Copyright © Paula Meth, Sarah Charlton, Tom Goodfellow and Alison Todes 2024

The right of Paula Meth, Sarah Charlton, Tom Goodfellow and Alison Todes to be identified as the authors of this work has been asserted in accordance with the Copyright, Designs and Patents Act 1988.

An electronic version of this book has been made freely available under a Creative Commons (CC BY-NC-ND) licence, thanks to the support of the Economic and Social Research Council (ESRC), which permits non-commercial use, distribution and reproduction provided the author(s) and Manchester University Press are fully cited and no modifications or adaptations are made. Details of the licence can be viewed at https://creativecommons.org/licenses/by-nc-nd/4.0/

Published by Manchester University Press
Oxford Road, Manchester, M13 9PL

www.manchesteruniversitypress.co.uk

British Library Cataloguing-in-Publication Data
A catalogue record for this book is available from the British Library

ISBN 978 1 5261 7121 4 hardback

First published 2024

The publisher has no responsibility for the persistence or accuracy of URLs for any external or third-party internet websites referred to in this book, and does not guarantee that any content on such websites is, or will remain, accurate or appropriate.

Typeset by Newgen Publishing UK

Contents

List of figures	vii
List of tables	ix
Acknowledgements	x
List of abbreviations	xiii
Introduction – Paula Meth, Sarah Charlton, Tom Goodfellow and Alison Todes	1
1 Visions of the urban periphery: Ethiopia and South Africa – Alison Todes and Tom Goodfellow	46
2 Investment and economic change on the urban periphery – Alison Todes, Sarah Charlton and Tom Goodfellow	65
3 Jobs and livelihoods: Accessing work within and beyond the periphery – Alison Todes, Tom Goodfellow and Jennifer Houghton	87
4 Governing the urban peripheries – Tom Goodfellow, Yohana Eyob, Paula Meth, Tatenda Mukwedeya and Alison Todes	112
5 Housing in Addis Ababa: Policy, programmes and lived experience – Zhengli Huang, Tom Goodfellow and Meseret Kassahun Desta	133
6 Housing, history and hope in South Africa's urban peripheries – Sarah Charlton, Alison Todes and Paula Meth	154
7 Peri-urban transformations: Changing land markets and (in)security in peri-urban Accra, Ghana – Divine M. Asafo	186

8 Transport and mobility – Tom Goodfellow, Paula Meth and Sarah Charlton	207
9 Producing places: Services, infrastructure and the public realm – Paula Meth, Sarah Charlton and Alison Todes	226
10 Social differentiation, boredom and crime in the peripheries – Paula Meth, Metadel Sileshi Belihu and Sibongile Buthelezi	252
11 Supermarkets, retail and consumption in peripheral areas – Sarah Charlton and Meseret Kassahun Desta	280
Conclusions – Paula Meth, Sarah Charlton, Tom Goodfellow and Alison Todes	298
Bibliography	313
Index	339

Figures

0.1	Gauteng case studies	17
0.2	eThekwini case studies	19
0.3	Addis Ababa case studies	20
0.4	Living the Peripheries team working at Mangwa, South Africa	23
2.1	Declining Ekandustria	72
2.2	Condominium sites and informal settlements in Addis Ababa	79
2.3	Tulu Dimtu area	82
2.4	Yeka Abado area	84
3.1	Informal economic activity in Yeka Abado	95
3.2	Agricultural activity in Checkers, Winterveld	106
4.1	Political party poster, Waterloo, northern eThekwini	120
5.1	Construction materials and condominium housing in Yeka Abado	144
5.2	View from interior of Tulu Dimtu condominium housing showing incomplete construction	147
6.1	Map of apartheid Bantustans relative to contemporary provinces and metropolitan areas	158
6.2	Forms of self-built or locally constructed housing in Madibeng Hills	163
6.3	Housing improvements in Ekangala	167
6.4	Housing in Molweni	171
6.5	Waterloo	177
6.6	Hammonds Farm	178
6.7	Lufhereng	180

6.8	Canelands with the Verulam railway bridge in the distance	182
7.1	Map of GAMA showing the selected study communities	194
7.2	Different platforms for advertising land sales	200
7.3	Land delivery channels and the issue of legitimacy	203
8.1	Minibus taxis at road intersection, Greater Ekangala	208
8.2	Buses and shared taxis in Yeka Abado	211
8.3	A donkey cart with *bajaj* in the background, Tulu Dimtu	212
8.4	Unsurfaced roads in Rethabiseng	219
8.5	Pavements in Tulu Dimtu	223
9.1	Country Club Developers, Legetafo, Addis Ababa	233
9.2	State provision of ablution facilities, Canelands and Coniston, northern eThekwini	234
9.3	Bus shelter in Molweni	241
9.4	Incomplete public space in Tulu Dimtu	248
10.1	Informal church in Waterworks	257
11.1	Informal micro-retail in Hammonds Farm	285
11.2	Retail space in Yeka Abado	287
11.3	Protea Glen Mall	292

Tables

0.1	Summaries of all cases	14
0.2	Common and differential characteristics of urban peripheries	26
7.1	The range of prices of land in peri-urban Accra	195

Acknowledgements

Writing this book has been a lengthy task and has drawn on the skills, knowledge and generous support and labour of a wide group of people. We would like to thank these people and organisations and acknowledge the part they played in bringing this book to fruition, while taking full responsibility for the arguments contained herein.

The book is based on a research project, Living the Peripheries: Investment, Infrastructure and Economic Change in African City Regions, funded by the UK's Economic and Social Research Council (ESRC) and South Africa's National Research Foundation, in terms of the Newton Urban Transformation Programme over the 2016–19 period. Without this funding, the research would not have been possible.

We would like to thank members of the international advisory board for the original project, who provided valuable advice at various stages. These include the late Professor Vanessa Watson (University of Cape Town (UCT)); Professor Paul Jenkins (Wits University); Dr Rob Moore (Gauteng City-Region Observatory (GCRO)); Rashid Seedat (Gauteng Provincial Government); Dr Geci Karuri-Sabine (South African Cities Network (SACN)); Dr Mark Napier (the Council for Scientific and Industrial Research (CSIR)); and Professor Cathy Sutherland and Glen Robbins (the University of KwaZulu-Natal (UKZN)).

Our understanding of the Addis Ababa context was supported by Dr Ephream Gebremariam; Eyob Balcha Gebremariam (University of Bristol); Professor Fasil Giorghis, Tesfaye Hailu and Dr Elias Yitbarek Alemayehu (Addis Ababa University); Dr Selamawit

Acknowledgements

Robi (University of Sheffield); Dr Ezana Haddis (University of Manchester); Dr Robin Bloch (ICF International); Dr Tim Conway (formerly of the Foreign, Commonwealth and Development Office (FCDO)); Dr Alazar Ejigu (academic and freelance architect, Sweden); Dr Jason Mosely (independent researcher); Dr Marco di Nunzio (academic, University of Birmingham); Dr Sabine Planel (the National Research Institute for Sustainable Development (IRD), Paris); and Dr Sarah Vaughan (University of Edinburgh). We are very grateful for their various inputs.

Although some are co-authors of this book, we want to issue a wide and big thank you to the various researchers in multiple cities who supported our collection of data, data analysis and follow-up support hosting stakeholder events, photographic expeditions and writing. We thank Dr Jennifer Houghton, Dr Tatenda Mukwedeya, Dr Zhengli Huang, Dr Meseret Kassahun Desta, Metadel Sileshi Belihu, Fikile Masikane, Sibongile Buthelezi, Israel Tesfu, Yohanna Eyob and Dudu Khumalo. We could not have completed this book without you!

We'd like to thank researchers who supported our stakeholder events, post-data collection analysis and tidying up of draft texts and referencing, including Spencer Robinson, Isabella Langton Kendal, Mitchell Chikowero, Dr Cara Mazetti Claasen and Anna Williams.

We are indebted to the various community leaders, residents, academics, government officials and other urban actors who offered both their time and energy during our inception events, participated in our data collection and then attended our different city stakeholder events and provided constructive and insightful feedback on our earlier findings and their relevance for local and policy audiences. The project and this book would not exist without their efforts.

We thank staff at the South African Research Chair on Spatial Analysis and City Planning (SA&CP) at the School of Architecture and Planning, Wits University, including Dr Margot Rubin, Professor Phil Harrison and GCRO staff including Dr Richard Ballard, Dr Ngaka Mosiane and Graeme Gotz, for their input into the project, including initial project conceptualisation, case study selection, survey preparation and contextual understanding.

Thammy Jezile from SA&CP supported administration of the research project for several years.

The affiliated students on the wider project at Wits University – Abraham Abijade, Jasmine Ramoseu, Thandi Foto, Siya Dywili, Tsebe Hanyane, Unathi Kabale, Kimberley Khumalo, Thabang Dolo, Adelaide Nkoane, Nonhlanhla Mathibela, Nonhlanhla Nkosi, Sarah Makwebo and Tinyiko Ngomane – undertook linked research and provided valuable insights. We also thank the University of Sheffield for supporting the funding of Dr Divine Asafo, then a doctoral student affiliated to the project and ultimately a key contributor to this book – his insights and understanding in the Ghanaian context have been invaluable.

We are deeply grateful to Mark Lewis, a professional photographer who captured the peripheries within Ethiopia and South Africa for the peripheries project; through Mark we've learnt the power of the visual, and his role in supporting an exhibition of the images and expanding engagement with our understanding of the peripheries cannot be overstated.

We would like to thank Michela du Sart and Frank Sokolic from EduAction for several of the maps and geographic information system (GIS) analysis, Progressus Research and Development Consultancy for the South African survey and Thomas Zenawi and his team at TZG General Development Research for the survey work in Ethiopia. Alexandra Appelbaum undertook some mapping and GIS analysis, conducted several interviews and set up the website for the project: www.wits.ac.za/urbanperiphery.

We are very grateful to the editors and staff at Manchester University Press, including Tom Dark, Shannon Kneis and Laura Swift, for their support, guidance and advice. We would also like to warmly thank Pete Gentry (Pete Gentry Editorial) for copy-editing our manuscript, Derika van Biljon (Lexia Language Service) for her indexing work, and Sarah Rendell, Gail Welsh and Tanis Eve (Newgen) for leading the book's production.

Finally, we would like to thank our families for their support and patience while we have held countless 'peripheries book' online meetings and for giving us the time and space to explore this topic in depth.

Abbreviations

AACA	Addis Ababa City Administration
AAGHP	Addis Ababa Grand Housing Programme
AAHDPO	Addis Ababa Housing Development Project Office
ADLI	Agricultural Development-Led Industrialisation
ANC	African National Congress
BEPP	Built Environment Programme Plans
BNG	Breaking New Ground
BRT	Bus Rapid Transit
CCD	Country Club Developers
CBD	central business district
CLS	Customary Land Secretariate
COJ	City of Johannesburg
COT	City of Tshwane
DA	Democratic Alliance
DTP	Dube TradePort
EFF	Economic Freedom Fighters
EPRDF	Ethiopian People's Revolutionary Democratic Front
EPWP	Expanded Public Works Programme
ETB	Ethiopian birr
GAMA	Greater Accra Metropolitan Area
GIZ	German Technical Cooperation (formally GTZ)
GTP	Growth and Transformation Plan
IHDP	Integrated Housing Development Programme
KDC	KwaNdebele Development Corporation
MEGA	Mpumalanga Economic Development Agency
MSE	micro and small enterprises

NDPP	Neighbourhood Partnership Development Programme
PASDEP	Plan for Accelerated and Sustained Development to End Poverty
PSNP	Productive Safety Net Programme
PWP	Public Works Programme
RDP	Reconstruction and Development Programme
SA	South Africa
SACN	South African Cities Network
SASSA	South African Social Security Agency
SDF	Spatial Development Framework
SEZ	special economic zone
SSA	sub-Saharan Africa
UPSNJP	Urban Productive Safety Net and Jobs Project
URP	Urban Renewal Programme
ZAR	South African rand

Introduction

Paula Meth, Sarah Charlton, Tom Goodfellow and Alison Todes

Living the urban periphery: an introduction to the introduction

This book builds on the burgeoning interest in urban peripheries, suburbs and frontiers: the spaces in which much contemporary global population growth is being made. While the megacities of Asia and Latin America and their varied forms of spatial expansion have spawned a substantial literature, the literature on African urbanisms (particularly beyond the central city itself) is still nascent. Such areas are often viewed as a geographic extension of the dynamics of marginality, informality and unplanned urbanisation that characterise African cities in general. Where African urban peripheries are considered in their own right, the literature often focuses on specific challenges associated with urban sprawl and peri-urban development, such as transport, informal construction and infrastructure deficits, or traditional land systems and land use change. This book takes up the challenge of examining African urban peripheries holistically, not just as spaces on the city edge but as new socio-economic environments that give rise to distinct patterns and dilemmas of urban life.

We argue that these urban peripheries cannot adequately be understood from a bird's-eye perspective that views them primarily as products of urban expansion; rather, they are formed by a number of distinct *logics* enacted by states, private developers, households and communities. Moreover, while these logics are identifiable in the way different urban peripheries are evolving, this is only half of the picture. Since the evolution of these places is often contingent and unpredictable, we also need to dig deep into the *experience* of life in the periphery to understand these urban formations and their implications. *Living the urban periphery* therefore employs a dual focus on logics of the periphery and experiences of the periphery, and how these intersect (and diverge) on the ground. It argues that this dual lens provides novel insights, illustrating how urban peripheries are spaces in which dynamism and stagnation can co-exist in ways that cannot be captured by dominant ideas about either surburbanism or marginality.

We explore these dynamics through the experiences of city-regions in two strategically selected countries – Ethiopia and South Africa – with supplementary material from Ghana. This gives the book substantial continental breadth, encompassing cases in East, Southern and West Africa respectively, as well as highly divergent precolonial, colonial and postcolonial experiences. Yet the decision to base this study primarily on South Africa and Ethiopia also reflects a deliberate choice to focus on countries where there have been particularly notable large-scale policy initiatives that have transformed urban peripheries, either deliberately (as in Ethiopia and in some South African cases) or largely as a side effect of efforts to overcome urban spatial legacies (as in post-apartheid South Africa). Rather than this making these two countries exceptional, we argue that substantial amounts of investment in urban peripheries – paired with significant neglect of others – represent the experience of many African cities writ large, or ahead of time. The state investment and private speculation on the urban fringe that these cases present therefore offer a lens on processes that are unfolding, albeit at varying paces, across the continent. Moreover, choosing these cases allows for exploration of urban peripheral dynamics beyond those that dominate the existing literature, which are centred on processes of incremental change, auto-construction and informality. These things exist in our cases, certainly; but we also emphasise the need to see peripheries as places of (sometimes massive) state investment, grandiose speculative endeavours as well as inherited governmental obligations. If urban peripheries are where African futures are being made, then such futures are unfolding particularly vividly and variously in Ethiopia and South Africa.

The book makes a number of key contributions. First, it provides a significant conceptual contribution, by tying together a body of literature focusing on urban peripheries (including that examining the peri-urban, frontiers, suburbanisms, etc.) and exploring the analytical value of these in relation to African cities. It offers a fresh conceptual framing of African peripheries in the form of five logics of the periphery which are used to structure and interpret much of the subsequent analysis.

Second, the book makes an important empirical contribution, by analysing and engaging with a substantive body of fresh empirical data and through the inclusion of authors researching African peripheries. As such, it helps to address the paucity of data and debate on peripheral spaces within African cities, given the more common focus on the central districts of large cities or the tendency to explore distinct urban processes, such as housing, informal development, transport or the politics of land. The book offers the reader understanding and knowledge of spaces, processes and experiences of urban peripheries at multiple scales (namely national, city-region, neighbourhood/settlement and house), and it uses a mix of visual, numerical and qualitative data to reveal key findings.

Third, the book offers an important example and exercise in urban comparison, both within city-regions and countries and between different countries. This intellectual and methodological approach advances wider calls (see Robinson, 2016, 2022) for comparative urbanism which supports 'a more global urban analysis', given that African contexts are still under-represented in comparative discussions. It is primarily focused on comparisons between Ethiopia and South Africa, and across cases within these contexts, but includes a contribution from a scholar working in Ghana. Comparison is facilitated by the conceptual framework and methodological approach detailed below and is used to contrast wider structural processes shaping urban peripheries as well as to note similarities and differences in residents' experiences of these urban changes.

Fourth, the book illustrates the intellectual and methodological value of adopting an everyday lens to understand processes of urban transformation in African cities, relevant to cities globally. It makes a strong case for the benefits of privileging residents' voices, understanding their perspectives and concerns, and using these to really interrogate wider narratives of urban change and illustrate how growth, investment, decline and infrastructural change actually translate on the ground. Through this methodological approach the book reveals how what appear to be concrete urban outcomes are experienced in highly diverse ways, as well as embodying deep tensions, contradictions and openness to change. This challenges conceptualisations and categorisations of places and practices which often seek fixed labels and interpretations, and we argue that a more fluid and textured analysis is required.

Finally, the book speaks to urban actors, policymakers, government officials, planners, community organisations and those working to shape urban transformation in city peripheries at multiple scales. It reveals how state and other interventions have unintended consequences, how legacies of historical policy choices play out decades after implementation and how policy disjunctures and contestations at local levels impact on residents, commonly the urban poor. The book details examples of successful or meaningful urban practices including governance arrangements, neighbourhood scale designs and micro-infrastructures which positively shape everyday life. It also points to the absence of policy or infrastructural interventions which could significantly alter residents' lives for the better and examines the consequences of these absences for urban lives that increasingly play out in the periphery.

Locating the book: existing conceptualisations of urban peripheries

A growing literature has emerged to capture and explain urban transformations occurring on city edges. Propelled in part by studies showing the significance of urban expansion in urban spatial change (Angel *et al.*, 2011, 2016) and their diversity, drivers and dynamics, new literatures on suburbanisation (Keil, 2018; Keil and Wu, 2022), peri-urbanisation (Follman, 2022; Follman *et al.*, 2022), 'peripheral urbanisation' (Caldeira, 2017) and new cities (Van Noorloos and Kloosterboer, 2018; Cote-Roy and Moser, 2019) have emerged to understand processes of change. Recent initiatives to reconceptualise and provide new vocabularies for 'planetary urbanisation' (Brenner and Schmid, 2015) have also been generative in exploring forms of urban peripheral growth (Schmid *et al.*, 2018; Howe, 2022; Sawyer *et al.*, 2021).

Earlier conceptualisations of urban peripheries focused on their location on the edge, either in the classic form of the late-twentieth-century Euro-American suburb (e.g. Schnore, 1957; Fishman, 1989) or as places transitioning from rural to urban on the city's 'fringe' (Pryor, 1968). While distant from economic cores, these spaces were often seen as providing developers with strategic opportunities to maximise profits (Henderson and Mitra, 1996). Processes of change might occur incrementally or through larger developments, enabled by the lower cost and availability of land. Hence the urban periphery was inevitably seen as a moving edge.

With regard to Africa and the Global South more generally, the broad concept of 'peri-urbanisation' has been important in exploring this urban-rural interface and the associated changes in land uses and livelihoods (Simon, 2020). Follman (2022) argues that the term 'peri-urban' has been used loosely and taken on different dimensions in Global North and Global South contexts, with the former exploring the mix of urban and rural uses and the latter emphasising unplanned, informal, illegal and incremental growth on the urban edge. Within the literature on peri-urbanisation, considerable attention has been given to the way tenurial systems shape these processes of urban spatial change, especially in African cities where customary forms of tenure are prevalent (Mbiba and Huchzermeyer, 2002). Ghana, where customary tenure reaches deep into cities, has been a particular focus (Gough and Yankson, 2000).

While earlier literature emphasised that these less regulated spaces provided cheaper housing for the urban poor, and urban access for rural migrants (Simon, 2004), more recent studies point to the growth of middle-class housing in urban peripheries (Mercer, 2017), including in some contexts on traditional authority lands (Bartels, 2019/20), patterns also evident in the South African context (Mbatha and Mchunu, 2016). Research on Ghana shows the intricate relationships between the state and traditional leaders in land development and how commodification of customary land is enabling large-scale property development there and leading to exclusion of those who might once have had usufructuary rights to land (Aakateba, 2019; Anane, 2021). In the face of these changes, authors are exploring more complex conceptualisations of peri-urbanisation, encapsulating a more diverse set of processes which often produce substantial precarity on the periphery even as they also enhance infrastructural connectivity (Kanai and Schindler, 2022).

As Follman (2022) argues in a review of the peri-urbanisation literature, existing conceptualisations of the peri-urban tend to focus on one of three vectors. The first involves *territorial* dimensions (such as distinct planning processes and boundary issues), the second *functional* ones (such as flows and interactions between rural and urban spheres) and the third *transitional* dimensions (such as the process of urban growth and the fluid/'frontier' nature of these places). In fact, Follman argues, it is difficult to distinguish the process of 'peri-urbanisation' from the process of urbanisation itself, people tending to adopt the former term when they want to focus on the specific spatial dynamics of places 'beyond city limits' and because they want to highlight some of the contingent and fluid ways in which urbanisation occurs in the Global South specifically (Follman, 2022).

When we move beyond the term 'peri-urban' to think about the 'urban periphery' more broadly, we are also confronted with a range of social, economic and political questions associated with peripheries and peripherality. These include the issue of social class. The growth of middle-class housing and major developments on the periphery present challenges to literature equating geographic peripherality with poverty and economic marginality. Mosiane and Gotz's (2022) work on Gauteng further argues that places that might have been born out of displacement and marginalisation on the urban edge can nevertheless become spaces of 'displaced urbanism' with levels of entrepreneurial 'bottom-up' dynamism. A simple core–periphery binary is also questioned by Peberdy (2017) and Pieterse (2019) who note the deep poverty and social marginality in central cities within Gauteng and the complex multidirectional patterns of movement and living within the polycentric region. These critiques are important in avoiding simplistic assumptions about the spatial periphery, who lives there and why. Yet, given that geographically peripheral areas are so complex and often rapidly changing, we need to go further to understand the places themselves and the diverse lived experiences there.

Like Peberdy (2017), who draws on Wallerstein's conception of periphery as social and political rather than spatial, Caldeira sees peripheral urbanisation as 'a way of producing space' (2017: 4), equating it with auto-construction that unfolds 'transversally in relation to official logics, and amidst political contestations'. This can involve dynamism, entrepreneurialism and collective action, including on urban edges but not only there. Caldeira's account is important in focusing on one of the significant processes through which urban areas grow and change, but it does not tell us specifically about processes on the spatial periphery and their multifaceted dynamics. As we argue in this book, notwithstanding the importance of social and political peripheralisation and how this affects the production of urban space, it is important not to lose sight of the specific dimensions of *geographic* peripherality within cities and city-regions, which have profound and concrete effects on the lives of people in the urban outskirts.

While several of these conceptions focus largely on incremental growth, literatures emanating initially from the USA in the 1990s pointed to the emergence of major new economic centralities on the urban edge (Garreau, 1991) and the growth of new forms of residential and mixed-use estates (including gated communities), much of it driven by the private sector or through public–private partnerships. These processes are also evident in the Global South, including in Africa and on customary land, and are increasingly documented in the peri-urbanisation literature as well, with attempts to expand the concept to include these processes. The 'Global Suburbanisms' project from 2009 set out to explore the many forms of non-central growth now emerging, expanding the concept of 'suburban' beyond its North American middle-class/mid-twentieth-century associations (Keil, 2018). A key focus has been the physical growth at scale of residential neighbourhoods across diverse urban localities worldwide, as well as the transformation of existing suburban space (Güney *et al.*, 2019), emphasising differentiation among and within suburban spaces. Ren (2021) examines the growing body of global suburban studies and identifies through analyses of urban peripheral India, Latin America and China how infrastructure failure, transforming governance and popular resistance reveal a broadened politics of suburbs and facilitate a broadened, international and comparative approach to urban peripheries.

Taking an African focus, the review of Bloch *et al.* (2022: 306) for the Global Suburbanisms project[1] highlighted city peripheries as places 'where the constant movement of urban frontiers is not merely extending the existing city but creating new configurations and spaces for different urbanisms'. This challenges the idea of an ever-expanding 'edge'. They go on to emphasise that 'older areas ... reveal very rapid changes of people and buildings, and activities', while at the same time 'new centralities have emerged, since both peripheral expansion and redevelopments in older areas destabilised former centralities as they remade patterns of urban life and movement'. Bloch (2015) pointed to growth of the middle class and economic expansion underpinning new forms of urban development on the periphery – trends echoed by Mercer (2017, 2020). The relevance of 'suburbanism' in African contexts has been debated (Bloch *et al.*, 2022). Andreasen *et al.* (2017) and Mercer (2017) embrace the term 'suburb' in the context of Dar es Salaam, arguing that it better describes households moving from the centre to the periphery to build housing incrementally than peri-urbanisation does. Writing about Lagos, Sawyer (2014), on the other hand, argues that suburb has little meaning for households on the periphery, where forms of 'piecemeal urbanisation' are occurring that bear little resemblance to the idea of the suburb. Karaman *et al.* (2020) argue that these and similar processes across the world are better described by the concept of 'plotting urbanism'. The process of 'plotting' refers to the commodification and subdivision of land plots to create constantly adapting spatial arrangements rooted in territorial compromise and conflict. This is not exclusive to urban peripheries, but often dominates within them. By contrast, Buire (2014) finds that urban peripheries are providing new 'orderly' suburban lifestyles and homeownership in large, new, state-led apartment developments some twenty–thirty kilometres from Luanda. Across diverse forms of state-sponsored housing in Southern African urban peripheries, including in Maputo (Melo, 2017), Durban and Johannesburg (Charlton and Meth, 2017), there are complex resident experiences that reflect the 'everyday realities' of establishing lives in new edge localities (Lemanski *et al.*, 2017). While these studies suggest that different forms of housing and lifestyles are emerging in urban peripheries, they are all associated with very long commutes exacerbated by poor infrastructure, suggesting that being *spatially* peripheral produces distinctive experiences of the urban.

Importantly, it is also now widely recognised that the geographic peripheries of cities are not necessarily places of gradual and piecemeal change but also sites of sometimes dramatic renewal and city 'visioning', including on the part of central and local states. Indeed, a key aspect of contemporary urban peripheries is the extent to which these areas are 'outside exclusive state control but at the same time ... reflect state developmental intention' (Wu and Keil, 2022: n.p.). Recent literature points to the growth of 'new cities' (mainly satellites) in Africa (e.g. Van Noorloos and Kloosterboer, 2018; Cote-Roy and Moser, 2019). Linked to 'the assumption that African markets are poised for unprecedented growth' (Cote-Roy and Moser, 2019: 2359), new cities are being promoted by both private developers in search of profitable real estate markets (Van Noorloos and Kloosterboer, 2018) and entrepreneurial states seeking to attract investment by re-imaging their cities (Cote-Roy and Moser, 2019). In practice, most developments are large, upmarket, residential schemes, despite claims that they will be inclusionary and multifunctional (Cote-Roy and Moser, 2019). In contrast to previous 'new town' approaches, contemporary forms are more often residential (sometimes coupled with special economic zones (SEZs)), driven by private developers or through partnerships (Harrison and Todes, 2017). Even where 'new cities' are not a feature, ideas of 'infrastructure-led development' have become increasingly important to the logic of urban expansion and interconnection (Schindler and Kanai, 2021), often transforming previously peripheral locations directly or speculatively through 'promises of connectivity' (Kanai and Schindler, 2019).

While much discourse around new cities emphasises economic growth and modernisation, the history of satellites as places of failed growth, decline or economic instability needs to be noted (Kanai and Schindler, 2019). More generally, much of the literature on urban peripheries emphasises new growth, or the consolidation of rural or informal settlements that might have emerged incrementally. There is less work on the transformation of large existing housing estates and 'townships' on the urban edge, which emerged in the context of earlier histories (but see Lemanski *et al.*, 2017; Güney *et al.*, 2019). Previous urban edge development is important in South Africa, given apartheid histories, but not unique to it. The spatial inheritance of urban peripheries, and how this can relate to decline as well as growth, is thus significant. As Follman (2022) argues, along with attention to 'the *not-yet-urban*' (which is implied in peri-urbanisation discourses), we need also to consider places that might have long been urban, and even those that could be considered '*not-urban-any more*'.

Recent research on peri-urbanisation, suburbanism and urban peripheries has generated considerable debate and new conceptualisations of the extensive processes of change occurring. Researchers have proposed extending concepts of peripheralisation, with even the Global Suburbanisms project ultimately turning away from the idea of the suburb. In the case of China, for example, they argue that 'the urban periphery, with its salient feature of heterogeneity, is becoming a more meaningful category' (Wu and Keil, 2022: n.p.). In the project's final edited collection, peripheral change is framed not as suburbanism but as 'a form of planetary and extended urbanization … that is sensitive to historical temporality and geographical contingencies' (Wu and Keil, 2022: 12). The 'planetary urbanisation' concept itself, and associated projects drawing on the Lefebvrian idea of 'extended urbanisation', generated diverse concepts to think about specific forms of urban transformation on the periphery. These range from the 'plotting urbanism' discussed above (Karaman *et al.*, 2020) to 'bypass urbanism' (Sawyer *et al.*, 2021), 'toehold' and 'aspirational' urbanisation (Howe, 2022) and more. This surge in literature on diverse urban peripheries around the world, and how they might be better described, demonstrates Wu and Keil's point that we live in a world of 'variegated forms of peripheral urbanization' (Wu and Keil, 2022: 29), which are likely to continue to evolve, posing challenges for dominant understandings of urban form.

Our work contributes to this growing scholarship to inform grounded, contextualised understandings of peripheral urban change. We conceptualise urban peripheries in a way that is both spatial and deliberately broad: as geographical edges of cities or city-regions that may have their own internal centralities and margins, may be 'new', 'old', rich or poor and can have varied histories as rural or urban spaces – but crucially are perceived by residents as being in some sense remote and having limited accessibility to a primary 'core' or relevant urban hubs. This breadth allows us to unpack the varying logics that shape different kinds of periphery and to differentiate the overall concept from other associated concepts in the literature. Thus, the periphery can encompass spaces at much greater distances from traditional 'cores' than are associated with the term 'suburb', including places at the edge of city-regions beyond reasonable commuting distance, and sometimes infrastructurally disconnected from the urban core rather than contiguous. However, peripheries are not necessarily *marginal* in that they may themselves be economic hubs and spaces of new centralities (Mabin *et al.*, 2013; Keil, 2018). Nor are they necessarily *frontiers* in the sense of being spaces imagined as previously vacant, in which the state seeks to establish new territorial authority and socio-spatial reordering (Simone, 2011; Rasmussen and Lund, 2017; McGregor and Chatiza, 2019). In short, an urban periphery *may* be a suburb, marginal or frontier space, but equally might be none of these – or all of them.

As this review of the literature has shown – and Keil and Wu (2022) have recently argued – most of the current and recent literature on urban peripheries focuses on questions of land, infrastructure and (to a lesser extent) governance. The latter issue is certainly an area for further exploration because of both the significant role of regions and regional administrations in governing large urban conurbations (Keil *et al.*, 2016) and because of the often complex boundary issues associated with the spilling of metropolitan areas beyond municipal and city borders (Beall *et al.*, 2015; Cirolia, 2020; Goodfellow and Mukwaya, 2021). As Horn (2022) notes with respect to La Paz, Bolivia, it is often not state absence that defines development in the urban periphery but the lack of clarity around boundaries and consequent 'hyper-regulation' by multiple scales of authority. But even aside from these formal governance challenges, it is often far from clear who the key actors are in governing urban peripheries, and when collaboration or collusion among these actors tips into conflict and contestation. The presence of state agendas in urban peripheries, alongside a significant absence of state authority in many cases, produces 'intertwined modalities of governance' (Wu and Keil, 2022) that require further analysis.

Our book contributes to unpacking these dimensions of the periphery, while also expanding on a dimension that is sidelined in much of the above literature: the everyday lived experience of living and working in African urban peripheries. We turn now to detail the methodologies informing our embrace of the everyday as a critical lens into African peripheries, before outlining our conceptual framework which structures much, but not all, of our analyses in subsequent chapters.

Our book's methodology: using a lived experience comparative urban approach

A lived experience approach, where on-the-ground experiences of places and of urban change are centrally positioned within data collection, analysis and interpretation, underpins the entirety of this book. Indeed the conceptual framework of this text is derived from a foundational grounded analysis approach, where our varying logics emerged through an engagement with the stories and accounts of residents living in peripheral spaces of African cities. This intellectual and methodological appreciation of lived experiences has substantial traction within geography, urban studies and planning. Work in these disciplines is frequently inspired by urban anthropology (De Boeck and Plissart, 2004; Ross, 2010; Bank, 2011) and sociological studies (Mosoetsa, 2011) which observe how people work, live, move, consume, eat, sleep, parent (Meth, 2013), love and die in different places. In contrast, much research of the urban, especially studies informing meta-scale urban interventions, often establishes quantitative outcomes through a reliance on survey instruments. Elsewhere, we have argued against the paucity of understanding of the social outcomes and lived experiences of major infrastructural interventions, as well as more micro-scaled material transformations (see Charlton, 2018b; Goodfellow and Huang, 2021; Meth *et al*., 2022). These interventions are powerful drivers of change at the local scale and can include state-provided housing, investments in transport and the provision of sanitation facilities in informal settlements, among others. We've examined how state housing directly shapes livelihood challenges, capacities to move and travel, experiences of safety and identity, which themselves are structured by gendered differences impacting on relations of power, and violence (Meth and Charlton, 2016; Charlton and Meth, 2017). In this book we advance these insights into the lived experiences of key drivers of urban change through an explicitly grounded approach, resting on strong research collaboration, case study urban comparison and engagement with residents and other key urban actors. The book's arguments draw on a methodological logic where differentiated everyday experiences of urban change are examined comparatively.

Lived experiences through case studies

All the chapters in this book draw on a case study approach to understand urban change and the lived experiences thereof in the African urban peripheries. Chapter 7 focuses on the city of Accra and draws on four distinct case studies, namely Oyibi, Abokobi, Achiaman and Oshiyie, using a qualitative methodology to examine peri-urban land markets and land transaction practices therein. Methodological detail and case descriptions are presented within the chapter (and see Figure 7.1 which shows their location within Greater Accra beyond the Accra Metropolis boundary). The cases reveal that landownership is predominantly customary but also includes religious institutions and individual families. All other chapters draw on data generated through the Living the Peripheries project, which adopted a comparative and multinodal case study approach. Seven case study areas across three city-regions (Addis Ababa, Gauteng and eThekwini) were selected, containing distinct nodes. Each node was characterised differently but commonly included varied housing forms, revealing different classes of residents with diverse histories of urban presence and experience. See Table 0.1 for a summary of all the cases.

Although the Living the Peripheries project eschewed strictly uniform criteria for case selection, location within a geographic periphery, where some form of investment (broadly defined) had occurred, was a key criterion. Case selection included areas of decline, including those of historic investment and current collapse. The seven cases are not necessarily comparable in terms of the geographic areas they cover, their population numbers, etc.; rather, they are variously multinodal, capturing a diversity of lives on the periphery.

Diversity of everyday life is not unique to urban peripheries, and neither is the variety of urban change evident therein. However, what is specific to urban peripheries is that these trajectories of

Table 0.1 Summaries of all cases

City-region	Case study	Characteristics
Accra	Oyibi	Lying to the north-east of Accra, Oyibi is a rapidly growing peri-urban settlement dominated by private individual houses and several gated communities. Haphazard development is evidence of intense contention over land among landowners (see Figure 7.1).
Accra	Abokobi	Abokobi, a peri-urban settlement situated north of Accra, plays a crucial administrative role as the capital of the Ga East district. Complex tenure insecurities and haphazard development are consequences of the rapid and unguided transformation of the customary land market (see Figure 7.1).
Accra	Achiaman	Located north-west of Accra, Achiaman constitutes indigenous peri-urban settlements with vast land for housing development. The expansion of the community into new areas is characterised by different housing structures built by mostly middle-income and high-income individuals; however, many of these structures experience intense tenure insecurities (see Figure 7.1).
Accra	Oshiyie	Located in Accra's north-west, Oshiyie is an indigenous and thriving coastal community witnessing rapid expansion towards its inland territories. Characterised by vast available land, housing is commonly at different levels of completion, evidencing the challenges surrounding property ownership (see Figure 7.1).
Gauteng	Lufhereng/ Protea Glen/ Waterworks	Located to the west of Soweto in the city of Johannesburg, Lufhereng is a mixed housing development with substantial RDP housing; Protea Glen is privately

Table 0.1 (Cont.)

City-region	Case study	Characteristics
		owned, lower-middle-income housing; Waterworks was an informal settlement, now demolished (see Figure 0.1).
Gauteng	Ekangala/ Rethabiseng/ Dark City	This set of settlements is located in eastern Tshwane near Bronkhorstspruit and the declining Ekandustria industrial park. Ekangala was an apartheid relocation site. Post-apartheid housing is largely RDP with informal Phumekaya included (see Figure 0.1).
Gauteng	Winterveld	Lying in northern Tshwane, this is an extensive, mostly low-density area produced through historic displacement. It includes Checkers, with large plots and a mix of RDP and informal housing, and informal Madibeng Hills, falling within neighbouring North West Province (see Figure 0.1).
eThekwini	Northern eThekwini	Located just north of the economic hub of Umhlanga/Gateway, this northern node includes Hammonds Farm, an RDP settlement; Waterloo, an area of consolidated state housing; informal Canelands and Coniston; and Verulam, a former economic centre (see Figure 0.2).
eThekwini	Molweni/ Crestholme	Located to the west, land in Molweni mainly falls under traditional authorities. Housing is mixed, comprising traditional housing, some RDP structures, owner-built houses and rental row housing. Crestholme is middle to upper income with much substantial housing (see Figure 0.2).
Addis Ababa	Yeka Abado/ Legetafo	Located in Addis' north-east, Yeka Abado contains a substantial state condominium settlement of 18,000 units. The area contains informal and displaced farmers'

(continued)

Table 0.1 (Cont.)

City-region	Case study	Characteristics
		housing, as well as a very high-end gated community in Legetafo, located just beyond the city boundary in Oromia region to the east (see Figure 0.3).
Addis Ababa	Tulu Dimtu	This lies in the south-east of Addis, partially over the border into Oromia. As well as a major condominium housing site (10,000 units), it contains a very large but less dense area of cooperative housing and some informal settlements (see Figure 0.3).

growth, decline and mixed settlement are accompanied by geographic distance from urban cores, presenting challenges and also opportunities commonly associated with poorly serviced land which is cheaper and less dense. This chapter, and indeed the entire book, asserts the benefits of analysing urban change at the scale of the periphery through a lived experience perspective, and it is to these particular urban scales and cases that the chapter now turns.

Five cases in total were located within urban South Africa. In Gauteng province three distinct cases (see Figure 0.1) were examined. The Lufhereng/Protea Glen/Waterworks case consists of three different settlements located to the west of Soweto, Johannesburg, on and just beyond the municipal boundary. Lufhereng is a state-subsidised 'mega-human settlement' of mixed-income (including 'RDP')[2] housing located on formerly agricultural land. It was planned for around 20,000 households, and initial phases primarily accommodated beneficiaries from nearby informal settlements. Protea Glen is a lower- to middle-income private sector development with a shopping mall, and Waterworks was an informal settlement marked for relocation to the neighbouring municipality (at the time of the research) and then subsequently demolished. Despite reflecting state and private sector investment, this periphery is distant from the priority growth areas of the municipality, and plans to develop here surfaced city versus provincial governance tensions and competing planning visions (see Charlton, 2017, and Chapter 2).

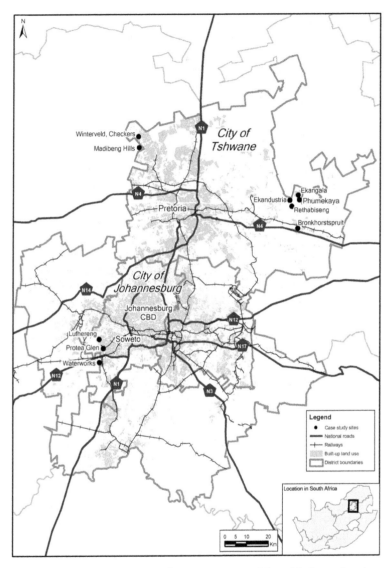

Figure 0.1 Gauteng case studies (source: copyright with the authors)

Ekangala/Rethabiseng/Dark City forms the second Gauteng case, located near the eastern boundary of Tshwane municipality and the town of Bronkhorstspruit. These settlements are a direct product of the apartheid plan to achieve 'white only' urban settlements elsewhere, serving as relocation sites for black people moved into what were then remote locations. The case study site incorporates Ekandustria, established through associated apartheid industrial decentralisation policies (see Chapters 1 and 2), which despite declining remains an economically significant industrial park. Established and more recent RDP properties are abundant in this case alongside private housing forms, and it includes the informal settlement of Phumekaya.

Winterveld is the third Gauteng case, predominantly located in northern Tshwane although also crossing a boundary into the north-west province. This is a sprawling and often poorly serviced site, again a function of apartheid homeland (or Bantustan) policies of forced relocation which produced displaced urbanisation, targeting and peopling peripheral locations. This case includes Checkers, which is a sparsely populated area in the north, and the Madibeng Hills informal settlement located just over the provincial border. A key feature of this case study is the dominance of larger plots, many of which have been illegally subdivided. RDP housing again dominates, alongside informal properties.

Two further cases were located in eThekwini municipality, South Africa (formerly Durban; see Figure 0.2). The northern eThekwini case is located just south of the King Shaka airport and close to the city's growing economic node of Umhlanga/Gateway. This particular case illustrates the idea of relative geographic peripherality owing to its proximate positioning, while the friction of distance persists. The multinodal case includes Hammonds Farm, a recent two-storey RDP housing settlement built on former farmland; the consolidated state housing area of Waterloo; the informal settlements of Canelands/Coniston; and parts of the older commercial and service centre of Verulam. The areas of Molweni and Crestholme form the second eThekwini case. These are located far to the west of the city-region. Peri-urban Molweni dominates the case study in population numbers and scale and includes a mixture of traditional authority land with traditionally constructed houses, frequently on larger plots enabled by tenurial arrangements, as well as some RDP

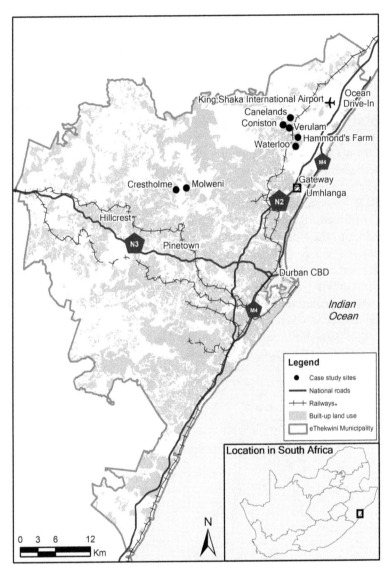

Figure 0.2 eThekwini case studies (source: copyright with the authors)

housing and rental row housing. Crestholme is nearby: this wealthy settlement consists of private and gated properties on substantial plots afforded by relatively lower land prices targeting upper and middle classes. The area contains a recently built shopping mall, also the focus of looting in 2021 (see Chapter 11).

Two multinodal cases were selected in the city-region of Addis Ababa, Ethiopia (see Figure 0.3). Yeka Abado/Legetafo is located in the north-east of the city. It straddles the federal border with Oromia and is predominantly characterised by a substantial new settlement of state-subsidised condominium housing. Around 18,000 housing units are located on former farmland. Unlike the RDP housing units in South Africa, these condominiums are not distributed for free, despite subsidies. Their financial arrangements relate to their distinct housing typologies: the majority are '20/80' condos (where a 20 per cent deposit is needed, with the remaining 80 per cent taken as a bank loan), while the remainder are '10/90' condos (with only a 10 per cent deposit needed), which are much smaller units targeting low-income and displaced households (see UN-Habitat, 2011; Ejigu, 2012; Planel and Bridonneau, 2017; Kassahun and Bishu, 2018). The case study area includes some informal housing areas, displaced farmer settlements and very

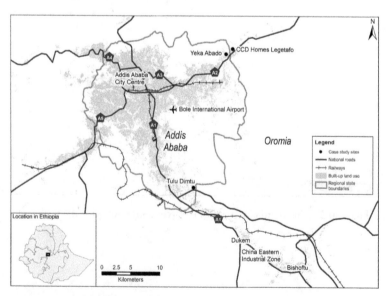

Figure 0.3 Addis Ababa case studies (source: copyright with the authors)

wealthy, upmarket gated communities – including the substantial CCD Homes estate which is located in the neighbouring Legetafo area to the east of the city border.

Tulu Dimtu is the second Addis Ababa case and is located in the south-east of the city. The area also straddles the border with Oromia. Tulu Dimtu encompasses a substantial area of new condominium houses (10,000 units, all of which are the 20/80 type) again built on former farmland. The condo development is bifurcated by a major arterial road. The case includes informal housing and an expansive area of cooperative housing: multistorey, multi-household units developed by residents collaboratively in small groups through a government-sponsored scheme. Although not part of the case, various industrial parks, including a significant Chinese-owned establishment close to the town of Duken, lie just beyond the municipal border. These are within relatively easy reach of Tulu Dimtu, although this case represents significant geographic isolation from the centre of Addis more generally (see Chapter 9).

Methods of data collection and urban comparison

All the cases discussed in this book drew on a mixed-methods approach dominated by the collection of qualitative data in order to undergird an understanding of the lived experiences of urban change in African peripheries. In the four cases within Accra (discussed in detail in Chapter 7), interviews with various actors (e.g. land sellers and house builders) and observations (including of court hearings) were employed to discern the proliferation of actors in the rapidly changing land market and their experiences thereof. Within South Africa and Ethiopia, data collection included initial stakeholder and community workshops to support case study selection and topic focus. These were followed by soliciting around fifty diaries from residents in each case (achieving about 350 in total). Residents were invited to write over a two-week period about their everyday lives in their peripheral settlement, including offering observations on changes or challenges they'd witnessed or experienced over time. A smaller number of residents provided photographs to illustrate issues shared in their diaries, with a few even submitting videos. The research team used these materials to structure subsequent interviews with all participating residents to deepen our understanding of their lived experiences. Interviews were conducted in the local language and translated into English transcripts. As was the case in Accra, Ghana, in both South Africa and Ethiopia, key stakeholders were interviewed, including developers, community leaders, political leaders and planners, to enhance analyses of urban change in the peripheries. Note that quotations from these diaries and interviews used later in the book are all rendered verbatim. Quotes are frequently translations, and we have sought to maintain the integrity of how data was received from research assistants by not tidying up the phrasing significantly.

In the South African and Ethiopian cases, qualitative findings were supported by surveys generating quantitative data. Two hundred surveys were carried out with residents in each case study area, capturing the varying nodes of each case, producing 1,400 surveys in total. Surveys explored residents' movement histories and household composition, employment, quality of housing and services. Our wider analyses were also informed by available statistics and maps, and visual insights through professionally produced images of all the cases by Mark Lewis, a Johannesburg-based photographer.

Our practices of comparison were dynamic and iterative. The book's comparative approach was informed by Robinson's (2016) tactics of 'genetic' and conceptually 'generative' comparison. Our genetic tactics were alert to 'the strongly interconnected genesis of often repeated urban phenomena' (Robinson, 2016: 6) and examined interconnected but differentiated (2016: 18) historical processes, drivers of change and everyday experiences within and across our cases. Alongside this, we employed conceptually generative tactics, namely the choice of 'cases with shared features to generate and revise concepts' (2016: 6), to bring the specificities of cases with their similarities and differences into conversation. These generative tactics were marshalled explicitly to facilitate conceptual innovation.

Opportunities for genetic and 'generative comparison' of all the material analysed within this book were achieved through engaged and collaborative scholarship. Dr Asafo's work on Ghana was an integral component to the overarching Living the Peripheries project, offering a critical intra-African point of comparison. Ghanaian trends, particularly in relation to landownership and state interventions, were read alongside events in South Africa and Ethiopia through multiple conference presentations, seminars and doctoral exchanges with researchers from the University of Sheffield and Wits

University. At the same time, the South African and Ethiopian findings themselves were compared and conceptualised through numerous project team meetings where data and findings were interrogated, multiple joint presentations delivered and writing tasks (Meth *et al.*, 2021b) and targeted stakeholder engagement events completed. The work was further enriched through two exhibitions of photographs commissioned to support our study. These all served to 'provoke and enrich' (Robinson, 2016: 18) our analyses and to underscore the comparative insights, which were frequently visually arresting in their contrasts. These multiple collaborative practices facilitated ongoing comparative discussions on the epistemologies of the peripheries, informing our strategies for interpreting disparities between our quantitative and qualitative data, our disciplinary positions shaping data interpretation and navigating the subtle differences between written and orally narrated accounts of living the peripheries. It was through all these collaborative moments that multiscalar comparisons and divergences were identified, where analytical trends were contested, thrown out, revised and negotiated, where theoretical interconnections were advanced and where we co-produced the conceptual framework detailed subsequently, which informs the wider analyses of this book (see Figure 0.4, one such collaborative moment where our 'conceptual breakthrough' occurred).

Figure 0.4 Living the Peripheries team working at Mangwa, South Africa
(source: Paula Meth, 2018)

The urban periphery as a spatial phenomenon: one concept, five logics

In our discussion of existing conceptualisations of African peripheries above, this book explicitly embeds our understanding of peripheries in terms of geographic particularities understood in part through the lived experiences thereof. We recognise that 'being peripheral' is subjectively experienced and determined, and not necessarily tied to spatial coordinates. However, this book specifically examines the geographic fringes of cities, while not preconceiving these spaces as necessarily politically, economically or culturally peripheral within the wider city-region. We recognise that these fringe spaces include key sites of power, wealth and prestige. Emphasising the geographic qualities of urban peripheries invariably means emphasising distance. The cases discussed in this book, including in Accra, are largely located on the urban edges of cities or city-regions, and accessibility, visibility (particularly by the state) and mobility are central concerns in all areas. However, although all of the cases are distant in commuting terms from a primary urban core, we understand their 'location' in relative terms, taking into account other urban hubs, 'new centralities' and actual and desired destinations, as well as what these distances mean in terms of lived experience. We see these geographic elements of urban peripherality as producing particular urban expressions, and we consciously note the implications of these geographies throughout the book. These speak to our wider claim regarding the empirical and theoretical value of studying urban peripheries, as processes and lived experiences are intimately shaped by the geography of peripheral living. Urban peripheries are therefore relational spaces. This is not just about how people perceive their relationship to 'the city'; there are relational qualities evident at multiple scales. Even within one peripheral area, strongly contrasting neighbourhoods or settlements exist (e.g. wealthy gated estates versus impoverished informal housing) which draw their identities in contradistinction with one another. Moreover, differentiation and relationality also occur between streets and individual plots with varying access to transportation and services, or histories of landownership (evidenced so clearly in the analysis of Accra), which prove to be important axes of inequality.

This book employs our conceptualisation of urban peripheries outlined in Meth *et al.* (2021a) (detailed below) which explicitly builds from the spatial, but together with conceptualising peripheral *areas* of cities also seeks to incorporate and understand *urban processes and practices* and urban *experiences* of different parts of the city. We briefly outline our intellectual journey informing our conceptualisation of urban peripheries, but before doing so we note that this conceptualisation is not the only conceptual 'show on the road' employed in our book. Given the breadth and complexity of this book, with examinations ranging from histories of planning and urban investment to governance, land, housing, transport, conflict, social relations, retail and urban infrastructure, it invariably draws on a wider scholarship informing the lived experiences of urban change in African peripheries. We have taken the choice to detail these wider conceptual debates in particular chapters rather than summarise them here or draw any out for particular distinction. Suffice to say, as we outline our journey towards our dominant conceptual framework now, we acknowledge the significance of multiple other concepts which have proved productive in our interpretation and analysis.

Through collaborative and generative comparison, we mapped out common features across all peripheries (i.e. what makes the urban periphery relevant and meaningful as a generic concept) as well as the factors which differentiate peripheral spaces from each other (see Meth *et al.*, 2021a). These commonalities and differentiating features of urban peripheries are summarised in Table 0.2. This practice facilitated sense-making of the paradox of peripheries being so diverse and yet still a coherent and distinct spatial category for analysis. Some of the individual features identified as common are obviously present in other urban (or rural) areas that we might not consider urban peripheries, but together they are constitutive of urban peripheries. Meanwhile, the binary opposites we identify (some of which co-exist in the same spaces) illustrate the spectrum of variation within and between urban peripheries.

Drawing on our data and analyses, we then identified five 'logics', which each refer to specific sets of practices, processes and experiences associated with urban peripheral spaces. The logics are not all-encompassing or absolute; neither are they hierarchical or exclusive. Instead, they operate in hybrid and overlapping

Table 0.2 Common and differential characteristics of urban peripheries

Common characteristics	Differentiating characteristics
Distant from primary urban 'core'	Proximal to economic hubs/distant from all hubs
Changing forms of land use, often combining urban and rural	Dynamism/stagnation
Actual and perceived distance from job opportunities	Opportunity/marginalisation
Relatively low economic density	Residential density/sparsity
Relatively cheap land; sites of potential or actual speculation	Wealth/poverty Acquisition/dispossession
Infrastructure and service deficits; incremental or unfinished built environments	State absence/state presence; consolidated/unfinished environments
Challenges of accessibility for some residents	Transport options/transport difficulties
Associated with boredom and slower pace of life	Tranquillity/exposure to violence
Place identity defined partly in relation to proximity or access to urban hubs	Connected/isolated; visibility/invisibility

ways: any one case study area may have one or more logics applied to it. These logics operate as interpretive tools for making sense of urban periphery experiences and processes of change. The logics can be thought of as corresponding to 'quintessential types' of urban periphery, none of which exist in pure form anywhere, but which serve as useful heuristics for interrogating the dynamics of changing spaces at the urban fringe. Temporality is a key element of these logics, as our conceptualisation attends to change over time and offers ways of making sense of changes to urban space.

We conceptualise our five logics as follows: i) the speculative periphery; ii) the vanguard periphery; iii) the auto-constructed periphery; iv) the transitioning periphery; and v) the inherited periphery. We now discuss each of these in turn.

The speculative periphery

This logic describes processes of speculation adopted by urban actors in relation to peripheral areas (including homeowners) and speaks to the more general trend of 'speculative urbanism', which is manifesting in particularly stark ways in parts of Africa and Asia (Goldman, 2011; Goodfellow, 2017a, 2022; Gillespie, 2020). Investment is multiscalar and commonly undertaken by customary landowners, private developers or small or large institutions (such as estate agents, as is evident in Accra), sometimes in partnership with the state as co-developer (and/or significant funder of underlying infrastructure). A critical point is that the range of actors engaging in speculation is diverse and diversifying. As argued in Chapter 8 in relation to Accra, new groups of actors, including landguards, estate agents and various associations, have joined customary leaders and landowning families in practices generating profit from peripherally located land. Speculation and investment can also occur in a more abstract manner through urban planning policy and visions for urban change. Commonly, the purpose of these practices is profit generation through investment into land purchasing or leasing, and building construction or acting as intermediaries to prepare land (e.g. resolving its ownership and tenurial claims) to enhance its profitability, as in Accra. The outcomes in built form vary significantly and may include the division of plots of land, incrementally constructed individual houses which may include on-site rental properties, small or substantial housing estates, commercial properties, light or heavy industry, agribusiness, retail facilities (particularly shopping malls) as well as multi-use developments and new cities. Investors originate from diverse contexts – local, national and international.

The logic of speculation in urban peripheries bears witness to the common perception of the availability of relatively cheap land in large parcels and the idea that access to such land might be quicker (or gained through clan connection or social networks) and less obstructed by planning, NIMBYism or historical ownership claims. Or, as is the case in Accra, although ownership is frequently contested, the presence of often aggressive landguards serves to facilitate speculation through multiple land sales. The varied use of farmland for urban expansion across multiple cases evidences at times both the profit-seeking practices of powerful large-scale farm owners alongside the weakness of poorer farmers to contest land expropriation, and also the pressure on customary landowners to release land to alleviate housing shortages but also generate profit. Equally important is the expectation that demand will grow in these areas and therefore land will increase in value, often radically, as seen in the Greater Accra region. This can be heightened by related processes of urban expansion or nearby planned or actual developments (Shatkin, 2016). Whether such increases actually materialise is variable and uncertain. Being situated on or adjacent to administrative boundaries can contribute to these benefits, facilitating different regimes of municipal taxation and planning. Land on the periphery may fall beyond municipalities' planning visions or just over the boundary with adjacent municipal authorities who have different plans or more limited capacities, potentially rendering them more open to investor-controlled development, such was the case historically in northern eThekwini (Todes, 2014a). Boundaries may produce opportunities for profit as relative access to the urban core alongside differential planning controls can prove attractive, as with our Legetafo case of high-end luxury housing across the border of north-eastern Addis. Indeed, the speculative periphery may also be associated with different governance regimes, where large developments, including gated estates and new cities, are managed and regulated wholly or partially outside of (weak) municipal systems (Van Noorlos and Kloosterboer, 2018). While land speculation is clearly a pervasive feature of urban development across the world, it is these specific dynamics of land pricing, anticipated demand, boundary effects and overlapping governance regimes that give the speculative periphery a distinct logic.

The speculative periphery also references changes in urban power relations, as investments generate power for institutions (such as developer conglomerates or partnerships) and often cement power for particular governance structures (e.g. municipalities, national government) through the promise of tax revenue and onward investment chains. Yet speculative practices can also undermine the capacities of weaker governance structures who wish to manage urban change according to shared principles (e.g. sustainability or inclusive planning) or whose institutional capacity to deliver basic services such as water can be weakened by speculative landowners.

Bureaucratic institutions may lack the capacity to challenge both investors and politicians around speculative intentions and decisions. For example, the economic development of northern eThekwini occurred following national, provincial and private sector pressure, despite significant limitations in its sanitation infrastructure and its defiance of the municipality's plans for containing city growth (Sim *et al.*, 2016).

The logic of the speculative periphery is also evidenced through small-scale speculative practices, including those managed by individuals or small organisations who target peripheries for their profit-making potential or whose presence within the peripheries places them in prime positions for speculation or profit generation. These varied actions can be both problematic and productive for residents living in these spaces and for residents urgently trying to find affordable housing within cities, particularly where weak political control by the state (at varying scales) renders certain areas more prone to predatory speculative initiatives. In this book we document various examples of such activities. In Accra the practices of landguards working to secure income through controlling or illegally selling parcels of land, or via offering protection of contested land, reveal how violence and intimidation are employed to achieve these ends. Their actions can benefit potential land buyers, or existing house builders, but the rise in multiple land sales and contestation over ownership suggests these speculative practices are deeply unsettling for urban periphery dwellers. Within South Africa, in both Winterveld and Ekangala there is evidence of local 'big men' who control whole areas and provide housing and access to electricity. This offers a significant service and resource to residents unable to access formal housing, or who live off the national grid, but is accompanied by complex power relations which shape a climate of fear and dependence. These kinds of practices can also contribute to dynamic urban change as the provision of informal housing and electrification can transform a barren uninhabited space into a relatively dense settlement. Similarly, we discuss in this book evidence of small-scale speculation occurring through the sale or rental of government-provided housing in both South Africa and Ethiopia. In Lufhereng, Johannesburg, for example, adverts in the secondary market of state-subsidised housing emphasised rental possibilities. Meanwhile, in the peripheries of Addis Ababa an extremely vibrant market in (often illegal) resale of condominium housing units is a key site of speculation, particularly with the periodic announcement of new condominium projects shaking up the housing market. Despite the benefits that some actors reap from speculation in the peripheries, these benefits are highly selective: those lacking the skills to work in new enterprises or resources to hold on to or acquire land or housing often find themselves on the sharp end of speculation-driven change.

The vanguard periphery

The vanguard periphery is a logic in which major investments led or facilitated by the state – often in the form of mass housing, infrastructure, a large-scale industrial or commercial venture or some other flagship investment – are undertaken by way of stimulating the broader development of an urban periphery. These may not in themselves be profit-making or directly motivated by economic gain, sometimes instead constituting political projects to gain support among key urban groups or project a particular image on the national, regional or global stage. Both apartheid and post-apartheid housing projects on the urban periphery might be seen in this way. However, vanguard investments often pave the way for the logic of the speculative periphery described above, such as the continued expansion of private housing developments in Protea Glen (Butcher, 2016). As Shatkin (2016) notes with respect to Asian megacities, the state often makes strategic investments in peri-urban infrastructure to stimulate the monetisation of land. In other cases vanguard projects on the periphery are smaller and more experimental in nature, effectively using the periphery as a testing ground for new ideas and practices. In yet others vanguard investments can follow speculative practices that have demonstrated the value or significance of a particular area or site. The intertwining of vanguard, speculative and other logics can therefore happen in a variety of ways.

Included in this categorisation are practices of urban policy experimentation which may reflect multiscalar or national state ambition or commitment. These may be bound up with election promises or constitutional obligations. In our study, examples include new forms of state housing, particularly those that experimented with mixed, integrated forms of housing and design, such as Lufhereng in Johannesburg. In this case new low-income housing designs were implemented in close proximity to middle-income dwellings in order to produce a more textured neighbourhood as well as overcome the monotony associated with previous state housing developments. In Addis Ababa the construction of differently financed (and hence differently sized and designed) condominiums on the periphery aims to provide a varied housing offer to the city's residents, but also to perform a vanguard function by stimulating new private developments in the surrounding area and new urban economic hubs.

These substantial investments by the state are assumed to be *generative* in that their purpose is to attract and produce new developments in time: for example, new housing estates will draw in small businesses and services. Temporality and the fulfilment of a future vision is a key aspect of their existence (Meth *et al.*, 2022). In Lufhereng, planning and delivery of state housing was accompanied by investment into infrastructure to underpin housing for purchase by lower-middle-income residents: together, these diverse dwelling types and income groups would help stimulate new local production of goods such as steel windows and cupboards, the accompanying economic plan assumed (Charlton, 2017). In Addis Ababa the design of condominiums with around 10 per cent of ground floor space designated for retail meant that businesses were quite quickly attracted to these new sites of high-density residence. Moreover, in Tulu Dimtu particularly, condominiums have been sited deliberately far from the urbanised part of the city (with open farmland in between) but strategically close to emerging industrial corridors. The intention is that the space between city and periphery will be 'filled in' over time in response to this vanguard investment (Goodfellow *et al.*, 2018).

The vanguard periphery, like all our categorisations, must not be viewed in isolation or as a bounded spatial intervention. Rather, it constitutes a logic that reflects, facilitates or responds to concurrent urban changes occurring elsewhere in the city, such as inner-city regeneration, gentrification or land use change. In Addis Ababa, condominiums on the city edge are a response to efforts to 'renew' central Addis Ababa and formalise the city more generally (Abebe and Hasselberg, 2015; Haddis, 2019) and are thus linked to displacement and relocation. Tied to this are efforts to densify the city and to maximise and capture land value. Meanwhile, Hammonds Farm in eThekwini is a significant state investment carried out partly in response to the demands of a private landowner to the north of the city, whose land (Ocean Drive Inn) was illegally occupied by informal residents for many years. Her desire to develop her land in view of other recent investments nearby meant that the state was obliged to step in and rehouse residents on former farmland designated for residential development.

As with the selective benefits of speculative development, vanguard investments similarly benefit particular individuals and not others, or have contradictory impacts. Residents in Tulu Dimtu suffer a lack of transport provision, with overcrowded and slow services the norm. This directly affects their daily routines and capacity to engage in trading or work, attend school or access services (Belihu et al., 2018; Meth et al., 2022). In Hammonds Farm, very few residents own cars and depend on informal taxis to access work and services. Despite being reasonably well located in relation to the newish northern economic hub of Umhlanga/Gateway, residents feel spatially isolated, particularly from employment opportunities (Meth and Buthelezi, 2017; Houghton, 2018). Long-running tensions between taxi and bus companies make travel costly. In this case wider infrastructural provision has failed to meet the significant housing provision.

Vanguard practices may also include those with explicit political intent tied to opportunities associated with borders or boundaries, or to disputes over territory or governance. In contrast to the speculative logic identified above, in these cases the primary motivation may be political (e.g. to control land, access voters, establish power bases and political allies, reduce power blocs or overcome conflict) rather than simply as a profit-generating operation (Kinfu et al., 2019; McGregor and Chatiza, 2019). Some of the investments in condominiums in Addis Ababa may be viewed in this way in the context of the government's desire to regain urban support after losing almost all parliamentary seats in the capital after 2005 (Di Nunzio, 2014; Planel and Bridonneau, 2017). However, the approach to vanguard investments in the periphery of Addis Ababa has changed in recent years. Following the attempt to implement the Addis Ababa and Surrounding Oromia Special Zone Integrated

Master Plan in 2014, major social unrest erupted in Oromia, ultimately contributing to the regime change in 2018 (Mohamed et al., 2020) and fostering a much more cautious approach to the periphery.

Sometimes vanguard investments clash with other state logics (e.g. between spheres or tiers of government), and vanguardism may evidence contestation, competing policies or disagreements relating to spatial strategy. The Lufhereng example illustrates this tension in multiple ways: the development of this site was contrary to the City planners' view of it as 'outside' of the desirable and developable city edge, but the City fell in line with the province to support the project, with housing delivery and other imperatives overruling locally derived planning principles (Charlton, 2017). Furthermore, Lufhereng's peripheral location means that it is problematic for poor people who live marginalised lives, unable to easily access services and employment (Williams et al., 2021). Thus, residents' experiences of vanguard peripheries may be as relatively isolated, slow-to-consolidate places lacking facilities, jobs or other economic opportunity, in contrast to the grand ambitions behind them. In South Africa these kinds of spatial practices are possible in part because welfare payments and social support enable people to try to survive there.

The auto-constructed periphery

This third logic partly draws on Caldeira's (2017) conceptualisation, identifying the significant role of unauthorised development in shaping the spatial form and lived experiences of many peripheries. It also bears resemblance to the concept of Schmid et al. of 'popular urbanisation', which describes 'the material transformation of the urban territory with strong participation of the inhabitants' (2018: 35). This logic involves informal efforts to produce and occupy space, largely (but not exclusively) enacted by the urban poor, many of whom are migrants from other countries, cities, neighbourhoods or rural hinterlands who are seeking to secure an urban footing. This logic is also productive for understanding some of the ways in which land and affordable housing is secured and incrementally constructed by individual house builders in urban peripheries, including those occupied by the working poor or the middle classes. The acquisition of this land outside of the formal planning channels underscores its 'auto-constructed' nature. The auto-constructed periphery incorporates multiple forms of accessing water, electricity or power, alongside the construction of innovative forms of housing, and structures for retail.

Again, these built forms can occur in central areas as well as peripheries, as evident in many cities and as Caldeira's conceptualisation demonstrates. However, the combination of auto-construction and peripheral location poses distinct challenges for accessing work, services and broader urban life. This book examines (to varying extents) some of the distinctive challenges of living in these auto-constructed peripheries (in Ethiopia, South Africa and Ghana) compared with other built forms. The combination of distance from an urban metropolis, extreme poverty and very poor access to infrastructure and services worked to produce highly precarious lives. Within South Africa the case of the Canelands/Coniston informal settlements in northern eThekwini illustrate efforts by urban residents to set up home in spaces that are relatively well located adjacent to an industrial park but which lack individual piped water, electrification or formal housing. The site has unsurfaced tracks and is built among dense vegetation. This auto-constructed periphery is critical in providing a relatively low-cost option to residents to potentially gain an income from being located 'near' to the city and to survive on meagre wages by walking to avoid transport costs (Houghton and Todes, 2019). Within Accra the self-building of houses on the urban periphery speaks to the exceptional demand for affordable housing. Yet financial limitations and the drain of resources through landguardism often mean housing is constructed very slowly or is built in compromised form (Asafo, 2022). Owners also struggle with poor access to employment opportunities and limited or absent infrastructure.

Noted already in relation to incremental housing construction, the auto-constructed periphery can have particular temporalities associated with its spaces and practices. For some these can be experienced as spaces of temporariness, particularly where there are threats of eviction or change owing to external pressures on the land or the enforcement of particular planning policies. In Waterworks (near Lufhereng) in Johannesburg, residents have been rehoused elsewhere to make way for private sector investment, despite long years of occupation. In many parts of the Addis periphery including our case of Yeka Abado, the character of auto-constructed settlements has transformed as they have had to incorporate (or found themselves adjacent to) settlements of farmers displaced from the land on which the condominiums were built (Belihu *et al.*, 2018). Temporalities also vary in relation to the time it takes for informal spaces to receive services or to be granted legal title. In Winterveld in northern Gauteng, some residents experienced significant delays in accessing any form of security (services/titles) over decades.

More positively, auto-constructed spaces can also represent hope, opportunity and possibility, with residents expressing expectations for future investment, and can include more middle-income forms of housing. Auto-constructed spaces can be central to reducing pressure on housing affordability in rapidly expanding urban spaces. Clearly, the logic of auto-construction incorporates wealthier forms of investment (overlapping our speculative logic detailed earlier) which may ignore planning conventions, environmental concerns or building bylaws. Finally, this logic also points to forms of opportunistic governance by 'strongmen' who use the informal allocation of land and services to build power, as noted above in relation to Winterveld and Ekangala.

The transitioning periphery

Our fourth logic is that of the 'transitioning periphery', used to capture more incremental consolidation and change. Key here is change in land use or evidence of parallel land uses and sociospatial arrangements from rural and agricultural to, or alongside, more urban uses, including formal residential, institutional or retail. Transitioning areas commonly have long histories of settlement (for varied reasons), and ensuing changes may also speak to processes of formalisation, or indeed those of decline and loss. In several African contexts the establishment of middle-class houses alongside significant densification on land previously or still managed by traditional or customary authorities is an important process (Asafo, 2020; Bartels, 2019/20; Mbatha and Mchunu, 2016; Sim *et al.*, 2018), including in all of the Ghanaian Accra cases, and Molweni in eThekwini, South Africa, discussed in this book.

Transitioning peripheries often involve the co-existence of multiple systems of landownership and regulation, echoing the concept of Karaman *et al.* of 'plotting urbanism', in which the allocation and changing use of land proceeds through incremental land commodification in contexts characterised by 'overlapping modes of territorial regulation, land tenure and property rights' (2020: 1122), with the four case studies in Greater Accra a classic example. The transitioning peripheries can point to a proliferation of actors involved in land protection, sales and purchase (see Chapter 8 on Accra) where multiple and contested ownership rights emerge including outside of formal planning and registration institutions. Our concept of the 'transitioning periphery' also highlights specific dynamics of the densification of the built environment in geographic peripheries. These include associated reductions in plot sizes, including where owners are forced to divide plots to overcome ownership disputes (Asafo, 2020), and a growth in housing (often more formal in character but not necessarily in terms of titling) alongside a rising presence of retail facilities. These transitions are commonly characterised by the introduction of services and infrastructure which transform space through dedication to bulk services, electrical facilities, bus shelters and pavements. Yet infrastructural transitions can also be more individualised with a growth in individual homeowners sinking boreholes or acquiring generators on newly acquired plots of land. Road and transport investments influence access to employment opportunities and retail spaces, particularly malls, as these develop. These transitions relate to differentiated socio-cultural and economic change which residents experience as significant; for example, in Molweni and Waterloo in eThekwini, the arrival of supermarkets and a shopping mall fundamentally altered residents' spatial-temporal realities (Charlton, 2018a). Yet, despite changes in land use, access to land for agricultural purposes (e.g. for growing food) remains critical, as is evident across multiple cases. The availability of land in transitioning peripheries also sees rising pressures on land for subdivision and provision of rental accommodation.

This logic also highlights continuity and gradual forms of change. For example, a township settlement may be undergoing less dramatic change than in the case of vanguard or speculative logics, through investments in institutional facilities, roadworks or small-scale housing interventions. Such areas are better seen as *consolidating* or *transitioning* rather than *transforming*. Waterloo in Northern eThekwini illustrates this as it has shifted from a housing estate to a more textured and mature 'township'. Other forms of transition may include areas of state housing that experience second waves of beneficiaries, the inflow of tenants and new forms of occupation and investment. Again, the temporal aspect comes to the fore, as areas developing through a 'transitioning' logic may have previously been 'vanguard' spaces but over time have been reshaped in more incremental and less planned ways. Changes can include varying degrees of 'informalisation' of older or more recent formally delivered neighbourhoods through unauthorised construction and land uses, significant particularly in South African low- and mixed-income housing developments but also in some Addis Ababa condominiums. While these transitions are not specific to geographically edge developments, they can be significantly present there and may be influenced by mobility costs, distance and weaker governance or urban management, in addition to other factors. We thus see this logic in broad terms, reflecting not just rural to urban changes but other forms of transitions – and rather than representing a singular transition from one form to another, a characteristic of this logic may be the sense of a periphery in constant transition. The gradual filling of retail units in the Addis condominium developments is an example of transition afforded by earlier vanguard housing investment and relative dislocation from alternative sources of consumption.

Transitions also refer to changing or hybrid forms of governance stretching across traditional leadership to democratically elected municipal structures or to the arrival of other actors shaping everyday decision-making (as in Accra's changing governance of land markets). Changing governance may also involve party political changes which then impact on peripheral spaces by either blocking or promoting particular visions of change. In Addis Ababa, for example, the establishment of committee structures in condominium developments facilitates small-scale transitions in local representation, managing urban gardens and controlling crime. Yeka Abado provides an example of a relatively 'matured' peripheral transition, partly facilitated by local governance changes (Goodfellow *et al.*, 2018). For residents, the transitioning periphery can account for minor but significant adaptations over time which make residents feel that change is underway or that their demands as citizens are being heard. In Accra the collapsing authority of customary landowners in shaping land allocation (see Chapter 7) illustrates how control, governance and profiting from transitioning peripheral spaces in the fringes of Accra is rapidly evolving, with authority secured through violence and intimidation in many cases but also through strong social networks in others. In Molweni, South Africa, residents clearly articulated their sense of shifting from living rural lives to those more akin to township dwellers as a result of progressive investments in roads, housing, electricity and transport. Here a surprising coherent partnership emerged between co-existing traditional authorities and the relatively strong eThekwini municipality. However, residents living in the traditional authority-governed area identified numerous deficiencies as a result of different funding mechanisms and their seeming exclusion from wider beneficial municipal policies (Meth et al., 2021a; see also Sim et al., 2018). This illustrates the challenges for municipalities managing urban–rural divisions in transitioning areas.

The inherited periphery

Our fifth and final logic is that of the inherited periphery. Areas typified by this logic often exist as spaces of obligation for the national and local state and are a function of specific histories through which political practices at multiple scales attempted to mould areas and people. Such spaces are often now the victims of failed policy initiatives. Our case of Winterveld, in northern Tshwane, historically produced through apartheid's violent forced relocation programme, endures as a site of tragedy requiring state attention in order to combat very high levels of poverty, high crime rates and economic failure. Ironically, many of these places have had significant state investment in the post-apartheid South Africa context, underpinning their population (but not economic) growth, and there may be initiatives to revitalise old state-supported industrial spaces, such as Ekandustria in our Ekangala case. For many weak authorities, these kinds of spaces exert a significant pressure on both their budgets and capacity. This logic extends to colonial practices elsewhere, or other faltering vanguard-like interventions which leave a troubled legacy.

These inherited spaces often show evidence of decline (commonly in economic terms) or they reveal an inability to progress in different ways, including in relation to levels of basic infrastructure, the extent and type of investment and employment opportunities. In these areas the range of opportunities for work may be narrow as well as highly vulnerable, and prone to change if structural and local factors unfold in particular ways. Wage levels may be depressed or work irregular. This was strongly evident in Ekangala where deindustrialisation has significantly impacted on residents' lives. Industries that previously received some state subsidy under apartheid now stand abandoned, and unemployed residents describe their perpetual frustrations with seeking work in an increasingly competitive and limited pond (Houghton and Todes, 2019).

Many residents experience spatial marginalisation compounded by weak, expensive and unreliable transport. Relative distance from urban cores is critical here, as is evident in Winterveld, a sparsely populated settlement far from most economic hubs. Residents frequently express negative emotions: they feel neglected, trapped and marginalised, pointing to years of stasis with little hope of improvement. They describe their loss of faith in the state to deliver on election promises, and they struggle to see pathways out of poverty. Importantly, the term 'inherited periphery' does not label the residents in these spaces or their actions as problematic or intrinsically marginal but instead speaks to the historical origins of the areas' marginality and the consequences of this, including the trend towards declining levels of service or employment. It is worth noting that even major 'vanguard' investments in key sites on the urban periphery can become part of the 'inherited periphery' at later points in time, particularly if the surrounding areas do not develop in the ways intended. In theory, therefore, sites such as Tulu Dimtu in Addis Ababa could become the inherited peripheries of the future if further investment in critical infrastructure fails to materialise and the nearby industrial activities fail to generate sufficient economic activity and jobs. Tied to the troubled sentiments expressed by residents in existing inherited peripheries is the overwhelming experience of boredom, signalling a lack of disposable income, development and entertainment opportunities, and the prevalence of poverty and immobility (Mukwedeya, 2018). For some residents, however, these qualities of desolation are matched by perceptions of peacefulness, fresh air, tradition and quiet. These 'boring' spaces are therefore not necessarily perceived in unidimensional ways, and geographic marginalisation may be accompanied by a rarer urban quality – that of space.

Weak governance institutions may be present in such areas, including traditional authorities within hybrid governance systems who complain of neglect, under-funding and sometimes significant hardship compared to neighbouring municipalities. Finally, inherited peripheries may be dominated by the 'informal strongman' mentioned earlier. These individuals can yield significant power locally and can prove highly effective at delivering key resources, including housing, electricity and employment. However, residents' narratives reveal high incidences of dependence on such individuals, alongside intimidation and violence, often unhindered by the state, as strongmen operate beyond their vision.

Book structure and key arguments

The book turns next to Chapter 1 which discusses visions of the urban periphery in South Africa and Ethiopia and how these have influenced development in our case studies. In the context of international policy debates over appropriate spatial policy, it draws on empirical material from key informant interviews and documentary analysis to demonstrate the complex ways in which urban spatial policy and implementation are shaped by (shifting) politics, institutions, agencies and actors. Although urban peripheries may be considered in spatial policy, little attention is given to their diversity, their dynamism and to the everyday lives of residents, which emerge in other chapters.

Focusing on Ethiopia and South Africa, Chapter 2 explores the dynamics and drivers of investment and economic change on urban peripheries in the case studies, focusing on areas where there has been significant private and public investment at some point. Taking each country in turn, it presents some of the general policy trends and frameworks shaping investment in each national context, and some of the ways in which these are experienced, before considering the city-regions and case study areas that are the particular focus of this book. Using empirical evidence, it highlights the diverse trajectories of these places, key actors and agencies and some of the specific major investment projects that have been shaping our case study peripheries. It adds substance to concepts of speculative, vanguard and inherited peripheries in relation to the case studies.

Chapter 3 explores lived experiences of access to work and livelihoods on the urban peripheries of South Africa and Ethiopia, relating these to the varying logics of peripheries. It contributes to debates on the extent to which new growth on the edge is likely to be associated with poor access to employment and a reliance on commuting, at least for the urban poor. It considers the extent to which major infrastructure and economic investment in vanguard and speculative peripheries result in better access to employment and economic opportunity, and the types of jobs and livelihoods generated in these and other areas. It suggests that while there may be higher levels of employment and more opportunities in economically dynamic areas, jobs available can be short term or inaccessible to the poor. Despite differences across areas, there is a significant reliance on commuting, diverse local livelihood strategies, social grants (in South Africa) and (often politically mediated) public works programmes, none of which are adequate to meet the challenge of secure livelihoods on the urban edge.

Chapter 4 uses data from key informant interviews, and resident diaries and interviews, to examine the varied governance structures shaping the peripheries in both South Africa and Ethiopia. It opens with a discussion of key conceptual framings relevant to understanding governance trends in urban peripheries and moves to review the multiscalar institutional bodies, administrative structures, local committees and key figures including ward leaders and 'strongmen' operating in, and responsible for, the peripheral spaces in city-regions. Within this review the chapter offers brief reflections on hybridity, the limitations of the state and the role of the private sector shaping decision-making. The chapter turns to an analysis of borders and boundaries as central to particular governance contestations and analyses state–citizen relations using the insights drawn from the book's overarching 'lived experiences' approach. Throughout the chapter, conceptualisations of the periphery, developed in the Introduction, are drawn on to analyse particular governance arrangements and practices, including new structures within vanguard peripheries, 'transitioning peripheries' possessing hybrid governance structures and auto-constructed peripheries where informalised mechanisms of leadership are evident, alongside weakened state structures which are obligated to serve 'inherited peripheries'.

Chapter 5 examines the evolution and 'lived experience' consequences of housing policy in Ethiopia in recent decades, which was radically transformed by the introduction of the Integrated Housing Development Programme (IHDP) from 2005. This was a major 'vanguard' investment aimed at transforming the economic and social character of the urban periphery. The chapter situates this programme in relation to broader developments in Ethiopian housing policy, including the cooperative housing programme that was initiated in the 1970s but continued into the twenty-first century. It then explores some of the tensions at the heart of the Integrated Housing Development Programme (IHDP), which set out to produce 'affordable' housing at the same time as being part of an economic growth and homeownership agenda, leading to escalating prices and rents as well as mass displacement. The lived experience of housing of various kinds in our case study areas is then examined. The chapter concludes that, ultimately, the apparent promise of the 'vanguard periphery' in these areas was partly undermined by limitations in infrastructural capacity but also by the simultaneous creation of auto-constructed, speculative and potentially future 'inherited' peripheries.

Chapter 6 locates the diverse forms of housing in our South African cases relative to a historical view of urban policy, contextualising the origins and contemporary dynamics of inherited as well as more recent peripheral settlements. Experiences and perceptions from residents' interviews and diaries explain their links to these areas and include expressions of hope and optimism as well as dejection with life there. The long shadow of apartheid colours but does not define people's continued occupation of areas that were intentionally dislocated from urban centralities, while post-apartheid state housing, often peripherally located, surfaces complex relationships with speculative development and economic activity or its absence. The chapter discusses also the differing roles played by informal settlements and other forms of auto-construction in our study sites. The lens of peripheral logics illuminates people's housing experiences and motivations, the pull of state and other housing-related investment, sometimes in contradictory ways, and the dynamism as well as sedimentation in this housing landscape.

An analysis of recent transitions in Accra's peri-urban land market is the focus of Chapter 7. The chapter explores pressures on peripherally located land in the context of significant affordability issues in wider Accra, and the ways in which land originally owned and managed by customary authorities in the main is increasingly the focus and object of a proliferation of new actors in the city's land market. Speaking to the speculative logic, the chapter distinguishes between primary land providers and delivery channels (including chiefs and family heads controlling customary land) and newer entrants including real estate companies, welfare associations, individuals, land agents and landguards. These 'secondary' land providers and intermediaries form part of the complex set of actors at the centre of rapidly rising land prices and stories of landgrabbing. Much of the housing being built is done so individually, outside of the formal land and planning mechanisms, and these changes to Accra's peripheries directly reflect the transitioning and auto-constructed logics of African urban peripheries.

Chapter 8 examines transport and mobility in the urban peripheries of South Africa and Ethiopia through an analysis of existing forms of transportation and arguing that the urban peripheries produce particular challenges around cost, time and infrastructure tied to the histories and logics of the varying peripheries. The chapter discusses investments in road and rail infrastructure and considers the significance and limitations of walking for residents, impacted by often very significant geographic peripherality. Stuckness and immobility are key concepts underscoring the experiential realities for residents, and the chapter calls for a relational understanding of these concepts to situate peripheral locations relative to more centralised environments.

Chapter 9 establishes from the perspectives of residents living in Ethiopia and South Africa what infrastructure is evident, what is absent and what the significance of this is for residents. It uses this analysis of infrastructure to understand how places on the urban peripheries are produced from an infrastructural perspective, with a particular focus on the material public realm and the online realm. Initially, the chapter explores the interconnections between the varying logics of the periphery to illustrate how particular peripheries foster particular forms of infrastructural realities, recognising that these interconnections are also context-specific and inconsistent. The chapter then considers the significance of micro-infrastructure in urban peripheries and argues that despite investment in some macro-scale interventions, their impact on residents is contested. The widespread unevenness to the nature of infrastructure, including the significant challenges of infrastructural absences or failings, and how this is experienced on the ground forms the focus of the rest of the chapter. Where relevant, the connections between the forms of investment and governance shaping infrastructural interventions or failings are detailed in order to provide some explanation for the unevenness identified across the cases.

Chapter 10 explores the social processes, differentiations and experiences of living in African urban peripheries through a focus on Ethiopia and South Africa. The chapter examines various facets of difference including gender, age and tenancy status, as well as explores the experiences of boredom and the dominance of crime and violence. It argues that urban peripheries are highly differentiated and that constructions of boredom are relational. Crime and violence are highly significant, particularly in the South African case study areas. Fundamentally, the chapter examines how urban change shapes social processes, and it evidences that African urban peripheries are highly differentiated spaces.

Chapter 11 focuses mainly on vanguard peripheries in Ethiopia and South Africa and draws on often spontaneous accounts in diaries and interviews of people's experiences of food and related retail in state-led housing developments. In South Africa the presence or absence of powerful supermarket chains feature prominently in our respondents' daily lives and imaginaries, including for crucial services and experiences they offer beyond grocery sales, but smaller shops are little encouraged in the residential neighbourhoods, although informal micro-enterprises emerge nevertheless. In Ethiopia, where large private supermarkets do not dominate as in South Africa, shops are encouraged on the ground floors of condominiums along key roads, assisting with mixed-use vibrancy and local purchasing for residents, although they also desire access to bigger markets which require travel elsewhere. In both contexts access to choice, diversity and cheaper goods can often only be found elsewhere or in the vicinity years after housing has been occupied. In the meantime residents' narratives make clear that the initial approach to facilitating retail opportunities in vanguard developments can significantly shape everyday lives.

The book's conclusions are briefly presented in the last chapter. Given that each chapter offers its own concluding reflections, this chapter returns to the question of urban comparison within African peripheries and considers the value of comparison for advancing understanding in these complex urban spaces. It briefly addresses the book's contribution to core literatures detailed at the start of this chapter, but primarily it returns to our conceptual framework and our five logics of African urban peripheries to consider its value and limitations. Finally, the chapter considers the policy implications, very generally, of some of the arguments and evidence presented in this text.

Notes

1 See Mabin *et al.* (2013) for an earlier discussion.
2 'RDP' stands for the ANC (African National Congress) government's Reconstruction and Development Programme of the mid-1990s. Government-funded low-income houses became colloquially known as 'RDP housing' (Charlton, 2018b: 99).

1

Visions of the urban periphery: Ethiopia and South Africa

Alison Todes and Tom Goodfellow

State spatial visions can play powerful roles in shaping urban peripheries. It is thus critical to understand these ideas and their effects. Whether or not they are realised in full, and whether or not they take the periphery as an explicit focus, the imaginaries behind urban policies and spatial plans condition lived experience in the urban periphery – albeit in ways that are rarely straightforward. International policy discourse has focused on debating the merits of urban compaction (e.g. UN-Habitat, 2009, 2016; Lall *et al.*, 2017) and ways of managing rapid urban expansion (Angel *et al.*, 2016), including the use of 'new cities'. In practice, however, urban spatial policies and their implementation are shaped in complex ways through particular histories, geographies, politics, institutions, agencies and actors.

This chapter explores visions of the urban periphery arising from national and local spatial policy in Ethiopian and South African cases. It considers the evolution of policies in the two countries and the specific city-regions in our study. It examines how these policies have been shaped historically and politically by key institutions and actors. In many respects the two countries are very different. While South African urban spatial policy focuses on compaction, it confronts a history of spatial apartheid and continuing inequality, which generates its own spatial logics. Urban peripheries themselves have varying origins and experience different processes of change, not all of which are directly considered in spatial policy. In practice there are challenges and shifting directions undermining the realisation of spatial imaginaries. Addis Ababa, by contrast, has experienced sharp shifts in spatial policies, from a focus on developing core areas to an explicit agenda for urban peripheries and back to prioritising core areas again. Processes of spatial change in the city, however, have generated their own peripheral dynamics. The chapter thus highlights the contextuality of urban spatial policy, its fluidity and its complex effects on urban peripheries.

South Africa

In South Africa, fragmented, sprawling, racially divided cities were the consequences of apartheid 'Group Area' visions from the 1950s, which extended existing forms of racial segregation (Smith, 1992). Large 'townships' for black people were created through relocations to the urban periphery, where they were accommodated in mass housing schemes. The creation of ethnic 'homelands' (or Bantustans) where black African people were expected to achieve levels of political self-rule exacerbated these patterns in cities bordering on them, such as those now part of the City of Tshwane and eThekwini municipality. In these areas townships were created and the informal settlements which emerged, sometimes on land held by traditional authorities, were usually even more distant from economic centres than Group Area townships, requiring lengthy commutes to work – a form of 'displaced urbanisation' (South African Cities Network (SACN), 2016).

In reaction to these patterns, and influenced by international urban compaction discourses (Dewar and Uytenbogaardt, 1990; Harrison *et al.*, 2008), post-apartheid policies proposed to restructure cities towards greater compaction and integration (COGTA, 2016). Proposed approaches included the creation of urban edges, urban densification and the development of well-located, affordable housing in areas close to economic opportunity or along transit corridors linking townships to the rest of the city. However, most black people continued to live in peripherally located townships, including those in the former homelands. Further, the lower cost of land and its availability in large parcels on the urban edge has meant that the government's large housing 'RDP' (Reconstruction and Development Programme), mostly offering detached housing for low-income households, has delivered mainly in areas close to existing townships and other parts of the urban periphery (Charlton, 2014). Constituency politics and pressure to provide housing to communities 'where people are' (Todes, 2000) have enabled the development of such housing even in spaces of 'displaced urbanisation' (Marais et al., 2016).

In practice, policy to improve conditions in the former townships and new RDP housing areas on the periphery has been a significant focus of both national and local government. This has been facilitated by the creation of large metropolitan municipalities, replacing the fragmented and unequal administrations which previously ran cities and able to cross-subsidise from wealthier to poorer areas. This thrust has also been supported by national funding programmes to improve infrastructure and services and to stimulate economic activity in these areas. These include the area-based Special Presidential Lead Projects of the 1990s/early 2000s which operated in some areas, including in Winterveld (SACN, 2016); the national Urban Renewal Programme (URP) (2001–11), which focused on seven major townships in metropolitan areas (Todes and Turok, 2018); and the later Neighbourhood Development Partnership Programme (NDPP), which initially supported municipal initiatives to promote township development across the country. From 2014 to 2020 the NDPP refocused on a smaller number of nodes and their 'urban networks' in metropolitan areas and secondary cities. These were the few core centres in or adjacent to major townships, which had the potential to become significant competitive urban hubs well linked through roads and transport networks to central areas (National Treasury, 2013). None of our case study areas were defined as such nodes.

The urban network approach drew from earlier debates over national spatial policy, which had raised concerns about the perpetuation of inefficient and unsustainable apartheid spatial patterns, including the very long travel distances associated with displaced urbanisation. Focusing on national spatial patterns, the 2003 National Spatial Development Perspective, for example, argued for support for areas with competitive potential, particularly core economic agglomerations, and a space-blind approach offering basic services and social infrastructure to other areas (Oranje and Merrifield, 2010). Although this position was not sustained in national policy, with the National Development Plan (2011) and the National Spatial Development Framework (2022) adopting a more balanced approach, it was influential in the development of the NDPP's urban network approach (Interview, SA (South Africa) Government Official 1, National, 2013). From this perspective, more marginal distant townships on the periphery would be unlikely to be prioritised for major infrastructural investment beyond social need.

The urban network approach to township development went along with a new commitment in policy to urban compaction. The compact city idea was initially embodied in policy in the 1995 Development Facilitation Act and was taken up in metropolitan spatial frameworks. However, it faced constant challenges, in part due to the investment patterns of private developers towards middle-/upper-income gated enclaves on urban edges, the weak impact of spatial plans and the sometimes contradictory spatial outcomes of national and provincial policies. Initiatives to embed urban compaction more strongly came through the 2013 Spatial Planning and Land Use Management Act, the 2016 Integrated Urban Development Framework and the National Treasury's Cities Support Programme which put in place a system of grants for urban infrastructure development in metropolitan areas which could enable a more integrated approach to urban development (Duminy *et al.*, 2020). Its system of Built Environment Programme Plans (BEPPs) linked infrastructure investments and budgets to strategic spatial planning.[1] It required metropolitan municipalities to spell out their core spatial focus areas for investment in 'Integration Zones' focusing on spatial transformation through development around public transport routes linking townships with major city economic nodes:

> Integration Zones form the core prioritised areas that link to the primary township hubs, key informal settlements, extremely marginalised areas and finally the strategic areas of current and future employment or economic nodes. These spatially targeted areas should form the focus areas for intergovernmental planning, co-ordination and investment. This does not mean that most of the expenditure is focused in these areas, but that a significant amount of public funds are well planned and co-ordinated in these areas, while the basics of infrastructure repairs and maintenance, operating costs, etc. are still adhered to. (CSP, 2016: 14)

Yet, as an evaluation report noted, there is an evident tension in the emphasis on 'spatial targeting' towards greater efficiency and 'providing existing households with access to basic services' (DPME,

2015: iv) – in effect the treatment of what we term 'inherited peripheries' remained unresolved. An SACN (2016) study of 'displaced urbanisation', for instance, argues that municipalities need to appreciate the complexity of these places and their varying roles, while Mosiane and Gotz (2022) argue for seeing them as sites of 'displaced urbanism', not residual spaces. National policies do not define different types of urban peripheries and how they might be addressed in policy, leaving this level of 'detail' to be considered within provincial and municipal plans. Further, most state policies, such as those focused on poverty alleviation, do not explicitly consider urban peripheries.

While there have been initiatives in the state to consolidate urban compaction policies, frustration at the slow pace of housing delivery and the lack of spatial transformation has led to contrary thrusts towards 'new cities' (Ballard and Rubin, 2017), mirroring recent international discourses (see the Introduction). This approach was driven initially by the national Department of Human Settlements' push for very large housing 'mega-projects' since 2014 (Duminy *et al.*, 2020), but it also sees these projects as part of larger schemes containing higher-income areas, economic nodes and more. Given the scale of land required, these are likely to be in peripheral areas, as has been the case for some recently proposed housing-led developments. In 2021 Lanseria, on the edges of Johannesburg and Tshwane, was announced as South Africa's first 'smart new city'. While this initiative has some economic base and is in a growing region, the rationale for new cities in other parts of the country more distant from urban economies is less clear. There are also initiatives to use spatial industrial policy to promote forms of economic decentralisation, including within cities (Farole and Sharp, 2017). For instance, some special economic zones (SEZs) are on the edges of cities, close to former townships, although in some cases this location or relationship is incidental. The Revitalisation of Industrial Parks Programme seeks to improve infrastructure and hence the prospects for economic development in several former industrial decentralisation points, some of which were deconcentration points close to former homeland townships. More recently, since 2020 the National Treasury's Cities Support Programme has shifted to a broad-ranging approach to enabling township economic development, focusing particularly on small entrepreneurs.

Hence there are changing and sometimes contradictory visions of urban peripheries in the state.

Municipal planning and visions

These visions, and the differences and contradictions between them, play out in municipal plans, which also embody their own contextually defined tensions and politics. The City of Tshwane covers a particularly large area, being an amalgamation of several local administrations, including parts of former homeland areas. It was expanded through the incorporation of the former Metsweding municipality in 2011, which brought in the Ekangala area, among others. The area is run through seven regions, each of which have their own spatial plans, within the context of an overall spatial framework. Academics interviewed for this research argued that planning in Tshwane is 'like a Jackson Pollock image ... blobby' (SA Academic 1, 2018), reflecting different interests and a lack of strategic focus: the municipality is quite fragmented internally, with differences between departments (Interview, SA Academic 2, 2018). Further, 'every ward councillor wants to know that their ward has been presented on the plans, and they want to know that something is being done for them' (SA Government Official 4, City of Tshwane, 2018). The spatial framework presents a version of urban compaction with an urban edge (COT, 2021), and an 'integration zone' focused on transit-oriented development within a 25 km radius of the central business district (CBD), encompassing the large townships closer to the centre where most of the population lives. The major city projects, including the Tshwane Automotive City in Rosslyn, are within this area (Interview, SA Government Official 3, City of Tshwane, 2018). However, while planning focuses on compaction, housing and related services account for a large part of the capital budget, much of which occurs on the periphery where land is available, even in traditional authority areas beyond the urban edge. As one interviewee noted,

> we're a city; we can't just include or exclude certain areas. We have to attend to the whole city, and unfortunately Tshwane is huge. Even though we do have ... the principle of compaction ... the reality is we have people very far off, and it's a peculiar way people are settled there with this big rural area ... in between. (Interview, SA Government Official 3, City of Tshwane, 2018)

Basic services are also to be provided in 'rural' areas, although urban expansion is to be contained (COT, 2021). With the political shift to the opposition Democratic Alliance (DA) in 2016, local elections, poverty alleviation strategies and service delivery in poorer areas were emphasised, extending the focus on peripheral areas (Interview, SA Academic 1, 2018). Further, some of the 'new city' initiatives such as Lanseria and Mooikloof, a middle-income housing development, had to be incorporated into municipal planning (Interview, SA Government Official 7, City of Tshwane, 2021).

SA Academic 2 (Interview, 2018) argued that the municipality didn't know how to deal with the sprawling north and east. Although Winterveld had been prioritised in the early 2000s, also as an area of in-migration, requiring RDP housing (Interview, SA Government Official 4, City of Tshwane, 2018), it is now out of the planning prioritisation zones. Nevertheless, it has received significant municipal funding for basic infrastructure and services, in part since there are some large provincially planned housing projects close to the area (Interview, SA Government Official 4, City of Tshwane, 2018). While Ekangala had been an important township hub in Metsweding, it was now a more minor secondary core within the larger municipality (Interview, SA Government Officials, 3 and 4, City of Tshwane, 2018). It is part of an integration zone, but not in the main transit-oriented development urban network. At certain points the area was considered as a possible site for a mega-housing project and an SEZ, but these ideas have given way to more limited ambitions and expectations. Economic development in this 'city in the east' (Interview, SA Government Official 4, City of Tshwane, 2018) was supported by the municipality, which mounted a food and energy project in the area in 2016, but it has performed poorly (Interview, SA Government Official 5, City of Tshwane, 2018). Ekandustria, the former homeland industrial decentralisation point adjacent to Ekangala, is one of the sites targeted by the modest Revitalisation of Industrial Parks programme, while the major industrial focus is now on Rosslyn and the Silverton SEZ.

Compared to the City of Tshwane, spatial planning in the City of Johannesburg has been more coherent and integrated over time (Interview, SA Academic 2, 2018), although it has also faced internal policy contradictions, differences with national and provincial departments and the impact of political shifts (Todes, 2014b;

Harrison and Todes, 2020). Since the early 2000s, spatial planning has cohered around a focus on urban compaction through the use of an urban edge, inner city revitalization, development around a transit-focused corridor linking the major township Soweto to the centre and areas in the north, along with improving living conditions in 'marginalised' former townships. The most recent planning (COJ, 2016, 2021) presents a polycentric compact city model, recognising links to adjacent municipalities as part of a broader city-region. It defines a number of zones of focus, including its prioritised 'transformation' zone, embracing the inner city, Soweto, and the 'Corridors' project linking these areas and the dense Alexandra township through to Sandton (Johannesburg's newer upmarket CBD). It also suggests prospective new corridors linking across areas in the north. While Soweto and Alexandra form part of the 'Integration Zones', several other 'marginalised' areas distant from regions of employment fall out of the area of focus, particularly in the far south. The strategy for these places is to improve public transport, basic services and infrastructure, creating 'liveable and sustainable human settlements' (COJ, 2021: 20), but they are not seen as areas of expansion or a priority for major new investment.

While the City of Johannesburg has attempted to lead development through spatial planning, and was an early innovator in linking infrastructure investment, budgets and spatial planning (Todes, 2012), sustaining this approach has been challenging in recent years. The unseating of the ruling African National Congress (ANC) by an alliance of the opposition DA and the radical Economic Freedom Fighters (EFF) from 2016 to 2019 weakened the link between plans and budgets, with a greater focus on investing in areas of poverty. More recently, unstable, shifting coalitions have undermined spatial policy and its power. Further, as in other municipalities, the drive to deliver low-income housing has resulted in further development close to existing townships or other parts of the edge (Charlton, 2014), although in a rapidly growing polycentric city, some of these places are better located than often assumed. The recent provincially driven housing mega-project and new city ideas, however, present a challenge to the City's compaction ideas. Lufhereng, one of our case studies, is the outcome of a contradictory policy of this sort (Charlton, 2017; see Chapter 2). While Lufhereng is relatively well located in relation to Soweto and within the larger Soweto transformation zone (although still beyond public transport routes), a more peripheral project in the south and the proposed Lanseria smart new city were incorporated into Johannesburg's 2021 Spatial Development Framework (SDF) (COJ, 2021), against the advice of planners.

Strategic spatial plans considering future spatial visions at the level of the Durban city-region (now eThekwini municipality) have emerged since the late 1980s. These initiatives, and the strategic spatial plans of the metropolitan councils set up from 1994, largely embraced compaction ideas and the use of corridors to structure growth. Some of these early plans accepted the idea of major growth in the north, which at the time was largely under sugar cane, or in settlements and small towns, including an upmarket residential and tourist area on the edge of Durban. A site for a new airport had been purchased by the state in the 1970s. A vision of growth along corridors and nodes in the north was produced in a 1989 strategic planning process initiated by the major landowner and sugar producer in the area, Tongaat Hulett, drawing in oppositional academics and political leadership, among others (Todes, 2017). It was facilitated by prevalent assumptions of population growth rates of 4–6 per cent over future decades, and hence by high expected demand for its relatively flat land in a city dominated by incised, hilly topography. A north–south imbalance, where many people lived in the north of the city and in townships in the north-west, while jobs were largely located in the centre and the south, was also influential in arguments for economic development in the north.

In early post-apartheid planning, the north was promoted as the 'jewel in the crown' by local politicians and landowners (Todes, 2000), offering Durban the potential to become more competitive. However, with consolidation into a unitary municipality, municipal officials raised concerns that the growth of the north might undermine the already declining CBD and southern industrial areas. Through negotiated political processes, the growth of the area was ultimately accepted and incorporated into planning (Todes, 2017). Provincial ambitions to stimulate the economy through developing the airport site as a new city airport – initially in conflict with municipal plans – later led to the urban edge moving beyond the airport site to the edge of the municipality in the north. Hence, much of the north has come to be viewed as an area of growth, despite its significant infrastructural costs (Robbins, 2015) and the fact that population growth rates have been far lower than expected (Todes, 2017). Nevertheless, the language of compaction is still used, and an urban development phasing line has been put in place to contain the extent of infrastructure spending in the area (Sim *et al.*, 2016).

eThekwini is structured around the two major highways which intersect to form a T shape along a coastal plane and from the centre through to Gauteng. Areas closest to the T were reserved for whites under apartheid, with black areas more distant and more likely to be located on the most difficult terrain for development. Recent spatial frameworks divide the area into an urban zone (2–4 km from major routes associated with the T), a suburban zone and a rural zone, placing emphasis on the former. The urban zone contains 90 per cent of jobs and 48 per cent of residents, and includes a Prime Investment Corridor and catalytic projects, including an Integrated Rapid Transport Network. It also includes a former industrial decentralisation point and homeland area en route from the port to Gauteng, which contains major new logistics sites. Hence, what might once have been seen as a peripheral area is being repurposed in terms of the new spatial vision (eThekwini, 2020). Much of the northern area, including our case studies there, are within this 'urban zone'.

The focus in the 'suburban zone', 1–2 km beyond the urban zone, is on improving the quality of services and facilities there, and on enhancing connectivity to the urban zone. It includes many of the former townships and informal settlements (eThekwini, 2020). An urban development line is intended to contain development in 'rural' areas, both commercial farmlands and areas administered by traditional authorities. Only basic infrastructural services suited to lower-density development are available in the latter, and municipal rates and regulations do not apply. There have been complaints about the applicable service standards, particularly in densifying areas where middle classes are building large houses in agreement with traditional authorities – a pattern also evident in Ghana. In response a recent SDF opens up the possibility of a more differentiated approach to these areas (eThekwini, 2020).

Hence, there are variations in how different types of urban peripheries are understood and envisioned in national and municipal spatial policies, which have also shifted over time. While compaction ideas are evident in all three contexts, and likewise in the challenge of dealing with histories of apartheid spatial fragmentation, planning responses are shaped by the local spatial contexts, by key actors, institutions and politics.

Ethiopia

In contrast to the mostly gradual change in policy approaches in South Africa, urban peripheries in Ethiopia have been subject to sudden policy shifts, reflecting political tensions and the fractious dynamics of the country's ethnic federalism. Addis Ababa occupies a unique position within this system, being (alongside Dire Dawa) one of two 'federal cities' that have distinct status under the 1994 Constitution. Addis Ababa is by far the larger of the two, and its growth and expansion into the peripheries has been complicated by the fact that it is entirely surrounded by Oromia region: the region in which anti-government protests took root from around 2014, culminating in the change of regime from 2018 and the collapse of the pre-existing political order. Amid this protest and conflict was substantial tension over the direction and management of the capital city's urban periphery. In this section we explore how, after a century of gradual evolution along a particular spatial trajectory, the city's urban form was turned inside out through two distinct processes in the late twentieth and early twenty-first centuries.

The evolution of Addis Ababa's urban form in the twentieth century

To fully understand the nature of Addis Ababa's urban peripheries in Ethiopia, it is necessary to delve into the country's urban history. In the era of Ethiopia's emperors – particularly under the long reign of Haile Selassie from 1930 to 1974 – Addis Ababa's development had been characterised by an unusual level of socio-economic intermingling in space (Pankhurst, 1961; Duroyaume, 2015). This contrasted with the colonial cities in surrounding countries, with their often extreme spatial segregation, and most obviously with apartheid South Africa. Dignitaries were granted large land concessions by the Emperor and gradually sold parts of these off to the growing administrative and commercial classes. These urban middle-class groups would often then construct properties at the rear of their plots, thus offering rental housing to new urban dwellers (Duroyaume, 2015: 398). Hence, the city became characterised by a pattern of 'sumptuous dwellings alongside hovels of wattle and daub' that was unusual in Africa (Duroyaume, 2015: 398). The city was highly unequal – for example, by 1962, 58 per cent of land in the city was owned by just 1,768 individuals (UN-Habitat, 2011: 2) – but this inequality was largely mixed together in space, particularly in central areas of the city (Di Nunzio, 2019: 36). There was some expansion into the peripheries since the city was growing apace, with its population reaching around 800,000 by 1970 (Burton, 2001: 21; Zewde, 2005). However, at this time there was little intentional development of peripheral or 'suburban' areas, which only from the 1960s started to be seen as desirable for dwelling (Zewde, 2005).

Following the communist revolution of 1974, which led to the seizure of power by a military junta known as the Derg, major land reforms were passed in 1975 through which both urban land and all 'extra houses' were nationalised (Tiruneh, 1993). Since Ethiopian towns at this time primarily constituted nobles' grand houses surrounded by many smaller ones built for renting out, nationalising extra houses was a radical step that abolished landlordism overnight. New housing construction also virtually ground to a halt. The imperial urban structure was effectively 'frozen' (Duroyaume, 2015: 400), but the political economy underpinning it transformed. Rents that city-dwellers had paid to landlords were now paid directly to the state at fixed rates. This freezing of rents also meant it was forbidden to develop or structurally augment properties without obtaining special permission, perpetuating the problem of extremely substandard housing. Nevertheless, some suburban housing development did take place in Addis Ababa – particularly in the CMC area to the east of the centre (named after Cooperativa Muratori Cementisti, the Italian contractor that built it), which was established for civil servants during the Derg period.

Throughout this period, a protracted civil war was fought against the Derg regime, led primarily by rebel groups in Tigray and Eritrea. When the rebels finally took power under the banner of the Ethiopian People's Revolutionary Democratic Front (EPRDF) in 1991, they were faced with major decisions about whether to privatise land. This was the course of action preferred by their Western supporters, but being of a Marxist-Leninist persuasion themselves, the EPRDF could not countenance full privatisation. Existing land use was governed by a permit system in which the government would issue permits to use particular plots of land for indefinite periods in exchange for minimal amounts of rent. The EPRDF wanted to unlock the value of land but also combine this with continued state landownership, and in pursuit of this objective, the Addis Ababa City Authority developed a system of land-leasing along the lines of other countries transitioning from socialism. Proclamation number 80/1993 allowed the government to transfer rights over land for specified periods in exchange for market-based land-lease fees, while retaining the ultimate title (see Yusuf et al., 2009 and Goodfellow, 2015 for discussions of different modalities of land-leasing). This turbocharged the real estate market in the capital (Frew Mengistu, 2013) as well as introduced new dynamics to peri-urban areas (Adam, 2014, 2020).

The city turned inside out (and back again?)

As a consequence of these changes, in the 1990s the peripheries of Addis Ababa became places in which a nascent real estate industry took its first steps in experimenting with land commodification and the development of private property. This real estate activity in the periphery helped to build the construction and property development sectors (Himmelrich, 2010), and the peripheries became spaces of middle-class and elite aspiration as large-scale private residential real estate developments flourished on the eastern peripheries (Di Nunzio, 2022a). There was in this sense a gradual shifting of investment from the centre to the emerging suburbs on the part of the few who could afford such real estate.

Despite this, there was very little interest in Addis Ababa or in urban development generally during the first decade of EPRDF rule; indeed, their whole identity was partly predicated on waging war against an urban-based Derg regime and prioritising rural development. Yet the EPRDF's interest in Addis Ababa grew from the early 2000s in the context of an internal political crisis in 2001 and the loss of parliamentary seats in the capital. Despite the sense that urban areas were turning against the EPRDF, the party decided to allow a significant opening of political space in advance of the 2005 election (Pellerin, 2018), leading to the loss of virtually all their seats in Addis Ababa, followed by major protests over the election process and a violent crackdown. These events prompted an acute awareness of the power of the city's population to mobilise and inflict serious political damage on the EPRDF, which generated a new appreciation of the potential of urban investment as a tool to limit opposition and bolster the regime's social legitimacy (Lefort, 2007; Di Nunzio, 2014; Oqubay, 2015; Planel and Bridonneau, 2017; Gebremariam, 2020; Goodfellow, 2022).

This new governmental attention to Addis Ababa manifested in a range of policy initiatives that unfolded on a grand scale over the subsequent decade, alongside a dramatic closure of democratic space (Aalen and Tronvoll, 2009). From this point onwards, urban areas became a priority in the national development plan, the Plan for Accelerated and Sustained Development to End Poverty (PASDEP) (MOFED, 2006; Gebre-Egziabher and Yemeru, 2019). The government established the Ministry of Urban Works and Development in October 2005, and the seeds were sown for large-scale urban investments in infrastructure and housing. This had profound implications for the urban periphery, both by default and by design.

In contrast to the real estate development on the periphery, the new urban infrastructure and housing development drives initially focused on the city centre (Planel and Bridonneau, 2017). The government's Integrated Housing Development Programme (IHDP) – discussed in detail in Chapter 5 – aimed to construct 400,000 condominium units, the first blocks of which were all in central areas of Addis Ababa (UN-Habitat, 2011). By late 2019 over 175,000 had been built in Addis Ababa with 132,000 more under construction (Larsen *et al.*, 2019), and a rate of production of around 30,000 units per year,[2] with waiting lists of over a million people. The programme delivered houses via a lottery scheme through various modalities targeted at different income groups, as explained in Chapter 5. While the first condominium projects were located in central areas, this changed as the government's parallel ambition to turn the city centre into the 'Diplomatic Capital of Africa' gained pace. This vision effectively envisioned central Addis as a 'new city', replacing its distinctive heritage of mixed-income development (Haddis, 2019; Kloosterboer, 2019), and discouraged residential development in the centre. Thus, while the drive towards commercial real estate investment and renewal became increasingly trained on the city centre, the housing programme was reimagined through two complementary logics: on the one hand there was the need to rehouse people displaced by these very processes (Di Nunzio, 2022a), and on the other there was an agenda to locate IHDP housing estates closer to new peripheral industrial projects that were central to the government's broader economic vision (Oqubay, 2015). These included the country's very first industrial park – the Chinese-owned and financed Eastern Industrial Zone, which opened in 2007 close to the town of Dukem in the city's south-eastern periphery – and its first public industrial park (Bole Lemi), which opened in 2014 at the eastern edge of the city's built-up area. In this way construction in the periphery became dominated by the condominium programme, while the commercial redevelopment of the centre gathered pace. As the latter progressed, the city government set out a new structure plan in 2017 and established the City Centres and Corridors Development Corporation to facilitate the development of 'a high-density CBD over 350 ha' of land for higher-value development, including 60 ha of serviced land 'for modern office facilities, retail & recreational facilities and Multinational Corporations' and 15 ha as a regional commercial and transportation hub (Interview with City Government Officials, August 2018). Between 2002 and 2020, there were repeated slum clearances in the centre to make way for major commercial development projects, dispersing the population into the periphery in the process (Terrefe 2020; Weldeghebrael, 2022; Weldegebriel et al., 2021).

However, there are a number of reasons why expansion into the peripheries has been challenging and contentious in Addis Ababa. The first relates simply to the city's physical geography: areas to the immediate north and west of the city are mountainous; hence most of the expansion, industrial parks and residential development (and relatedly our case study area choices) have been in the city's south and east. But the constraints are also political: since Addis Ababa is fully surrounded by the troubled ethnic state of Oromia, expansion into the peripheries has been highly controversial (Lavers, 2023). In 2014 the government unveiled its Addis Ababa Integrated Master Plan (sometimes known as the Addis Ababa and the Surrounding Oromia Special Zone Integrated Development Plan), which proposed to integrate planning between Addis Ababa and a substantial portion of Oromia. This sparked massive fears of land-grabbing and displacement of farmers[3] and generated an explosion of protest (Abate, 2019) that snowballed into the 2014–16 'Oromo protests' focused on a broader range of issues, ultimately leading to the demise of the EPRDF in 2018.

In response to this controversy, grand visions for the urban periphery were downscaled as the new government refocused its attention on transforming the urban core and allegedly promised to rehouse displaced people in centrally located housing projects rather than on the urban edge. Thus, since the 1990s, government-funded housing development has shifted from core to periphery and back again, while private real estate investment began in the periphery and then gravitated towards the city centre. Meanwhile, the peripheries continued to evolve as the peripheral housing programmes were characterised by high levels of tenant turnover, cooperative and private property development continued to expand and farmers displaced by the condominium project often made homes in informal settlements nearby.

Infrastructure and job creation on the periphery

The EPRDF's agenda for Addis Ababa from the mid/late 2000s was sophisticated and multifaceted, encompassing not only city centre renewal and the housing programme discussed above but also major investments in urban roads and rail (Rode *et al.*, 2020; Goodfellow and Huang, 2021), as well as investment in health and education facilities (Duroyaume, 2015), new microfinance and entrepreneurship schemes for small-scale businesses and urban youth (Di Nunzio, 2015) and subsidised urban food distribution (Gebremariam, 2020). Fuelled by the land lease system, in the early–mid 2010s the city was in a process of constant spatial evolution and churn as vast construction projects overturned its history of largely incremental and low-rise development.

This agenda was not only about promoting Addis as a 'diplomatic capital' and investment site and addressing the housing shortage, but also job creation. As well as aiming to build 400,000 housing units, the housing programme aimed to create 200,000 jobs and promote the development of 10,000 micro and small enterprises (MSEs), enhancing the capacity of the construction sector (UN-Habitat, 2011). In some cases, such as Tulu Dimtu and Koye Feche – the largest and most recent major condominium site with 60,000 housing units – there has also been an attempt to link these sites to industrial zones and corridors. However, despite the 'integrated' rationale of the housing programme, officials involved in developing the programme freely admit that the consideration of broader socio-economic considerations came very late: only a few years before the eventual winding down of the programme after 2018.[4] This is arguably because the housing programme was above all designed to build a class of urban EPRDF supporters rather than constitute a planning vision for the urban periphery (Planel and Bridonneau, 2017). In consequence, infrastructural connectivity and livelihood options were highly constrained, as the remainder of this book will show.

The developments described above have left the peripheries of Addis Ababa in a state of limbo. Though the decade from the late 2000s to the late 2010s saw a significant turn towards reimagining the city's edges as spaces of industrial development and residential relocation, this was never articulated as an integrated vision for the periphery. Moreover, moves towards closer integration of the wider city region, promoted through the 2014 Addis Ababa Integrated Master Plan, were radically cut short by the political controversy over the plan and the subsequent snowballing of protests from the city's periphery to the country at large. Under the new regime of Abiy Ahmed from 2018, there was a further shift away from an emphasis on peripheral industrial development towards city centre megaprojects and luxury real estate (Terrefe, 2020). In the context of spiralling civil conflict and concerns about the potential dissolution of the Ethiopian state, visions for the periphery are now low on the political agenda – despite their continued growth as recent 'vanguard' investments evolve side by side with informal settlements, speculation and private real estate development.

Conclusion

This chapter has provided an overview of visions of the urban periphery in South Africa and Ethiopia, and in relation to our case study cities. In South Africa, visions of the urban periphery have been shaped by policies to redress the history of spatial apartheid, which have been informed by compaction discourse. These visions are translated in different ways in the various cities, shaped by their local socio-spatial geographies and politics. While the broad idea of urban compaction has held sway, policies have had to contend with the reality of sprawling cities and fragmented settlements arising from a history of homelands and racial segregation. Such inherited settlements have had their own dynamics, and many of them have continued to grow post-apartheid, as we demonstrate in later chapters. Further, compaction policies have been contradicted by other policies and processes which have resulted in new growth in urban peripheries, as other chapters show – by vanguardist housing and new city projects, by the speculative initiatives of private developers and by forms of auto-construction. Hence, while compaction policies have in some respects consolidated and become more sophisticated over time, urban peripheries have continued to expand. Ironically, visions of urban peripheries themselves have been partial, in many respects residual: although there is an increasingly developed idea of the transformation of former townships, and there are visions of new cities, imagined futures of inherited spaces on the far peripheries and on traditional authority lands are lacking. Nor are urban peripheries specifically considered in national policies.

In contrast to South Africa, sprawl has not historically been a major concern in Ethiopia, with the history of urban growth having been relatively compact. However, Addis Ababa's periphery has been subject to sudden policy shifts, reflecting political concerns – in particular the pressures of ethnic federalism and a new ideological approach since 2018. Private investment in real estate began on the periphery in relatively unplanned ways but then moved towards the centre, particularly in terms of commercial property development encouraged by the vision of the city as Africa's 'diplomatic capital'. Meanwhile, state-funded residential development shifted decisively from centre to periphery – though in the context of contestation over the city's boundary, it is now set to move back towards the centre through new forms of densification. The city's infrastructural and political challenges have therefore produced pendulum swings between expansion and contraction. At the same time, peripheries have developed their own growth dynamics and processes of change, which are not addressed by policy. Our research thus raises questions about the future of these peripheries half-formed by the state. Will they become 'inherited peripheries' that the state is obliged to support, as seen in some of the South African cases?

In both Ethiopia and South Africa, visions of the urban periphery have been part of a broader set of urban spatial policies and strategies. Spatial visions themselves, however, have been highly political, and there are often contradictions between spatial planning and other policy priorities. Despite attempts to put in place more coherent forms of planning in some contexts, fully integrated approaches have been lacking. Further, urban spatial policy coherence often loses out to politically appealing grand interventions based on top-down governance and planning, and to shifting priorities. However, although urban peripheries are an element of urban spatial policy, their diverse logics, their dynamism and the longer-term implications of spatial and other policies for these areas and for people living there remain to be fully considered. The rest of the book makes some contribution to these ends.

Notes

1 BEPPs were later phased out, but their planning approach was to be incorporated into SDFs (Duminy *et al.*, 2020).
2 Interview with government adviser, 24 November 2017.
3 Despite the controversy, the planners involved maintain that this was rooted in fundamental misunderstanding since the plan was never to actually annex surrounding land or extend the boundaries of the city but rather to integrate the master plans for each surrounding area with that of Addis Ababa (Interview with planner in the Addis Ababa Integrated Development Plan Office, 30 September 2014).
4 Interviews with housing and planning officials in Addis Ababa in 2017 and 2018.

2

Investment and economic change on the urban periphery

Alison Todes, Sarah Charlton and Tom Goodfellow

Investment and economic change are two of the key drivers shaping places on the urban periphery, and people's experience of them. Literatures exploring these dynamics range from the earlier work on edge cities and later explorations of new forms of economic and residential development on the edge, to older work on satellite cities and recent work on new cities (e.g. Van Noorloos and Kloosterboer, 2018; Cote-Roy and Moser, 2019) to the more recent suburbanism research (Keil, 2018) which includes studies on the development of new centralities. Much of this work, however, focuses on understanding growth and large-scale investment on the edge – there is less attention to decline and to smaller-scale processes of economic change. Keil and Wu (2022) also note that there is little work examining the roles of various agencies and actors in peripheral urban expansion. This is particularly the case in African contexts (Mabin *et al.*, 2013), although South African literature has long considered the generic role of state-planning in driving peripheral growth (Harrison *et al.*, 2008; Charlton, 2014), and some of the 'new city' literature considers these issues.

This chapter contributes to this work and provides an understanding of the drivers shaping change in our Ethiopian and South African case studies, in all of which there has been significant private and public investment at some point, evidencing logics of a speculative and vanguard periphery. Some of these places are now experiencing economic decline and show logics of an inherited periphery. The chapter highlights and explains key investment and economic dynamics, focusing on formal sectors (with informal livelihood generation discussed in the following chapter). It considers the contribution of parts of the state and the private sector to investment and economic change and how this has evolved over time, locating the discussion of the cases in an overview of the economies of the two countries.

South Africa

The South African economy developed historically around a 'mineral-energy' complex (Fine and Rustomjee, 1996), with a relatively narrow economic base and a highly concentrated ownership (Philip et al., 2014; Black, 2016). In the post-apartheid era since 1994, the economy has shifted away from agriculture, mining and manufacturing towards services and finance, with the tertiary sector now accounting for the largest share of employment. Manufacturing growth has 'imploded in terms of both output and employment' (Bhorat et al., 2020: 11), with significant losses in labour-intensive sectors and growth mainly in more capital-intensive firms (Black, 2016). Employment has largely been in high-skill areas, while the demand for low-skilled and semi-skilled workers has declined. After a period of decline in the early post-apartheid period, social inequalities have risen and are some of the highest in the world (Makgetla, 2020). The state has 'compensated' the poor through social grants and programmes such as free 'RDP'[1] housing, but deep structural inequalities remain.

While South Africa's economic growth post-apartheid has never been rapid, its economic performance since the 2008 global economic crisis has been 'lacklustre' (Bhorat et al., 2020: 18), with growth rates averaging 1.7 per cent per annum between 2009 and 2018 (Visagie and Turok, 2020) and with sharp declines since then. Unemployment rose from 23.7 per cent in 2009 (National Treasury, 2019) to 29 per cent[2] in 2019 even before the impact of the Covid-19 crisis in 2020. Growth rates have declined through the impact of Covid and other shocks, and national unemployment rates have since risen to 32.9 per cent in 2023 (StatsSA, 2023). The effects of an energy crisis, weak governance, political conflict and corruption have also been significant (Swilling et al., 2017).

Spatial patterns of growth and decline within cities in the late-apartheid and post-apartheid era reflect these patterns of economic change and social inequality. Within eThekwini, Johannesburg and Tshwane, major private sector property investment has been concentrated in middle and high-end gated residential complexes, particularly on urban edges where large land parcels are available, and in decentralised office and retail centres, sometimes creating new centralities. Several older industrial areas have declined and lost employment, including those in or near former townships once reserved for black African people. At the same time, post-apartheid state investment in low-income housing projects has largely been on the edge but often close to townships. Hence, private 'speculative' and state 'vanguardist' property investments have been significant in particular types of peripheral growth, though not necessarily in the same spaces.

Within the context of our research, eThekwini north reflects patterns of both private speculative and state vanguardist investment, while Molweni is located some 10 and 20 km respectively from the growing Waterfall and Hillcrest economic nodes, which have redeveloped following upmarket residential property developments from the 1990s. In Johannesburg, private property development and the growth of new centralities have been concentrated in the north. Our Lufhereng case, in the west, reflects a form of vanguardist state investment, but it is also shaped by speculative private property development of a different kind to that evident in the eThekwini north case. Major areas of private property growth in Tshwane have been distant from our case studies. Ekangala, as discussed below, was the product of an apartheid, state vanguardist logic of investment in housing and industrial infrastructure but is now experiencing decline, while the Winterveld has been bypassed by significant private and state investment logics, although there has been a level of state investment in RDP housing and services, and more recently in the Mabopane station node, some 10 km away. In what follows we explain patterns of investment and economic change in eThekwini north, Ekangala and Lufhereng.

eThekwini north

Among all our cases, the logic of the 'speculative periphery' is most evident in the expansion of northern eThekwini, which was driven initially by the major landowner in the area, Tongaat-Hulett. The firm was a large sugar producer listed on the Johannesburg stock exchange, with operations in several countries. From the 1980s it began to pursue a property development strategy, strategically planning for and converting its land in the area to urban development. By 2021 around 3,600 ha had been released from agriculture, although not all in this area. It used its own planning initiatives (Chapter 1), its power as a major landowner and its position as one of the very few large, locally headquartered companies to gain acceptance for the idea of northern expansion and to shape how this was to occur. Hence, a series of largely upmarket retail, residential, industrial and recreational developments were approved from the early 1990s (Todes, 2014a). Tongaat-Hulett controlled the release of its land carefully to maintain property values and to realise its plans. By 2000 there was considerable congruence between Tongaat-Hulett's strategic plan for the area and actual development (McCarthy and Robinson, 2000). While its developments were largely upmarket, it later entered into a partnership with the municipality to develop Cornubia, a large, mixed, low-/low-middle-income housing development, to some extent countering the class-divided new city which was emerging in the north.

Logics of a 'vanguardist periphery' are also very evident in the development of the region. In the late-apartheid years, Waterloo was planned as part of the state's initiative to create very large townships for black Africans on the edges of cities, although it was only developed in the post-apartheid era as an RDP housing project. Hammonds Farm and Cornubia were also the consequence of post-apartheid state vanguardist planning to deliver low-income RDP and mixed housing (see Chapter 6).

The development of the new King Shaka airport, opened in 2010, is another kind of vanguardist investment logic initiated by other parts of the state. At a cost of R8b, it was one of the two largest infrastructure projects of the decade in eThekwini (Robbins, 2015). Although supported by the private sector, it was primarily driven as an economic initiative of the provincial government, initially contrary to municipal plans. Planned as 'an aerotropolis' focused on logistics and a state-supported special economic zone (SEZ) (Dube TradePort (DTP)), it was intended to provide a major economic stimulus to the region. Major state investment in road infrastructure supported these developments.

As a consequence, eThekwini north grew significantly as a site for new property development in the city, dominating such development in the city from 1996, especially in non-residential sectors (see Todes, 2014a; StatsSA, 2021 data[3]). The growth of economic activity in parts of the north is also evident in a Cities Support Programme (CSP) (2021a) analysis of spatial change in employment and firms from 2013 to 2017, although the central and southern areas of the city are still dominant (see also eThekwini, 2020). Economic growth within the north is more concentrated around Umhlanga than the airport, which has had a more limited impact than expected, giving support to concerns that it would not be economically viable and was 'premature' (Todes, 2014a). Hansmann's (2020) study shows that Durban's cargo and logistics industry remains focused on the seaport, while OR Tambo airport in Gauteng continues to dominate the air-related industry. Only 1,386 jobs had been created in DTP by 2019, most not focused on logistics. Hence, the effects of speculative and vanguardist investment have been uneven in their impact across the region, and socially, as we demonstrate throughout the book.

Nor is this growth ongoing or secure. StatsSA (2021) data show a sharp decline in private building plans passed from 2016 with a slight uptick only in 2021 in non-residential development, when eThekwini as a whole grew more rapidly. Several factors may explain these changes, including the performance of the economy as a whole and Durban's position within it, and the Covid pandemic from 2020. Whereas eThekwini municipality was once seen as competent, political divisions and conflict within the municipality in recent years, with accusations of corruption and fraud, have contributed to Durban's declining image as a place of investment. This has been exacerbated by concerns about municipal financial challenges, capacity losses and poor service delivery (Interviews, SA Academic 3, 2022; SA Councillor 1, eThekwini, 2022). Although development has continued to occur in the north, it is at a much slower pace as the demand for property, particularly offices and upmarket residential development, has declined (Interview, SA Private Sector 1, 2022). With Covid, the reduction in flights and passenger numbers affected the viability of the airport, and the development of DTP stagnated. Plans for DTP to double its land holdings and grow the number of large-scale tenants have not been realised since 2017. Nor has there been much state investment in housing in recent years (Interview, SA Councillor 1, eThekwini, 2022).

Importantly, Tongaat-Hulett itself, once the major driver of growth in the north, has experienced significant crisis affecting the region. Between 2015 and 2018, fraudulent accounting and misrepresentation of profits from land and property resulted in arrests of some executives, a loss of reputation and a sharp decline in the company's share price. Initiatives to restructure the company to reduce debt ultimately led to the loss of some 8,000 jobs across the firm, a decimation of the property development company, and the sale or bonding of assets and land holdings (Harper, 2022). By the end of October 2022, the company went into business rescue. With its decline and a weakening municipality, the former drive for investment in the region has been lost (Interviews, SA Academic 3, 2022; SA Private Sector 1, 2022).

A violent insurrection with Durban at the epicentre in July 2021 and major floods in April 2022 have also had devastating effects on Durban's economy and on the north. This has been exacerbated by municipal underspending on infrastructure maintenance, with little done to address the effects of these crises in the north and elsewhere (SA Councillor 1, eThekwini, 2022). Hence, the years of speculative and vanguardist development in the north seem to be over, at least for now, demonstrating the temporality of these processes.

Ekangala/Ekandustria

Ekangala and Ekandustria evidence logics of 'inherited peripheries', in this case the long-term consequence of historic vanguardist apartheid planning coupled with state investment to support the establishment of ethnic homelands (or Bantustans). Ekangala was created in 1982 by the East Rand Administration Board, which was responsible for controlling the 'influx' and settlement of black African people as part of the state's 'orderly urbanisation' policy. The area was later incorporated into the KwaNdebele homeland, which had been established in 1977. Ekandustria was established in 1984 through the apartheid state's industrial decentralisation policy, which offered large subsidies on employment to designated 'deconcentration' and 'decentralisation' points in or near homelands at the time. The policy had been established in 1960 and evolved in its aims and orientations until its demise in 1996 (Todes and Turok, 2018). However, its main focus in the apartheid era was to contain the growth of the black African population within the big cities through limiting industrial development there (and specifically the growth of labour-intensive industries) and encouraging its growth within or close to the Bantustans. Unions were banned in Bantustans, and minimum wages did not apply there, so wages could be lower than in the cities. The establishment of Ekandustria occurred in a period when the state was extending the policy, increasing levels of subsidy to businesses there as part of its 'state reform' to divide the black African population between those with urban rights in the cities and others who would be 'citizens' of Bantustans.

Ekandustria was run by the KwaNdebele Development Corporation (KDC) and expected ultimately to support a population of around 300,000. Harrison and Dinath (2017) note that although this was never achieved, it grew relatively rapidly in the early period, attracting a range of industries, offering around 10,000 jobs by 1991. Industries included a large contingent of Taiwanese firms, attracted in part through proactive recruitment by the nearby Bronkhorstspruit municipality and their establishment of a residential area for Taiwanese residents (Hart, 2002; Harrison and Dinath, 2017). Taiwanese firms, which accounted for half of the new jobs created in decentralisation points in the 1980s (Lin, 2001; Xu, 2019), were also drawn to apartheid South Africa by its diplomatic relations with the Taiwanese state and by structural changes in its economy, which undermined the viability of low-wage industries (Hart, 2002).

Conditions changed in the post-apartheid era with the South African state severing ties with the Taiwanese government and with the withdrawal of industrial decentralisation policy and incentives. The rapid dropping of international tariff barriers also had its effects. Ekandustria, like many other industrial decentralisation points, experienced severe decline as firms moved out. There was some revival and investment by new firms in Ekandustria from the late 2000s (Harrison and Dinath, 2017), but overall employment has declined (CSP, 2021b), especially since 2015. Interviews with City of Tshwane officials (SA Government Officials 2, 5, 2018) indicated that firms were moving out, and it was difficult to attract new companies into the area: firms were seeking more central locations, accessible to major highways, and more skilled workers. The poor state of infrastructure – graphically demonstrated in Figure 2.1 – and the levels of criminality (including the operation of gangs) also underpinned decline. A 2018 figure of 6,000 jobs given by the deputy minister of the national Department of Trade and Industry (ePropertyNews, 2018) seems high in the light of the apparent state of the area but nevertheless showed considerable decline. By 2019 only 56 per cent of the sites were occupied (Industrial Property News, 2019). Part of the problem has been that while the area was incorporated into the City of Tshwane and Gauteng in 2011, Ekandustria itself is still managed by the Mpumulanga Economic Development Agency (MEGA), which inherited the assets of the KDC. MEGA amasses revenue from the area but has not been using it to maintain infrastructure there. A programme to revitalise the area by improving infrastructure was launched by the Department of Trade and Industry in 2019, but there are concerns that it has not been effective as the governance problems remain.

In this case, investment in the area has been driven by the state with varying logics, with changing responses by private industrialists. Meanwhile, state investment in RDP housing and related infrastructure in the area has continued. In this and other later chapters,

Figure 2.1 Declining Ekandustria (source: Mark Lewis)

we explore the social implications of these dynamics and how they have been experienced in the area.

Lufhereng

Along the edge of Soweto on the western boundary of Johannesburg, diverse forms of residential development include a vanguard state-sponsored housing development, a long-standing speculative initiative incubated decades ago under apartheid (Butcher, 2016) and a precarious auto-constructed settlement at the time of our research undergoing relocation to make way for commercial development. Although reflecting significant government and private sector investment, this expansion of the city is at odds with spatial plans and economic trajectories in Johannesburg, as the subregion is disconnected from priority growth areas and was identified as an area where further extension should not be supported through state infrastructure (Ahmad, 2010; Charlton, 2017). This anomaly is at least in part explained by the relationship between its vanguard aspects in the form of the state-driven, mixed-income housing project Lufhereng and the longer-rooted speculative component, the large Protea Glen development. It illustrates close private–public connections historically but also differing priorities, political relations and power dynamics between levels of government.

The privately driven development of Protea Glen contains multiple extensions of mostly mortgage housing for ownership, often aimed at first-time homeowners. Butcher (2016) shows how the plan for the area originated under apartheid and resulted from a perceived but also constructed opportunity. Township Realtors, with connections to the governing National Party and involved in its spatial tactics, started acquiring land in the area in the 1980s with an eye to future residential property demand from black urban residents. This aligned with a change in political strategy during the late-apartheid era from preventing to promoting urban homeownership, discussed in Chapter 6. Township Realtors saw an opportunity to build housing on inexpensive land, available as it was undesirable or uncontested for other development (Butcher, 2016). While the land had some unfavourable geotechnical aspects, the plan would attract 'no white NIMBYism to prevent it' (Butcher, 2016: 57). However, even the state took some persuading to support the development: for decades expansion of Soweto to the west of the natural boundary of the Klipspruit water system was considered inappropriate, with the company itself noting that 'it took four years to persuade the then Department of Community Development to grant [us] the right to develop across the Klipspruit' (Township Realtors Land Developers, n.d.).

In 1990 the first 1,315 stands in Protea Glen were serviced, and over time a further twenty-seven extensions with over 34,000 residential units were built. By 1996 the developers had secured Nelson Mandela to do the ceremonial opening of Extension 11 of the development, seemingly securing a post-apartheid stamp of approval despite the area's location. More than thirty years later, the area now includes a large shopping mall, many smaller shops and government investment, including the Rea Vaya rapid bus transit route and wi-fi service. As we discuss in Chapter 6, for some people it is now a highly desirable area to live in, a successful example of the development strategy of a core group of private sector players operating across the city: what Butcher (2016) describes as the network of developers, financiers and landowners that is shaping the city by how and where they build affordable housing. Responding to a demand for low-cost residential units, these new schemes are often in peripheral areas where established developers have acquired land over decades, capturing a market that has almost no alternatives in their price range in better locations (Butcher, 2016).

On this western edge of Soweto, the affordable housing momentum of Protea Glen has arguably drawn in a major vanguard development. A few kilometres away, the flagship mixed-income project of Lufhereng began construction in 2008 but had been mooted by provincial authorities at least a decade before (Urban Dynamics, n.d. a). Celebrated in its early stages as 'the biggest single planned development area in the country' (Urban Dynamics, n.d.b), it was anticipated to eventually house between 65,000 and 100,000 people (City of Johannesburg, 2015) in both fully subsidised and mortgage-linked accommodation, aimed at easing some of the pressure on state housing waiting lists and in particular the housing backlog in Soweto (Urban Econ, 2014; Charlton, 2017).

Provincial planners and their consultants contend this area is 'a natural extension of Soweto' (Charlton, 2017), close to Protea Glen and 'a natural extension of the Dobsonville and Protea Glen communities' (Urban Econ, 2014: 95). However, the location was not supported in city spatial plans. Despite their opposition, city officials speak of having to fall in line with, invest in and support the Lufhereng development as it was pushed by the provincial sphere of government (Charlton, 2017), often politically dominant. For the province, wider interests beyond the housing demand in Johannesburg come into play: neighbouring smaller municipalities affected by the decline in the once thriving mining industry are also under pressure to deliver the housing benefit to poor communities, and more generally they seek to connect with the relative strength and dynamism of the Johannesburg metropolitan municipality (Interview, SA Government Official 8, Gauteng Province, 2018). Edge developments of various kinds both in the metro and across its border help the province to foster these ties, and the province is supporting other 'mega-human settlements' in the wider area. Though a contested view, these are couched by the province as contributing to the spatial transformation of the Gauteng city-region, with renewed calls to somehow ensure the necessary economic opportunities and social facilities are created and function in these developments (Gauteng Department of Human Settlements, 2022). At the same time, there are paradoxical actions by authorities: residents in the auto-constructed informal settlement of Waterworks to the south of Protea Glen were accessing precarious, low-paid jobs within walking distance just across the border in Johannesburg but have now been relocated (at least those who qualified for the housing benefit) further away into the Rand West municipality, in anticipation of a private shopping centre development near the land they had occupied.

These peripheral developments have a high price. Concerns with Lufhereng include the huge investment in infrastructure needed to develop this former farm and mining land, and significant delays have manifested while the city attempts to fund this and to overcome technical difficulties on site. Residents who have moved into the early phases of subsidised housing experience its disconnect from existing transport infrastructure, its distance from significant economic opportunities and the difficulty of stimulating local economies. A confident-sounding economic development plan produced for the Lufhereng area by consultants envisioned agricultural activities, small-scale manufacturing linked to household needs and the provision of goods and services to the local residents (Urban Econ, 2014). But there is little evidence of this economic activity to date, with provincial officials fearing it will take decades to materialise. This leaves virtually indigent beneficiaries of state housing largely disconnected from income-generating opportunities and affordable transport. In Protea Glen decades of promotion by a private sector with the power to channel what is termed 'affordable housing' development into certain parts of the city has eventually resulted in a more consolidated set of neighbourhoods with retail and other investment; however, the viable realisation of the follow-on, state-led development of Lufhereng is lagging far behind.

Ethiopia

The Ethiopian economy has been the subject of significant fascination in recent decades given its tumultuous history alongside recent world-leading levels of economic growth. Following centuries of imperial rule during which there was little investment in urban centres or manufacturing, the first factories were established in the 1920s and 1930s, along with inter-city roads and a renewed attention to the banking sector (Bekele, 2019). These activities increased during the Italian occupation from 1936 to 1941, with the occupiers upgrading major roads to asphalt as well as investing in a range of industries in Addis Ababa and Dire Dawa (Zewde, 1991). When Haile Selassie returned to power in 1941, there was a period of significant American influence during which foreign capital began to trickle into import-substituting industries in the mid-twentieth century as the Emperor attempted to pursue a transition to a modern, capitalist economy (Markakis, 1974). This, however, was radically cut short by the 1974 revolution and the radical socialist policies of the Derg regime, which instituted a range of sweeping nationalisations not only of key industries but also, as noted in the previous chapter, of land and 'extra houses'. By the end of the Derg period in 1991, as well as the formal capitalist property market having been shut down through state ownership, the majority of key industries were controlled by the state – including large proportions of transport and communications, mining, construction, electricity, banking and communications (Lefort, 2015). The Ethiopian

People's Revolutionary Democratic Front (EPRDF) thus inherited a state-dominated economy in which there had been very little investment in physical infrastructure and technological innovation (Oqubay, 2019).

Economic policy under the EPRDF has been extensively documented, both in terms of how it sought to find a path between its Marxist-Leninist ideological orientation and the neoliberal prescriptions of eager foreign donors (Demissie, 2008; Vaughan and Gebremichael, 2011; Clapham, 2018) and in terms of its success in producing sustained economic growth rates of over 8 per cent from the early 2000s until 2018 (Lefort, 2015; Oqubay, 2015; Cheru et al., 2019). Central to the trajectory of investment was a shift from a relatively unsuccessful policy of raising agricultural productivity through the paradigm of 'Agricultural Development-Led Industrialisation' (ADLI), initiated in 1993, towards an increased emphasis on direct support to industry and infrastructure. This began with the Industrial Development Strategy in 2002, followed by a more concerted focus on infrastructure investment under the Plan for Accelerated Development to End Poverty (PASDEP) from 2006 and a further ramping up of public investment under the Growth and Transformation Plan (GTP) from 2010 (Cheru et al., 2019; Oqubay, 2019).

It was with PASDEP and the GTP that major investments in critical infrastructure such as roads, rail, power generation and irrigation soared, with the aim of stimulating an industrial transition (Ali, 2019). In 2015 the GTP was supplanted by GTP-II, which explicitly recognised the importance of urbanisation for Ethiopia's industrial transition (Gebre-Egziabher and Yemeru, 2019). In the GTP-II period, gross fixed capital formation reached 41.3 per cent of GDP in 2019/20 (Manyazewal, 2019: 176). Much of this growth in fixed capital took the form of new roads, other infrastructure, housing construction and industry in the new peripheries of Ethiopian cities as Ethiopia experienced unprecedented levels of urban physical expansion.

Addis Ababa

The major investments in Addis Ababa in recent decades need to be understood against this historical and contemporary policy backdrop. However, there is also a distinct story to be told at the city scale. Having been founded by Emperor Menelik and his wife Taitu in 1886, Addis Ababa itself (initially conceived as another temporary capital in a long line of such temporary capitals) soon became the Ethiopian empire's permanent capital, following the growth of the state bureaucracy as the imperial boundaries grew and consolidated. A first major wave of investment into the urban built environment came in 1904–5 when the palace ordered the demolition of all wood and mud houses with thatched roofs, before having them rebuilt in stone with corrugated iron roofs – a move that was seen as an important harbinger of urban modernity (Bekele, 2019: 22). The city's growth was given a major impetus by the Addis Ababa–Djibouti railway, which was initiated in 1896 but only reached the Ethiopian capital in 1917. The railway became the primary means through which Ethiopia was integrated into the world economy (Zewde, 1991), and consequently the city flourished and became a space of substantial investment in housing of various kinds. By the second decade of the twentieth century, Addis Ababa had overtaken Harar to be the most significant city in the Ethiopian empire (Bekele, 2019). The Italian occupation, though only five years long, had a disproportionate effect on the city – not only in terms of expansion and investment in some infrastructure but also with regard to the racial policy that resulted in the dispersal of many Ethiopians to a large new 'native' area of the city around a new marketplace (*Merkato*). Following this, Haile Selassie's own modernisation drive involved a massive expansion of the state bureaucracy, bolstering the city's population with large numbers of people on the government payroll as well as a growing student population (Zewde, 1991; Clapham, 2017; Bekele, 2019).

As discussed in Chapter 1, a rentier economy evolved under the emperors that fuelled the property market as the city's bureaucratic and emergent middle classes expanded but which was abruptly halted by the Derg's land and housing policy from 1975. Under the Derg there was little incentive to invest in properties that one did not own – and indeed there was a range of regulations and restrictions that prevented properties from being substantially improved, as well as some limiting how much new housing was built (Tiruneh, 1993; Duroyaume, 2015; Zewdie *et al.*, 2018; Larsen *et al.*, 2019). This had profound effects for the housing shortages that have shaped investment decisions in Addis Ababa in more recent years, with the major undersupply of property even for middle- and higher-income residents driving the majority of domestic and diaspora investment into the real estate sector (Goodfellow, 2017a). At the same time, the nationalisation of land – and the EPRDF's decision to maintain state ownership despite the introduction of a leasehold system – has enabled the government to distribute large amounts of land for priority investments with relative ease. This too has had profound consequences in the peripheries. As noted in the previous chapter, in the first decade and a half of its rule, the EPRDF showed little interest in urban areas – but from 2005 onwards the peripheries became spaces of expansion and speculative real estate investment, followed by large-scale vanguardist government projects. Figure 2.2 illustrates how condominium sites have come to be concentrated in the city's eastern peripheries particularly, while over the same period the concentration of the population in mud and wood houses in central areas has declined.

Our two Ethiopian case study areas demonstrate some similarities but also contrasting dynamics when it comes to both vanguardist and speculative private sector investment, as we explore below. In general, however, it is difficult to overstate the degree to which

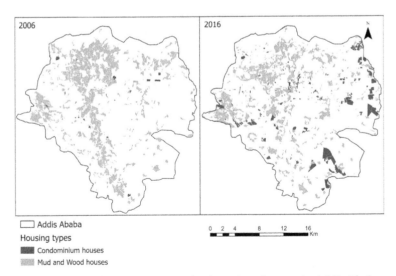

Figure 2.2 Condominium sites and informal settlements in Addis Ababa (source: Larsen *et al.* 2019: 10, adapted by Tilahun Fikadu, 2023)

the Integrated Housing Development Programme (IHDP; discussed in Chapters 1 and 5) has impacted on the extent and rapidity of public investment in these areas more generally, including with respect to roads, water and sanitation infrastructure, telecommunications and other infrastructural systems (see Chapter 9). Accompanying this in both areas have been rather different dynamics of private sector investment, which has flourished particularly around Yeka Abado, with the emergence of gated communities that, in general, are uncharacteristic of Ethiopian urban development.

Tulu Dimtu

Tulu Dimtu was selected as a location for major government housing and infrastructure investment partly because it was close to existing industrial areas in an area called Akaki in Oromia, along the corridor between Addis Ababa and the nearby town of Dukem. The condominium settlement at Tulu Dimtu, which consists of around 10,000 households, sits at the intersection of two major expressways, including the recent $612m Chinese-built and financed Addis Ababa–Adama Expressway, as well as the older A1 road that runs through various towns and industrial areas. The scattered industrial investments along this corridor culminate in the Chinese-owned Eastern Industrial Zone, a very large (223 ha), privately run industrial park and the first of its kind in Ethiopia. This zone, which became operational in 2013, has generated significant amounts of investment and employment – at least 8,000 local jobs according to one study (Fei and Liao, 2020: 633) – while also playing a major role influencing Ethiopia's broader industrial park development strategy and ushering in further Chinese investment (Brautigam and Tang, 2014; Lin *et al.*, 2019; Goodfellow and Huang, 2021). It has, however, been criticised on the basis of not building sufficient linkages with the wider economy (Giannecchini and Taylor, 2018). Around the same distance from Tulu Dimtu is the first government-run industrial park, Bole Lemi, a 156-ha site operational since 2014, the second phase of which (186 ha) is under development (Ethiopian Academic 1, 2018).

Even closer to the Tulu Dimtu condominium site, less than 5 km due north, is Kilinto Industrial Park. This has been under construction since 2016 on 279 ha of former farmland and is aimed specifically at stimulating the pharmaceutical industry (Ethiopian Academic 1, 2018; Ethiopian Consultant 1, 2018). However, in the context of Ethiopia's civil strife since 2018 and ongoing disputes between the Industrial Parks Development Corporation, the city government and the electricity utility, both Kilinto and Bole Lemi phase II are still not operational despite having received $425m in financing from the World Bank and apparently being '98% complete' as long ago as 2018 (Endale, 2022). Meanwhile, alongside these vanguard investments there have been some private investments in industrial zones and large factories, including an IT park and a Heineken beer factory. In keeping with the industrial and IT focus of investments in the area, the new Addis Ababa University Technology Campus (where 30,000 students study) is also very close by, midway between Tulu Dimtu and Kilinto (Ethiopian Consultant 1, 2018). Moreover, while the area to the north of Tulu Dimtu was until very recently primarily farmland, this has radically changed with the construction of Koye Feche condominiums, which is by far the largest single condominium site with some 60,000 housing units. Koye Feche condominiums are clearly visible as the largest single block of condominiums (see Figure 2.2 above, where the substantial block is evident in the bottom-right corner of the map). The creation of space for transport infrastructure has also been a feature of investment in Tulu Dimtu, which is close to some of the most significant transport routes out of Addis Ababa, including the railway to Djibouti and the expressway to Adama, which runs via a major dry port at Mojo (as is evident in Figure 0.3 in the Introduction).

Although we found it difficult through our key informant interviews to establish a clear rationale for Tulu Dimtu condominiums being sited so far out on the Oromia border, there is therefore a logic to the overall focus of investments in the wider area and the function of a large housing settlement within this. These developments also mean that the construction sector – including many small and medium-sized enterprises – and construction workers themselves are a feature of the area. Moreover, the displacement of farmers has resulted in new displacement sites in which former farmers and construction workers often live side by side, right next to the condominium site, as indicated by the area circled on the very right-hand side of Figure 2.3. Also evident in Figure 2.3 is the

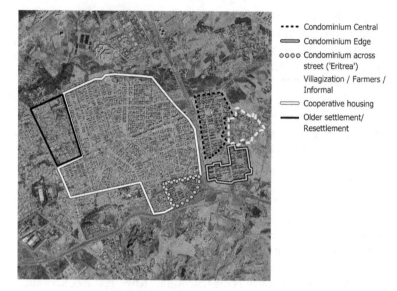

Figure 2.3 Tulu Dimtu area (adapted from Google)

extent to which the Tulu Dimtu condominiums border an area of cooperative housing to the west, which is much more geographically expansive than the condominium site itself. This kind of housing, which involves small-scale private investment by families and groups that come together to form cooperatives under a specific government scheme, will be discussed in Chapter 5. As is also evident from Figure 2.3, there is a stark spatial divide within the condominium settlement between the areas east of the main road and junction and the area to the west – nicknamed 'Eritrea' due to its isolation from the main part of the settlement.

Yeka Abado

While Yeka Abado has seen similar dynamics in terms of public investment in trunk infrastructure associated with the IHDP sites, it is more of a residential and service-based area, with significant private investment in housing and real estate of various kinds. This in many ways is a natural extension of the explosion of property development in the Ayat area to the east of the city centre and the more general eastward expansion of residential development in the city where there are fewer geographical constraints to expansion than in the north and west. Yeka Abado has thus been described as a 'showcase' for real estate development that can attract significant domestic and private investment, as well as somewhere with relatively little pollution and noise and with pleasant mountain scenery (Addis Ababa Housing Official 2, 2018). Seen increasingly as an area for middle-income settlement, Ayat and the surrounding areas have seen a massive property boom both through the allocation of land to private real estate developers and through various condominium sites around the city's east and north-east fringes, including Yeka Abado condominiums themselves at the very edge. Straddling the border with Oromia, Yeka Abado condominiums incorporate 18,169 units that house over 100,000 people in 746 separate housing blocks across 250 ha of land. Most of these are five storeys high and of the 20/80 typology (see Chapter 5), though with some 10/90 and some 40/60 blocks as well. To give some sense of the scale of activity involved, 287 separate contractors were involved in the construction of this condominium site, though with 668 micro and small enterprises (MSEs) playing a role if all of the materials and infrastructure provision are taken into account, and around 12,000 people were employed in the process (data provided by the IHDP branch office, 2018). Despite this large-scale public investment in housing and infrastructure – on an even larger scale than in Tulu Dimtu – Yeka Abado is seen as an area in which private investment dominates over public investment to a much greater extent than Tulu Dimtu. There have been some major investments in real estate in the neighbouring Legetafo area bordering Yeka Abado but on the Oromia side of the border – most notably the Country Club Developers' (CCD) gated community, clearly visible as the largest of the contiguous blocks of development outlined on the top right-hand side of Figure 2.4. According to the Developers' website, a fully finished, four-bedroom house in CCD currently retails at around 30,000,000 Ethiopian birr (US \$560,000).[4] West of this is an older and somewhat less upmarket real estate project (Ropak). Being in Oromia, both projects have been controversial in view of concerns about the expansion of the city into Oromo territory, which fuelled protest movements in Oromia from 2014. On the Addis Ababa side of the boundary, the growth and transformation of Yeka Abado areas were so substantial as to lead the city

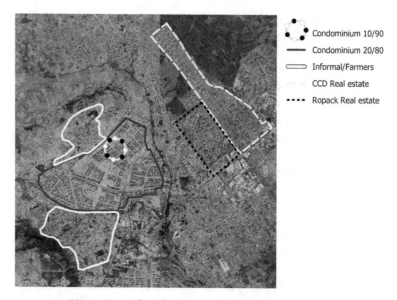

Figure 2.4 Yeka Abado area (adapted from Google)

government to carve out a new sub-city (Lemi Kura) in October 2020 to ensure that residents could have access to improved services and administration (see Chapter 5).

The rapid expansion of the Yeka Abado area has again meant that both displaced farmers and construction workers need to be accommodated, which mostly takes the form of establishing temporary or permanent homes in informal settlements, visible in the circled areas on the left-hand side of Figure 2.4. Like most of the city's eastern and southern peripheries, Yeka Abado was predominantly agrarian land held by Oromo farmers through forms of rural tenure.[5] Policymakers in Addis Ababa conceded that farmers were made landless as a result of these processes and that inadequate attention was given to the wellbeing of these people – with one commenting that 'we created a huge mess in the peripheries' (Addis Ababa Labour Official 1, 2018). Compensation was widely agreed to be inadequate, with monetary compensation generally being offered to farmers without sufficient guidance and support regarding how this might be used to establish a new livelihood (see Chapter 3). Moreover, while some people displaced from city centre areas under the urban renewal drive discussed in Chapter 1 were offered small condominium units in Yeka Abado, this was not the case for displaced farmers who usually ended up in informal settlements (Ethiopian Government Official 2, 2018). Despite these challenges, and the political upheavals since 2018, the area has continued to see widespread investment in facilities such as health centres, schools and business centres and is considered a thriving part of the city (Addis Ababa Housing Official 5, 2022).

Conclusion

This chapter has shown the diverse trajectories and dynamics of investment and economic change in the case studies, the various actors and the agencies involved. All of the cases show the significant role of a vanguardist state in driving investment – very often in housing but also through infrastructure development. Some of this infrastructure development has been focused on promoting economic development. Airports and industrial sites have been developed, transport infrastructure has been created and in some cases other strategies have been put in place to support economic development, with varying degrees of success. In eThekwini north and Yeko Abado, some state-led housing projects have followed or come after economic activity on the periphery, although they may also have been driven by other logics.

The private sector has also been key in investment and economic change on the periphery – as speculative landowners, through their long-term strategies to revalorise property on the periphery, and as property developers and investors in (often upmarket, gated) housing estates, large industrial zones, offices, retail and tourist developments. Direct investment in transport infrastructure has also been evident in the Ethiopian cases. Different parts of the private sector have been involved, with variations in the scale and sector of firms and encompassing both foreign and domestic companies. In some cases, as in Yeko Abado and eThekwini north, private investment dominates in the region or has driven growth in the area. But there are also intricate, varying and changing relationships between the state and the private sector. The state is not monolithic either: different sectors of the state and spheres of government may play diverse and sometimes contradictory roles, promoting competing agendas, as the South African cases demonstrate.

In the following chapter we explore the experience of these developments from the perspective of jobs and livelihoods. The extent to which economic development has occurred in these speculative and vanguard peripheries varies. In some cases these areas have become stable parts of the city, with diverse activities. Some industrialists have been drawn into the public and private industrial sites developed on the periphery, especially in the Ethiopian cases where considerable new industrial growth is occurring. In other instances promises of 'economic development' have not materialised or private sector responses to the creation of industrial zones have been more limited than expected, or have declined after a period of growth. Some areas are predominantly housing areas, forcing people to rely on commuting. It is not certain that economic activities will emerge there or that existing ones will remain there over time. There is a temporality, and continuous change. The flip side of 'development', of course, may be the displacement of people and their place-centred economic activities, as farmers, waste-pickers, domestic workers and more – as the Ethiopian and Lufhereng cases demonstrate. These dynamics, and the social implications of investment and economic change, are explored more fully in later chapters.

Notes

1 After the Reconstruction and Development Programme – free housing for those earning under R3500 per month. See Chapter 7 for more detail.
2 On the narrow definition of unemployment which includes actively looking for work.
3 See figures for eThekwini and eThekwini north in spreadsheet in Statistics South Africa (StatsSA) (2021).
4 Source: Country Club Developers (www.ccd-homeseth.com/housetype/block-a) (accessed 14 November 2022).
5 See Lavers (2018, 2023) for a discussion of the tensions between rural and urban tenure in peri-urban areas in Ethiopia.

3

Jobs and livelihoods: Accessing work within and beyond the periphery

Alison Todes, Tom Goodfellow and Jennifer Houghton

A significant literature has focused on the implications of living on the urban periphery for access to jobs and livelihoods. It is a key aspect of understanding lived experiences there. Earlier literatures on urban peripheries assumed that they were largely residential spaces, with those living there commuting to urban cores. Lloyd-Jones and Brown (2002), among others, argued that the peripheral location of low-income households in cities of the south undermined their livelihoods, even if it enabled them access to better housing and more space. Research on satellite cities developed with the intention of growing around local economies found that local economic development was uneven and often unstable over time (Gaborit, 2010, 2013), and that extensive cross-city commuting was common (Cervero, 1995). More recent work points to the growth of new economic centralities on the urban edge (Keil, 2018), raising questions about the kinds of jobs and livelihoods that are emerging there. However, there has also been a wave of large public and private housing developments on the periphery of cities in the Global South (Buckley *et al.*, 2016), with research pointing to long commutes to places of employment (e.g. Buire, 2014; Sawyer, 2014). Hence, different logics of peripheries and trajectories of development may have varying consequences for jobs and livelihoods.

In this chapter we explore the lived experiences of access to work and livelihoods in our South African and Ethiopian case studies. We examine the logics of peripheries in the case studies, how they play out in terms of jobs and access to work and the way infrastructure investment links to jobs. While in some of our case study areas there have been strategic job creation drives led by the state or private sector and linked to infrastructural and residential investment, these may have limited reach, and in other cases may be lacking entirely. In these contexts, we explore the everyday challenges of accessing work and the livelihoods that are generated within peripheral neighbourhoods, and consider aspirations for the future.

These processes and experiences are shaped by the different national contexts. South Africa's structural economic problems and consequent high unemployment, discussed in the previous chapter, affects jobs and livelihoods of low-income people (especially unskilled workers and youths) in urban peripheries. Outside of privately developed middle- and upper-income residential areas, the proportion of adults in formal employment in our case studies ranges from 17 to 35 per cent, except for one informal settlement where over 51 per cent work in poorly paid construction and factory work.[1] There is also a significant reliance on social grants as sources of income in South Africa. At the time of the study, around 31 per cent of the national population received social grants paid by the state as a form of poverty alleviation (SASSA, 2021).[2] Thus, similar experiences of work-seeking and jobs are evident across case areas in South Africa. However, there are also differences across and within cases, which are influenced by their histories, locations and by local economic dynamics. In addition, class and income differences affect experiences within case areas.

Data on employment in Ethiopia can give misleading impressions, with official unemployment rates being deceptively low. Nationally, official unemployment was just 4.5 per cent in 2013, rising to 8 per cent in 2021, but this includes rural areas where – officially – unemployment is negligible. When it comes to urban unemployment, the official figure in 2021 was 18 per cent (Geda, 2022: 3). Moreover, there is a stark gender divide, with 25 per cent of urban women being unemployed compared with 11 per cent of men, and youths are over-represented with 23 per cent (29 per cent of women and 16 per cent of men) (Geda, 2022: 3). Data from our own survey should also be treated with caution. Only 4.6 per cent of 1,321 household members across both sites were reported as unemployed, with 19.8 per cent formally employed, 13.9 per cent informally employed (though this varied substantially from 18.3 per cent in Tulu Dimtu to just 9.4 per cent in Yeka Abado), 8.6 per cent self-employed, 8.3 per cent doing unpaid work in the home and a further 8.6 per cent either being retired or studying.

However, for a large proportion of respondents (29.7 per cent), the question on employment was not responded to in the survey, and many of those people could either be unemployed or depending on some form of casual work. Hence, the qualitative material presented in this chapter is important for really understanding the dynamics of employment and income generation in the peripheries of Addis Ababa.

There is a literature that highlights the refusal of work in Ethiopia linked to expectations of decent, dignified work and the awareness that during Ethiopia's long economic boom, waged work constituted a form of 'adverse incorporation' (Mains, 2011; Di Nunzio 2022b). Dawson's (2022) work on Johannesburg suggests a similar refusal among South African youths to work for low wages, leaving this to foreign migrants. Yet at the same time, surviving in Ethiopian cities without a wage is much harder than in our South African cases because the kinds of social grants that play such a significant role in urban South Africa are absent in urban Ethiopia. While there have been celebrated social protection initiatives, including cash for public works (discussed below), until recently this was limited to rural areas (Lavers, 2019). The social protection and entrepreneurship programmes that do exist in urban areas are limited in reach and sometimes highly politicised (Gebremariam, 2020).

In the sections below we explore intentional forms of job creation in the urban periphery, both through government job creation programmes and through major investments in infrastructure, industry and housing, as well as consider employment dynamics more generally in case study areas. We begin with a discussion of how job creation programmes formulated at the national level in South Africa and Ethiopia have played out within our cases, before turning to consider the ways in which jobs have been created through the different peripheral logics and the limitations of these efforts. We then explore how people access livelihoods in practice in the urban periphery given the widespread absence of secure waged work.

Job creation programmes and the urban peripheries

In South African peripheries where access to formal work is scarce, national public works and other employment schemes function as an important source of employment. This work is low paying and contractual – often only employing residents for six–twelve months – but is identified as a critical source of income for households. The Expanded Public Works Programme (EPWP), for example, is in operation in all the South African case study areas. This programme offers work such as street-sweeping, litter collection, construction of pavements and gardening to community members. In almost all the case study areas in South Africa, there is evidence of community members gaining employment through these programmes, with access to the work contracts arranged through the local ward councillor or traditional leader (sometimes in combination with community-based organisations). The process of allocation of work to specific individuals in a community or ward varies. There is evidence of a leader calling for the identification of the neediest households or individuals in a community in order to prioritise access to work to those who are most vulnerable. There are also practices in place for rotating job allocations through a community to try to spread access to income across households over time. The sheer number of unemployed people within the urban peripheries offers an absorptive challenge to these programmes.

Accessing work scheme programmes is not always a benign process and can be highly competitive. Data from peripheries in eThekwini and Gauteng show strong evidence of links between volunteerism, political patronage and accessing employment contracts within municipal wards. In these cases, local politically negotiated work schemes benefit party 'faithfuls' who have volunteered, campaigned and supported the election and terms of office of the locally ruling party, namely the African National Congress (ANC) and the Democratic Alliance (DA). 'The jobs available, you get in based on who you know and where you're affiliated to. Like the jobs of fixing the roads are done by the ANC and so you need an ANC membership and to know people to get in' (Ekangala Dark City BM 05 Interview). Furthermore, not all job allocations are fair, 'And it's the same people; since they introduced PWP [Public Works Programme] it's the same people; they haven't changed them. They said after two years they'll change them but they never did.'

Volunteerism and political patronage can contribute to job insecurity in relation to public works and other job creation schemes, particularly when there is a change in political leadership and existing hierarchies, systems and actors are shifted or deposed. For instance, in Ekangala a DA councillor was elected to replace an ANC councillor in 2016. The DA mandate to stop corrupt ANC practices halted the allocation of EPWP work to ANC volunteers. In addition, new 'fairer' selection processes and job allocation systems were put into place over the course of months following the DA election win. This meant that those already employed in the work scheme lost their employment and that those who had invested time and effort in campaigning for the ANC in the hope of securing future employment were not able to do so. In addition, those who had volunteered for the DA pre- and post-election were left without any guarantees that once new systems were in place they would benefit. Similar experiences are evident across most communities in northern eThekwini, with reports that 'Since the DA has taken over we believe nothing [i.e. work] is going our way because we did not vote for them' (Waterloo MG Diary). Efforts to volunteer are therefore a job-seeking activity which is widely taken up but which remains tenuous and can be unrewarded – regardless of which party's patronage is sought.

Ethiopia has also been increasingly reliant on public works programmes. The Productive Safety Net Programme (PSNP), initiated in 2005, has been widely celebrated as a pioneering social protection programme which draws on the 'productivist' social policies associated with East Asian 'developmental states' (McCord, 2012; Lavers, 2013, 2019). While not a job creation programme per se, it is a sort of 'workfare' system predicated on cash and food transfers in exchange for participation in activities such as the development and maintenance of community infrastructure (e.g. irrigation or local roads). It was motivated by food security concerns and focused on chronically food-insecure households in rural areas, so it held little relevance for Addis Ababa. However, since 2016 the World Bank has been supporting an Urban Productive Safety Net programme based on similar principles, which is claimed to be the first of its kind in Africa with an estimated cost of $530m in the first five years (Lavers, 2019). Although intended to cover 600,000 people (of whom 60 per cent should be women) in eleven regional capitals, at the end of 2018 some 70 per cent of the budget had been allocated to Addis Ababa (Ethiopian Government Official 1, 2018).

One official involved in the implementation of the programme explained that it aimed to identify the very poorest residents – people earning under $1 per day – and primarily in households with four or more people. Participants were identified through a local development committee including representatives of women, youths and elders. As well as being given cash for participating in public works and 'beautification' projects, they are encouraged to save, and under certain conditions the government will match their savings to help them invest in livelihoods development (Ethiopian Government Official 1, 2018). Results of recent studies indicate that while the programme has indeed reached hundreds of thousands of people, a majority of participants remain food-insecure (Derso et al., 2021) and the programme has faced significant challenges including political intervention, lack of transparency, insufficient coordination among partners and delayed payments (Dechassa and Jalata, 2021). The next phase of the project is set to be focused more directly on job creation, being renamed the Urban Productive Safety Net and Jobs Project (UPSNJP) and expanding the existing programme by an additional $400m targeted at youth employment and the inclusion of host and refugee communities (World Bank, 2021). This builds on earlier urban entrepreneurship drives such as the Micro and Small Enterprise Strategy and the Revolving Youth Fund, the latter of which was established specifically in response to the wave of protests that erupted (particularly in Oromia) from 2014 (Gebremariam, 2020). Such programmes have been critiqued for being used as a tool to co-opt people into Ethiopian People's Revolutionary Democratic Front (EPRDF) party membership while actually having very limited potential to transform the lives of urban youths (Di Nunzio, 2015; Gebremariam, 2020).

Job creation in the vanguard and speculative periphery

Vanguardist and speculative logics within our South African case studies produce mixed outcomes in terms of job creation and employment. In most of our case studies there has been significant state vanguardist investment in housing under apartheid and/or in the post-apartheid era, as discussed in Chapter 2, so access to this housing rather than jobs is usually a key reason for location for low-income households. Where state-provided housing has been developed, longer-term planning sometimes includes plans to foster and support job creation within and near to newly settled places, but these do not materialise quickly enough (or at all), limiting the ability of relocated residents to access jobs, as has occurred in Lufhereng, for example (see Chapter 2).

Both vanguardist and speculative logics are evident in eThekwini north (see Chapter 2) where investment in the airport, housing, retail, tourism and manufacturing has resulted in a wider range of employment opportunities compared to many of our other case studies, and somewhat lower levels of unemployment,[3] although they are still high compared to the rest of the city (see Todes and Houghton, 2021). As might be expected, considerable employment is generated in the construction phase of infrastructure and property development and is not sustained thereafter. Further, while there are more jobs in the region, employment is not necessarily available to local people due to skills mismatches, because hiring occurs centrally without regard to the local area or since companies bring their existing staff when they relocate to or establish in an area, such as has occurred with the King Shaka airport, perhaps the most striking infrastructure investment in the South African cases. Residents in northern eThekwini were able to cite some who had found work at the airport, including tenants who had been attracted into the area to access work, but they also noted the extent to which those working there were from other parts of the city. Waterloo, a more established area with higher overall incomes than Hammonds Farm and the informal settlements, is in a better position, although skills mismatches are still noted there. Some residents, including tenants, had moved to the area over time to access nearby job opportunities emerging as projects in northern eThekwini have progressed. For instance, ZD (Waterloo 09 ♂ Interview) states 'I decided to live in Waterloo because of the large number of job opportunities available in Sibaya, Cornubia and La Mercy.' By contrast, local micro-infrastructure projects to improve water, sanitation, roads and local facilities, and public works projects largely employed local workers, providing an important but temporary and poorly paid source of employment in our case study areas.

Proximity to Verulam also meant that residents across all northern eThekwini areas could access jobs as domestic workers, a significant source of employment according to the survey, particularly for those living in one of the informal settlements. Unemployment levels in most informal settlements across the study were particularly high, but some had developed around specific local employment opportunities. In northern eThekwini, one of the informal settlements afforded good access to poorly paid work in factories, security and construction. Workers were able to walk to work, saving considerable costs. Hence, levels of unemployment were somewhat lower than elsewhere, and a high proportion of those living there had moved to the area to access work – in contrast to most other areas in our study. Nevertheless, incomes were very low, as was the case in all informal settlements.

In our Ethiopian cases, the extent of government and private sector investment would lead one to expect a major boost to job creation, and to some extent this has materialised. With the early–mid 2010s involving a particularly intense frenzy of activity in the construction of condominiums, by 2015 370,000 new job opportunities had reportedly been created as part of the Integrated Housing Development Programme (IHDP) (Keller and Mukudi-Omwami, 2017). Residents living in the large area of cooperative housing adjacent to Tulu Dimtu condominiums (see Chapter 5) commented on how lots of jobs in construction and services were being created in the area, with government agencies also engaging in registering youths for the specific purpose of job creation (Tulu Dimtu RG 034 ♀ Interview; Tulu Dimtu BA 085 ♀ Interview) in activities such as cobblestone road production (Tulu Dimtu AA 083 ♂ Interview; Tulu Dimtu DY 084 ♀ Interview). One condominium resident even said that

> Everyone is doing something; some are shining shoes; others are giving satellite dish installation services or doing plumbing work. You don't see any jobless person sitting around. … I think job opportunities are created for all. From what I see of my family, I feel like the same is true for others. (Tulu Dimtu KF 012 ♂ Diary)

Figure 3.1, depicting a water vendor, illustrates one of the many forms of livelihood generation characterising these areas.

This was not, however, a view widely shared by condominium residents in Tulu Dimtu. Once the construction period was over, there was a dearth of livelihood opportunities as far as many residents were concerned. Joblessness was described as 'one of the ugly faces of the area' (Tulu Dimtu ME 011 ♀ Interview). The kinds of

Jobs and livelihoods

Figure 3.1 Informal economic activity in Yeka Abado
(source: Mark Lewis)

jobs that many people migrated in to pursue in the construction phase were relatively unskilled, meaning that they could be taken up by people with relatively little education – but now those same people struggle to find work in the emerging service economy of these areas or other parts of the city they can easily access (Tulu Dimtu KT 026 ♂ Interview; Tulu Dimtu TZ 031 ♀ Interview; Tulu Dimtu M 075 ♀ Interview; Tulu Dimtu DY 084 ♀ Interview). This problem was exacerbated by the limited capacity transfer between big international companies brought in for other kinds of infrastructure and the local micro and small enterprises (MSEs) working on the housing programme, constraining the development of the local MSEs and the future job prospects of local construction workers. The slump in construction activity once condominiums were finished had further knock-on risks for local income generation; owners of nearby cooperative housing who rented properties to construction workers were fearful that the rental market in the area would collapse, depriving them of an income (Tulu Dimtu DY 084 ♀ Interview). The cooperative housing settlement was an area that particularly attracted 'jobseekers from various ethnic backgrounds' due to the low rents (Tulu Dimtu AM 083 ♂ Interview), but it is clear that the situation was fragile given the limited job opportunities in reality, sometimes resulting in outbreaks of violence (Tulu Dimtu AM 083 ♂ Interview).

Moreover, despite the range of industrial parks and other industrial areas close to Tulu Dimtu (detailed in Chapter 2), industrial jobs barely featured in most residents' lives. Some were unaware that this might be an option, and one even wrote in their diary that 'There are no industry parks in the area' (Tulu Dimtu HG 058 ♂ Diary). In any case the pricing of IHDP housing is beyond the reach of the income levels of most factory workers. In Tulu Dimtu the average monthly condominium rent easily exceeds ETB1,800 according to our survey data; yet in the nearby factories the best wage for unskilled workers was only slightly over ETB1,500 (Schaefer and Oya, 2019). The housing programme was therefore not targeted at one of the country's most significant urbanising social groups, evidencing a mismatch between vanguard investments in housing and infrastructure at the condominium sites and economic opportunities sited in surrounding areas. The idea that job creation in the industrial parks would benefit residents of Tulu Dimtu seemed to exist only in the realm of hope. Indeed, hope was discussed quite often by Tulu Dimtu residents with respect to job opportunities; as one commented, 'There is no change yet but there is hope' (Tulu Dimtu RG 034 ♂ Interview).

In Yeka Abado similar dynamics exist with respect to the substantial number of jobs generated through infrastructure and housing construction that then evaporated once the condominium site was complete. This was even more of a feature in Yeka Abado given that the amount of housing units is almost double that of Tulu Dimtu. There was also a sense that people had moved into their housing units at a time of economic opportunity and perceived momentum, but that this promise has not been fulfilled. Comments such as 'The number of people without jobs is increasing' were common in the area (Yeka Abado 015 OR ♂ Interview), with one resident noting that 'Job opportunities are not like before. Around the time houses were assigned there was a lot of work' (Yeka Abado ED 002 ♂ Interview). Again, the fact that former construction workers often lack the skills and capital to benefit from the commercial, retail and service provision opportunities in the area comes through in this diary entry:

The big issue of joblessness and the fact that there is no improvement coupled with the closing of commercial units and the rise in number of people without jobs is a big challenge. The fact that the area is only suitable for living but not for livelihood provision has made commercial activities accessible only to those with financial capital. (Yeka Abado ED 002 ♂ Interview)

Job creation in the inherited, transitioning and auto-constructed periphery

In contrast to growing northern eThekwini, the impact of industrial decline was evident in Greater Ekangala, an inherited periphery, and levels of unemployment were much higher. Residents' diaries and interviews were filled with discussions of the significant loss of jobs as firms had moved out of the area or closed, and the difficulty of accessing employment. Nevertheless, some low-skill industrial jobs remained in Ekangala, and there are levels of local employment in public services such as schools and clinics and in areas such as retail and construction. Some also commute to employment in Bronkhorstspruit and Pretoria. The area is, however, differentiated, with particularly high levels of unemployment in the informal settlement, and much lower unemployment and more jobs in the service sector in the more established older area of Ekangala, where employment in the formal sector is most prevalent.

Unemployment rates were also very high in Winterveld, another inherited periphery but one with a different history, requiring lengthy and costly travel to jobs in 'Mabopane Pretoria Rosslyn' (Winterveld GK 09 ♀ Interview). Lack of qualifications and skills affects access to jobs, but even youths with matric struggle to find work. Lack of job opportunities was mentioned often in diaries and interviews. Only some government work, public works and service delivery projects (as in other areas) provide a form of formal employment, 'So if there are no projects at all, it means people won't be working' (Winterveld JJ 17 ♂ Diary).

Molweni, a transitioning periphery, experienced much higher levels of unemployment than the other eThekwini cases, similar to those in Winterveld. However, jobs were available as domestic workers in middle-income suburbs nearby and in a wider range of activities in economic centres in the region such as Hillcrest,

Pinetown and Waterfall. Within Molweni some employment is generated through schools and public facilities and in public works schemes and piece work on development projects, such as building toilets and digging roads. Speculative developments such as that of a new mall in Waterfall, an area which neighbours Molweni, offer some job opportunities; for instance, VN (Molweni 29 ♂ Interview) says 'there are so many people who have jobs at the mall they can't even count'. Others, however, were less enthusiastic, noting the distance to Lower Molweni and limited transport, or that jobs were mainly available in the construction phase or only to young people or those with experience.

In Addis Ababa the question of livelihoods in the transitioning and auto-constructed nodes within our case studies is intrinsically linked to nearby vanguard investments such as the condominium housing programme and industrial parks – not least because of the displacement of farmers and rural livelihoods that has resulted from these investments. One of the major challenges of livelihood creation in both Tulu Dimtu and Yeka Abado has therefore been how to support displaced farmers in finding a new livelihood. Around 35,000 displaced farmers had been identified in the peripheries of Addis Ababa by 2018 (Ethiopian Government Official 2, 2018). Little had been done to help these displaced farmers at the time of our research. As one source commented:

> For the farmers, the money they received as compensation was not enough to help get their lives back on track. We did not plan that aspect properly. Since we did not give thorough thoughts on the management and transformation of their livelihood, those farmers who received the compensation money alone did not bring any change. The kind of inclusivity they deserved was not seen and applied in the city development plans. (Ethiopian Consultant 1, 2018)

This sentiment was widely echoed, including by many government officials, one noting that 'some wise farmers used the compensation money to initiate a different livelihood but majority are now jobless, homeless and also without sustainable livelihood' (Ethiopian Government Official 1, 2018). While multiple sources thus admitted that not enough had been done to support them, by 2018 there was a new drive to help rehabilitate these people's lives by training them in technical and vocational skills, including with respect to construction work (Ethiopian Government Official 2, 2018). As part of this, displaced farmers were grouped into five categories: incapacitated people unable to work (such as the sick and elderly); people who should be supported with some grants and loans temporarily while they are trained to establish their own livelihood; people who receive an income that is too low to survive and can be supported while they develop a business plan; middle-income farmers; and higher-income farmers. All of these groups were entitled to some support to establish new livelihoods but with the ratio of grant to loan differing by income group (Ethiopian Government Official 2, 2018). Given the dramatic political change and turmoil in Ethiopia since 2018, it is unclear how much this has been followed through and the extent to which it has been successful.

In both Tulu Dimtu and Yeka Abado, the decline in job opportunities related to the construction of the condominium sites has to some extent been mitigated by the other ongoing construction, development and increased commercial activity in the area – particularly in Yeka Abado. The relative dynamism of this area in terms of commercial activity and infrastructure investment, being part of the city's general eastward expansion, means that there is constant physical growth and smaller-scale construction outside the condominiums. The building of new asphalt roads and the widening of existing roads have thus provided opportunities for some (Yeka Abado EM 041 ♀ Diary). However, as explored in the following sections, there certainly was not enough of this kind of work to go around, as well as the construction sector and some other local opportunities being heavily gendered.

Everyday challenges of accessing work

As noted earlier, there is a general lack of job opportunities in peripheral areas in South Africa, and attempts to address this are not successful in creating sufficient employment or work that is adequately stable and sustainable. As a result, those seeking employment experience deep and ongoing challenges. Interview and diary data highlight the predominance of insecurity of work, a continuous search for jobs and poor working conditions. As a characteristic of peripheries, the distance between job opportunities, work and home increases the overall challenge of accessing work.

Available employment is often insecure and short term, with diary and interview respondents describing regular changes in their place of employment. Daily work that may be secured in a factory or construction site is typically manual labour and low paying. Where work has been accessed, these characteristics play a role in limiting the benefits of employment. For example, in Ekangala, northern eThekwini and Lufhereng, some local employment is linked to construction of low-cost housing, infrastructure upgrades or green fields development – depending on the peripheral logics at play. The benefits of employment creation through construction processes are evident, but these are seen as short term and often do not extend beyond the main period of construction. Residents in peripheral areas experience and predict a lack of work after projects are completed.

In declining peripheries where manufacturing and other forms of employment have been (and continue to be) declining due to the relocation or closing down of factories and businesses, the search for employment is ever more lengthy and demanding. One resident of Rethabiseng recalled seeking employment in nearby Ekandustria:

> I travel to the firms to ask for jobs and the firms say that they will call but they never do. … I used to work in a firm for two years; however, the firm closed down. Many of the firms are moving from Rethabiseng as the rent is too expensive and are going to Joburg. If the firms come back … it would be much better; if not people will fight for more jobs. (Ekangala Rethabiseng MB 11 ♀ Interview)

This is a story that is repeated often.

Concerns regarding unpredictable and low-paid work are further visible in the questions raised by those employed in Ekandustria. One respondent noted that 'There are people who get paid R8 [per hour], there are people who rate R11 and there are people who rate R10. So now that amazes us that why is this happening, but we are doing the same job … we work together; we are all doing pick-ups' (Ekangala Dark City KT 08 ♀ Interview). In 2017, when this data was collected, these rates of pay were on or below the legal minimum wage for South Africa. Also, these are extremely low rates of pay when the distance and associated costs required to travel to work and the limited options for alternative employment are considered.

Access to work is time-consuming, and efforts have no guarantee of success. For example, in Ekandustria there are numerous reports of jobseekers walking from their homes to Ekandustria or travelling to other potential places of work such as Bronkhorstspruit and queuing up outside factories for daily work for months and not being contracted in any secure way. In some cases queueing up on a day results in gaining one day's work, with the process repeated on a daily basis and without the guarantee of success each day. Sometimes, prospective employees have been employed via short contracts or have a history of being employed on shifts by a particular company but find that their planned contracts do not materialise – 'I can go during the day to sign up for weekend work and when you arrive they turn you away but you signed up for the weekend' (Ekangala Dark City KT 08 ♀ Interview).

In northern eThekwini one of the reasons that residents of Coniston and Canelands have chosen to live in these informal settlements is their location near to established areas of manufacturing. Here, within a speculative and growing periphery, respondents believe that work is relatively easy to access (and is comparatively more available than in Ekangala) but is low paying and often insecure. Walking to work from a nearby settlement is an important means of accessing workplaces at no financial cost, making work more worthwhile than in peripheries such as Lufhereng where distance from work has created a barrier to employment.

Poor working conditions and ill health are at times associated with limited access to employment opportunities. In a peripheral context where unemployment is high and formal work is insecure, the pressure to keep a job means that those who are employed sometimes endure inadequate health and safety measures at work rather than pressing for improved conditions. For instance, a lack of appropriate clothing in cold rooms, a lack of masks in flour-filled industrial bakeries as well as limited provision of safety gear in factories raise the risks of injury and chronic illnesses (Ekangala Dark City KT 08 ♀ Interview; Ekangala Dark City LS 16 ♀ Interview; Ekangala DM 05 ♀ Diary). When injuries or illness occur, contracted or daily workers have no secure access to medical benefits or compensation and must rely on limited state healthcare options or supportive responses of employers, or tackle long bureaucratic processes for accessing support through the application of labour regulations. At times the conditions of work are so detrimental to health that employed people have given up their jobs rather than face ongoing debilitating illness.

The geographical peripherality of the case study areas creates challenges for jobseekers and for those needing to travel long distances to their place of work. Often, searches for professional as well as low-skilled work opportunities require that work is sought away from the residential areas on the periphery as there are limited local opportunities, especially in the declining or abandoned peripheries. Work-seekers must pay high transport costs in their travels to submit work applications and participate in interviews, etc. Furthermore, the costs of simple work-seeking activities such as accessing formal identification documents and the printing of application-related documents is expensive for jobseekers as without much competition, service providers can charge higher rates. 'Some of us had to borrow money to do the CVs and to submit them. It's R30 for the CV and it gets more if you make copies. They charged us R10 per page' (Ekangala Dark City BM 05 Interview). Furthermore, those who are employed in the wider urban region rely on commuting to access jobs. For example, some residents of Dark City in Ekangala have found employment in the broader region working on the construction of the Khusile power station in Mpumalanga province. They rely on transport provided by the construction company to access the power station site. Middle-class residents of Ekangala are employed largely in administrative or commercial jobs, or service provision such as teaching, nursing, etc. A number of these residents travel long distances on their daily commutes, typically traversing the city in privately owned vehicles or minibus taxis. The pressure of daily commuting costs and the possibilities of needing to relocate are particularly high immediately upon beginning a new job. Prior to earning a first salary or wage, new employees must fund their commutes, limiting opportunities to take up positions. In addition to the challenges created by distance, the poor transport services within the urban periphery (see Chapter 8) operate as a barrier to accessing work, increasing the time and costs associated with commuting and raising the risks associated with travel, especially where road infrastructure and vehicles need maintenance.

In some post-apartheid Reconstruction and Development Programme (RDP) settlements, such as Hammonds Farm and

Lufhereng, households were relocated from informal settlements which were close to local sources of work to these new places, affecting access to jobs. The costs of commuting from these newly developed housing estates on the urban periphery to existing places of employment were found to often negate the benefits of earning an income from low-paying work. For instance, Lufhereng residents lamented how they are now further away from Lenasia, where many used to secure various forms of piece jobs. 'In Protea South there were many jobs … Lenasia … was near so people could work and get temp jobs … This place [Lufhereng] is far … in Protea South they used to walk. … Even gardening jobs they used to get. You do gardening well, and in the evening you come back carrying something' (Lufhereng EN ♀ Interview). In Hammonds Farm some respondents explained that they had given up their jobs because the costs of travel were too great. The mediating role of distance in accessing work opportunities is not an unusual dynamic internationally but is exacerbated by peripheral location relative to hubs of economic activity.

In Addis Ababa, despite the various job creation programmes discussed above, the reality is that many people are unable to find work locally and cannot resort to the same kinds of livelihood activities that had previously been relied upon. As one official involved in urban policy noted:

> in old neighbourhoods, many poor people used to use their house as a site for their informal businesses. Now, they cannot use the condominium-housing unit to prepare traditional drinks and generate income through selling it. I am hearing a lot of economic disruption among many poor women and families who used to engage in informal business. (Ethiopian Government Official 1, 2018)

Consequently, they are forced to divert significant amounts of what little resources they have in order to spend it on transportation, either to commute to wherever they worked before or to access other work in more central areas. In this respect the challenge of accessing work is closely linked to the challenges of transportation discussed in Chapter 8: because many people have no choice but to go back to places in the centre where they can find work, they 'are forced to wait for buses early in the morning in the cold and rain' (Tulu Dimtu ME 011 ♀ Diary). These challenges equally apply in

Yeka Abado, which feels somewhat less peripheral in the sense that it is more contiguous with the main built-up area of the city but is equally if not more affected by transport congestion that contributes to lengthy commutes. As one resident commented, 'When the government built these houses, it should have considered workplaces. The big problem is not seeing your family from 6 in the morning until 8 in the evening' (Yeka Abado BA 072 ♂ Diary). As discussed in Chapter 8, accounts of having to leave the house as early as 5 a.m. every day are widespread.

Livelihoods generated in peripheral neighbourhoods

Livelihoods in peripheral neighbourhoods are generated through multiple forms of employment, speculative and informal income generation and self-employment. In our South African and Ethiopian cases, this is especially evident where formal employment levels are low and there is little prospect for accessing secure and well-paid work, thus largely following the expected forms of livelihood strategies for the poor and marginalised in southern cities.

There is little evidence of speculative income generation activities in our South African cases, but where this does exist it is typically linked to property development, largely in the form of housing. In South African cities overall, there has been a dramatic growth in 'backyard housing' in former black townships and RDP settlements, taking the form of both shacks and brick buildings (Scheba and Turok, 2020). This provides a source of income for those renting structures but is more prevalent in areas closer to places with access to transport and employment. According to our social survey, a very small proportion of households in our study areas – generally less than 10 per cent – were renting such structures or hiring out rooms in the house, and this hardly emerged in the diaries and interviews. Backyard rental was most evident in Protea Glen and Waterworks, and to a lesser extent in Waterloo, Ekangala and Winterveld, while a few households in Hammonds Farm and Canelands rented rooms within the house.

Opportunities for income-generating activities and multiple modes of self-employment can be somewhat attributed to the lower urban densities in the South African peripheries. Distance from commercial centres also plays a role in creating a market for locally produced goods and the offering of services that would otherwise not be readily available. In northern eThekwini, diaries and interview data indicate that migrant entrepreneurs are flourishing relative to other areas in the city. This is due to higher skill levels and rapid development of the area with little competition from bigger formal companies (e.g. for the installation of television networking and the operation of internet cafes). In Lufhereng, Hammonds Farm and Waterloo, older people and the unemployed with an inability to access formal work do recycling as a means of generating income. This involves gathering large quantities of recyclable plastics, glass, paper and cardboard, moving these collections to a central collection point and then selling on to recycling companies which operate in the formal sector.

'Urban' farming is a common undertaking, with residents growing vegetables and fruit as well as raising chickens, pigs, goats and some cattle. Produce is widely used on a subsistence basis, but a number of small-scale farmers sell their crops, livestock and eggs to generate an income. Where housing densities are lower and formal supermarkets are less easily accessible, and in generally poorer urban peripheries, communities rely more heavily on locally produced food. This is especially true for the formal and informal neighbourhoods in Ekangala, Winterveld and Molweni (see Figure 3.2). Small-scale farming as a means of generating an income can take the form of cooperatives which are supported by the local state through a provincial programme of fostering cooperative, focused economic development. This communal form of farming has had some limited success. In Waterloo, northern eThekwini, an interview respondent explained:

> When I was still trying to build my house the company closed down, and I had to be an unemployed mother up until I talked with the Councillor Mxolisi who advised us to start a cooperative. We did that but it was still difficult because at times we will get some money and sometimes we did not. (Waterloo TN 020 ♀ Interview)

As with the opportunities for backyarding and urban agriculture in detached or semi-detached housing, informal 'spaza' shops and taverns operate as small, informal businesses which are usually incorporated into a house or built separately on the properties.

Figure 3.2 Agricultural activity in Checkers, Winterveld
(source: Mark Lewis)

The multiple and integrated activities that are undertaken collectively form a livelihood strategy which allows poorer households to survive. Livelihood activities can be thought of as a means of 'hedging' for some. This is particularly true in poorer areas and in cases where there is speculation that proposed or ongoing development provides the prospect of future sustainable and secure employment. In informal settlements such as Coniston and Canelands in northern eThekwini, the settlements and the work of residents can be understood as an 'urban estuary', providing a foothold in the city and an entry into the wider economies and livelihoods of the city. Even in declining peripheries where job losses have increased vulnerability and forced households to try varying and multiple means of generating their own income, residents are hopeful of the benefits of future formal stable employment. For example, in the case of Rethabiseng and Ekangala, residents express hope that with the incorporation of the area into the Tshwane municipality and industrial revitalisation efforts, firms will return to Ekandustria and provide renewed opportunities for employment, potentially reducing or negating the need for informal and survivalist income-generating activities.

Multiple modes of livelihood are also a feature of the ways in which people attempt to make a living in the peripheries of Addis Ababa. However, the pace of farmland conversion, a restrictive regulatory environment in the condominium settlements, highly politicised city boundary issues and ethnic rights over land on the Oromia side (Lavers, 2018, 2024) create numerous challenges for the diversification of livelihoods. The nature of the regulatory environment was alluded to quite specifically by some condominium residents, with one, for example, saying: 'The local enforcement doesn't allow you to generate money to survive. Why don't they let everyone work as much as they can and provide for themselves?' (Yeka Abado NA 050 ♂ Interview). In particular, activities such as market-vending in allocated spaces, known locally as *gulit*, are highly constrained – with one resident noting that when it comes to allocation of spaces for such activities, 'they give areas where its almost desert … These areas they give are just spaces to not profit' (Yeka Abado NA 050 ♂ Interview).

Despite these challenges, some of the most marginalised groups such as displaced farmers eke out a living as day labourers on construction sites, as well as in some cases engage in MSEs. Although it has generated mass displacement, on the positive side the new infrastructure investments have 'facilitated the emergence of new markets in those areas for those who want to engage in the service industry', particularly in terms of selling consumption goods. This is rarely highly lucrative or transformative for their lives, but can enable them to survive (Ethiopian Government Official 1, 2018). At the same time, the uplift in land values has generated significant resources for some, and farmers who remain around the peripheries can benefit from the new market for food in these densifying areas (Ethiopian Government Official 1, 2018).

Meanwhile, in the condominium settlements, the virtual evaporation of job opportunities after the end of the construction period has led to a situation in which many residents simply hang around waiting for opportunities to emerge. These often relate to the processes of moving in and out of the neighbourhood; as one resident noted, 'When one comes to the neighbourhood with items there will be about ten young adults fighting to take your stuff up for you' (Tulu Dimtu ME 011 ♀ Diary), an experience she described as 'very scary' (Tulu Dimtu ME 011 ♀ Interview). In Yeka Abado there were similar dynamics: one condominium resident commented that 'whenever someone is moving in or out there is a fight over who gets to do the job' (Yeka Abado OR 015 ♂ Interview). The sense that physical health and strength were required in order to survive in the area was underlined by one cooperative housing resident with health problems, who noted that 'for someone who has the strength, there is work' (Tulu Dimtu DY 084 ♂ Diary).

These conditions force people to be quite creative in finding opportunities for work and income, often through making some improvements to aspects of condominium life or maintaining community resources in exchange for some money pooled together by several households. For example, in one case condominium residents employed four people to guard the area and supervise parking, 'and this is done from the contribution of residents' (Yeka Abado TM 016 ♂ Diary). Another resident described how they had put up grill fencing in the corridor for drying clothes, and this was one of the ways in which he made an income (Yeka Abado ED 002 ♂ Interview). Yet the limitations of this kind of sporadic, piecemeal work are very clear, with the same respondent noting that although he had been living there for two months, he had not yet been able to put doors in place in his unit and was waiting for the next job before he could afford to do so. In some cases people have been allocated some land 'in a far-out area' that they can use to grow and sell produce. One resident spoke of how he and his wife attempted to use this as a livelihood option but failed:

> We talked of options with my wife and decided that she should work on vegetables so that we can also use the unsold items for our household consumption. I gave her one thousand birr as a capital and she started working there, but there weren't any customers. And so we abandoned the idea and the land with it. (Yeka Abado OR 015 ♂ Interview)

The gendered dynamics of work are also significant, with one Yeka Abado resident noting that 'if you see all the neighbours, only few of both couples are working, mainly office work. Other than that, women usually stay in the house' (Yeka Abado ED 002 ♂ Interview). One male resident noted that his wife gave up a factory job because her wages were equal to paying for childcare (Yeka Abado OR 015 ♂ Interview).

Conclusions: joblessness and aspirations for future fulfilment

Our findings across both countries and all case study areas have shown not only the intense precarity of livelihoods and incomes in the urban periphery but also the particular sacrifices that people make in terms of personal wellbeing and time spent with family as they struggle to access any kind of work. In the Ethiopian cases, where there are no adequate lifelines in terms of social grants, we also see significant initiative and even ingenuity in the generation of income streams from various collectively funded activities and odd jobs, though this is often accompanied by insecurity and the risk of violent competition.

In all the South African areas, there are public works schemes and also efforts by councillors and other local players to generate and distribute work through projects to improve services and infrastructure in the area. There are efforts to direct such employment to locals where possible. These processes are recognised and discussed in resident diaries and interviews, and are particularly pronounced in the eThekwini cases. In northern eThekwini there are also some efforts to enable or promote local business, for instance the Mayibuye Business Association in Hammonds Farm, which encourages people to start their own businesses. Reference is also made to some skills development programmes, for instance in Waterloo.

In the absence of job opportunities – and in many peripheries this absence can come to feel like a long-term or even permanent situation, viewed as the norm – one of the few resources that residents have recourse to is hope. As people eke out a living in the condominium sites of Yeka Abado and Tulu Dimtu, unfavourable comparisons with previous homes and locations are commonplace; residents often rely on hope for a better future to sustain themselves. When asked whether living in the area had allowed them to be a better version of themselves, one Yeka Abado condominium resident replied:

> No, I believe it has even lessened me. Because in the area I used to live before, even if you live in a small space, you can find a job easily. I am living in hope things will get better. Other than that it's really difficult living here. People assume because you live in the condominium that everything is fulfilled, but you see there are a lot of missing gaps when you live in it. (Yeka Abado NA 050 ♂ Interview)

One of the most significant 'missing gaps' is clearly the source of an income. In some cases people directed their hope towards lofty dreams of fame and wealth, for example as a sportsperson (Yeka Abado M 097 ♂ Interview). While it is easy to see such hopes and dreams as futile, the expectation of increased opportunities in the future is perhaps not so irrational when one considers how rapidly these peripheral areas are changing, as discussed in Chapter 2.

However, the sense of momentum that may be found in some 'vanguard peripheries' is not felt by everyone and is certainly not always present in areas subject to other peripheral logics. Indeed, the quite pessimistic analyses offered by Lloyd-Jones and Brown (2002) in terms of poor access to employment and a reliance on commuting seem to be borne out in both countries. This also echoes the findings of Buire (2014) on Luanda and Sawyer (2014) on Lagos, reinforcing critiques of the creation of large residential developments and satellite cities on the edge (Gaborit, 2010; Harrison and Todes, 2017; Houghton, 2019; Todes and Houghton, 2021). There are somewhat better conditions in places where new economies are emerging on the edge, but levels of employment and absorption of local workers are still limited, reflecting the extent of employment creation as well as skills mismatches and other factors. Large-scale infrastructure investment in industry, airports and housing projects provide some level of employment but mainly short term. Ironically, small-scale, ongoing micro-infrastructure projects are more generative, at least in the South African cases, where they may be linked to public works schemes. In Ethiopia small businesses seem to have responded more to the local opportunities created by distance and local density than in South Africa, where the dominance of large corporates limits prospects (Philip *et al.*, 2014, and see Chapter 11 on retail and consumption), densities are lower and grants provide some level of basic income. Nevertheless, the cases do suggest the limits and problems associated with policies actively encouraging new growth on the edge.

Notes

1 Survey figures indicate that the share of formal employment in all sources of work ranges from 22 per cent to 72 per cent. Formal employment includes jobs in public works schemes. Figures were: 42

per cent in Hammonds Farm, 63 per cent in Waterloo, 36 per cent in Canelands, 44 per cent in Coniston, 47 per cent in Molweni, 60 per cent in Lufhereng, 44 per cent in Winterveld, 72 per cent in Ekangala, 47 per cent in Rethabiseng and 33 per cent in Phumekaya.
2 The most significant grants numerically and financially are the child support grant and the old-age pension. The importance of grants was evident throughout the study as the main source of income for between 14 and 31 per cent of adults outside of residential areas developed by the private sector. The grants are particularly relied upon in Greater Ekangala areas and in Winterveld, regions where unemployment rates were highest.
3 Unemployment rates in areas other than privately developed residential areas ranged from 25 per cent in Canelands to 55 per cent in Phumekaya, according to our 2017 survey. Other rates were: Hammonds Farm (36 per cent), Waterloo (37 per cent), Coniston (43 per cent), Molweni (42 per cent), Lufhereng (41 per cent), Winterveld (46 per cent), Ekangala (43 per cent) and Rethabiseng (54 per cent).

4

Governing the urban peripheries

Tom Goodfellow, Yohana Eyob, Paula Meth, Tatenda Mukwedeya and Alison Todes

This chapter examines the varied governance structures shaping urban peripheries in both South Africa and Ethiopia and argues that these spaces can produce and support distinctive governance practices and foster new structures, networks and citizenship relations. At the same time, peripheral spaces evidence some similar governance arrangements found in central urban contexts, although the friction of distance hangs over how these function and intersect with peripherally located residents. Conceptualisations of the periphery developed in the Introduction of the book are drawn on here to analyse particular governance arrangements and practices, including those of 'transitioning peripheries' possessing hybrid governance structures; the carving out/annexing of new municipalities or 'sub-city' governments that sometimes occurs in 'vanguard' peripheries; the informalised mechanisms of leadership often evident in 'auto-constructed' peripheries; and weakened state structures which are obligated to serve 'inherited peripheries'. The chapter covers cases from across South Africa and Ethiopia and opens with comments on theorising governance, then briefly details key governance structures in both contexts relevant to our peripheral cases. It considers governance issues in the context of boundaries and borders and the significance of state–citizen relationships on Africa's urban peripheries.

Theorising governance in the urban periphery

The theoretical literature exploring urban governance is extensive, taking off in the mid–late twentieth century when urban political scientists and sociologists developed ideas about pluralistic political power, urban growth coalitions, urban regimes and urban social movements (Dahl, 1961; Castells, 1983; Logan and Molotch, 1987; Stone, 1989). Meanwhile, the literature on changes to urban form – and specifically on suburbs – has been more concerned with spatial and social dynamics of these 'new' urban spaces than with governance. The question of suburban – or peri-urban – governance has thus been relatively absent in the literature, at least until recently (Ekers *et al.*, 2012). Moreover, all of this literature on both urban governance and suburban socio-spatial dynamics was very Global North (and particularly US)-centric. The question of peri-urban governance has also been rendered more complex by the emergence of extended urban conurbations, 'megalopolis spaces' and 'new centralities' that reconstitute the idea of the periphery (Lang and Knox, 2013; Keil, 2018; Bloch *et al.*, 2022) – and, relatedly, by recent interest in forms of 'extended urbanisation' that challenge conventional ways in which urban space is defined and delimited (Brenner and Schmid, 2015; Wu and Keil, 2022).

Regardless of these complexities, in much of the world there is a central tension at the heart of peripheral governance between decentralising and centralising impulses. On the one hand there is a natural affinity between urban peripheries and the decentralisation of governance to respond to local needs in these areas; but on the other the expansion of cities beyond existing municipal boundaries creates the need for higher-scale, metropolitan tiers of governance that in practice are often tightly controlled from the top down by central or state-level government agencies (Cirolia and Harber, 2022) and/or may marginalize local concerns in the periphery. Moreover, Ekers *et al.* (2012) note that some forms of *private* governance emerging in suburban spaces – such as gated communities and quasi-autonomous development agencies – are often authoritarian in nature. They argue that 'suburban governance' takes place primarily through three overlapping modalities: the state, capital accumulation and 'private authoritarianism'.

The association of the urban periphery with forms of private governance dates back to US-inflected ideas of the suburb as the sphere of private investment and the subdivision of greenfield lands (Keil, 2018: 184). This has contemporary – and more global – echoes in ideas such as 'plotting urbanism' as the process by which urban space is created and commodified in places such as Lagos, Istanbul and Shenzhen (Sawyer, 2014; Karaman *et al.*, 2020). Yet in 'vanguard', 'speculative', 'transitioning' and 'inherited' peripheries, the public realm of governance can loom large too. The state's role is often framed in terms of infrastructure-led development (Ekers *et al.*, 2012; Schindler and Kanai, 2021), though states may be *responding* to private investment and speculation as much as leading it. Moreover, the extent to which state involvement in the periphery can produce and exacerbate conflicts between different tiers and spheres of state authority is crucially important – particularly in contexts of rapid urban growth and underfunded city authorities, which are common in sub-Saharan Africa.

In such contexts administrative boundaries and scales of authority are points of particular contention, as illustrated in Chapter 2 of this book in relation to Lufhereng in South Africa. Rapid urban growth gives rise to disjunctures between city-level governance institutions and functional urban territory, and the often massive disparities in power and resources between city authorities and surrounding districts are also common sources of tension (Gómez-Álvarez *et al.*, 2017; Goodfellow and Mukwaya, 2021). This inevitably exacerbates institutional fragmentation and the challenges of 'fractured fiscal authority and fragmented infrastructures' (Cirolia, 2020). The creation of metropolitan authorities to try and overcome these tensions can be seen as a form of 'scalecraft' (Fraser, 2010; Cirolia and Harber, 2022), which 'typically dilutes local and democratic control' over key functions of urban governance (Cirolia and Harber, 2022: 2441). Moreover, the challenge of spatial/infrastructural integration is not exactly the same as that of *institutional* integration (Klopp *et al.*, 2019; Cirolia and Harber, 2022: 2441), and efforts to integrate, for example, transport institutions do not necessarily overcome the broader tensions and conflicts that characterise the governance of peripheral spaces.

The third of the three modalities of 'suburban governance' identified by Ekers *et al.* (2012) is capital accumulation itself – something that intersects with both state action and private governance but is, they argue, a distinct 'governing force' (Ekers *et al.*, 2012: 413). Building on the seminal work of Harvey (1982) and Logan and Molotch's 'urban growth machine' (1987), this foregrounds the opportunities offered by urban peripheries for the operations of capital to actively reshape these areas (e.g. through mortgage-based suburban residential development or the relocation of industries).

While the role of the state and forms of 'private authoritarianism' differ substantially between our five peripheral logics, capital accumulation of some kind plays a fundamental role in all of them, albeit at very different scales. However, unlike in the prototypical American suburb, land tenure regimes may be in flux (as is explicitly argued in Chapter 7 focusing on Accra), capital relatively scarce and the reach of state institutions highly limited. Keil notes that claiming space on the periphery 'has always been an intricate dance whose steps are part condition of land tenure and legal rules created by authorities and part free improvisation, sly moves around the status quo' (2018: 188). In rapidly growing African urban agglomerations, this 'status quo' may be tenuous, while the legal rules are often outdated, colonial or unfinished, rendering such 'improvisation' all the more significant in the overall process of urban governance.

In the specific contexts considered in this book, these dynamics of state control, private governance, capital accumulation, scale and boundary issues take on distinct qualities relating to their unique histories of state-building and urban development. Throughout, this chapter incorporates considerations of the lived experiences of these processes and includes a focus on citizenship and state–citizen relationships, drawing on Lemanski's (2020) work in relation to infrastructural citizenship, given the dominant role that infrastructure provision plays in how residents see and judge the state. It also employs ideas of auto-construction (Caldeira, 2017) which inform our framing of 'auto-constructed peripheries' to understand informal governance arrangements, including 'strongmen' and the politics of governance in areas dominated by shack housing and low service delivery.

Key governance structures in the urban peripheries

Referencing the conceptualisation of the five logics of the peripheries detailed in the Introduction, this section sets out the key governing structures in our case study areas in Ethiopia and South Africa. It reflects on how residents are governed differently, or at least experience governance differently, depending on their status as homeowners (often in 'vanguard peripheries'), tenants, migrants or political party supporters – distinctions that will be elaborated further in the arguments about difference in the urban peripheries presented in Chapter 10.

Key governance structures in the peripheries of Addis Ababa

The Addis Ababa City Administration (AACA) is subdivided into eleven sub-city administrations (following the creation of Lemi Kura Sub City in 2020), which in turn are comprised of 117 *woreda* administrations (the most local level of official administration). According to the AACA revised charter of proclamation number 361/2003, the city government's organs of power are the city council, the mayor, the city cabinet, the city judicial organs and the office of the city chief auditor. The sub-city- and *woreda*-level administrations replicate similar organs of power, having a council, chief executive and standing committee, while *woredas* also have an additional organ of power in the form of the 'social courts'.

Sub-cities have their own cabinets and elected councils. They administer the *woredas* under their jurisdiction and are responsible for law and order in their respective areas. The *woreda*-level administration engages in the everyday lives of residents by providing a wide range of services central to the socio-economic needs of the community. According to the constitution of the Country and City Charter, *woredas* should have elected councils and executive committees that are responsible for local governance, provision of public services and socio-economic development. Since both sub-cities and *woredas* have elected councils, they have dual accountability to their councils and upward to the city government. With a relatively stable administrative future now possible in the peripheries of Addis, following the decision on new administrative boundaries (discussed below), the above administrative structure and functions are expected to be consolidated and maintained.

The housing development and administrative agency under the city administration is the organisation responsible for the development of condominium houses in the city under the Integrated Housing Development Programme (IHDP). Within the condominium settlements, there are forms of semi-formal community governance. Once they have taken up occupation, condominium owners are expected by law to create a Condominium House Owners'

Association to coordinate communal development works in order to create unified and secure communities. The central association is comprised of representatives at block and cluster levels, depending on the size of the site or the number of condominiums. The associations receive cascading support from housing development and administration agencies through the sub-city and *woreda* administrations. In close collaboration with the residents and *woreda* administrations, the homeowners' associations coordinate security, registration of renters, management of communal buildings, greening, fencing works with a monthly contribution collected from residents and a special contribution collected at different times when further finances are required for special development works.

Some respondents in the case study areas indicated that groups of volunteers become involved in the community policing works to support the formal police and security structure in the *woreda* (discussed further in Chapter 10). This involvement especially helped people living in the condominiums built at the peripheries to know each other better and to protect their community to overcome their vulnerability to security threats arising from living in areas with unfulfilled infrastructure far from city centres. As our findings in Chapter 3 show, in some cases it also appears that activities such as the provision of fencing and security are not purely voluntary but provide a trickle of income for some residents who supervise these activities.

These general governance structures apply in the peripheries more or less in the same ways as they would in other parts of the city, though the role of the housing agency looms especially large in our case study areas due to the large proportion of these regions devoted to condominium housing. However, in peripheries specifically it is important to understand the challenges and conflicts that have been associated with the demarcation of the city's boundary. For many years the lack of a clearly demarcated administrative boundary between Addis Ababa and Oromia Regional Government has generated complicated and conflictual political, social, economic and spatial dynamics in Addis Ababa's peripheries. Back in 2016 when it was newly built, Tulu Dimtu was officially within the boundaries of the city: it was integrated within Akaki Kaliti Sub-City under AACA, and the investments made in the area in terms of IHDP condominiums, services and infrastructure were made by

AACA. However, by 2022 the situation had completely changed, and Tulu Dimtu is now administered under Oromia Regional State and has become one of the *woredas* within Koye Feche Sub-City, under the Sheger City Administration in Oromia. We explore this further below in the section on 'borders and boundaries'.

Key governance structures in the peripheries of Gauteng and eThekwini

South Africa's urban peripheries evidence a wide variety of governance practices, actors and scales of power and influence. Governance within cities occurs within the framework of a municipal structure, which has varying responsibilities back to the broader provincial and national levels of the state. In South Africa post-apartheid, as explained in Chapter 1, metropolitan areas were consolidated into large, single, metropolitan, municipal authorities as a way to redress apartheid fragmentation and inequality. Each metropolitan municipality (in our cases eThekwini, Johannesburg and Tshwane) has a single tax base, integrated development plan and budget, enabling spatially redistributive governance. A single administrative system pertains, although levels of regional administration occur for particular areas. These have evolved in different ways in the three municipalities, with weak regions embedded in centralised administration in the case of Johannesburg; experimentation for a period with area-based development in eThekwini, some of which remains; and the use of seven regions to administer the very large City of Tshwane area, alongside central departments. Winterveld falls under Region 1 and Ekangala under Region 7 within the City of Tshwane. Tshwane's size and composition means that many areas are disconnected and far away, creating significant challenges for governance:

> it's just very, very, very big ... there is peripheral to the built environment [Pretoria urban area] and there is peripheral to the municipality ... Tshwane is a brilliant Jackson Pollock creation; it is just so incredibly blobby and not focused ... the new administration is trying very hard to show that they can do service delivery, so it is not really solving the blobby; it is just making the blobby areas better. (Interview, SA Academic 1, 2018)

In South African municipalities, representation occurs through a combination of ward-based councillors and councillors represented through political party-based proportional representation, each of which account for 50 per cent of councillors. Overall, the system is centralised, but as our discussion below demonstrates, the space for influence by local politicians, developers and other actors is greater than might seem apparent. Further, while the system in theory enables spatial equalisation, the reality is more complex, as this and Chapters 1 and 2 show.

Ward councillors were consistently key local scales of governance, yet their roles varied significantly. Some operated as local brokers of a developmental state or as mere local social peacekeepers occupying relatively weak positions alongside party structures (Benit-Gbaffou, 2012). Their leadership rests on locational particularities and their power base, shaped by the financial and political clout of their wider municipality, and their political party's power. There is partial evidence ward councillors in more peripheral peri-urban spaces are afforded some degree of power because of the possibility of access to key resources, particularly land and housing. In Molweni, for example, strong citizen support was evident as development was occurring and residents could point to benefits gained, including in accessing housing and accessing land. In contrast, in northern eThekwini and Ekangala, ward councillors are described as weaker. In very poor and remote wards, on the edge of municipal boundaries within inherited peripheries, with constrained resources and where access to land is distorted by borders and boundaries with other municipalities, wards may be extensive in scale and lacking in revenue. In such cases, such as Winterveld in Tshwane, ward councillors' capacities are highly circumscribed. The great distances from a significant urban centre, such as Pretoria, further reduces local employment and resultant wealth circulating in the ward.

Ward councillor positions are highly vulnerable to local government elections (see Figure 4.1 showing political party campaigning in the Hammonds Farm/Waterloo Ward Councillors office). In 2016 numerous wards changed party leadership through boundary changes but also evidencing growing frustration with the long-ruling African National Congress (ANC) party. Northern eThekwini changed from ANC to Democratic Alliance (DA) leadership, and in Ekangala in Tshwane it transitioned from ANC-led to a mixed DA–ANC ward. Ward councillors are thus key governance

Figure 4.1 Political party poster, Waterloo, northern eThekwini
(source: Mark Lewis)

actors, whose power can be enhanced by peripheral location, but are more commonly marked by generic a-spatial vulnerability.

South Africa's post-apartheid multiparty democracy has largely been dominated by the ANC party, with growing challenges from competing parties. This evidences rising voter dissatisfaction and anger about state capture and corruption. Clientelistic practices, not unique to peripheries, were evident in our case studies, particularly in relation to land, housing and work: 'If you don't fall under the ANC you won't get his signature on your proof of residence when you go look for work' (Dark City, Ekangala MS 20 ♀ Interview). Party politics also shaped politically affiliated civic groups such as South African National Civics Organisation (SANCO), cited as a significant governance institution in Ekangala controlling the delivery of key resources in the area.

The reach of the South African state is comparatively powerful (e.g. in contrast to many other African states), yet arguably peripheral locations facilitate the invisibility of self-selected local leaders from the state. In Tshwane, distant 'inherited peripheries' assume semi-political autonomy where politically 'independent' male leaders rise. We label them here as 'strongmen' to articulate their modes of governance including coercion, violence, respect, fear, dependency and power. Controlling local resources, particularly land, housing and access to employment, fuels their power. In Phumekaya informal settlement in the Ekangala area (see Figure 0.1, Introduction), one man chairs the Concerned Residents of the Ekangala group. He and his unelected committee are described locally as the 'government', performing state-like functions (taxing businesses, providing land and shelter) in an auto-constructed periphery. Leadership is secured via threats of violence. The informal settlement of Madibeng Hills (in Klipgat municipality, North West region, bordering Winterveld – see Figure 0.1) was established by two men in around 2010 who parcelled out stands to residents. They lead road-grading, stand-planning and the provision and maintenance of electricity. Their unity was challenged after the 2016 elections where divided party affiliations proved unsettling. Overall, their leadership evidenced relatively coherent auto-constructed (Caldeira, 2017) governance.

Hybrid leadership in the 'transitioning' peripheries

Hybrid governance is common within African urban peripheries, where democratic institutions sit alongside traditional leadership (Beall, 2006; Sim et al., 2018). The confluence of urban tenures and ownership patterns collide with rural and traditional systems of land control and management. These 'transitioning' peripheries evidence hybridity through mixed historic claims to land producing a patchwork of overlapping governing structures. In South Africa, particularly the region of KwaZulu-Natal (where eThekwini is located), the duality of hereditary traditional authority alongside post-apartheid democratic governance structures is constitutionally defined and legitimated through the Ingonyama Trust. However, its history and current practice is fraught with tension (Beall, 2006). The challenges and potentialities of hybridity are evident in the case of Molweni (eThekwini), where traditional leadership operates alongside a ward councillor. The responsiveness of the then ward councillor was largely agreed, but frustrated residents identified governance gaps and frictions, particularly when governed by local chiefs:

> you find that the Inkosi says that this is my land and the municipality say another story. We do not have the land to build our house. We are still renting with my family. If you tried to build the house here,

the municipality will come and take down your house. The Inkosi is asking R500 for the title deed, and we are not sure what to do now. Inkosi needs meat, alcohol and drinks. (Molweni VN 029 ♂ Interview)

Differing agendas underpin this governance hybridity extending also to investment practices. Despite an overarching celebration of development locally by residents, specific chief-governed areas such as Nogxaza were perceived as 'left behind' with interventions lacking. This unevenness produces a 'periphery within the peripheries'.

Significance and limits of a 'transformative' state

Todes and Harrison (2015) argue in the post-apartheid era, with the loosening of spatial controls, there is growing evidence of spatial change (such as densification) in South Africa being shaped by actors (including private enterprises and people) other than the state. Their use of the concept of 'a loosening state' is productive for analysing peripheral spaces, where investments in gated complexes for wealthier residents (and their associated governance regimes) has entrenched patterns of low-density development. Despite this, the state's transformative practices were evident across all cases, changing residents' lives daily through key interventions. Changes are, however, often uneven, and peripheral contexts matter. Histories of peripherality often mean state interventions are strongly appreciated, but where interventions are partial and unintegrated, they can compound hardship. In Molweni, historic non-investment means recent interventions are celebrated: 'The development of the area is now much better because this area now looks like a township instead of a rural area' (Molweni NS 04 ♀ Diary). These relational evaluations contrast 'rural' hardships (e.g. no water, no electricity, no toilets, no schools, no buses, no tarred roads, etc) with evident improvements. In contrast, greenfield settlements, such as Hammonds Farm in northern eThekwini and Lufhereng in Johannesburg, Gauteng, contain residents moved from consolidated townships or informal settlements which often contained services or locational advantages (see Sutherland and Buthelezi, 2013; Meth and Buthelezi, 2017; Charlton, 2017). Associated losses in services reflect the limitations of a transformative state propelled by a poorly integrated housing agenda. Similarly, residents in informal settlements not earmarked for upgrading may find small-scale interventions limited and inadequate: 'I have noticed only the toilets and showers in this area' (Coniston AM 01 ♀ Interview). Many residents interviewed in Ekangala were extremely frustrated by their living conditions and felt abandoned by the state.

Peripherality often signals the poor reach of the state, reducing the state's capacity to be transformative but posing advantages for some. Strongmen are discussed above, but foreign migrants also benefit. Self-employed and operating retail and service businesses, migrants' wellbeing was enhanced through freedoms from police demands to present legal papers. Migrants described the area as 'friendly to foreigners'. The limited presence of the state proved welcoming.

Private sector investment and governance relations

The power of private sector organisations to drive particular governance regimes and urban development plans – often in areas we consider 'speculative peripheries' – is discussed in Chapter 2. In northern eThekwini this is significant, although highly fluid (see Chapter 3). There, Tongaat-Hulett is the substantial landowner dominating decisions relating to the aerotropolis, retail and high- and middle-end housing as well as industry. Houghton (2013) conceptualises eThekwini's wider public–private partnerships as evidencing 'entanglement', noting divergent goals of economic growth imperatives alongside efforts towards redistribution. Key here is how these partnerships and negotiated entanglements shape peripheral spaces through investments in infrastructure, work opportunities and housing. Furthermore, peripheries as 'frontier' (McGregor and Chatiza, 2019) spaces for investment may lack services but boast cheaper land and lower business rates. Both can prove enticing. State support of investment is often politically determined with the DA unsurprisingly urging a strong facilitatory role:

> government ... should make it okay for business to operate. (Interview, SA Councillor 2, eThekwini, 2018)

> the municipality should ensure there is provincial bulk infrastructure creating a climate which is conducive for business development to happen and the private sector will come into that development to do business with people (Interview, SA Government Official 9, eThekwini, 2018)

Chapter 11 examines the quasi-governance roles played by shopping malls in the disbursement of welfare payment, illustrating the interconnectedness of governance and private sector institutions.

Borders and boundaries

Geographic peripheries of city-regions inevitably invoke and construct border identities and spatialities because of their proximity to, or occupation of, land and people divided by political and legal (and perhaps semi-/illegal) boundaries. These operate at various scales, including between municipalities, states, regions and between city and region. They can signify or work as 'frontier' spaces if they are located at the far reach of uneven spatial zones, often necessitating migration (e.g. migration from Zimbabwe into Winterveld) or where they perform a frontier function because of an often unequal shift in resourcing, governing or institutional framing beyond a border of some kind (as in the case of the relationship between Addis Ababa and Oromia).

Here we argue that the concept of urban frontiers as spaces of territorial struggle and legal ambiguity (McGregor and Chatiza, 2019) has relevance when applied to our cases. The significance of the periphery in terms of institutional overlap and mismatch is captured by the idea of 'betwixt and between'. This is a governance concern because of the layering and frequent tension in institutional frameworks, personnel, resources, legal expectations, policy landscapes and political allegiances which can be found in such geographic spaces. Across our seven cases, the presence of significant boundaries was evident in five cases specifically, often at very different scales. Here we analyse what it means to be 'bordered' or to have boundary markings crossing through a case study area in order to understand some of the complexities of governing the periphery more clearly. In the first instance, we consider the case of Ekangala, before turning to a more detailed focus on Addis Ababa. Many of our arguments regarding the significance of municipal and provincial boundaries relating to Ekangala could be applied to that of Winterveld and Lufhereng discussed above. We do not revisit the case of Molweni here, discussed above in relation to hybrid leadership, although the case is marked by the presence of boundaries between Ingonyama Trust land and land belonging to eThekwini municipality.

The wider Ekangala case to the east of Tshwane municipality (see Figure 0.1, Introduction) is a classic example of the urban periphery occupying fragmented and shifting boundaries, which directly impacts on the governance of residents, services and businesses in this area. With a history based on homeland industrial policy (Ekandustria) and segregation (black residents living in Ekangala and white inhabitants in Bronkhorspruit), Ekangala and Ekandustria fell under the Mpumalanga province, but within the cross-border municipality of Kungwini, where some of the rest of the municipality fell within Gauteng.

The entire area has since been consolidated within Gauteng; however, the process to arrive at this consolidation has been highly complex with amalgamation remaining problematic (Kabale, 2020). In the post-apartheid era Bronkhorstspruit–Ekandustria had fallen under the Metsweding District Municipality and the Kungwini Local Municipality. These were poorly resourced local authorities that struggled to provide adequate planning and management for the area. In July 2008 the Municipal Demarcations Board took the decision to incorporate Metsweding, and its two local municipalities, into the jurisdictions of the Tshwane Metropolitan Municipality with effect from the date of the municipal elections in April 2011 (Fin24, 8 May 2011). As Kabale notes, this amalgamation was burdensome to Tshwane given how weak municipalities such as Kungwini were, with historic debts (2020: 105). There were also adjustments to the provincial boundary to correct a 'technical error' in the original demarcation process which placed Ekangala in Mpumalanga, separating it from Bronkhorstspruit. However, as identified in Chapter 2, Ekandustria remained under the control of MEGA (Mpumalanga Economic Development Agency), yet revenue from this region has not translated into maintaining infrastructure in the area, in part contributing to it becoming run down over time (Todes and Houghton, 2021; Chapter 2).

With the wider area now in Gauteng province and under the Tshwane metropolitan council, the prospects for integrated development should have been significantly better, although as noted by Kabale (2020), poorer areas within the former Kungwini Local Municipality (wherein our case Ekangala is located) continue to perform badly with high levels of local protests over the lack of services evident and also in relation to anger over increases in service costs, such as the implementation of prepaid meters for electricity. Amalgamation can mean bigger municipalities are less responsive to local needs, input and demands (Kabale, 2020: 106–9).

In Addis Ababa the boundary issue has been particularly explosive in recent years – indeed, it was central to the eruption of protests that eventually spread and led to the demise of the Ethiopian People's Revolutionary Democratic Front (EPRDF) regime nationally. In 2008 the Oromia Special Zone Surrounding Finfinne (an Oromo name for Addis Ababa) was created with a view to developing a framework to regulate and plan for Addis Ababa's urban growth. When in 2014 a master plan for Addis Ababa and the surrounding Special Zone was released, this triggered protests due to widespread perceptions that it meant expanding the boundaries of the city itself and the likely displacement of thousands of Oromo farmers. These protests, which flared up repeatedly from 2014 to 2016, eventually spiralled into the broader uprising that ultimately led to regime change.

Throughout this, there has, however, been a joint committee sitting with the intention of demarcating a new boundary between Addis Ababa and the Oromia Special Zone. This committee consists of people from the Oromia Special Zone, AACA and the federal government and has conducted seven years of research, leading finally to the announcement of a decision about new boundaries on 10 August 2022. The decision has made various area reshuffles between Addis Ababa and the Oromia Special Zone. According to the decision, the areas where Koye Feche, Tulu Dimtu and part of Jemo 2 condominiums are located (all of which were built by AACA) are now allocated to Oromia. On the other hand areas up to Karsa River, including other condominium sites built by the Oromia government, will now be within the AACA boundary. In a very recent development to the situation, at the time of writing, it was decided that the Oromia Special Zone surrounding Addis Ababa will be considered as one city administration to be administered by a single municipality called Sheger City. The Sheger City administration is moving ahead with the creation of sub-cities and *woredas* of its own, with Tulu Dimtu becoming one of the *woredas* organised under the Koye-Feche Sub-City. Yeka Abado, being much further north, was not affected by the boundary restructuring and remained in the jurisdiction of Addis – however, it too has seen some governance changes with the creation of a new sub-city in 2020, Lemi Kura, which encompasses Yeka Abado (Addis Ababa Housing Official 5, 2022).

The boundary decisions announced by the mayor of AACA and the president of Oromia regional state are presented by the two bodies as being of historic significance, providing long-lasting and sustainable solutions to many years of lingering challenges and conflicts in the peripheries of the two areas. However, there have been different opinions and commentaries on the decision and the process, with some stakeholders objecting that it was not participatory and was a top-down decision, in addition to the assignment not being carried out by the appropriate body, the Administrative Boundaries and Identity Issues Commission established in 2018. On the other hand AACA and the Oromia regional state believe that the decision will solve problems people previously faced in terms of mal-coordinated and absent government services in those areas, the challenge of expanding important services and infrastructure and most importantly the existence of excessive land-grabbing, informality and the lack of an organised structure to implement rule of law and accountability. This has at times led many people in the peripheries to flee their homes, families and communities, leading to economic, social and psychological crisis – particularly in the tumultuous years after our main research was undertaken in 2018.

Without having a clear administrative boundary, the AACA and the Special Zone found it difficult to implement integrated and collaborative development works. This was believed to be a persistent challenge in the area before now, with the lack of efficient public services and infrastructure and the expansion of wide-scale informality and illegal practices. Upon the implementation of the above decisions, an intermediate governing structure with an overlapping and collaborative effort of the two sides will remain in place to make sure that there is continuity in service delivery, with special attention given to completion of ongoing projects in the respective areas and the delivery of collaborative security works. Yet as of 2022, peripheral areas such as Lemi Kura Sub-City still lacked clear decision-making structures to guide infrastructure investment (Addis Ababa Housing Official 5, 2022). Boundary disputes exist on a much more local scale, too. A complaint often arises among residents about the lack of 'ownership map certificates' for residents, which they believe would enhance a sense of ownership and reduce conflict in border spaces within the condominium sites, as well as with local farmers; currently, 'There is no existing legal framework to settle disputes between farmers and condominium owners' (Addis Ababa Housing Official 6, 2022).

State–citizen relationships

In the context of the governance structures and boundary issues described above, which reflect both rapid population growth and long-term political tensions, state–citizen relationships have been complex and challenging in these areas. Our interviews in Addis Ababa show that the city administration was clearly not prepared for the sudden increase in population in Yeka Abado, for example. In 2018 the local administration was trying to set up a new administrative unit, the Woreda 14, based on the demand from the new tenants in the area. The sudden increase of the over 100,000 residents in the area, mainly driven by the IHDP housing provision, formed a significant challenge to the local administration. At the time of our research, there was deemed to be a huge gap between citizens' demands and the capacity of the new *woreda* to respond, and little clarity on how well it was functioning. The arrangements in place in both Yeka Abado and Tulu Dimtu, where in each case the whole area was being governed under one new *woreda* that was subject to enormous demands, were considered problematic and provisional even by those involved in city governance. As one key informant noted, 'we are trying to consider how we can better organise these areas in terms of governance structure' (Ethiopian Consultant 1, 2018).

These problems were not lost on residents themselves, with one in Yeka Abado commenting that the 'lack of integration and cooperation by the relevant stakeholders has made simple problems more complicated' (Yeka Abado KA 069 ♂ Interview). Residents also sometimes felt 'dumped' in these areas with a highly unresponsive local government; one in Tulu Dimtu noted that 'the officials are fully aware of the situation, but they seem not to care that much to improve the area' (Tulu Dimtu K 077 ♀ Interview). Unsurprisingly, the perception of government responsiveness is worst of all for people living in the informal/displaced farmers' settlements. Both female and male residents of one such area in Yeka Abado stated that none of their needs were met in terms of service delivery (Yeka Abado M 043 ♀ Interview; Yeka Abado AA 046 ♂ Interview), with one stating their belief that government agencies in the area gave 'special preference to the condominiums and not the villages' in the area (Yeka Abado AA 046 ♂ Interview), despite them being virtually next to one another. That said, other residents of such settlements were seeing positive changes as services such as electricity, water and telecommunications were being extended, with one commenting that such services were coming to them 'because we are paying taxes, and this makes me happy' (Yeka Abado FG 047 ♀ Diary). In this respect, despite all the challenges, there were signs that a growing sense of urban citizenship (tied to infrastructure as per Lemanski's 2020 framing) and inclusion was possible even for the most marginalised in these areas.

Within the condominium sites themselves, the Condominium House Owners' Associations are a particularly interesting form of governance, not least because of the way in which these associations often have to be built 'from scratch' and made effective very quickly by communities who have been thrown together by the lottery system and relocation. Our interviews in Tulu Dimtu, for example, showed how the improvements in social ties among condominium owners led to enhanced collaboration with regard to registering and monitoring renters, with tangible impacts on the incidents of petty crime (see further discussion in Chapter 10). The tension between decentralising and democratising impulses on the one hand and top-down authoritarian ones on the other is very clear in the condominium sites. With regard to the latter, the planning phase for these settlements 'did not include residents' (Addis Ababa Transport Official 1, 2018) and the residents' committees arguably cascade government decisions downwards to a greater extent than they channel residents' demands upwards. However, contrary to the idea that suburbs are spaces of 'private authoritarianism', in these peripheries we see examples of participatory and relatively democratic private forms of governance, as residents come together to make collective decisions about how to develop and protect shared resources such as green spaces and children's play areas, as well as address crime and improve social relations.

Admittedly, some of these activities are linked to the pooling of funds, and participation is therefore contingent on financial contributions, but there is little evidence that these arrangements are exclusionary or authoritarian in nature. Many residents commented on the collective nature of decision-making with regard to which local works should be prioritised (Tulu Dimtu MK 025 ♂ Interview; Tulu Dimtu BY 028 ♂ Interview), with some Tulu Dimtu residents even noting that the sense of community power was growing through the activities of the committee (Tulu Dimtu KT 026 ♂ Interview; Tulu Dimtu RG 034 ♀ Diary). In some of the most spatially cut-off areas in our cases, such as the 'Eritrea' node within Tulu Dimtu, the sense of community-driven change was having a real impact on people's wellbeing. One resident echoed the sentiments of many when they said that 'The changes have brought hope for me. When I moved here I was depressed for fifteen days. Now that I see change I feel better' (Tulu Dimtu BA 030 ♂ Interview).

Across the five South African cases, what it means to be a citizen varies significantly, in part paralleling the distinctive levels of development and state intervention across these spaces. Residents observe 'recognition' of the state, subsumed often by the monolithic descriptor 'the government' which works to obscure the scaled nature of governance interventions. These recognitions are significant, however, not least because of their political implications for ensuring votes but also through their direct association with infrastructural provision (Lemanski, 2020): 'we do have the good things such as toilets and showers … That shows that the government is listening to people's needs' (Canelands NK 11 ♂ Diary). Gratitudinal recognition illustrates residents' desperation and consequent relief when intervention occurs, but also the paternalistic nature of the state–citizen relationship: 'That councillor of the ANC to me is like the Moses from the bible who help the people of Israel from Egypt to the promise land because he able to take me from the muddy house to the formal house' (Hammonds Farm MM 13 ♂ Diary). The state's agenda shapes expectations. Residents living informally (often waiting for Reconstruction and Development Programme (RDP) housing) expressed a sense of abandonment by the state on account of their lack of formal housing and services.

Yet not all citizens express their relationship to the state in such terms, and some acknowledge that part of citizenship is responsibility: 'We have to stop that habit of expecting things from other people, them doing things for us. It is time now for us to wake up and work hard' (Hammonds Farm NM 04 ♀ Diary).

Residents also performed citizenship through a defiance of governance rules and conventions through practices such as the illegal use of electricity, the auto-construction of informal houses and the individualised use of RDP housing in ways not condoned by the state. These include illegal renting out, abandonment and through landlord practices in RDP houses or plots (see Charlton, 2018b). Protest and violence were practised in some cases to effect governance change and pressure (as discussed in Chapter 9). In Ekangala this method of citizen engagement was frequently described by residents detailing attacks by locals of infrastructure and services in the area as a protest against failed promises and slow delivery.

Conclusion

This chapter has analysed varying governance practices across a range of peripheral contexts in Ethiopia and South Africa. Multiscalar and multistructured governance structures and practices were analysed, including institutions and individuals from the private sector, the state (both historic and current), traditional authorities, organised residents' committees, political parties and also people's actions and reactions. Beyond providing an overview of governance, the chapter also sought to consider what it is about peripheral areas that makes these governance practices distinctive and significant. We suggest that urban peripheries are spaces where the tension between decentralising and authoritarian impulses are thrown into especially sharp relief (particularly in the Ethiopian cases), and the role of administrative, political and sometimes also social boundaries is significant here. Relatedly, they are spaces in which the simultaneous absence and presence of the state are keenly felt by residents. In some peripheral areas, shifting absences come to the fore (i.e. absences of sophisticated state machinery, adequate work, investment, access, visibility and some services), whereas in other areas – or even in the same places but in different ways – we see shifting presences of governance (in the form of land allocations, housing provisions, relations of dependence between citizen and state, the presence of traditional authorities, the reproduction and long shadow of boundary politics and operating as recipient spaces for new urban migrants). These varying absences and presences structure governance and citizenship relations, the extent to which private forms of collective governance come to the fore in place of the state and the ways in which communities navigate the social and political challenges of being 'on the edge' of both administrative and functional boundaries.

5

Housing in Addis Ababa: Policy, programmes and lived experience

Zhengli Huang, Tom Goodfellow and Meseret Kassahun Desta

When trying to understand the evolution of Addis Ababa's urban peripheries over the past decade, the Integrated Housing Development Programme (IHDP) looms larger than any other policy measure, investment or residential form. As discussed in Chapters 1 and 2, this programme comprised one of the most significant 'vanguard' investments of the late Ethiopian People's Revolutionary Democratic Front (EPRDF) period, and easily the most significant when it comes to housing. There are peripheral areas of the city where IHDP is not a major feature – particularly in the western and northern edges of it where mountainous terrain has prevented major expansion – and we intentionally selected case study areas with major IHDP sites. These areas are broadly representative of the most dynamic, changing and far-flung peripheries in the city, providing us the best possible sense of the opportunities and challenges of life in the orbit of contemporary Addis Ababa.

The IHDP was an important element of the EPRDF's broader urban development strategy, which – particularly after 2005 – involved various efforts to both build an urban support base and reimagine Addis Ababa as a city of 'renaissance' and the 'Diplomatic Capital of Africa' (Planel and Bridonneau, 2017; Di Nunzio, 2019; Gebremariam, 2020; Weldeghebrael, 2022). The massive amount of housing built under the state-led housing programme has irreversibly changed the landscape of Addis Ababa, especially in the peripheries, and the way people live in the city. This chapter will discuss how the IHDP, as the country's dominant approach to housing in the periphery since 2010, has become an essential tool of physical and social transformation in the peripheral areas in Addis Ababa, and how it has driven the formation of new localities and helped to produce particular forms of land development in the city.

Despite the centrality of the IHDP to housing policy in recent times, it is also important to consider other key elements of housing policy and programming that preceded it and existed alongside it. This includes the Cooperative Housing Programme, which remains important to this day and of particular significance in the Tulu Dimtu area. The chapter begins by situating the IHDP in relation to broader trends in public housing provision in the Global South, as well as in Ethiopian recent history – including cooperative housing. It then explores how the EPRDF government attempted to address the increasingly glaring housing crisis through its distinctive approach to low-cost housing, and how the affordability question relates to other goals of the housing programme. The following sections will then examine the growth goal and the space-restructuring goal of the IHDP, and how they gave shape to the physical and social landscapes in the periphery of Addis Ababa. In this chapter we combine a review of academic and policy literature with first-hand empirical evidence collected in our two peripheral case study areas in Addis Ababa – Tulu Dimtu and Yeka Abado. We argue that the tensions and compromises between housing provision for the poor on the one hand and the pursuit of land value rise, urban land restructuring and the building of a potential middle class on the other have made the urban space in Addis Ababa increasingly unequal. This has contributed to a situation in which social stability in the periphery has become increasingly precarious.

The evolution of housing policy in Ethiopia

The IHDP programme does not meet conventional, strict definitions of 'public housing', which generally define such housing as being owned by the state and rented at subsidised rates to relatively low-income tenants, due to the fact it is actually based on owner-occupation. However, it is 'public housing' in a broader sense, given that it is funded up front by the Ethiopian government and substantially subsidised through a progressive logic in which the smaller units targeted at the poorest residents are the most heavily subsidised. Since the late 1960s, housing advocates have advised governments of developing countries to abandon their policy of direct public housing provision and transform to act as an 'enabler' of self-help and community-based housing activities (Pugh, 1994; Mukhija, 2001). Consequently, state-owned public housing that is rented to urban tenants has declined as a global form in recent decades, though the recognition of the importance of rental housing to many urban dwellers in practice – including informal rental housing (Scheba and Turok, 2020; Lombard et al., 2021) – is leading some scholars to urge governments to pay greater attention to the provision of rental housing options (Bredenoord et al., 2014; Gilbert, 2016). In the past decades most African governments have shifted from housing provision to a more complex approach which emphasises the service management and infrastructure provision (Stren, 1990; Jones and Datta, 2000; Ogu and Ogbuozobe, 2001). While they differ in terms of their modalities and tenure systems, the literature on public housing programmes in developing regions suggests very mixed results (see Olayiwola et al., 2005; Etim et al., 2007; Charlton, 2009; Oldfield and Greyling, 2015).

In the case of Ethiopia, the EPRDF regime was also seeking to shift away from the emphasis on public ownership of housing that had characterised the Derg regime preceding it. Under the Derg not only was there an emphasis on state-provided housing remaining in national hands, but any second homes were also nationalised (see Chapters 2 and 3), with small amounts of rent being paid to the *kebele* and much of the old housing in the city remaining this way to the present day. In the late-Derg and early-EPRDF period, very little new formal housing was built of any kind, such that between 1984 and 1995, 80 per cent of new housing units built were unplanned, informal and often auto-constructed (Shiferaw, 1998). Against this backdrop, as part of its developmental drive the EPRDF government wanted to stimulate housing provision. However, its first efforts to do so were not through direct investment in housing but through pushing the development of housing by cooperatives.

The Cooperative Housing Programme was first initiated under the Derg regime shortly after it came to power in 1974 as a policy measure to address the housing shortage for low- and middle-income households after decades of land speculation and profiteering by imperial elites. Under this programme, land was allocated for free for the construction of owner-occupied units on plots of a maximum of 500 m² for individuals and households who organised themselves as cooperatives, none of whom could already own a house (Tesfaye, 2007). In 1986 there was an attempt to make the programme more efficient by initiating a full Department of Cooperative Housing within the Ministry of Urban Development and Housing, reducing interest rates, committing the government to provide physical infrastructure and reducing the maximum plot size to 250 m². The Housing and Savings Bank provided loans for the cooperatives collectively at interest rates substantially lower than were available to individuals, while the Housing Construction Corporation provided assistance in materials and construction (Zewdie et al., 2018). The subsidies were generous – not only was land free, but construction materials were provided at a 60 per cent subsidy (Masumoto and Crook, 2021: 41).

From 1975 to 1992 the cooperative movement produced 40,539 housing units – an average of 2,252 annually (Tesfaye, 2007: 31). This, however, satisfied only a small proportion of demand for the period, and the processes for securing loans and acquiring permits were slow and cumbersome (Tesfaye, 2007: 31). Despite its drawbacks, as a modality of housing delivery it continued to exist and evolve, remaining one of the main mechanisms of housing delivery under the EPRDF. However, land was no longer given entirely free (being instead allotted at a benchmark price under the lease system), and interest rates became significantly steeper due to liberalisation reforms in 1994 (Matsumoto and Crook, 2021: 15). To benefit from the scheme it is also required that these individuals pool their capital so that 50 per cent of the planned construction cost was set aside in a blocked Commercial Bank of Ethiopia (CBE) account prior to registration (Zhang et al., 2019: 42). This meant that those able to engage in cooperative housing construction were mainly middle- and upper-income groups.

The cooperative housing system delivered 24,820 cooperative houses in Addis Ababa between 1996 and 2003 (UN-Habitat, 2011: 4), an estimated 60 per cent of which were in the peripheries (Zhang et al., 2019: 41). This was a far higher number than the 7,409 units built by the state in this period, or the 3,520 built by real estate developers, as well as being slightly higher than the 22,225 houses built formally by individuals and just under the estimated 30,000 informal dwellings (UN-Habitat, 2011: 4). Combined, this estimated 88,000 was, however, still nowhere near meeting demand, given that Addis Ababa had accumulated an estimated housing backlog of 233,000 units by the early 2000s (Delz, 2014).

Given the relative failure of the cooperative housing policy to generate anything like sufficient amounts of housing, the EPRDF reached a decision – in line with its broader turn towards large-scale investment in urban infrastructure and fixed capital (Goodfellow, 2022) – to invest massively in housing that could then be divested to city dwellers. The Cooperative Housing Programme was officially suspended in Addis Ababa in 2005, partly due to concerns about speculation facilitated by the preferential land allocation for cooperative housing (Masumoto and Crook, 2021: 41) but also due to the fact that by this time the IHDP was the centrepiece of the government's housing policy. The IHDP has facilitated the building of around 300,000 housing units in more than thirty sites in Addis Ababa alone.[1] As discussed in Chapter 1, as the programme advanced, the new sites were pushed further towards the edge of the city and this led to widespread evictions of farmers and informal settlers. The sprawl of housing land to the periphery and the swift relocation of low-income households into these disconnected sites have often led to loss of incomes, interruptions of children's education and current social ties, and challenges in access to public services (Abebe and Hesselberg, 2015; Ejigu, 2012; Megento, 2013; Gebre-Egziabher, 2014; Keller and Mukudi-Omwami, 2017).

The fact that the IHDP has had some negative consequences, including large-scale displacement, should come as no surprise when one considers the multiple functions served by the programme. Contrary to the understanding of housing policies as the government's efforts to solve housing shortages, these policies have always been an 'ideological artefact', more often than not being directed towards maintaining political or economic order rather than merely addressing housing shortages (Marcuse and Madden, 2016: 184). Although 'affordability' and 'housing the poor' are central to the rationale for the programme, the decision-making on the IHDP (like many other large-scale housing programmes) has been 'negotiated' among different interest groups and entities, driven by a set of varying political interests and rationalities at different levels that inevitably generate contradictions and tensions between targets, procedures and results (Huchzermeyer, 2001; Charlton, 2009; Marcuse, 2013).

Given that such housing programmes are often multifaceted and riven with inconsistencies, in this chapter we examine the IHDP programme from a range of different perspectives. We argue that despite a core focus on housing affordability, the programme embeds much more complex social and political goals. As such, the IHDP was not only a housing programme but also a key element of a broader 'developmental' idealism in the EPRDF's Ethiopia. As an official document from the Ministry of Works and Development pointed out, 'The IHDP envisages ... the utilisation of housing as an instrument to promote urban development, create jobs, revitalise the local urban economy through MSE development, encourage saving and empower urban residents through property ownership, and develop the capacity of the domestic construction industry' (Ministry of Works and Urban Development, 2008).

There are at least three goals that the housing programme aimed to achieve besides housing provision itself. First, the Ethiopian government has been using the programme as a tool for economic growth through investment in the construction sector and related industries, as also examined in Chapters 2 and 3. Second, the IHDP has been central to the cultivation of a 'property-owning' class that could provide a long-term support base for the EPRDF in Addis Ababa (Planel and Bridonneau, 2017). Third, the IHDP has been a tool of spatial restructuring of the capital city of Addis Ababa through the change of land uses and density redistribution. Proceeding in parallel with the attempt to disperse residential populations out of the city centre (discussed in Chapter 1) while remaining within politically and institutionally manageable boundaries, densification has been a driving concept behind the design of the IHDP condos (UN-Habitat, 2011: 20). While the first condominium buildings were 'ground plus four storeys' (G+4), later ones, including those developed at Yeka Abado, are up to G+7. As one of the city government officials put it, 'bringing scattered people in one space and making very compact kind of lifestyle might [make] good value on land use' (Ethiopian Government Official 1, 2018).

The continued effort of inner-city renewal and peri-city housing projects in Addis Ababa has therefore resulted in an increase in density on residential land in the city. Indeed, the average population density in residential land in Addis Ababa increased from 170 people per ha in 2006 to 201 people per ha in 2016. In the meantime the percentage of informal housing occupation of the total residential areas has decreased significantly from 58 per cent to 38 per cent (Larsen *et al.*, 2019). The housing programme has thus been an integral part of the urban renewal programme to clear the city centre and densify communities at the edge to avail central land for high value-addition investment. In the following sections we analyse these different layers of the housing programme and their effects on the periphery of Addis Ababa, as well as some of the aspects of the lived experience of condominium housing and the other housing forms that surround it in our case study peripheries.

Housing crisis, affordability and the multiple rationales of the IHDP

By the mid 1990s the sense of a housing crisis in Addis Ababa was acute; various studies showed that only 21 per cent of the city's housing stock met definitions of 'acceptable' housing, with 80 per cent of the population living in conditions designated as crowded (Shiferaw, 1998). 57 per cent of housing units were publicly owned (a figure later estimated at 70 per cent (UN-Habitat, 2011: 15), with levels of deterioration of these houses reaching a critical state in the majority of cases (Shiferaw, 1998). Throughout the 1990s, transformation of existing housing was the primary means through which housing was provided for the burgeoning city population (Shiferaw, 1998), notwithstanding some new housing production through various modalities outlined above. Although the EPRDF had made an effort to unleash the urban economy by leasing public land to increase government revenue and open up the housing sector to the private actors (Goodfellow, 2017b; Zewdie *et al.*, 2018), this in itself could not rapidly address the housing backlog – particularly for affordable housing. Housing development was constrained by limited land availability, soaring prices for land that was released for auction and severely limited access to finance (Goodfellow, 2017b). Thus, despite efforts by the government and assistance from the international organisations to support self-help housing, the housing backlog persisted.

Facing the significant housing deficit, in the early 2000s the government of Ethiopia started its collaboration with German Technical Cooperation (GTZ, since renamed GIZ) to explore low-cost construction technology, and initiated what was initially called the Addis Ababa Grand Housing Programme (AAGHP) – the predecessor of the IHDP. This was a particular priority of Arkebe Oqubay during his time as Mayor of Addis Ababa from 2003–05. With GIZ support, a pilot project was carried out in the Bole-Geji in eastern Addis Ababa in 2004, where 750 housing units (with one–two bedrooms) were constructed along with some office and commercial units. The major work was completed within eight months, though elements of the housing blocks were left intentionally incomplete (e.g. floor tiling and interior plastering was left to residents themselves), and the delivery of infrastructure was beset with problems of coordination and quality (UN-Habitat, 2011). However, despite its limitations, the pilot provided an important learning curve, and these challenges did nothing to dampen the government's enthusiasm for taking the programme forward. Once established, the AAGHP facilitated the design and planning of more than 60,000 units in one hundred different sites through the newly established Addis Ababa Housing Development Project Office (AAHDPO) (Delz, 2014). In 2005 the EPRDF government scaled it up and rebranded it as the IHDP, with the official aim of building 396,000 housing units during the first phase up to 2010 (MoUDHC, 2014: 45).

The initiation of the AAGHP, and its successor the IHDP, reflected two major characteristics of the government's new approach to housing: 1) massive provision to address the housing crisis, and 2) subsidisation, particularly of smaller units, to promote affordability. The programme proved able to deliver a significant number of housing units within a limited timeframe through the channelling of an impressive amount of public resources. By the designated deadline of Phase I, the programme had delivered 142,802 units in total, of which 62,557 (43.8 per cent) were built in more than thirty sites in Addis Ababa (MoUDHC, 2014: 45; UN-Habitat, 2017). By 2015, 245,000 units had been built in total (Keller and Mukudi-Omwami, 2017), and by 2019, 175,000 had been built in Addis Ababa alone, with another 132,000 under construction (Larsen et al., 2019). Moreover, in the early stages at least, the programme largely delivered on its overriding aim of building condominium housing at low cost: the cost of the pilot programme was ETB886/m^2, as compared with an estimated ETB2000/m^2 on the private market (UN-Habitat, 2011: 18). As well as providing basically no finishing in the interior of the units, new technologies were adopted:

> The LCH [Low Cost Housing] technology's main measures to reduce costs and increase efficiency consisted of designing a new and cheaper hollow block size; creating columns without formwork by inserting reinforcement inside the hollow blocks, combining both strip and slab foundations, and introducing a pre-fabricated formwork-free slab system using beams and hollow blocks. Overall, this resulted in construction costs of ETB 500–800 (USD 59–95) per square meter, a 40% reduction of average building costs in Ethiopia at the time. (Delz, 2014)

To further regulate the cost of constructing condominiums and to enhance support to the MSEs, the government restricted the condominium housing contracts to domestic companies (Interviews with City Government Officials, 2018). Despite the government's effort to reduce construction costs, the affordability of the housing units was increasingly called into question as the programme continued to expand. Even from the outset, the intention to actually deliver housing affordable to poor urban residents was somewhat contradicted by a manual published by GTZ and the Government of Ethiopia (GoE) in 2003, in which it is stated that the targeted beneficiaries are people with an income range of between 300 and 1,300 birr, those who can afford a down payment equalling half of the construction cost or those who 'have a fixed employment as civil servants or within the private sector' so that they can access the credit system of the banks (Ministry of Federal Affairs, 2003). Later development of the programme further demonstrated that affordability has not been the top priority of the IHDP. Originally funded by the Addis Ababa City Administration (AACA)'s own resources, when it expanded to national level in 2006, the CBE agreed to provide finance for the IHDP housing through a bond agreement with the government (UN-Habitat, 2011). At the distribution end, the housing unit recipients are supposed to make a down payment upon allocation of the housing unit and pay back the loans over the long term with a concessional interest rate. This finance-distribution mechanism could be traced to the Cooperative

Housing Programme discussed in the preceding section, though the finance for the condominium housing is directed towards individual households and the payment mechanism is more complex. There are three modalities in terms of deposit/loan ratios, each associating with particular housing modalities. The cheapest units, targeted at the lowest-income households, pay 10 per cent as a deposit and are loaned the remaining 90 per cent, which they can repay over twenty-five years at an interest rate of 9.5 per cent. The units under this scheme are studios or one-bedroom apartments. The 20 per cent down payment/80 per cent loan option is associated with more spacious two-bedroom apartments. The 40 per cent down payment/60 per cent loan option is targeted at middle- and high-income groups for bigger apartments and attracts a higher interest rate (MoUDHC, 2014). In all cases, houses are delivered via a lottery scheme, with applicants having to demonstrate they can afford the down payment before being able to sign up. The primary exception to lottery-based delivery is that some of the 10/90 units are allocated to low-income groups evicted from settlements – usually in the city centre – that have been appropriated by the government for urban redevelopment.

The rationale of the financing system is that the buyers of the housing units will pay back the loan and economically benefit the CBE; indeed, the intention is that the whole programme can deliver 100 per cent cost recovery. By the end of 2011 the government had raised ETB3.2 billion (USD153 million) from CBE through bonds for implementing the IHDP (MoUDHC, 2014). To achieve this cost recovery, the government is willing to compromise the tenure of the housing units. In other words, while it was intended as a programme to create owner-occupancy, it is recognised that this is not possible in many cases given that the cost of loan repayments is beyond the capacity of many beneficiaries of the lottery scheme:

> No credit or income checks on potential beneficiaries are undertaken. The assumption is that if beneficiaries have the financial capacity to meet their mortgage obligations, they will do so. If not, they will rent out their unit and finance the mortgage through this income. The CBE refers outstanding mortgage repayments to the HDPO, who, depending on the grace period, in turn may replace the household with another household who has the ability to pay. (UN-Habitat, 2011: 19)

Our survey in the two sites of Yeka Abado and Tulu Dimtu, where the majority of the IHDP condos fall under the 20/80 financial scheme, has shown that renting of the condominium housing is indeed a common practice. Among condominium residents surveyed in Tulu Dimtu, 36 per cent were renting, while in Yeka Abado this figure was even higher at 52 per cent. This far exceeds the percentage of the rental tenants in the private real estate development adjacent to the condo sites in Yeka Abado, in which only one in six of our respondents were renting. Interviews show that there has not only been informal renting in the condominiums but also informal selling of the condo houses immediately after allocation – which is contrary to the rules in place that officially prohibit resale within five years: 'Those who can afford to live in it are living in it and those who can't or prefer not to are selling their properties and earning enough for their plan' (Yeka Abado NA 050 ♂ Interview). The housing officials in the city government also recognised that informal sales of the condominium housing have become a popular practice (Addis Ababa Housing Officials 1 and 3, 2018).

As the financial mechanism and the practices on the ground show, the IHDP is not designed for maximum provision of suitable shelter and tenure for the poor, but rather to facilitate flow of capital into the housing market. The economic implications weigh heavier than any other elements in the housing programme, and there is a clear pursuit of broader economic development goals above the realisation of housing rights for the poor. These goals include the boost to construction sector activity (see Figure 5.1) discussed in Chapters 2 and 3; yet, as is clear from our findings in relation to jobs and livelihoods, the stimulus to these sectors was often temporary and also resulted in the formation of new informal workers' settlements with poor living conditions that then became permanent, co-existing in tension with the government's drive to progressively formalise housing in the city.

Another element of the IHDP that raises the question of long-term economic impact of the programme is its vigorous promotion of homeownership, which aims 'to not only improve one's housing conditions but also to take advantage of ... [the] extremely secure private asset' (UN-Habitat, 2011: 38). Experiences in other countries have shown that the growth of housing ownership does encourage savings and may contribute to wealth accumulation

Figure 5.1 Construction materials and condominium housing in Yeka Abado (source: Mark Lewis)

and the formation/consolidation of a middle class, as well as potentially strengthen social stability (Lim et al., 1980; Dupuis and Thorns, 1998; Rohe et al., 2013). However, recent studies have also challenged the correlation between homeownership growth and economic development in the 'late' homeownership era (Forrest and Hirayama, 2018). In Ethiopia the demand for private ownership of condominium units has also proved to be lower than anticipated outside of Addis Ababa. While the IHDP was planned to be a national programme, in 2010 the programme was suspended in all cities outside the capital because of low effective demand and highly constrained ability to pay for the housing (UN-Habitat, 2011: 19). This suggests that a programme predicated on an abrupt shift towards private ownership has limited potential to meet the housing backlog, especially outside Addis Ababa, throwing the overall approach into question. In reality the promotion of homeownership and the objective of housing affordability always exist in tension, given that the wider economic prosperity generated by homeownership depends on the rising value of assets, while housing affordability relies on cost control (Ortalo-Magné and Prat, 2014).

The lived experience of housing in the peripheries of Addis Ababa

Life in the condos

Despite the stated aim of creating homeownership, our survey data shows the high rates of renter-occupiers in the condominiums. Out of the 204 people surveyed in the Tulu Dimtu area, 136 were condominium residents, 85 of whom were owner-occupiers and 49 renters (36 per cent). In Yeka Abado, where 131 out of 204 residents surveyed were based in condominiums, 63 were owners and 68 renters (52 per cent). The data also presents a very mixed picture when it comes to people's feelings about whether their lives have improved since relocating to these areas. In both Tulu Dimtu and Yeka Abado, around half of the interviewees across all housing types in the area consider that their lives have improved after relocating there (50 per cent and 51 per cent respectively), but the ratio of condominium owners specifically who acknowledge life improvements is slightly lower (45 per cent in Tulu Dimtu and 46 per cent in Yeka Abado). Although the difference is relatively minor, one might expect a programme designed to enhance housing conditions to result in higher levels of satisfaction regarding life improvement.

While this suggests that becoming a condominium owner does not necessarily translate into greater satisfaction with living conditions, there were plenty of owners for whom that fact of homeownership was highly significant. When discussing their positive feelings about homeownership, residents cited reasons such as the freedom to settle in one place with a sense of continuity/stability, including in social and religious relationships and affiliations (Tulu Dimtu MM 090 ♂ Diary). Owning one's own home was associated with pride and increased confidence (Tulu Dimtu RG 034 ♀ Diary). In perhaps the most striking quote on this issue, one resident of the part of Tulu Dimtu known as 'Eritrea' (due to it being cut off from the main site by a major road) said that 'Not living in a rental house is like moving to heaven for me' (Tulu Dimtu DT 029 ♀ Diary). Similar religious imagery was used by condominium residents in Yeka Abado, with one resident saying they would 'like to thank God who has delivered us from rental housing and gave us a home of our own' (Yeka Abado TB 001 ♂ Diary).

This sense of gratitude for a house of their own was particularly marked among some of the very poorest residents, who had been allocated small and relatively cheap 10/90 condominium units (Yeka Abado EN 014 ♀ Interview; Yeka Abado ZW 049 ♀ Interview). Related to the pride of homeownership was the sense of dignity associated with having one's own facilities such as a toilet, a water supply and a kitchen. As one resident noted, 'We're very lucky that God gave us this kind of house which gives us unshared facilities' (Tulu Dimtu TZ 031 ♀ Interview). Freedom was also often cited by residents as one of the great merits of living in (and especially owning) a condominium unit, particularly for those who have experienced various forms of housing in which they had been constrained by communal life and community pressures. One male Yeka Abado resident noted that his biggest source of joy was the freedom his family has in the house where they now live (Yeka Abado BA 072 ♂ Diary). Some people were so happy with life in the condominiums that they said there was nothing at all they weren't happy with (Tulu Dimtu KF 012 ♂ Interview), though this was relatively rare. Around half of condominium owners surveyed also cited a reduced cost of living as a benefit of being an owner-occupier in a condominium.

However, most of these positive assessments of the quality of the living environment, facilities and cost of condominium life were countered by people saying the opposite. In terms of cost, for many residents in the condominiums, 'the rise in everyday expenses [has become] a major issue' (Yeka Abado SM 042 ♀ Interview), including due to the increased spending on transport (see Chapter 8). The costs were often significantly higher for renters given the rapidly escalating cost of the rental market in the condominiums. As one condominium resident in Tulu Dimtu noted, 'There are many people who rent in Tulu Dimtu and the rental prices are constantly increasing so that third parties can make commission from them' (Tulu Dimtu ME 011 ♀ Diary). Rents of around 2,500 birr per month were cited by residents of a typical condominium in Tulu Dimtu – significantly higher than the figures of 671–1,500 per month (depending on size) paid by owner-occupiers repaying their CBE loans. The increases in rents are striking: in just two years, one Yeka Abado resident reported their rent increasing from 600 to 2,000 Birr (Yeka Abado MK 022 ♂ Interview). These rapid increases perpetuated the high turnover among renters, leading people to 'hop' from one condominium site to another, newer or less well-located one in pursuit of cheaper rents. As in Tulu Dimtu, brokers were held responsible for pushing up the rents by demanding ever higher commission (Yeka Abado MK 022 ♂ Diary).

A further factor contributing to the cost of living in an IHDP condominium relates to the unfinished nature of the units at the point of distribution, discussed previously (see Figure 5.2). While the units were considered to be 80 per cent complete, the cost of finishing the remaining 20 per cent was hugely burdensome for many residents, especially when added to loan repayments. Some residents complained of the large amounts they had to spend just to make the apartment liveable given the poor quality of the materials and lack of fixtures and fittings (Tulu Dimtu BA 030 ♂ Diary; Tulu Dimtu BA 032 ♂ Interview; Tulu Dimtu RG 034 ♀ Diary). The sense that the various elements of the apartments were not joined up – with, for example, drainpipes that didn't connect with the guttering – was widespread. The cost of interior decoration and renovation was cited by some interviewees as amounting to 50 per

Figure 5.2 View from interior of Tulu Dimtu condominium housing showing incomplete construction (source: Mark Lewis)

cent of the overall cost of owning the unit (Yeka Abado TB 001 ♂ Interview). One resident noted that the condominiums were also 'not comfortable for children' (Tulu Dimtu RG 034 ♀ Diary), and the sense that they could be difficult for family and communal life echoes findings from elsewhere (Ejigu, 2012).

Meanwhile, regular cuts in water and electricity, as well as noise and disturbance from construction and interior decoration, impeded people's enjoyment of their property even when they were broadly positive about condominium life. Some residents of Tulu Dimtu condominiums – where our survey indicates that basic services such as water and energy provision was particularly poor at the time of our research – commented that they only received water once a week, and even then there was not enough water pressure to reach the third and fourth floors (Tulu Dimtu MH 092 ♂ Diary; see Figure 3.1 of a man carrying water containers in Yeka Abado). Water provision was notably better in Yeka Abado, though concerns about quality remained. In general, life on the higher floors was particularly hard, a problem felt especially acutely in the top floors of the tall G+7 blocks in Yeka Abado. Here, elevators had not yet been installed, hazardous drops in elevator shafts were commonplace and disabled and elderly people – though in principle supposed to be allocated lower floors if they won the unit in the lottery – struggled with long staircases (Yeka Abado ED 002 ♂ Diary; Yeka Abado KT 017 ♂ Diary). Residents commented on being shocked at seeing elderly people regularly having to deal with these staircases, which lacked crucial fixtures such as handrails (Yeka Abado KT 017 ♂ Diary).

Meanwhile, some residents – particularly in Yeka Abado where there were very high numbers of renters – commented that they had to 'give up' on some of the freedoms and values they deemed desirable in a place of residence, including cleanliness in the shared areas. As one Yeka Abado resident noted:

> When you live in a condominium house there is no point of cleaning your house alone because not everyone is clean and cares about cleanliness like you do. For example, on our floor there are ten houses; except our house the other nine are renters. Most renters don't care and most are single men or women; these usually leave in the morning and come back in the evening. (Yeka Abado TB 001 ♂ Diary)

Similar complaints were made about theft in shared areas of the condominium blocks. Meanwhile, there was a clear sense that even one's own private space, nurtured through months and years of decorating and care, could turn suddenly from being a treasured haven into somewhere very unpleasant if the infrastructural and service failures were too severe. The following quote captures well this duality between pride and pleasure in the home, and its capacity to go wrong at short notice due to factors beyond your control: 'A condominium house is comfortable for living. Nevertheless, if there is a problem of water shortage and power cut, a condominium would be among the very worst places to live in. Especially the smell of toilets, carrying water up, smell of the fridge from rotten food is very ugly' (Yeka Abado AA 068 ♀ Diary).

Life outside the condos

Of course, condominium housing is by no means the only type of housing in our case study peripheries; as well as cooperative housing in Tulu Dimtu and substantial private real estate development in Yeka Abado, both areas have informal settlements that house (among others) construction workers, former construction workers and displaced farmers. As alluded to in earlier chapters, one of the dark sides of the condominium programme has been the large-scale displacement of farmers, which – by the government's own account – was not adequately accounted for either with respect to livelihoods (see Chapter 3) or alternative housing provision. According to our key informant interviews in 2018, the IHDP only started to include the dislocated farmers fifteen years into the implementation of the programme, following the recognition that a significant number of farmers could not sustain their lives with the compensation they had been given (Ethiopian Government Official 2, 2018). Koye Feche, the most recent condominium site to be completed and by far the largest, has resulted in the displacement of about 1,925 farmers in order to build over four hundred four-storey housing blocks accommodating 600,000 housing units (three times the size of Yeka Abado).[2] The consequent homelessness of many of these farmers significantly contradicts the programme's aim to address a lack of shelter in the city for the poorest and most vulnerable.

For many such people, small mud houses in the interstices between the condominium sites and other land uses are typically where they have ended up living. Some people reported being happy in these houses – for example, appreciating the wider area, their status as owners and the freedom to decorate them as they choose (Tulu Dimtu BA 085 ♀ Interview; Yeka Abado YG 064 ♀ Diary). Others are much less positive about them, with one resident in a Tulu Dimtu informal settlement saying they 'don't like the neighbourhood or house' as it 'doesn't fulfil their needs' – lacking a water supply or toilet (Tulu Dimtu AM 083 ♂ Interview). For many residents of such areas, there is 'no comfort', and living with children in such housing is very difficult, not least due to an absence of their own water or power supply, leading to a heavy dependence on other people (Yeka Abado GS 048 ♂ Diary). Others still were ambivalent, with one resident commenting that they 'feel nothing about their house' (Tulu Dimtu HT 081 ♀ Interview). For some in these areas, the sense of hope for a better future – given the rapid development of the surrounding area – was palpable, with the housing considered 'okay for now, until I get better options' (Yeka Abado TA 040 ♂ Diary). Even in these areas, which constitute the most vulnerable and under-serviced housing in our case study peripheries, the cost of rent was often increasing every month despite no improvement to the quality of the house and quality of life (Yeka Abado SF 045 ♀ Interview). These areas are thus far from immune to the upward push of rents, with one Yeka Abado informal settlement resident noting that 'when you stay too long at that house they assume that is it because the rental prices is cheap for you and hence always look for a reason to increase the price' (Yeka Abado AA 046 ♂ Diary).

In the cooperative housing area of Tulu Dimtu, part-constructed buildings (usually just one or two storeys) housing multiple households are the norm. Multiple household occupancy is unsurprising given the conditions attached to developing cooperative housing, which required between ten and twenty people to come together in the formation of a cooperative, while the unfinished nature of buildings is also a consequence of the official discontinuation of support for the programme after 2005 (Masumoto and Crook, 2021: 27, 41). Although one study found that the majority of inhabitants of cooperative housing are actually from the top two income quintiles

(Zhang *et al.*, 2019: 42), our research suggests that the experience of living there can be insecure and 'scary' due to the perceived social instability of these multiple-occupant households, which often house temporary renters seeking scarce work (Tulu Dimtu S 060 ♂ Diary; Tulu Dimtu AA 083 ♂ Interview).

More generally, both informal settler residents and cooperative housing residents share many of the condominium residents' concerns about rising living costs due to lack of access to markets and supplies (Interviews with Tulu Dimtu Residents in March 2018). Although land belongs to the government, there are widespread informal transactions of landownerships (or user-ships) among farmers in the periphery, and land value has seen a rise since the construction of the IHDP buildings in these sites (Interview with Various Government Officials, Addis Ababa, December 2018). The change of land use and the rising price of farmland are part of the structural change in the development of Addis Ababa, which whether through the cost of acquiring land or the cost of rent has had a profound impact on the living costs of the peripheral urban dwellers, as well as their livelihood opportunities.

Meanwhile, the residents living in Country Club Developers (CCD) – the large, gated, real estate development adjacent to Yeka Abado condominiums (see Figure 9.1) – noted their appreciation of the quietness, clean air, cleanliness and beauty of the area (Yeka Abado M 100 ♀ Diary). The contrast here with people in the informal settlements primarily housing displaced farmers could hardly be more stark, with many such families forced to live in one-room houses (Yeka Abado FB 039 ♀ Interview) as well as under the constant threat of eviction due to the illegal status of their dwelling (Yeka Abado AT 037 ♂ Interview).

Conclusions

Urban Ethiopia – and especially Addis Ababa – has been the site of some of the most remarkable housing policies on the African continent in recent decades. The country's tumultuous modern history – involving abrupt shifts from imperial rule and landlordism to radical communist revolution, and then a form of developmentalist state capitalism – has meant the gradual adding of new housing policies and programmes on top of (very different) older ones, but without the older ones being fully extinguished. The sedimentation of different housing types over time – from the conversion of backyard dwellings in nobles' houses to state-owned *kebele* housing, to the introduction of cooperative housing, the birth of the IHDP, the gradual opening up of private real estate and the proliferation of informal settlements for displaced farmers – has produced a unique urban built environment. All of these housing types exist in the urban periphery. They often rub up uncomfortably against one another while at the same time sharing many similar challenges of distance, poor connectivity and (in all but the case of the wealthiest real estate enclaves) major challenges in basic services and material qualities.

The IHDP originated as a technical solution to address the housing shortage by using low-cost building techniques to house the urban poor on a massive scale. It expanded to a national level and was integrated into the state's broader developmental goals to achieve a set of social and economic targets, and the aim of providing shelter for the poor intertwined with other social and political interests at city and state levels. The competing and contradictory interests and stakes within the strategy have, however, undermined the efforts to achieve 'integrated' results and led to mixed outcomes. The government planned to use the construction of massive housing sites as a way to stimulate growth of the construction sector and accumulate a potential property-owning middle class. Yet the job creation effect of the programme has not been sustained (see Chapter 3), and a lack of linkages with the private sector has limited the overall economic development effect of the housing programme. The combination of the housing programme and inner-city urban renewal schemes relocated thousands of inner-city residents to the periphery and fundamentally changed the structure of the land use in Addis Ababa. But the lack of physical and social connectivity has led to the formation of isolated and often fragmented localities in the peripheral sites, in which many residents face huge challenges in everyday life and highly uncertain futures, while new and growing forms of urban inequality are etched into the urban landscape. In this sense the promise of the 'vanguard periphery' in these areas has been partially undermined not only by its own over-reach in terms of infrastructural capacity but also by the simultaneous creation of auto-constructed, speculative and potentially future inherited peripheries.

Indeed, without more sustained job creation, farmers' rehabilitation and more widely affordable housing, the peripheries will surely continue to be places of poverty and exclusion even if aspirant middle classes come to 'capture' the condominiums themselves. The IHDP has now been discontinued, with Koye Feche the last major site to be built (and mired in scandal over the allocation of its units). Yet the rise and fall of the IHDP has shown the challenges of trying to combine the welfare role of state housing with the value creation function. While the 'integrated' nature of the programme made sense in terms of Ethiopia's range of development challenges, housing cannot be truly 'affordable' to the majority so long as it is primarily seen as a tool of economic development and a means of building an urban middle-class political base.

Notes

1 By 2015 the programme was able to build 245,000 units (Keller and Mukudi-Omwami, 2017), and the last and biggest IHDP project in Koye Feche will provide 60,000 more apartments, according to our informant interviews in February 2018.
2 www.ethiopia-insight.com/2021/06/21/pushing-boundaries-in-ethiopias-contested-capital

6

Housing, history and hope in South Africa's urban peripheries

Sarah Charlton, Alison Todes and Paula Meth

Housing is a highly charged and politicised issue in South Africa, deeply embedded in the racialised social, economic and spatial history of the country. Peripheral settlements linger from the apartheid era, but new dynamics are shaping them and other edge localities have emerged. This chapter analyses diverse housing circumstances in our five South African cases in relation to policy as well as household practices. We discuss housing investment and typologies, why residents live in these peripheral places and relationships to the peripheral logics. The discussion is broadly chronological in relation to when our study sites emerged, though original drivers are layered with subsequent processes of consolidation or resettlement. The logics of the peripheries (identified in the Introduction) help explain patterns and relationships, such as long-term residence tied to historical coercion often evident within inherited peripheries, a limited ability to move elsewhere found in auto-constructed and inherited peripheries, opportunities among constrained choices found in spaces shaped by auto-construction or vanguard logic and residential preference tied to speculative, auto-constructed and transitioning peripheries. Across all logics and cases, there is evidence of residents hopeful for the future of these areas and their lives there, as well as those frustrated and despondent. We begin by outlining the urban historical context before introducing the specific legacy of homelands (or Bantustans) in close proximity to cities relevant to three of our case study sites. We then turn to late-apartheid and post-apartheid settlement dynamics reflected in our cases of developer-driven neighbourhoods, state-funded housing and informal settlements.

Housing in the first half of the twentieth century

Urbanisation accelerated in South Africa in the latter part of the nineteenth century, linked to mineral extraction, labour recruitment and later the hollowing out of black people's rural livelihoods through land dispossession and the increasing reach of urban capitalist relations (Mabin, 1992). In the early part of the twentieth century, public health crises prompted relocations from congested urban neighbourhoods and the separation of populations racially and spatially (Parnell and Mabin, 1995; Mabin, 2020). Black people in cities were in effect regarded as labour for white capital, and soon urban homeownership was effectively prohibited in terms of the 1923 Natives (Urban Areas) Act. Davies (1981) contends, however, that over the years segregating policies and practices were unevenly exercised, and by the 1930s laxness in the urban order heightened the pressures emerging from increased urbanisation. These stresses contributed to the hardening of urban policy and practice after 1948 towards an apartheid city form, argued in part to result from an earlier void in 'coherent urbanisation policy' (Mabin, 1992: 17).

Modernist planning ideals such as land use separation met racial separationist imperatives in these growing cities (Parnell and Mabin, 1995). With black urban dwellers 'a politically mute and landless class', urban residence, particularly for family units, was increasingly restricted through legislation (Davies, 1981: 65). Many African workers were accommodated 'in compounds, barracks and hostels', in domestic worker rooms or in shacks and shanty towns mainly on the urban edges (Davies, 1981: 65) but also in municipally provided houses in segregated areas (Mabin, 2020). Nationally there was growing policy emphasis on creating separate African locations or townships (Davies, 1981). Davies' diagrammatic representation of the 'Segregation City' reflected his argument that 'in essence, dominance–dependency relations in society were repeated in a core–periphery relationship in intra-urban space' (Davies, 1981: 64, 65).

The first decades of apartheid housing

The National Party gained power in 1948, and, buoyed by a period of economic growth (Hindson *et al.*, 1994; Mabin and Smit, 1997), apart-ness for black South Africans was ambitiously inscribed from the 1950s to the 1970s in a complex set of spatialities, including remote rural reserves, reservations closer to but outside of urban areas and mass housing delivery in segregated parts of cities. Practices of segregation or clustering followed tribal as well as racial designations in the belief that 'race and cultural differences in society are incompatible and that contact between ethnic groups leads to friction' (Davies, 1981: 69). In urban areas the Group Areas Act of 1950 followed the Population Registration Act and facilitated not just future but retrospective spatial ordering (Davies, 1981). Forced relocations to achieve racial and ethnic homogeneity ensued, mostly enacted on black people but also to an extent those designated as Coloured and Indian (Davies, 1981).

A programme of mass house-building by the state responded to huge deficits in urban worker accommodation and plans for spatial ordering. Large new neighbourhoods formed or expanded townships designated for different sections of the 'non-white' population (Davies, 1981). By the 1970s economic constraints, among other factors, shifted the emphasis to the promotion of 'homelands' for different black ethnic groups: separately administered rural localities, often with non-contiguous portions of land, claimed to have the potential to be developmentally equal to white South Africa, but typically impoverished, overcrowded areas with scant economic activity.

The multiple efforts by the apartheid state to direct where and how the population should live reinforced an urban structure of white occupation closest to the core of cities and black occupation most peripheral (Davies, 1981). Economic, social and spatial order was temporarily maintained through a relatively efficient, highly authoritarian system in which forms of resistance were crushed (Hindson *et al.*, 1994). For black South Africans, 'housing was about control. It was about excluding people from urban areas. It was about regimentation. It was about the administration of deprivation' (post-apartheid Minister of Housing Joe Slovo's address to Housing Summit, Botshabelo, 27 October 1994, cited in National Department of Human Settlements, 2014: 16).

Homelands and urban peripheries

The promotion of homelands complemented legislative tools such as Influx Control or 'pass laws' giving limited and temporary urban rights to some black workers and rendering illegal others. The 'Bantustans' were built on earlier rural 'reserves' into which many Africans were pushed during the 1960s through relocation from white-owned land or shifts in agricultural practices displacing labour tenants (Mabin, 1992). Ten different homelands were created, six of them 'self-governing territories' which remained part of the Republic of South Africa but were administered locally (Smith, 1992). The other four homelands had 'independence' conferred between 1976 and 1981. As explained further in Chapter 2, paralleling this policy, the apartheid state developed its industrial decentralisation strategy promoting labour-absorbing activities close to some homelands, or 'border industries', to foster African employment opportunities away from urban areas.

All of the 'independent republics' and self-governing territories consisted of variable portions of land, sometimes far apart from one another, all with 'white South Africa' in between. For historical reasons some were in relatively close proximity to major urban centres (Figure 6.1), and workers unable to achieve urban residency rights took to travelling daily from the edges of these areas in lengthy and debilitating commutes, such as from the KwaZulu homeland border into Durban (Haarhoff, 1980, in Davies, 1981). Land owned by churches provided similar access to white urban areas, and the commuting phenomenon from these border localities challenged and expanded the conception of peripherality (Mabin, 1992). Ostensibly within reach of cities, these constituted 'a form of deconcentrated urban settlement' (Hindson et al., 1994: 329) or 'hidden urbanities' (SACN, 2016: 2). However, demand for labour declined in the economically sluggish 1970s (Mabin, 1992), and much African labour became 'surplus to requirements' and increasingly a political problem to be managed (Work in Progress, 1979: 56).

The legacy of Bantustans remains strong in contemporary South Africa and in some of our case studies. We now turn to Winterveld, reflecting most directly its history as a labour reserve in the vicinity of a city economy.

From historic to ongoing struggles in Winterveld

Winterveld,[1] some 50 km to the north-west of Pretoria (SACN, 2016), is an extensive area of variable, often dispersed forms of

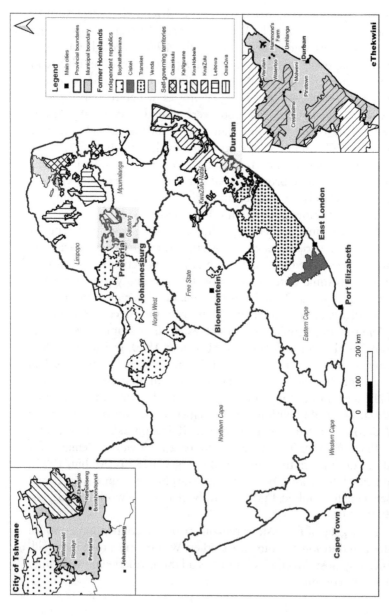

Figure 6.1 Map of apartheid Bantustans relative to contemporary provinces and metropolitan areas (source: produced for the book, 2022)

settlement covering about 120 km² (Simone, 2004). It constitutes an 'inherited periphery' posing difficult challenges for Tshwane municipality, an area with a complex and tragic history but also with contemporary auto-construction, some inward migration as well as a level of state investment in recent decades.

From 1938 and into the 1950s, black landowners from diverse backgrounds and ethnicities acquired plots in Winterveld, declared 'a released area' in terms of the 1936 Land Act (Work in Progress, 1979; Simone, 2004). The start of 'the urbanisation of the area' (Simone, 2004) is linked to forced removals from Pretoria in the 1960s to the township of Mabopane just to the south, in 'white South Africa' (Horn et al., 1992). Seemingly due to shortages of accommodation in Mabopane, government trucks offloaded many people on to the adjacent black-owned land of Winterveld, with dire long-term consequences for these relocatees (Van Gylswyk, 1981).

Further resettlement from 'black spots' around Pretoria and much further away (Work in Progress, 1979; Horn et al., 1992) increased movement to Winterveld because of a lack of rights to white-controlled areas or as part of seeking jobs in Pretoria (Van Gylswyk, 1981). Local black landowners were considered exploitative for charging high rentals and selling borehole water to tenants (Moseki, 1979; see also Black Sash, 1976; Van Gylswyk, 1981). As the profits of 'tenant-farming' outstripped that of agricultural usage (Van Gylswyk, 1981), the large southern portion of Winterveld became an extensive informal settlement (Horn et al., 1992).

In 1977 Winterveld was incorporated into Bophuthatswana, granted 'independence' in the same year (Horn et al., 1992). But many people in Winterveld – 90 per cent of whom were tenants (Horn et al., 1992) – were not Tswana (Van Gylswyk, 1981), making this homeland 'a geographic anomaly in the system of grand apartheid' which emphasised ethnicity in its balkanisation (Horn et al., 1992: 113). Many non-Tswanas were neither able to acquire 'citizenship' of Bophuthatswana nor move to nearby townships in white South Africa, and were denied access to facilities such as schools and grazing land in both (Ntema and Van Rooyen, 2016), a brutal and farcical homeland situation that attracted fierce anti-apartheid activism (Van Gylswyk, 1981: 1). In 1978 some people were relocated to nearby Soshanguve within white South Africa, but others were evicted to KwaNdebele homeland more distant from Pretoria, transforming employed relocatees into ultra-long distance commuters or labour migrants (Van Gylswyk, 1981). Other residents left Winterveld and its repressive conditions of their own accord, victims of the vicious cycle of 'no legal residence – no citizenship – no residence permit – no work' (Van Gylswyk, 1981).[2]

For those remaining in Winterveld, meagre services included a police station, a tar road and subsidised buses to facilitate labour commuting into white South Africa (Van Gylswyk, 1981). Notoriously poor conditions fed into malnutrition and cholera (Black Sash, 1976; Work in Progress, 1979). Winterveld's ethnic complexity and history led to some local development cooperation between the Bophuthatswana and South Africa governments, though most efforts were 'experimental and superficial' (Horn *et al.*, 1992: 114). The homeland state started building some housing near Mabopane and elsewhere in the area (Horn *et al.*, 1992; Simone, 2004), and the southern Klippan area was declared 'urban' in 1986 with an urban council established in 1990 (Horn *et al.*, 1992).

In 2001 the area was incorporated into the newly created metropolitan municipality of Tshwane, demanded by residents reluctant to remain within the adjacent municipality in North West province (SA Academic 1, 2018). This had been associated with poor service delivery implicated in population outflow from Winterveld in the late 1990s, a trend that shifted after 2001 with improvements in infrastructure (Ntema and Van Rooyen, 2016). For the metro the basic dilemma of this inherited periphery was how to improve the conditions of thousands of people living there, many impoverished, while grappling with its relative spatial and economic disconnect from contemporary priority growth areas. The Rosslyn industrial area established in the late 1970s as an industrial decentralisation point is relatively close by (20–35 km) and is now part of the Tshwane Automotive City focused on vehicle manufacturing (Chapter 1), offering some jobs for more skilled workers. The challenge is complicated by new settlement in parts of Winterveld. Winterveld was declared a presidential priority project in 2004, with a provincial housing drive and basic infrastructure delivery extending important practical as well as symbolic benefits (Ntema and Van Rooyen, 2016). Some economic development initiatives have occurred, and significant social facilities include schools, clinics and the Dube police station. The state continues a subsidised bus service to other parts of Pretoria, albeit now through a different mechanism that makes the service less viable for both bus companies and commuters (SACN, 2015).

However, Winterveld remains in effect a 'displaced settlement' at some distance from an economic core, poorly integrated with Pretoria and with some rural characteristics (SACN, 2016: 6). Winterveld is not a priority area of the municipality for spatial investment targeting: 'Winterveld didn't even make it on to the map as a node … because the city's view is always … "let's just formalise for the people who are there but we are not going to be making huge investments to try and make this input a core … it's too far"' (SA Government Official 4, City of Tshwane, 2018). Struggling with this contradiction 'between service delivery and strategic spatial planning' (SACN, 2016: 51), the municipality is nevertheless drawn in more extensively: 'it is not one of our primary nodal areas, but we have spent a lot of money' (SA Government Official 4, City of Tshwane, 2018), mainly to support the housing delivery of the provincial government focused on 'meeting their mandate regardless of what the city is doing' (SA Government Official 4, City of Tshwane, 2018).

Despite its dislocation our data shows a number of relatively recent arrivals in Winterveld (since 2008), some connected to the area through relatives but many who did not mention these links. A number arrived in Madibeng Hills (or a particular sub-area called Marikana) between 2012 and 2015, an area informally established seemingly by a local strongman and technically falling within the adjacent province of North West but contiguous with Winterveld. Respondents cited a desire for independence (wanting a place of their own), a need to escape family or changes in family circumstances elsewhere. Some came from relatively nearby areas such as Soshanguve and Hammanskraal and indeed other parts of Winterveld itself – 36 per cent of survey respondents had previously lived in a different dwelling in the same settlement. Others came from more central parts of Pretoria and further afield, including Tembisa and Soweto in Johannesburg. These respondents spoke about buying plots for very low prices from 'an office' (Winterveld LM 15 ♀ Interview), or from the 'founder' of the area (Winterveld MM 22 ♀ Interview) – though later prices rose due to 'improvements in the area (Winterveld KM 13 ♀ Interview) – or purchasing from an existing resident (Winterveld PS 28 ♀ Interview). In our survey about 30 per cent of respondents had bought their house/land, 8 per cent had inherited and 18 per cent received their house and land from the government.

Other reasons given for living in Winterveld included being born there (Winterveld LM 16 ♂ Interview, in 1999), moving there decades ago to look after a grandparent's house when they passed on (Winterveld MK 18 ♀ Interview) and, for a much more recent arrival, moving there in 2017 when she did not have enough income to support herself in Johannesburg: 'a lot of people are moving to Winterveld because of the low cost of living' (Winterveld GK ♀ 09 interview), which in some instances means 'you don't pay rent or electricity' (Winterveld KM 11 ♀ Diary). In the survey 16 per cent had moved to the area because it was affordable, and 13 per cent indicated it was the only place they could find accommodation. For 14 per cent it was the place they had been allocated housing. Our survey showed the mean length of stay in current dwelling at fourteen years, and about 19 per cent of respondents had lived there for over twenty-five years.

Perceptions are of a significant number of non-South Africans in the area, some living there for more than fifteen years (Winterveld MD 24 ♀ Interview). Respondents claim part of the attraction is the less thorough policing of documentation than other places in Gauteng, as well as low-cost or free infrastructure. As noted in Chapter 3, across our cases Winterveld had one of the highest rates of unemployment at 46 per cent, and reliance on social grants was significant. Rosslyn and Pretoria were mentioned as places for employment. There is a sense that 'connections' and bribery are needed to get a job. Most respondents see transport out of the area to shop or look for employment as very costly, although at least taxis now service the area. The poor condition of roads was frequently mentioned.

Among the types of housing and ways of accessing it in Winterveld are purchasing a stand and self-building a shack or a house, being allocated a free state-funded 'RDP'[3] house as an existing resident and renting a room (cheaply relative to other townships, with an example amount given as R150 per month). In an echo of history, some respondents resent the 'OmaStandi/Mastande' (plot owners) for renting out space at perceived high rates. A resident explained that the municipality only recognises the main house on these subdivided stands; thus, tenants or buyers are relatively powerless and dependent on the plot owners for informal extension of services. In Madibeng Hills 'purchasing' a stand reportedly still requires subsequent obligations to 'the founder' who charges a R2,000 transfer-of-ownership fee on successive transfers (Winterveld MM 22 ♀ Interview). Our survey data showed over 75 per cent of respondents living in a brick or block house and about 20 per cent in a shack or informal dwelling, but typology is varied, with different structures in close proximity to one another in some areas – from corrugated-iron single rooms and modest brick buildings to suburban-style houses with garden walls and gateposts (see Figure 6.2).

Perceptions of life in Winterveld were generally fairly negative, a key concern being its crime rate though variable across different subsections and with differing but mostly negative perceptions of police effectiveness. A lack of street lights and criminals 'hiding in the bush' were seen as contributing factors. For some people there was a sense of being trapped by poverty in the area and a view that respondents would leave Winterveld if they could afford

Figure 6.2 Forms of self-built or locally constructed housing in Madibeng Hills (source: Mark Lewis)

to (Winterveld AD 02 ♀ Interview), or at least move to another section they perceived as better (Winterveld LM 15 ♀ Interview). Several respondents saw the area as 'boring' (a concept discussed in Chapter 10) and as inconveniently located. Some respondents deem Winterveld rural by comparison with services and facilities in other townships, with a few viewing this positively: providing a better environment for raising children (Winterveld NN 26 ♂ Interview) and for agriculture and livestock-farming (occasionally with government support), the latter chiming with an earlier study that farming is significant for many residents (SACN, 2016; see Figure 3.2). One respondent noted that people return to Winterveld to worship their ancestors and for spiritual powers, praying that they find a job or better their lives (Winterveld MK 18 ♀ Interview).

Overall, residents portrayed a largely negative picture of the changes they had experienced in their respective areas. A sense of stagnation owing to little government and private sector investment contrasts with key respondents in an earlier study indicating generally positive perceptions of change (SACN, 2016). Yet 77 per cent in our survey indicated they plan to stay in the area. For the state, this is an inherited periphery with ongoing dynamics, including movement into it, a large, unevenly serviced and connected area, with resultant 'peripheries within peripheries'. Winterveld remains an area without an economic base, with households largely reliant on social grants, small-scale agriculture or employment in fairly distant parts of the metropolitan area. With a somewhat different history but some similar dynamics is our Ekangala case study, which we turn to next.

Ekangala

Chapter 2 provided an overview of the history of Ekangala and Ekandustria as the result of apartheid urbanisation, homeland and industrial decentralisation policies in the early 1980s. Ekangala 'proper' was established as a model township in 1982, with a population of 5,000, and later incorporated into the KwaNdebele homeland.

Other formal residential areas were established subsequently in the area. Plans for Rethabiseng, some 8 km away but closer to the town of Bronkhorstspruit, were passed in 1989, but much of it was developed through post-apartheid RDP housing (COT, 2013). Dark City within Ekangala was established in 1991, with subsequent sections being added until the mid-2000s. Compared to Ekangala 'proper', which has wide tarred roads and medium-size stands with formal housing, Dark City was developed to lower standards, with narrower roads, untarred secondary roads and pit toilets, but infrastructural improvements have occurred since the City of Tshwane took over the area in 2011. COT (2013) notes that the area developed rapidly in terms of new housing in the 1980s and 1990s, but growth slowed in the 2000s, and particularly since 2010.[4] Some informal housing also developed, particularly with the growth of Phumekaya which emerged from 2012, following violent service delivery protests which included the demand for land. Community members then occupied an open space on the edges of Ekangala, and about 1,000 people built shacks in parcelled-out plots.

Despite the origins of the area as a relocation site, and employment decline in Ekandustria from the mid-1990s (see Chapter 2), in-migration continued in the post-apartheid area. By Census 2011 the population of Ekangala had grown to 48,493, and Rethabiseng to 10,960.[5] Our social surveys[6] suggest that access to work was not a significant motivation for migration to the area, with only 6.3 per cent of respondents in Ekangala,[7] 1.7 per cent in Rethabiseng and 2.4 per cent in Phumekaya giving this as a reason. Still, a few respondents in the qualitative study said they had at one point moved to the area to find work (Rethabiseng AC 06 ♂ Interview; Ekangala BM 09 ♀ Interview) or when a family member had secured a job (Phumekaya Group Interview).

The accessibility of the area, access to services and transport, also did not feature as a reason for migration in surveys, diaries and interviews. Rather, access to housing was a critical factor: some 45.6 per cent of respondents in Rethabiseng and 17.7% in Ekangala indicated that this was where they were allocated accommodation. Others came to Ekangala because housing was affordable (16.7 per cent), it suited their needs (17.7 per cent) or it was the only place where they could find accommodation (6.3 per cent).[8]

The churn of family life and household change was reflected as a key reason for location in the area as a whole and in specific areas in social surveys, diaries and interviews. Some 69 per cent of survey respondents in Phumekaya, 39 per cent in Rethabiseng and

35 per cent in Ekangala had moved there due to 'changing family circumstances'. Qualitative interviews and diaries revealed the complexity of these circumstances. For instance, JN (Rethabiseng 09 ♂ Diary) 'used to stay in extension 4, but I moved from there after I had a disagreement with my wife; I now have another wife'. MM (Rethabiseng 12 ♀ Interview) came to live with her mother when the grandmother she was living with in Bushbuckridge passed away, and EK (Phumekaya 07 ♂ Interview) moved to Phumekaya to live with his new wife and left the old house for his children from his first marriage.

'Changing family circumstances' were particularly significant in Phumekaya. Compared to Rethabiseng and Ekangala, the population of Phumekaya is much younger, household sizes are smaller and unemployment rates are much higher, suggesting that it is a place where often unemployed youths from the area can establish new households, typical in auto-constructed peripheries. It is also a place where land is available. For instance, DM (Phumekaya 08 ♀ Diary) indicated that they moved there because they didn't have anywhere else to go and they wanted to build a home for their children. Another respondent explained 'when you marry someone you can't stay at your home with them. So [my husband] found out that there is a new place that is open ... he found a stand that we could live in.' Some households also moved into Phumekaya to have greater autonomy or control over their lives while others moved following job losses: for example, JS (Phumekaya 05 ♂ Interview) moved to Phumekaya from Dark City because he could not pay rent after becoming unemployed: 'when the firms moved out, more shacks have appeared' (Phumekaya TL 01 ♀ Interview).

Rethabiseng and particularly Ekangala are now long established with a large proportion of households who have stayed there for many years. Mean lengths of stay were eighteen and twenty-two years respectively – the longest in our Gauteng surveys. By now, a considerable part of the movement was within the area, so 52.5 per cent of Rethabiseng and 44.8 per cent of Ekangala households had moved into their current houses from elsewhere in the region. Phumekaya in particular attracted mainly households from the immediate area (69 per cent). Other households had moved in from other towns and cities mainly within the province and broader region.

Whereas Rethabiseng and Ekangala were initially established through state housing schemes, a market has developed in Ekangala, where 41 per cent of households surveyed said they had bought their house. There is also considerable evidence of improvement and reinvestment in housing, particularly in 'Ekangala proper' (see Figure 6.3), which has become a more middle-class area. Some houses are relatively large compared to most of our other study areas, with a mean of 5.4 rooms in Ekangala and 4.6 in Rethabiseng, including backyard structures. As in other South African 'townships', backyard units (including for rental) have developed in the area. Census 2011 indicated that around 3 per cent of households in this area lived in such units (COT, 2013). In our surveys around 40 per cent of houses had some form of backyard structure in Rethabiseng and Ekangala, but these were mainly for family members and were not rented out. Only 6 per cent of Ekangala and 2 per cent of Rethabiseng households had tenants.

Some respondents in the qualitative study noted the insufficiency of housing in the area, leading to long waiting times for housing and conflicts within the community as well as with the councillor. However, some housing was being developed, and new stands

Figure 6.3 Housing improvements in Ekangala (source: Mark Lewis)

were being opened up in Ekangala. Respondents noted the varied housing conditions, with some highlighting the developments and improvements that had occurred in Ekangala. In our survey almost all houses in Ekangala and Rethabiseng had taps in the house or on the stand, electricity connections (although some were illegal) and flush toilets. Some respondents in the qualitative study saw their homes as 'good and comfortable' (for instance, Ekangala Dark City EK 07 ♀ Interview). Others, however, pointed to poor-quality construction, including of RDP housing (Rethabiseng NH 03 ♂ Interview; Rethabiseng GM 02 ♂ Diary; Ekangala Dark City TM 04 ♀ Diary) – a concern also raised in other parts of South Africa. As might be expected, conditions in Phumekaya were much worse, with no electricity and only pit latrines and communal taps. Conditions in shacks can be dusty, damp and crowded. For instance, 'there is no space for us to work or for the school children to do their school work … sometimes when it rains all night we have to take turns to mop out water and in the morning the school children will go to school tired' (Phumekaya JS 05 ♂ Diary).

How do residents see their future, particularly given declining industrial employment in the area? Of course some have employment in service sectors (including in more middle-class occupations) and some commute to work elsewhere, but unemployment rates are high (see Chapter 3). Some thought that they would continue to live in the area while others hoped to move on, mainly to places outside of the area. Better access to work and economic opportunities were given as reasons to move, for example, 'it's not a place that can accommodate young people … The young ones need to stay in townships like Mamelodi, Soshanguve you see; the jobs are near that side' (Ekangala KS 02 ♂ Interview).

Several interviewees said that they want to move to 'busy areas' that will be good for their business, such as Witbank, Johannesburg and Pretoria (e.g. Rethabiseng AC 06 ♂ Interview; Ekangala EB 01 ♀ Interview). Likewise, KS (Ekangala 02 ♂ Interview) said 'I do have plans, but my plans are not at Ekangala because I plan on opening a business.' Others sought to move to safer environments where drugs are not so prevalent, to the suburbs, and sometimes to more peripheral areas where there is more space. One respondent, ST (Ekangala Dark City 01 ♀ Interview), planned to build a house in Dark City and then lease it out to provide an income for her family.

While some, such as DM (Phumekaya 08 ♀ Diary), said that they live in the area because they do not have anywhere else to go, others see benefits in staying. The housing available makes MB (Rethabiseng 11 ♀ Interview) happy, although the lack of job opportunities and work is troubling. Likewise, LM (Ekangala Dark City 14 ♀ Interview) said that 'I can stay at another place but I am home; I see this place as good'.

Hence, while the origins of the area are firmly located in an apartheid history, and it might in this sense be seen as evidencing the logic of an inherited periphery, particularly in view of current dynamics of decline, residents have diverse experiences of living there. For some, it is a place to escape, to leave, while others have nowhere else to go. Yet there are residents for whom it is 'home', a place to return to and invest in.

Molweni

Molweni is located around 30 km west of the urban core in the Outer West area of the eThekwini Municipality. Historically, the area was inhabited by traditional farming communities and dominated by the Ngcolosi tribal group, with strong chief authority managing decision-making and land allocations. In-migration into Molweni has a long and varied history, in the search for work and land (Stavrou and Crouch, 1989). Much of the area was officially incorporated within the homeland of KwaZulu in 1977 when KwaZulu was granted self-government and formed one of the initial seventy (major and minor) nodes within the most fragmented of all homelands (Butler *et al.*, 1977: 8). This fragmentation meant KwaZulu was never territorially or demographically a 'homeland' given that much of its 'traditional' land and people fell within 'white' South Africa (Butler *et al.*, 1977: 6). Nevertheless, housing provision and taxation of properties became a responsibility of the new homeland government (along with the provincial and central governments) (Butler *et al.*, 1977: 142).

Molweni is relatively well located for key economic nodes, including Pinetown-New Germany, Hillcrest and also the Inanda/KwaMashu/Ntuzuma complex. However, its steep topography, limited access routes with reliance on the single, recently upgraded Inanda Road bisecting the settlement, and location adjacent to the

Umgeni River position the settlement as 'remote and inaccessible' (UDIDI, 2012: 14). It is composed of a mix of tribal authority land (with 53 per cent of all tenure in our survey falling into this category) alongside land managed by the municipality. Its resultant mix of smaller and larger plots of land alongside significant areas of undeveloped steeply sloping land accounts for the area appearing peri-urban in form and rural in parts.

Access to land and housing varies significantly. Many residents have a long settlement history in the area, with our survey revealing a 26.6-year mean average. Local chiefs (*Inkosi*) have controlled the allocation of much of the land, and ongoing requirements to pay *Inkosi* for plots fuelled resentment of *Inkosi* practices (Molweni DM 10 ♂ Interview). Others were allocated land and temporary accommodation initially in containers and then two-roomed tin housing in the area of Congo after being relocated from KwaNgcolosi for the construction of the nearby Inanda Dam in the late 1980s (Molweni MC 03 ♀ Interview). Some residents already living locally acquired housing through the government's BNG[9] programme from around 2012 onwards, although provision through this scheme appears relatively sporadic, tied in part to a significant storm that hit the Molweni area in 2008 destroying many houses. Investment in services and infrastructure is highly variable, seemingly determined by which authority residents fall under, with the area of Ngoxaza (managed by local chiefs) repeatedly reporting underinvestment: 'my area I feel [is] excluded because few weeks ago we were attending the meeting about the development of Molweni, but Ngoxaza was [left] out from that development' (Molweni NS 38 ♀ Interview). At the same time, in this transitioning periphery many other properties have benefited from electrification and improvements in sanitation and water provision.

Housing form varies significantly throughout the area. Much is in the form of homesteads or multiple structures on single plots, including a mix of round, traditional structures adjacent to rectangular buildings (see Figure 6.4). Houses constructed of brick and concrete account for 91 per cent of property types, but overall typologies include state-provided RDP/BNG housing and individually constructed houses, ranging from more formal with services, including row housing with shared facilities, to less formal and poorly serviced, to traditional houses (9 per cent) to informal

Figure 6.4 Housing in Molweni (source: Mark Lewis)

shack housing. The 2019 Spatial Development Framework (SDF) identified around 3,000 informal structures in different sections of Molweni. There is relatively little backyard shack construction, accounting for only 1 per cent in our survey, with rates of renters and of other persons occupying stands very low. 42 per cent of households are female-headed, and income levels and high levels of unemployment reveal significant poverty. Various large detached properties on large plots of land also indicate some local wealth.

Homeownership and late apartheid

From settlements in or near homelands that subsequently consolidated, attracted or retained populations, we turn to another driver of housing on the urban periphery, the homeownership initiative of the late apartheid era. By the late 1970s it was increasingly clear that the apartheid system was both financially and politically unsustainable (Hindson *et al.*, 1994). As apartheid unravelled in the violent 1980s, a variety of housing initiatives took root across government, the business sector and ordinary people. In some places organised groupings occupied vacant land near townships (Hindson et al., 1994), with some settlements eventually achieving some security against eviction and basic service delivery (Mabin, 1992). By the late 1980s, site and service schemes were also introduced, some which later grew rapidly into large settlements while others had little take-up. Some upgrading of informal settlements was also initiated. Spatially, however, these victories in permanent occupation largely underlined apartheid divisions (Mabin, 1992). With similar spatial limitations (Hindson et al., 1994) but significant in terms of land tenure and urban legitimacy were the attempts from the early 1980s to encourage an emerging black middle class into privately financed homeownership, aimed also at stabilising politically volatile townships (Parnell, 1992). The U-turn government strategy recognised the inevitability of long-term urban residency but arguably targeted 'class divisions within urban black residential areas' (Morris and Hindson, 1992, cited in Hindson et al., 1994: 333). By 1986 influx controls were dropped and replaced by a strategy of 'orderly urbanisation' and the creation of large new townships on the edge of cities, part of attempts to manage social and labour conditions. However, heightened political contestation resulted in both rental and repayment boycotts across various housing types, part of the opposition strategy of making the country 'ungovernable'. Although unsuccessful as a political stabilisation strategy (Mabin and Smit, 1997), some of the homeownership initiatives born at this time – many of them on urban peripheries (Hindson et al., 1994) – have had long-term spatial influences, as shown by Protea Glen on the western edge of Soweto.

Protea Glen

As discussed in Chapter 2, Protea Glen emerged from a private company, Township Realtors, purchasing land on the edge of Soweto (Butcher, 2016), their eye on future residential property demand from black urban residents as apartheid crumbled. Using a location uncontested and unthreatening to white residents of Johannesburg, the company has made land available since the late 1980s to developers constructing houses for sale to generally first-time buyers (Butcher, 2016). As of 2022 some thirty-five neighbourhoods of Protea Glen have been developed, and the area now contains a shopping mall (see Figure 11.3) and other retail complexes, is now connected to other parts of Soweto and Johannesburg by the Rea Vaya bus service and has free wi-fi infrastructure, much appreciated by our respondents. However, it remains the outer periphery of Soweto, abutting mining and agricultural land. Yet for some of our respondents who had moved to the area from more rural parts of South Africa, it represented far greater accessibility: for example, changing life 'for the better' (Protea Glen GM 09 ♂ Interview, PG Extension 11). Mean length of stay was just under fourteen years, though notably some of our respondents had been living in the area for decades – for example, in Protea Glen 20 since 1993 – and some had moved from other parts of Soweto (e.g. Protea Glen SM 11 ♂ Interview).

Our respondents had mixed views on how far or proximate Protea Glen seems to urban opportunities, with some noting that it is too far from companies and job opportunities and complaining of transport costs (Protea Glen CC 08 ♂ Interview), and others commenting that transport is affordable and, with the new bus service, convenient (Protea Glen CT 014 ♀ Interview). Some respondents identify local job opportunities in retail and in government projects. There is a sense of the area growing, with 'new houses everywhere' (Protea Glen GA 04 ♀ Diary) and it feeling like a suburb (Protea Glen WM 20 ♂ Diary). The presence of the mall means convenient access to shops (Protea Glen VM 017 ♂ Diary; Protea Glen CC 08 ♂ Diary). However, typical of housing developments, the arrival of facilities lags behind residential expansion: respondents complained of only three primary schools and one clinic (Protea Glen TN 01 ♂ Diary) and a lack of playgrounds and sports facilities (Protea Glen WM 20 ♂ Diary). As with our other case study sites (see Chapter 10), the pervasiveness of drugs and crime was noted by many respondents, with some claiming people have left the area because of a failure of authorities to deal with crime (Protea Glen VM 17 ♂ Diary). Houses are formal, mostly detached, often with walls and gates around them, with a few low-rise rental apartments in addition. For some people, renting a room or even buying a house is considered affordable for those who work in the area (Protea Glen WM 20 ♂ Diary), but others comment that some people don't pay their housing bonds and so lose their homes or have them confiscated by the banks (Protea Glen ZN 10 ♀ Diary).

Overall sentiments reflect an area consolidating into a well-functioning and desirable place: 'Seven years back in Protea Glen, it was a place which many people did not like, but now it's a beautiful place because there are many things such as a mall, school and others' (Protea Glen 08 CC ♂ Diary). These sentiments, likely only achieved after several decades of investment and consolidation, contrasts somewhat with the nearby government-led housing development of Lufhereng, much newer and still lacking many facilities, amenities and public transport – still a relatively 'bare-bones' peripheral neighbourhood.

Post-apartheid housing policy and practice, post-apartheid peripheral experience

Both poorly located residential settlements lacking an economic base and vast shortages in housing were part of the burden and 'unenviable housing record' (Jones and Datta, 2000: 393) the new democratic government inherited in 1994. The promise of 'houses, security and comfort' from the Freedom Charter of the 1950s translated into the right to housing in the bill of rights of the post-apartheid Constitution. Housing policy was forged in a multiactor negotiating forum from 1992 to 1993, with analysts contending that the central outcome – homeownership through a serviced site with a very basic core house, later delivered as a complete house – was a compromise that didn't really suit any of the negotiating positions (Charlton and Kihato, 2006). However, the significance of land, homeownership and decent infrastructure after decades of apartheid repression and dire living conditions is not to be underestimated: now with waterborne sanitation in a state-funded house, PR rejoices that 'I flush like any other citizen' (Lufhereng PR ♂ Interview).

Post-apartheid spatial and housing policy, 'essentially modernist' in nature (Harrison *et al.*, 2008), advocated city restructuring, using better-located land to accommodate marginalised residents. But new subsidised housing-led suburbs have instead been critiqued for parallels with apartheid locations, with many built on cheaper and less favourable peripheral lands, without contributing to urban restructuring (Todes, 2003). In parallel with this state-funded delivery at scale, informal settlements have also multiplied as well as densified, reflecting housing demand exceeding supply but also housing location deficits as well as people's efforts to minimise living costs.

In both apartheid-era townships and new housing developments – which post-2004 have been increasingly realised as mixed-income developments including mortgage housing – householders have constructed backyard dwellings to increase room-space for family members or for rental income. Variable in quality, these have contributed significantly to densifying these neighbourhoods. Our Waterloo, Hammonds Farm and Lufhereng cases illustrate vanguard peripheries of late- or post-apartheid housing interventions but reflect different project approaches and spatial locations. After discussing these we turn to informal settlements in our study sites, part of the growing phenomenon of unauthorised settlements since the 1980s.

Waterloo and Hammonds Farm

Waterloo was established from the 1990s onwards about 25–30 km to the north of Durban's central business district (CBD). Housing is primarily detached, single storey and constructed from brick (92 per cent of the houses in our survey). Residents' mean length of stay was just under eleven years, and their origin is highly varied with participants moving in from further up the north coast, including locations such as Ballito and Tongaat but also from across KwaZulu-Natal more widely, including Pietermaritzburg (Waterloo DN 23 ♂ Interview). Mbatha's research in one part of Waterloo, namely Extension 5, reveals that state housing was constructed between 2000 and 2002 (Mbatha, 2018), an area described as economically vibrant with a relatively lower level of unemployment, where residents are employed in a range of private and public sector roles as well as informally. The wider area is clearly consolidated, with a mix of facilities including sports, schools and clinics, although when the first residents located there in the late 1990s, the site lacked any facilities: 'This place was awkward because there were no schools, no clinic, no shops. There was nothing. It was a sugar cane field' (Waterloo DN 23 ♂ Interview).

Our survey reveals that 54 per cent of residents purchased their properties, 19 per cent were renting and 15 per cent received both a house and land from the government. A further 8 per cent received only land from the government, aligning with Mbatha's findings that parts of Waterloo were originally the location of a government site and service scheme prior to the construction of RDP housing.

Resident DN offers extensive insights into the history and formation of the settlement, noting the various phases of development and how as these phases unfolded, house and plot sizes expanded from one to two rooms, up to 40 m^2 in Phase 5, with toilets included. He also explains that in 1996 when the settlement was first developed on former sugar cane land owned by Tongaat-Hulett, residents were offered either sites or one-room houses: 'People who were working decided to take sites and those who were unemployed to one-roomed houses. The government grant was R17,000 … they will take R7,000.00 for a site and give you R10,000,00 for material' (Waterloo DN 23 ♂ Interview). In his diary he notes that residents who received the initial very small one-roomed houses 'were very happy … because they were not [able] to afford to build it themselves'; however, '[they] were sleeping and cooking in that one room. Everything was located in one room, even the bathroom.' Later he suggests that the Department of Housing should rebuild these one-roomed structures as they were poorly constructed and insufficient in size (Waterloo DN 23 ♂ Diary).

As our survey suggests, and evidenced by Mbatha, there is a relatively high level of change of ownership in the area. However, the extent of resale of RDP houses was difficult to establish owing to reticence surrounding the sale of state housing, despite the houses in Waterloo falling outside of the eight-year ban on resale (Mbatha, 2018). A further challenge limiting an anticipated vibrant low-income property market was the absence of title deeds for many property owners, meaning resale was difficult, although Waterloo's relatively good location near the airport meant resale prices were healthy, recorded at between R20,000 and R65,000 (Mbatha, 2018). Many properties are extended or expanded, including some vertically or with the inclusion of garages and carports (see Figure 6.5). Mbatha notes that 25 per cent of his sampled 219 houses had undergone major improvements, and 21 per cent minor improvements (2018: 170). The settlement has an aspirational feel to it, as evidenced by resident DN: 'I believe that I can build my luxury house here in Waterloo because when I came here it was like a farm but look at it now. There are people who have built their beautiful houses here in Waterloo; I will do the same' (Waterloo DN 23 ♂ Interview). These trends support Mbatha and Mchunu's argument derived from research elsewhere in eThekwini about the peripheries as spaces of opportunity, particularly in traditional authority areas, with

Figure 6.5 Waterloo (source: Mark Lewis)

high levels of upmarket housing in 'job-poor' peripheral zones, which provide the benefits of affordable housing that 'job-rich' zones do not. On the one hand, people who cannot attain regular employment may relocate to the least expensive areas, which happen to be on the periphery. On the other hand, middle-class development thrives on a degree of informality and freedom from municipal constraints on the periphery. Periurbanisation blurs this distinction by mixing both middle-income and poor communities at the periphery in their quest for cheap land. (Mbatha and Mchunu, 2016: 12–13)

Waterloo's rental costs were considered to be relatively high, with resident BZ explaining that 'The two-roomed house is now R1,500 per month', in contrast to the R300.00 she paid previously (Waterloo BZ 19 ♀ Interview).

Very close to Waterloo, Hammonds Farm is an area of state-subsidised housing just south of the airport, built in the late 2000s. Controversy and allegations of corruption surround the sale of this land to the municipality as well as the tendering for housing development revealing the confluence of vanguard and speculative logics evident within the urban peripheries. The land was purchased in 2005 by a Mr Ravi Jagadasan (son of now deceased infamous property mogul Jay Singh) and within eighteen months was identified by the eThekwini Municipality as the site for the new Hammonds Farm housing development. The landowners secured decision-making over the appointment of contractors, and Jagadasan's father's company Gralio Precast was awarded the contract in June 2007 (Ellero, 2015) ultimately worth R400 million (Erasmus, 2013). Dardagan (2012) noted concerns were raised about the safety of the construction following the publication of the Manase report by the municipality in 2012 into financial and contractual irregularities, with the report describing 'Gralio Precast's work "shocking and unacceptable, dangerous, substandard"' (Erasmus, 2019). Ellero notes that the original costs for the development of Hammonds Farm escalated by R200 million 'due to environmental factors that would have been considered if a proper feasibility study had been undertaken before construction had commenced' (Ellero, 2015: 102).

Nonetheless, the site was developed with top structures put in place for 2,000 housing units (SLB Consulting, n.d.), with around 1,800 terraced, two-storey units constructed in around 2010–11 (see Figure 6.6). Many units were allocated to around 1,600 residents from the former Ocean Drive Inn informal settlement, located 17 km further north of eThekwini, who were living in dire conditions, whose land was reclaimed by its private owner and sold for development associated with the Dube TradePort (DTP) (Lewis, 2012). Other residents were moved into Hammonds Farm from surrounding townships and other informal settlements across the city and also

Figure 6.6 Hammonds Farm (source: Mark Lewis)

from nearby Waterloo. The properties contain two bedrooms on the upper floor, with an open-plan downstairs, including a lounge and kitchen area and a small bathroom alongside. Most properties have viable electrical and water connections, although the costs of these are significant for many residents. Perceptions of housing by residents were very mixed: many were grateful, delighted with the privacy, shelter and security, but frustrated by high costs and design limitations of housing (see Meth et al., 2022 for empirical details). The settlement does not contain any formal economic units, schools, creches, playgrounds, clinics or communal space. It is serviced by the nearby Spar supermarket (see Chapter 11) and the clinic and community hall located in adjacent Waterloo. The mean average length of residence in the settlement was around three and a half years at the time of our survey (in 2018), and 87 per cent of residents noted they received their duplexes from the government, with 10 per cent indicating they were renting properties and 2 per cent stating they'd bought or inherited properties. These figures align with the timings of the settlement's construction and occupation.

Lufhereng

Chapter 2 introduced the mixed-income housing development called Lufhereng on the western edge of Soweto, relatively close to the much older though still expanding speculative neighbourhoods of Protea Glen discussed above. Driven by the provincial government, Lufhereng was launched with great fanfare in 2010 with promises it would showcase viable new development (Charlton, 2017). Although geotechnical issues have reduced the anticipated yield, it still promises in the vicinity of 24,000 houses, with some of the fully state-funded housing occupied at the time of our research and the mortgage units mostly under construction. With design input from an architectural firm, the fully funded housing includes row housing and some semi-detached and detached single-story units (Figure 6.7). Planned to house people from surrounding farmlands of Doornkop, backyard rooms in nearby Soweto as well as others who had applied for state housing (Charlton, 2017), a number of our respondents had relocated from the informal settlement of Protea South some 10 km away and positively compared their new situations with their previous living conditions. 'I will say my house is a gift from God ... I was staying in a shack. Now even if it's raining I've got no worries for rain' (Lufhereng

Figure 6.7 Lufhereng (source: Mark Lewis)

NF 05 ♀ Interview). The neighbourhood as a whole was celebrated by some: 'It is only seven years old and has beautiful RDP houses, tarred roads, drain systems are on point. Everything here is almost perfect ... I love this place' (Lufhereng PD 01 ♀ Diary).

Our participants were appreciative of the primary school established (e.g. Lufhereng AM 04 ♀ Diary) but lamented the need to travel elsewhere for facilities such as a police station: 'you have to be the one who takes a taxi and goes to open a case' (Lufhereng VZ 20 ♀ Interview). In general the area's disconnection from formal shops, work and other opportunities was a significant problem, as discussed in Chapters 8 and 11 in relation to transportation and retail. Some of our respondents had relinquished work after relocation due to the cost of taxi transport relative to low wages (Lufhereng NF 05 ♀ Interview), particularly in comparison to train transport previously accessible from the informal settlement. Lack of affordability and constrained choice made mobility in general a problem for many (Williams et al., 2021), affecting jobseeking, viable earnings, further education and other activities requiring journeys: 'to me Lufhereng is a beautiful place ... the only problem is just the transportation' (Lufhereng PR 13 ♂ Diary). However, in our survey 66 per cent of respondents saw transport as improving in recent years. Some of our respondents saw Lufhereng as a rural area 'because it's a peripheral area ... the people go farming and they come back carrying wood ... [because] ... the electricity is not stable; it can go anytime, so they need firewood ... there are even cows walking about' (Lufhereng NM 04 ♀ Interview). Some participants had seized the opportunity to grow vegetables, and for many a permanent home and essential infrastructure were significant despite their joblessness and poverty (Charlton, 2017), though as in other low-income areas, outside rooms and home shops evidenced modifications needed to assist with a viable life.

Post-apartheid informal settlements: Canelands and Coniston, Waterworks, Phumekaya

Our cases of informal settlements in the auto-constructed periphery took diverse forms but often chimed with the view that they tend to be in 'peripheral areas, poorer areas where there is less urban management, there is less police presence; that's the easiest place to just stake your claim' (SA Government Official 4, City of Tshwane, 2018). Dwellings were often relatively provisional structures made of corrugated iron, packaging material and wood, but there are significant instances of more substantial investment, for example in Madibeng Hills in Winterveld, as shown in Figure 6.2 above.

Informal settlements perform varied functions. In Phumekaya, Ekangala, staking a claim in this low-density, very poorly serviced area was generally related to young households wanting independence from family homes. In Canelands and Coniston in Durban, as well as Waterworks near Protea Glen in Gauteng, residence was much more likely linked to jobs in the area within walking distance, though often low paying and marginal in nature. In Canelands and Coniston the very nearby light industrial area of Verulam provided some employment, though some respondents worked considerably further afield, and perceptions were that work is only gained through connections anyway. These are relatively dense settlements in a low-lying area affected by flooding (Figure 6.8), dramatically so in the extreme weather event the entire city experienced in April 2021, subsequent to our research. As explained in Chapter 9, there were much-valued, municipal-provided communal toilet and washing facilities (see Figure 9.2) but very poor refuse removal which strongly shaped people's experience of the area being a dirty and undignified living environment not suitable for families.

Figure 6.8 Canelands with the Verulam railway bridge in the distance (source: Mark Lewis)

Respondents spoke of leaking shacks and hazardous illegal electricity connections (Canelands SM 17 ♀ Interview). Despite their participation in political processes, some claim they are not respected and 'are looked at, as if we are baboons to be thrown away in the bushes to live there' (Coniston AM 01 ♀ Diary). Some respondents see their lives there as a temporary or short-term option and yearn for a 'proper house' like the RDP homes (Shintshani NM 10 ♀ Interview). Yet a few were positive about the area: 'In my eyes and my heart, this area is beautiful' (Coniston AM 01 ♀ Diary).

In lower-density Waterworks in Gauteng, with open grassland and bush around it, respondents spoke of very low-paying domestic 'piece jobs' in the more prosperous and historically 'Indian' suburb of Lenasia (a thirty-five-minute walk), and receiving charity from these neighbours. Residence in Waterworks resulted from, among other things, an inability to afford rental elsewhere, including other parts of Soweto (Waterworks N 06 ♀ Diary), eviction from other accommodation (Waterworks MK 04 ♀ Diary) or needing a cheap base from which to search for work (Waterworks MP 10 ♀ Diary). In our survey 46 per cent cited changing family circumstances (such as divorce or separation) as a reason for moving to the area. Some had lived in the settlement for more than fifteen years, with our survey showing a mean length of stay in their dwelling of over thirteen years, very similar to that in nearby Protea Glen. Although located along the same main road R558 giving access to Protea Glen, the settlement lay within neighbouring Rand West municipality, a factor apparently used to disqualify residents from certain work opportunities in Protea Glen (Waterworks LM 03 ♀ Interview). Plans were underway to relocate qualifying residents to state-funded housing deeper into Rand West municipality but with no arrangements for those not meeting subsidised housing criteria. Clearing the settlement was apparently linked in part to a subterranean water pipe traversing the area but also to retail and commercial development planned for both sides of the municipal boundary, the future speculative periphery trumping the current auto-constructed one. Dwellings were generally of corrugated iron or provisional materials (see Figure 10.1) with very basic services such as a communal tap and pit toilets infrequently emptied. Wood used for heating and cooking was a huge safety concern, with reports of shacks having burnt down. Flimsy construction accentuated vulnerability to break-ins: 'when I go to town I come back and something is always missing' (Waterworks MK 04 ♀ Diary) – and crime was pervasive, as discussed in Chapter 10. Some feel diminished by their status as an informal settlement resident: in poignant contrast to the access to waterborne sanitation celebrated earlier in the chapter in nearby Lufhereng, respondent PN (Waterworks 12 ♀ Interview) doesn't travel to nearby Protea Glen because 'I feel small there … because my kids are not used to the toilets and big TVs [so] they would sit there for a long time and play with the toilets'. This was a particularly impoverished and marginalised informal settlement, summarised by GN (Waterworks 09 ♀ Interview): 'what's there to like about this place? There's nothing here.'

Conclusion

Markedly different histories and diverse contemporary dynamics have shaped housing in our South African cases. Perhaps most striking are the indications of population inflow and of significant household investment in recent decades in areas intended under apartheid to keep black people out of urban areas. In the years since democracy, many people have remained living in these places, their lives and personal histories shaped by these contexts which are 'home'. Formerly neglected but dislocated areas have provided a vexing problem for authorities under pressure to deliver to households, and government investment has followed, mainly in housing, infrastructure improvements and some social facilities. But at least in the inherited peripheries of Ekangala and Winterveld, although these differ in perceived potential and categorisation in city spatial plans, the persistent lack of an economic base means these are not priority growth areas. Yet they are also transitioning peripheries: there is some state infrastructure investment, households alter homes, add rooms or establish businesses in their yards and there are whole areas of auto-constructed settlement, often for reasons of establishing households independent of family nearby or reducing living costs in a context of very few work opportunities. In the transitioning periphery of Molweni, also part of a former homeland, connections with the rest of the metro are strengthening through infrastructure improvements.

New post-apartheid housing developments can be found in locations driven by varying logics, sometimes in economically developing sub-regions of cities such northern eThekwini, other times in areas considerably more disconnected in economic terms such as Lufhereng. Some of these indicate the relationships between their vanguard logic and a less apparent speculative logic, through aspects such as land sale and promotion of location through nearby developments. They may also reflect uneven power relations between spheres of government, with the local level overridden in favour of provincial agendas out of kilter with local spatial plans. Relatively decent housing and infrastructure provision is generally valued by households in these areas despite what are often conditions of poverty and joblessness. In part because of these conditions, the more recently built developments indicate the start of similar reworking by households as their older counterparts, their formal visions edging towards transition under these adaptations. These processes of subsequent change to built form delivered as 'complete' reveal both the limitations of the state-provided housing (in that it needs to be modified) but also its importance as a resource for households (Charlton, 2018b). The post-delivery modifications add a distinct and significant dimension to the layering of people's agency with state logic, which Caldeira (2017) terms peripheral urbanisation.

Informal settlements may be found across a variety of peripheral locations, in some areas related to work opportunities but in others reflecting social or personal motivations, or a lack of alternatives. Across our different cases, housing typologies span from very provisional materials to very robust, formal construction and degrees of developer-driven, state and individual household investment. While only one of our South Africa cases included upmarket developments (see Introduction) also found on some urban peripheries, the range and diversity already reflected in the study sites reinforce the highly complex layering of past and present, and different actors and forces. Despite this diversity, the weight of history, contradictions in contemporary developments and the difficult circumstances of many respondents, 'hope' is also a cross-cutting theme, at least for some people: that further government investment will improve liveability, areas will develop and prospects for better, more viable lives will strengthen.

Notes

1 The name comes from its historical function as a winter grazing area for white 'pioneers' (Horn *et al.*, 1992).
2 For a more rounded picture of lived experiences of Winterveld over time, one would thus need to trace evictees from the area in addition to researching those currently living there.
3 'RDP housing' is a popular term that derives from the post-apartheid government's multifaceted Reconstruction and Development Programme.
4 These changes may reflect the shifting economy of the area (see Chapter 2), alongside population growth and local demand for housing. The role of Kungwini municipality in the earlier period may also have been significant.
5 On Census figures, growth rates were 3.1 per cent per annum for Ekangala and 6.8 per cent per annum for Rethabiseng between 1996 and 2011.
6 The question asked why households came to the area – respondents could give multiple responses.
7 Our survey for Ekangala covered the range of areas there, including both Ekangala 'proper' and Dark City.
8 Equivalent figures for Rethabiseng were: 8.5 per cent (suited needs), 6.8 per cent (affordable).
9 'Breaking New Ground' is the policy successor to the first-generation post-apartheid housing programme.

7

Peri-urban transformations: Changing land markets and (in)security in peri-urban Accra, Ghana

Divine M. Asafo

Introduction: peri-urban spaces and their land markets

The increasing transformation of customary land in sub-Saharan Africa (SSA) has opened up contemporary discourses around land use, landownership, land governance and land administration practices (Obeng-Odoom, 2016; Bansah, 2017; Akaateba, 2019; Chimhowu, 2019). Central to this discourse is the evolving land market and the associated (in)securities in the peri-urban areas of major cities in SSA. Wehrmann (2008: 75) reveals that the peri-urban land markets have become the 'most dynamic and most diverse in sub-Saharan Africa'. The increasing attention on customary land in peri-urban areas (defined as a space between urban and rural settlements and characterised with rapid spatial and social change) is informed by urban sprawl, rising demand for land, uneven power relations among different actors and the complex land governance systems (Wehrmann, 2008; McGregor et al., 2011). Consequently, the land market in peri-urban areas is now acknowledged and analysed in terms of uneven power relations, negotiation processes and competing interests among actors, especially in situations where land transfers and transactions have become highly contested (Ubink, 2008; Wehrmann, 2008; Arko-Adjei, 2011; Asafo, 2022).

In a recent review of customary land in SSA, including peri-urban land, Chimwohu (2019) presents new evidence of land transformation shaped by the interplay of global opportunities and complex state-informed neoliberal processes including commodification, privatisation, deregulation, re-regulation and flanking and support systems. He suggested that the outcome of these processes has resulted in a 'new' African customary tenure characterised by altered governance and institutional structures, and uneven power relations in land use and land management (see Chimhowu, 2019). Akaateba's work in Ghana reveals how exclusionary outcomes are evident as customary tenure regimes increasingly experience manipulation (2019). Empirical evidence reveals that countries including Rwanda, Zimbabwe, Mozambique, Zambia, Ghana and Nigeria have witnessed the establishment of institutions for land registration and the devolution of legal authority over land to facilitate access to land by private individuals (Chimhowu, 2019). A more significant feature of these transformations is the proliferation of different actors especially in peri-urban areas with either supporting or competing roles within land administration frameworks (Rakodi, 2006; Wehrmann, 2008; Obeng-Odoom, 2016).

While the literature on the rising number of actors in peri-urban areas has generally focused on land use, access, land delivery, governance and tenure rights (Larbi, 1996; Chimhowu and Woodhouse, 2006; Gough and Yankson, 2006), much is left unexplored about the proliferation of these different actors and how their actions shape the peri-urban land market. This chapter, therefore, investigates how these new actors are altering existing land transaction practices in the land market and their implications for tenure (in)security in peri-urban Accra. The intersection of rising speculation beset by conflict and insecurity by land-owning, intermediaries and land–seeking individuals in Greater Accra, the proliferation of housing production outside of legal and formal planning frameworks commonly for the purpose of satisfying the need for affordable urban accommodation, and changes in land use and processes of densification evident within peri-urban Accra speak to the logics of the speculative, auto-constructed and transitioning peripheries detailed in the Introduction of this book. Indeed, Accra offers a clear example of the ways in which different peripheries' logics are overlaid and bleed into each other (see Introduction and Meth *et al.*, 2021a). Speculation within this analysis relates not necessarily to the investment practices of large private sector institutions bent on profiting from Africa's new peripheral elite enclaves (Van Noorloos and Kloosterboer, 2018) but rather to the gains and potential for gains of various actors (customary leaders, local estate agents, individuals, landguards, welfare associations) from their control over or access to a highly contested resource, namely land, including at times through the use of force or intimidation. More generally, trust and social relations are key within these speculative practices, although speculation is often achieved through devious practices and multiple land sales. This chapter therefore offers an extension to the book's framing of peripheral logics through its analysis of the proliferation of actors engaged in speculative practices, its focus on transitioning peri-urban spaces driven by land market changes and its observation of the growth in unplanned housing structures.

Drawing on evidence from four peri-urban communities in Accra, the chapter is driven by the following questions: what are the emerging land transaction practices in peri-urban Accra? Who are the new actors in the land market? How are their activities shaping land transaction and tenure (in)security within the peri-urban land market? The interactions and outcomes of the various actors in peri-urban land markets not only reveal their interests but also how they influence the composition, dynamics and practices of land markets (Lombard, 2016; Asafo, 2020). Understanding these land market dynamics and how they are shaped contributes more broadly to the focus of this book on the drivers of change in African peripheries. This chapter offers a specific investigation of the role of land and land markets as central drivers of change and centres conflict as integral to peripheral transformation. Exploring these core components of the peri-urban land market is paramount to unpacking the different outcomes of land transformation and (in)securities, which is vital for policy reforms and improving the political economy of land in SSA.

The subsequent discussion is structured into four strands. The first provides the context to customary land in peri-urban Accra, Ghana, and this is followed by a discussion on the theoretical approach and the methods informing the study. The third section presents and discusses the results by providing empirical evidence on the theme from the case study communities, and the fourth and final section outlines key conclusions.

Land management and the peri-urban land market in Accra, Ghana

Similar to most countries in SSA, but distinct from both Ethiopia and South Africa, land in peri-urban Accra is collectively owned and largely controlled by customary institutions including the stool,[1] families and clans (Kasanga and Kotey, 2001; Ayee et al., 2008; Arko-Adjei, 2011). These institutions hold the allodial interest to land, while any transfer of land made to other entities such as individuals or groups is based on leasehold. While it is estimated that 80 per cent of the land is under customary authority, the remaining 18 per cent and 2 per cent is owned by the state and held in trust for the community through the state respectively (Kasanga and Kotey, 2001). Also, despite the fact that landownership is similar all across Ghana, there is a significant difference between land in peri-urban Accra and land in other parts of the country. In peri-urban Accra, for example, families and clans own the majority of land, whereas in other parts of the country, such as the Ashanti region, land is solely controlled by the stool (Mireku et al., 2016).

Customary control of land existed before prehistoric times; however, the footprints of colonial governance practices in Ghana have altered land management practices and, more significantly, changed the perception of land from a communal good to an economic good (Sackeyfio, 2012). This was evident through laws and policy reforms such as the Public Land Ordinance in 1876, which permitted state acquisition of land for public use. Sackeyfio (2012) revealed that this practice introduced elements of state control and commodification into the customary land market in Accra. Land policy reforms such as the Land Title Registration Law (PNDC 152) and the State Land Acts 1962 (ACT 125) are examples of this, as they established government institutions to provide tenure security through land title registration. The outcome, therefore, has been the co-existence of multiple institutions (state and customary) in land management in Ghana, especially in the Greater Accra Region, as is common across many African countries.

The co-existence of both the state and customary institutions in the management of land has not been on a smooth trajectory following the differences in their modus operandi. That is, while the state draws on set legal standards, formal land-titling and planning processes, customary institutions are characterised by flexibility, customs and social values such as trust and social networks in managing land (Leduka, 2006; Rakodi, 2006; Amanor, 2008; Chimhowu, 2019). The consequence of this has been complex administration problems, summarised by Ehwi et al. (2019) to include land acquisition challenges, land registration challenges and tenure security challenges. Policy interventions to enhance effective land administration include the Land Administration Programme I (2003–10) and II (2011–14), which established the Customary Land Secretariate (CLS), a hybrid institutional framework that complements state powers and customary authority in the management of customary land (Gough and Yankson, 2006; Gyapong, 2009; Arko-Adjei, 2011; Ehwi et al., 2019).

The land market in peri-urban areas is currently undergoing intense transformation as a result of the increasing urbanisation and urban sprawl, particularly in Greater Accra Metropolitan Area (GAMA), which is home to the majority of the urban population in Ghana (Asafo, 2022). This population is faced with increasing housing deficits and the high cost of rent, forcing people to seek refuge in peri-urban areas, which have relatively cheaper and available land (Asafo, 2020, 2022). Significantly, the informal nature of the peri-urban land market, that is, land transactions outside state regulations (Urban Landmark, 2010), has seen increasing purchases following the argument that the formal land market managed by the state has complex bureaucracies and high costs (Arko-Adjei, 2011; Obeng-Odoom, 2016). The resultant effect is rising land values in the peri-urban land market, as evidenced by Adogla-Bessa (2018) that a plot of land in Accra's peri-urban areas in the past ten years had increased by 450 per cent.

Nonetheless, complex uncertainties have characterised the informal land markets in the form of intense conflicts over ownership and access (Whermann, 2008; Arko-Adjei, 2011). A major outcome of this situation is landguardism, defined as the employment of individuals or a group of young persons who use 'illegitimate forces to protect land and landed properties as a service in exchange for cash or in-kind remuneration' (see Ehwi and Asafo, 2021: 3). Although landguardism has been banned through the Vigilantism and Related Offence Act, 2019 (ACT 999), Ehwi and Asafo (2021) argue that the fight against landguardism with vigilantism perceived as one holistic challenge is defeated given that landguardism is a long-standing problem characterised by complex causal factors as compared with political vigilantism, which is a current phenomenon informed by political interests. It is without a doubt that although landguardism is banned, the act continues to operate. Landguardism continues to be associated with insecurities tied to the land market in peri-urban Accra. The chapter turns now to an outline of its theoretical framework to explore these wider issues of changing land markets and insecurity, and the research methods underpinning the study.

Understanding the changes in the peri-urban land market through actors' access

One of the main elements underpinning the transformation of the peri-urban land market is the proliferation of different actors, whose varied interests shape access, control and use of land. To this end, the study draws insight from access theory to understand the factors influencing the control of land by various actors and how this influences land delivery, price modalities and associated insecurities. Access theory analyses the ability of actors to draw benefit from resources, in this case land (see Ribot and Peluso, 2003; William, 2013). Ability here constitutes what Ribot and Peluso (2003) called bundles of power, which either limit or facilitate the capacity of actors to draw benefits from resources. Considering that the peri-urban is a contested space characterised by intense struggles and uneven power relations over land (Ubink, 2008; Asafo, 2020), a careful analysis of how actors use different mechanisms to control land is relevant to understanding broader everyday politics and socio-economic changes that are affecting the land market. This focus also speaks to a wider interest of this book, which is to understand how African urban peripheries are lived and how the actions and experiences of different actors work to produce the peripheries in different ways.

The focus on access theory is a clear departure from the idea of property rights, which also informs access to resources (Ribot and Peluso, 2003; William, 2013). This departure follows the argument that the peri-urban land market is fluid and largely informal (Rakodi, 2006; Arko-Adjei, 2011; Chimhowu, 2019); hence, there are interrelated and complex underlying factors that influence access and control rather than rights. Although Sen's (1981) notion of entitlement underpins access theory (William, 2013; Myers and Hansen, 2020), Ribot and Peluso (2003) argue that property rights as an analytical tool for investigating the control of resources is limiting and does not consider the broad interplay of socio-economic and political factors that shape access. Other scholars (Arko-Adjei, 2011) have also argued that despite the entrenchment of customary land in entitlements and inheritance, the recent transformation within the peri-urban land market is characterised by social relations, negotiations and economic power (financial capital). These social characteristics constitute structures and social agencies that actors use in the quest to control land. With the largely informal nature of the peri-urban land market, Ribot and Peluso's classification of the mechanism of access into right-based access (legal and illegal mechanisms) and particularly the relational mechanism of access (see Ribot and Peluso, 2003 for a detailed discussion on each classification) offers a more nuanced understanding to the response in the land market by the state and customary institutions.

Context and methods

The study focused on peri-urban areas within GAMA. GAMA (see Figure 7.1) constitutes the geographical region that covers a much wider part of the Accra Metropolitan Area and accommodates peri-urban communities in the country's capital, Accra (Oteng Ababio et al., 2013; Agyeman, 2015). With GAMA's population growth rate of 3.1 per cent, this is said to be occurring in peri-urban areas as a result of its rapid integration with the city of Accra and the availability and cheaper cost of land which is compelling people to move into these areas (Bartels, 2019/20; Asafo, 2022). The implication for Accra's peri-urban land market therefore is rapid transformation, particularly the rise of different actors in the market (see Arko-Adjei, 2011; Asafo, 2020).

The specifics and drivers of Accra's transitions on its peripheries, including the configurations of actors, are in part distinct from but also map on to some of those detailed in the South African and Ethiopian cases elsewhere in this book. Accra's case parallels much of the rapid transition, particularly that which is informal or auto-constructed, evident across cities in SSA (see Mabin et al., 2013), including in Dar es Salaam where the demand for affordable housing pushes peripheral growth (Andreasen et al.,

2017), a trend noted in South African cities too (see Mbatha and Mchunu, 2016). Accra's cases and their use within this book hence work to illustrate the 'transitioning peripheries' logic (detailed in the Introduction) and provide insights into the kinds of dynamics which may become more evident in places such as Molweni, South Africa (see Chapter 6), where hybrid governance arrangements are in place but where there is less clear evidence of rapid changes in land markets as detailed in this chapter. In Ghana and Accra, a very large part of the city is customary land, whereas in eThekwini (and other South African cases where it exists), it is relatively small and the speculative aspects are less developed but emerging (see Mbatha and Mchunu, 2016 on eThekwini). This comparative focus on Accra is productive for how the book more generally understands trends relating to customary land in contexts such as South Africa, and it illustrates that the issue requires deeper exploration therein.

The study adopted a qualitative approach, using interviews and observations to gather data from key people on how the proliferation of different actors is shaping land in the peri-urban land market. The fieldwork, carried out between December 2017 and April 2018, focused on four communities in peri-urban Accra, namely Oyibi, Abokobi, Achiaman and Oshiyie (see Figure 7.1). The selection criteria of the cases include increasing land sales, parallel land management institutions (state and customary institutions), persistent cases of landguardism and land conflicts. In total, twenty-two key actors in the land sector constituting fourteen land sellers (at least three from each case study community), four chiefs (one from each case) and four municipal planning officers (one from each case) were interviewed.

Although the land is customary in the case study communities, some distinctions in the ownership composition are evident. For instance, in Oyibi and Achiaman the larger portions of the land are owned and controlled by families, followed by stools. In contrast, in Oshiyie the stool owns and controls larger land parcels, followed by the families. Conversely, the land in Abokobi is religious, largely controlled by the Presbyterian Church of Ghana (Zimmerman congregation), with other parcels of land owned by individual families. These distinct features highlight the complexities that exist within customary land in peri-urban Accra.

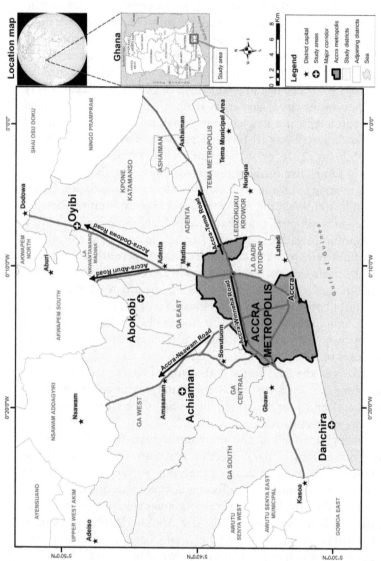

Figure 7.1 Map of GAMA showing the selected study communities (source: author's construct)

Land transaction practices in peri-urban Accra

Changing price modalities

Historical accounts of the four case studies point to the fact that there was no monetary transaction for land but rather the presentation of gifts and drinks (mostly alcoholic liquors), which depicted a symbol of allegiance and acknowledgement to landowners (Kusaana and Gerber, 2015). However, contemporary land transaction practices in the four case communities have seen a significant shift towards cash payments for the purchase of land. The majority of the land sellers in the study communities disclosed that this cash payment corresponds with the current market value of the land following rising demands which have intensified commodification.

The study discovered price variations in land (Table 7.1) as a significant feature of the land market in peri-urban Accra, which is consistent with the transformation patterns of land markets in Ghana, including flexible land transaction practices (Gough and Yankson, 2006; Ubink, 2008). The cost of land in the four case communities, for example, ranges from Ghc6,000 ($1,245) to Ghc55,000 ($11,458).

Arguably, these variations in land prices in peri-urban Accra reflect the colonial legacies of commodification and ineffectiveness of the formal land administration systems (Rakodi and Leduka, 2004; Chimhowu, 2019) which have given rise to the informal land market. A case in point of this informality is the pricing of land in peri-urban Accra, which is largely determined by socio-spatial and political factors alongside the forces of demand and supply. Observably, these factors do not operate in isolation, but instead they are interconnected and influence land prices across the peri-urban communities.

Table 7.1 The range of prices of land in peri-urban Accra (source: fieldwork (2018), compiled by Divine Asafo, 2018)

Community	Price of land per plot (70 × 100 ft, in Ghana cedis, ₵)	Price of land per plot (70 × 100 ft, in US $)
Oshiyie	6,000–20,000	1,245–4,166
Achiaman	7,000–35,000	1,458–7,291
Abokobi	9,000–40,000	1,875–8,333
Oyibi	15,000–55,000	3,125–11,458

Land sellers in Oyibi and Abokobi, for example, attributed the relatively high cost of land to the communities' increasing new developments, proximity to major trunk roads and Abokobi's political status as the municipal district capital of Ga East Area. In an interview discussion with the traditional authority in Abokobi, it emerged that the upgrade of Abokobi from a district to a municipal capital constitutes one of the major factors pulling new residents into the community. He argued that the community's political status is creating civil service jobs and other private employment opportunities, compelling people to relocate into the community.

In a more specific case, a land seller, whose opinion is shared by other land sellers, revealed that the high cost and increasing variation in land prices are due to a growing culture of land-grabbing, in which people invest in land with the intention of reselling it when the value increases, combined with the proliferation of local real estate companies. According to him the price of 70 × 100 ft land sold by these real estate companies is much higher than the price at which individual land sellers sell theirs. This influences individual land sellers to also increase their prices. Observably, the high cost of land by the real estate companies can be attributed to the provision of title and service plots in the market, which is hardly found with family and stool land. In Oshiyie and Achiaman, however, the relatively low cost of land compared to other study areas is attributed to their relatively small communities, which are also located far off trunk roads that connect the communities to the city of Accra.

More significantly, the price of land also varies within individual communities due to locational factors such as proximity to road networks and indigenous communities coupled with areas with high population densities. In an interview discussion land sellers from two different communities disclosed:

> though Achiaman is one community, the price of land differs and depends on where it is located. Within the community, it cost between ₵20,000 and ₵35,000, and when it is along a road, I sell it between from ₵30,000 to ₵45,000. And for the ones located in newly developed areas, I normally sell it for ₵7000. (Land Seller, Achiaman, 2018)

> our family land extends from the roadside inward and covers a very large area. So land within is sold for ₵15,000, and if it is roadside, it's ₵30,000 because builders in future build shops in front of their houses and make money. This is why we charge high when your land is close to the roadside. (Land Seller, Abokobi, 2018)

The high cost of land in locations such as 'roadside' is perceived to have potential economic values that offer residents future livelihood opportunities, reflecting the way speculative logics overlay development in these transitioning peripheries (see the Introduction). These narratives point to the socio-spatial factors shaping the economic value of land but, more importantly, the non-interference of the state in the peri-urban land market in Ghana (Anyidoho et al., 2007). This is evident in several land reforms which have largely focused on tenure security, governance and spatial-planning rather than developments in the peri-urban land market. The most recent of these reforms is the LAP I and II, which restructured the administrative procedure of the Ghana Land Commission and led to the establishment of the CLS to ensure efficient delivery of land (see Gyapong, 2009; Obeng-Odoom, 2016). Nonetheless, while landownership is largely controlled by the customary institutions, state control of the land market remains minimal. The consequence, therefore, is price hikes of land over time. The World Bank (2015b), for instance, revealed that land prices in Accra and Kumasi (the second most populous city in Ghana) have seen an increase from 460 per cent and 1,300 per cent within a decade, underscoring Citinewsroom's (2018) figure of a 450 per cent increase detailed earlier. These figures are bound to increase when the land market does not benefit from any institutional regulation.

Changing land delivery channels

Land delivery in Ghana continues to be largely managed by the customary authorities (stools, family or clan heads) (Akaateba, 2019; Asafo, 2020). In recent times, however, the land market has seen the proliferation of new actors who constitute a new land delivery channel in peri-urban Accra. This development was evident in all the study communities as the traditional authority in Oyibi, for instance, revealed that land sales have become a lucrative business and almost everyone is presently engaged in it. The expression 'almost everyone' highlights the new actors involved in land delivery, including real estate companies, organisations' welfare associations[2] (hereafter called associations), individuals, land agents and landguards who were non-existent in the past. To this end the study considers the new actors as secondary land delivery channels and the existing actors as primary land delivery channels. These actors have multiple social agencies, which enables them to transfer land in peri-urban Accra (Rakodi, 2006). These social agencies include economic capacity (financial capital), trust and social networks with state institutions in the land market. In contrast, other actors such as landguards take advantage of their role as stewards of contested customary land to gain control in land delivery. A family head in Abokobi recounts how a landguard sold 50 acres out of the 150 acres of land he was contracted to protect. Commenting on the rise of secondary land delivery channels and their associated characteristics, an official in Ga East Municipal Assembly, which hosts one of the case studies (Abokobi), stated that the power to engage in land sales is no longer the sole obligation of chiefs and family heads; rather, individuals, groups and other organisations are all using different mechanisms such as money, trust and networks to sell land.

These social agencies translate to Ribot and Peluso's (2003) concept of bundles of power, which enables access and control of resources, in this case land. Significantly, although the control of customary land is entrenched in entitlements and inheritance, the social agencies characterising secondary land delivery channels affirm the argument that the delivery of peri-urban land in recent times is driven by economic power, social relations and negotiations (Arko-Adjei, 2011). Additionally, the ability of landguards to use illicit and unsolicited means such as threats, assault, coercion and violence to gain land control in peri-urban Accra is an indication of the ability of an actor to control resources despite not being supported by rights (Ribot and Peluso, 2003; William, 2013).

As previously stated, the state's non-participation in customary land delivery, combined with the strict and complex bureaucratic procedures involved in acquiring state land (Rakodi, 2006; Anyidoho *et al.*, 2007), accounts for the influx of new actors in the Accra peri-urban land market. These secondary land delivery channels serve as an intermediary between the primary land delivery channels and the land market (Rakodi and Leduka, 2004) purposely to create an active land market but, more importantly, to mitigate tenure insecurities. For instance, land agents serve as middlemen who either find clients for the primary land delivery channels or vice versa. This is similar to the case of individuals, but largely, the individuals are involved in the sale of their own land which they acquired through inheritance or purchase. Additionally, the associations and real estate companies acquire the land in the name of the association or company and resell it to their members and clients respectively. This emerging practice is currently embraced by many people following the collective protection and land tenure security it offers to group members and clients (see Ehwi *et al.*, 2019). A daunting challenge associated with the aforementioned development is the increase in the cost of land in peri-urban Accra following the offer of titled and serviced land. This contrasts with the primary land delivery channels in peri-urban Accra, which are characterised by untitled, unplanned and unsecured land. Furthermore, the unregulated nature of this development has resulted in some real estate companies selling land fraudulently.

The operation of the secondary land delivery channels, largely based on trust and social values, positions the peri-urban land market as an effectively flexible and user-friendly entity in peri-urban Accra. A major element evidencing this is the varied payment arrangements, hereafter called *negotiated payments*, which allow buyers to pay for the cost of land in instalments. This payment arrangement has become necessary following the rather high market value at which land is sold in the study communities. During discussions with land sellers within the primary land delivery channel, it was disclosed that they offered one–six-month instalment plans to clients. In contrast, real estate companies and the associations had more flexible and structured payment terms of between twelve and twenty-four months. This means that individuals with monthly incomes can take advantage of these options to become landowners. A major impact of these characteristics of Accra's peri-urban land market is that it advances and extends access to land beyond the reach of the wealthy to the majority of people who would otherwise be unable to afford the full cost of land.

However, the negotiated payment plans by real estate and associations are costly due to the interest that accrues over the payment duration. These evolving land delivery channels, on the other hand, have created a more vibrant land market with evidence of different marketing platforms such as posters, websites, billboards, buildings and backs of vehicles for advertising land (see Figure 7.2). While these platforms create different avenues for the land market, the unregulated and mostly incoherent land information characterising such platforms create irregularities such as fraudulent land transactions in peri-urban Accra. Arguably, these negotiated payments and advertisement platforms do not merely reveal the evolving

Figure 7.2 Different platforms for advertising land sales
(source: Divine Asafo, 2018)

Peri-urban transformations

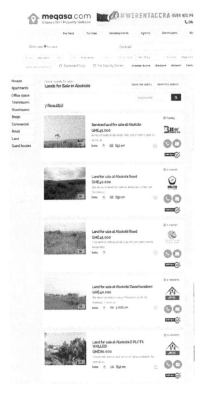

Figure 7.2 (Cont.)

commercial activities of the peri-urban land market but also highlight the competition between different actors in the land market in peri-urban Accra.

Land transformation and tenure (in)securities

Undeniably, the transformation of the land market in peri-urban Accra on the one hand is increasing access to land and on the other hand creating tenure uncertainties (see Wehrmann, 2008; Arko-Adjei, 2011; Asafo, 2020). These tenure uncertainties are underpinned by the rapid population increase and the sprawl of Accra, which have triggered the demand for land. In the four study communities, this increase in the demand for land is being met by indeterminate boundaries, multiple ownership, largely untitled land parcels and ineffective land administration practices. During an interview discussion with a family head in Ashaiman, it was disclosed that the rising demand for land in the community has caused the value of the land to increase, compelling most landowning families to cash in. This development has triggered the indiscriminate sale of land by some chiefs, family heads and clan heads without following planning regulations. Besides, given that many of these lands in the communities are not properly demarcated, there are increasing sales of encroached land, which is causing complex tensions between both the buyers and sellers (see Asafo, 2020 for a detailed discussion on land conflicts in peri-urban Accra). In Oshiyie, however, chieftaincy dispute is deepening tenure uncertainties as two families are claiming ownership of the chieftaincy title, which underpins the control of stool land (Ayee et al., 2008; Ubink, 2008). The implication of this for tenure is the multiple sales of the stool land to different buyers, which is generating intense conflicts between multiple buyers and sellers.

The breach of trust by some actors within the secondary land delivery channel is causing tenure insecurities and deepening existing ones. In one of the interview discussions with the traditional authority of Oyibi, it was revealed that many family heads and clan heads are entrusting their land in the hands of the secondary land delivery channels following the increasing trust they have built within the land market. Observably, the shift from primary to secondary land delivery channels highlights some degree of breakdown within the traditional institution, given its inability to keep up with the rapid evolution of the peri-urban land market (Lund, 2013). These secondary land delivery channels are expected to sell the land and reimburse the original landowners. Alternatively, due to rising land values, some secondary land delivery channels, such as real estate companies, purchase the land and pay off a portion of the purchase price, leaving the remainder to be paid later. However, on several occasions, some actors in the secondary land delivery channels (mostly land agents, associations and real estate companies) breach the contract by failing to pay off the land cost. Figure 7.3 illustrates how the breaches in the contract between these channels result in insecurities in the peri-urban land market in Accra. Anecdotal evidence from the field suggests that the negotiated payment mechanisms mostly

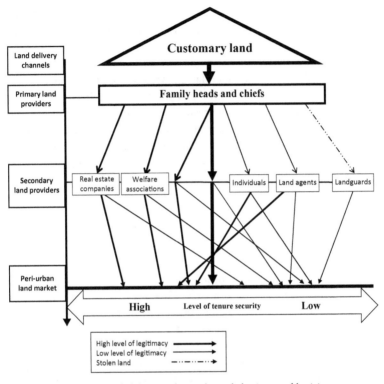

Figure 7.3 Land delivery channels and the issue of legitimacy
(source: author's construct)

used in the sale of such land do not enhance the recoup of the capital investment as it sometimes takes up to two years for clients to finish the payment. That notwithstanding, some of these secondary land delivery channels deliberately breach the contract, leading to disputes between the original owners. This situation highlights new dimensions of multiple land sales as most original landowners resell the land to other clients. These circumstances have resulted in complex tenure insecurities deepened by landguardism and litigations in court, which usually take years to resolve.

The act of landguardism was found as one of the challenges increasing tenure insecurities in the contemporary transformation of the land market in peri-urban Accra. Landguards are primarily responsible for offering protection to contested land. By extension of their activities, they also engage in extortion of informal levies such as 'digging fees' from housebuilders (see Bansah, 2017; Asafo, 2020). In most of the study communities, however, landguards were found to clandestinely engage in land sales (see Figure 7.3). Almost all actors who engaged landguards in the protection of their land recount how several parcels of the land have been sold without their knowledge. This has resulted in multiple sales of the same piece of land following the fact that the original owners do not have records of the land being sold. The consequence of this is a conflict that emanates between the original landowners and individuals who buy such land from landguards.

Conclusion

The land transformation in peri-urban areas in SSA continues to present significant opportunities for socio-economic investments, particularly in the area of housing. This has increased the demand for land and heightened commodification in peri-urban areas. In peri-urban Accra, Ghana, it appears the transformation of the land market has been shaped by colonial footprints and, recently, rapid and unguided urbanisation and the emergence of new actors. Consequently, the transformation of land in peri-urban Accra on the one hand is increasing access to land and on the other hand increasing tenure insecurities.

This study explored the transformation of the land market and its implications for tenure (in)security in peri-urban Accra, Ghana. Drawing on observations and interviews with key stakeholders in the land market, the study argues that the transformation of the peri-urban land market in Accra has resulted in a vibrant and more competitive land market. Indeed, despite the rising market value of land, elements of the land market, including the variation in land prices and the different modalities of payment for the land, have offered some flexibility for the majority of people to access land (Rakodi and Leduka, 2004). In Accra, where there is a rising housing deficit, a high cost of rent, coupled with the unlawful two-year rent taken by landlords, the peri-urban has become a new haven for people to escape the aforementioned urban challenges. Furthermore, the reliance on socio-spatial, political and locational factors, aside from the forces of demand and supply in determining land prices, unearths the entrenched role of informality that characterises the peri-urban land market in Accra and speaks to some of the dimensions captured with the auto-constructed periphery logic detailed in the Introduction.

The study further submits that the several land policy reforms in Ghana which appear to ignore the regulation of the customary land market coupled with deep-seated complexities of customary land have created an avenue for different actors to gain control over land delivery in the peri-urban Accra. These new actors (real estate companies, organisations' welfare associations and land agents) leverage on the ineffectiveness of these issues to offer wide-ranging services such as registered and serviced land to their clients. Resonating with the idea of access theory, these actors gain control of the land market drawing on economic power, social relations, legal backing, trust and in some cases coercion (by landguards). This implies that understanding the transformation of the peri-urban land market and how different actors gain control requires looking beyond rights and taking into account the complex social agencies that drive these practices. Additionally, considering how these social agencies shape power relations in accessing land is paramount to understanding the political economy of peri-urban land and its associated conflicts (Lombard, 2016; Asafo, 2020). As indicated above, overall transitions in customary lands speak to what this book terms transitioning peripheries, but it is evident how these transitions are shaped by speculative and auto-constructed logics too.

The overall conclusion of the chapter is that the flexibility and adaptability of customary land in peri-urban areas in SSA, especially Accra, reveal the diffusion of power to control land delivery shifting between multiple actors. This adds evidence to the fact that customary institutions, despite their dominant role in the land market, are gradually losing their power to control land in contemporary times, especially in the peri-urban. Certainly, the rather slow evolution of customary institutions to meet current land demands, especially in the peri-urban areas, constitutes a major factor in this situation. In the wake of rapid urbanisation, policy reforms and the influence of global systems (globalisation), closer attention to the transformation of the land market in peri-urban areas is critical in drawing positive outcomes, given the various socio-economic opportunities and challenges it presents. This chapter contributes an important focus on the significance of land markets in shaping and driving change on African urban peripheries to this book more generally and offers an important site of urban comparison around questions of land, housing affordability, densification, governance and insecurity across these spaces.

Notes

1 A stool represents the seat of a chief of an indigenous state and represents the source of power and authority. Land owned and controlled by such a state is referred to as stool land (Yankson and Gough, 2000).
2 These are groups of employees in an organisation who come together to purchase large portions of land and subdivide it among themselves. Payment is mostly done in instalments.

8

Transport and mobility

Tom Goodfellow, Paula Meth and Sarah Charlton

Weekends are, for some residents of the urban periphery, times to look forward to, not so much because of not having to work but because of not having to face the trials and tribulations of public transport. This chapter examines residents' experiences of transport infrastructure and associated mobility in the South African and Addis Ababa case studies, where these featured as a core issue. It shows the stifling impact of limited transport choice, high fares, long distances and congestion on people's mobility and access to opportunity, but also the significance of localised improvements to daily experiences in addition to large-scale infrastructure interventions. The chapter considers the political, economic and locational dynamics of mobility and transport, and charts shifting mobility and the impacts on peripheral lives in response to the implementation of various transport measures, as well as the impact of their failure or withdrawal or their delay in delivery. It includes consideration of the role of different forms of transport provision, noting how dependent and compromised residents living in peripheral locations are. Transport mode, trip-chaining and their attendant cost and safety implications are addressed through the lens of the everyday.

Provision and experiences of public transport

Primary modes of public transportation: the South African cases

Across the South African cases, public transport provision is dominated by a relatively thin network of publicly funded buses, often in concert or contestation with a much more substantive network of informal minibus taxis – which dominate public transport provision in all cases, though almost entirely unsubsidised (see Figure 8.1). The tensions between these modes of transport and the governance of their respective industries directly shape everyday experiences of mobility and dislocation for many residents living in the urban peripheries. In only one of the cases (Protea Glen in Gauteng), the city of Johannesburg's BRT (Bus Rapid Transit) system known as the Rea Vaya was used by some residents, noting it offered a safer service than informal transport. The BRT was inaccessible to residents in Lufhereng, because it was located around 5 km away. In Protea Glen some residents made use of the more affordable train by accessing the Naledi train station via taxis but found the taxi costs expensive, exemplifying financial and accessibility challenges of multimodal transport for those residing in peripheral locations. In the case of Waterloo, use of trains was mentioned but not by many residents, and it was noted that the train service was not convenient to this area.

The predominantly dual provision (buses and taxis) is also inconsistent and context-dependent. In Lufhereng the implementation of

Figure 8.1 Minibus taxis at road intersection, Greater Ekangala (source: Mark Lewis)

an effective bus network was not yet in place following the occupation of the new settlement by residents in state housing. This left them entirely dependent on expensive, often unsafe and unreliable taxis for transportation to work, clinics and nearby shopping spaces, and the nearest taxi rank was located on the other side of a busy road (Williams *et al.*, 2022). Yet the relative agility of the taxi industry to plug absences in the formal network illustrates the significance of informal transport provision for peripheral locations. The urban peripheries are frequently made liveable and accessible solely through this provision, including where major public transport plans have simply not materialised: in vanguard Lufhereng, private sector planning consultants lamented the stalled plans for a high-priority railway extension: 'the system only really works if all the infrastructure is there … rail is very important in the overall thing' (SA Private Sector 2, 2018).

In Rethabiseng, Ekangala and Dark City, in contrast, public buses service the areas, with some residents noting the provision as 'fine' (Rethabiseng GM 02 ♂ Interview). The journey from Rethabiseng to Bronkhorstspruit, where shops are located, takes around thirty minutes, costing R15, a price one resident describes as 'too much' (Rethabiseng MB 11 ♀ Interview). In Hammonds Farm and Waterloo, local buses previously serviced their neighbourhoods providing affordable and safer access to key urban locations. However, violent contestation between bus companies and taxi operators resulted in the former withdrawing services from this locality. As a result residents in both locations, places renowned for their steep topography, are entirely reliant on taxis which also selectively service the areas, prioritising those parts located nearer main roads or on less steep terrain.

The provision of public transport is highly fluid, with changes in choice and route evident, resulting in improvements or the worsening of experiences for residents. In Molweni residents noted an improvement in the routes that taxis would service, with drivers agreeing to drop commuters nearer to where they live instead of on the main road (as previously): 'It helps a lot because if you are coming from Pinetown or Hillcrest at night you are safe from the criminals … The taxi is helping the community' (Molweni DM 10 ♂ Interview).

The variable bus/taxi combination in South Africa also evidences changing governance practices and investments by local municipalities. In Molweni in outer-western eThekwini, the provision of buses to transport children to their schools daily was identified as a key marker of development and state recognition. The area is intensely hilly and semi-rural in form, and children were previously required to travel significant distances to access schools, often on foot.

Free bus transportation was also provided in parts of Winterveld, specifically Madibeng Hills, for children to access school. This arrangement was derived through community pressure on local government resulting in significant gains for some households, but for many others the time taken for children to get to school (a combination of walking and buses) remained unsustainable. Long journeys affected children's wellbeing and ability to function effectively through the school day. 'We'd like to have buses [for] our primary school kids whose schools are very far. A child cannot attend school tired' (Winterveld KM 13 ♀ Diary).

Primary modes of public transportation: the Ethiopian cases

As in the South African cases, relative physical immobility is one of the defining features of life in the peripheries of Addis Ababa. In Tulu Dimtu particularly there was a widespread sense that the transport in the area was very poor, as well as expensive. Yeka Abado, being more contiguous with the existing urban fabric, was less severely affected. Indeed, the relatively connected nature of Yeka Abado was one of the reasons the area was so popular and was thriving soon after the condominiums were allocated. As one resident noted, 'Since the rental price was low and since the transportation route was considered direct, there are a lot of people who moved here. You'll be amazed by the number of people you see every morning' (Yeka Abado EN 014 ♀ Interview). Despite this the rapid population growth outstripped provision, and the area was still beset with challenges of public transport under-provision and traffic congestion.

By their own admission, the authorities involved in planning the condominium sites did not adequately incorporate transport into the master plans for these areas and 'only thought about transport once the housing units were ready for [handing] over to condominium winners' (Addis Ababa Transport Official 1, 2018). Transport experiences are among the primary reasons why many residents are hesitant to make long-term plans to stay in the peripheral condominiums, and conversely, as noted by one condominium resident in Tulu Dimtu, improvements in transport and connectivity are one of the changes that could entice them to stay in the area (Tulu Dimtu MK 025 ♂ Diary). This is hardly surprising given that some residents report having to wake up as early as 3 a.m. in order to be able to get to work on time (Tulu Dimtu KT 026 ♂ Interview).

The primary forms of public transport provision consist of the bus services that operate in the area – including *Alliance*, *Higer*, *Anbessa* and *Sheger* – alongside para-transit in the form of shared minibus taxis and *bajaj* (three-wheelers) (see Figures 8.2 and 8.3). *Sheger* is a mass transportation system launched by the city administration as a public enterprise in 2008 and along with *Anbessa* is heavily subsidised. Bus provision is, however, far from adequate in the peripheries; for example, just forty buses were allocated to Yeka Abado, which has around 100,000 residents and no provision for bus terminals (Addis Ababa Transport Official 1, 2018). Problems with the minibus taxi system – which overall was the dominant mode of transport for city dwellers commuting in from

Figure 8.2 Buses and shared taxis in Yeka Abado (source: Mark Lewis)

Figure 8.3 A donkey cart with *bajaj* in the background, Tulu Dimtu (source: Mark Lewis)

the periphery – range from under-provision, unaffordable cost and severe overcrowding to certain locations being serviced at the expense of others. When it comes to transporting construction materials and other goods, as well as occasional passengers, carts drawn by donkeys or horses are still common (see Figure 8.3).

Despite the evident lack of sufficient public transport in areas like Tulu Dimtu, there was a palpable sense that things were improving: 'When we first moved here the transportation was almost non-existent; we were always frustrated. But now slowly, it's improving. When we moved here there was no taxi, and they used to charge us extreme amounts when they want' (Tulu Dimtu KF 012 ♂ Interview). By 2019 our engagement with residents and stakeholders indicated that transport was one of the things that had seen the most significant improvements (for example, in terms of increased provision of *Sheger* buses). However, transport into the city was much better provided for than transport in the other direction.

Notwithstanding some improvements, the everyday challenges that people face with respect to transport to and from work, and their effects on people's mental wellbeing, are often extreme, as is well captured by the following quote from a resident in the Tulu Dimtu area:

> Even before I leave home, when I think of the long line for a taxi, I don't feel so good. ... The queue was so terrible ... The long line coupled with the long interval between consecutive taxis has made people very frustrated. If there were no public buses, I could have waited there for an hour. (Tulu Dimtu HW 055 ♂ Diary)

Some respondents report having to wait as long as ninety minutes for a bus or taxi, only to have to endure a very uncomfortable journey on damaged roads (Tulu Dimtu BF 87 ♀ Diary). The paucity of public transport provision is so significant that some condominium dwellers resort to clubbing together to hire drivers to take their children to school. The severe shortage of schools in the peripheries – one of the problems that did not appear to be improving quickly, in contrast with the noted improvements in some forms of infrastructure – exacerbated transport challenges because people had little choice but to send their children on long journeys to other parts of the city to attend school.

Journeys that involve multiple stages and costs, contracting drivers and lacking fallback/alternative options are common occurrences. People also frequently have to be spontaneous and opportunistic just to be able to access the city, with the shifting and uncertain availability of transport options shaping the nature of their everyday encounters and experiences. Some respondents described queues for minibus taxis that are regularly over thirty metres long, which are 'exhausting even to look at' (Tulu Dimtu K 077 ♀ Diary), and even in the relatively better-served Yeka Abado area, residents sometimes have to wait two–three hours for a taxi (Yeka Abado AA 038 ♀ Interview). The process of queuing for transport itself produces spontaneous opportunities, as noted by one cooperative housing resident in Tulu Dimtu who negotiated an unexpected form of transport while in the taxi line:

> As I feared, there was a long line for a taxi. I was amazed by how long the line was and finally took a spot on the line. I started playing with the child of a woman who was standing in front of me; minutes have passed as I do this. A person driving a car that is a mix between a *bajaj* and a small car, noticing that the taxis are not coming constantly, invited us to board his car for 10 Birr each. The

price he offered was too much, and we all had to think a bit. After few minutes, a few of us hurried to the small car. I left the child I was playing with, and we both were sad. (Tulu Dimtu KN 059 ♂ Diary)

Helping each other out with transportation and fostering conviviality in the face of transport challenges were also noted by others, for example in the case of a taxi breaking down and passengers getting out to help fit a spare wheel, which led one Tulu Dimtu resident to note in their diary that 'My conscience was at peace when I saw how profitable assisting one another could be' (Tulu Dimtu K 077 ♀ Diary).

Cost, choice and accessibility of public transportation

Poor choice, high costs and restricted accessibility typified South African and Ethiopian residents' experiences across most case study locations. For most, their relative peripheral location was entrenched through weak networks of provision and a reliance on multimodal journeys incurring long delays and great costs. Invariably, cost of transportation was the most frequent complaint, as this example from Winterveld, South Africa, illustrates: 'Transport is a huge issue here; it is expensive. You first pay money to connect to the bus stop then money to get taxis to go to town. I spent R30 for a single trip to town. And I walk long distances to the bus stop so it's stressful' (Winterveld NN 26 ♂ Interview). This female resident in Ekangala explains how she opts for hitchhiking (which requires some payment) to overcome the cost challenges of multimodal travel: 'Yes a lot of people do hike because with hiking you pay less ... [the cost of getting to Bronkhorstspruit] really kills us so transport to go straight is fine, not this transport where you're going and getting off going and getting off' (Ekangala BM 09 ♀ Interview). In Addis Ababa, and especially Tulu Dimtu, the competition over scarce transport provision can often lead to pushing and even fighting as people scramble to access the bus (Tulu Dimtu H 008 ♂ Diary). The problem of overcrowding is a repeated theme in people's descriptions of their commutes, with an additional eight people often being crammed on to already full minibus taxis.

When discussing the challenges of public transport, some commuters into Addis Ababa considered cost to be a greater concern than the time it takes to access the central city. It was common for people to spend 20–40 Birr per day on transportation, or sometimes as much as 60 – significant amounts in the context of relatively low incomes. One resident even said that 'we are spending most of our income on transportation' (Yeka Abado MS 62 ♂ Interview). Costs were also commonly hiked in the evening rush hour, when minibus taxis 'make you pay more than the fare they should ask for, and that also is a concern' (Yeka Abado TK 066 ♀ Interview). For many others, however, the cost was less of an issue, but the question of time was much more distressing: 'We waste a lot of time on the road. Moreover, knowing the time it takes, we are not relaxed about our programmes elsewhere, and we mostly hurry back' (Tulu Dimtu KT 026 ♂ Interview). Another noted that 'I lose my time in transport. It's very tiresome' (Tulu Dimtu TZ 031 ♀ Diary). It was rare to hear about commutes of under two hours in either direction, and often they were even longer. For many, both cost and time were grave concerns; as one Tulu Dimtu condominium resident noted, 'I spend most of my time and money on transportation, and that makes me really sad' (Tulu Dimtu MM 090 ♀ Interview).

Due to the length of time it takes to travel between work and home, residents of the periphery are forced to make all kinds of arrangements and compromises that they had not previously needed to make, such as taking their children back to work with them after picking them up from school, leaving children with elderly relatives for periods of the day and waiting a long time for a partner in order to share a lift home after work. Some children and young people even stop attending school or college due to the distances involved (Tulu Dimtu TZ 031 ♀ Diary). A further dimension of the long times and significant costs of public transport are the effects these have both for livelihoods (see Chapter 3) and for accessing basic urban amenities, including marketplaces (see Chapter 11). The additional cost of taking a minibus taxi or *bajaj* to access what used to be local shopping or service opportunities is a significant drain on family resources (Tulu Dimtu BA 032 ♂ Interview).

The radius of potential employment locations for residents in most of the case study areas was circumscribed by transport costs and poor choice. Although by private vehicle several areas were relatively well located relative to potential job markets, the friction of distance impacted heavily on residents dependent on walking, buses or most commonly minibus taxis. In Molweni residents were opting to job search only in nearby Pinetown or Kloof rather than Durban central as transport costs were prohibitive. Movement to state housing in the urban peripheries significantly worsened access to employment for many. Several residents who moved to Lufhereng had previously benefited from domestic worker employment in Lenasia, accessible from their former informal settlement by foot. Moving 10 km to Lufhereng, with its weak transport connections, made the commute unaffordable, with the result that some workers became unemployed (Williams et al., 2022). In Tshwane, Pretoria offers good potential for employment, but exorbitant transport costs and commuting distances make this difficult for residents living in the Greater Ekangala area. BM (Ekangala Dark City 05 ♀ Interview) describes how commuters are 'working for transport' as a high proportion of their earnings are spent on the weekly bus ticket of R220.

Accessibility to key services is intimately linked to transport provision across the urban periphery. The location and presence of services such as schools are vastly undermined or enhanced by reliable and affordable transport. A consistent concern for residents in South Africa and Ethiopia was access for their children to schools, which were frequently not located near to their urban peripheral settlements. Transportation challenges were compounded by poor and insufficient provision of schools in some areas, leading to oversubscription. In Waterloo and Hammonds Farm this resulted in long walking distances (e.g. 10 km) for pupils (Hammonds Farm BR 03 ♂ Interview) and high costs for parents who pay for taxis to get children to school daily (Hammonds Farm MK 02 ♀ Diary; Hammonds Farm NM 04 ♀ Diary).

Safety and security concerns

The absence of reliable and affordable transportation provision across much of the urban periphery contributed directly to residents' urban insecurity and their fear of being a victim of crime. This was evident across both South Africa and Ethiopia, although particular areas were evidently more unsafe for travellers than others. Our primary data is littered with residents' anxieties about crime and violence while attempting to travel and to overcome distance, and multiple accounts of actual stories of criminal events while moving through and between spaces on the urban periphery.

If I want to take a taxi I have to go hike until I catch a taxi at Bronko after getting off from Bronkhorst. Sometimes I have to walk by foot them times at night and sometimes I get scared because one time I tried to take a shortcut coming from Rethabiseng. I took a shortcut but they mugged me and they took my phone. (Ekangala BM 09 ♀ Interview)

While levels of violence are generally not as high in Addis Ababa as in South African cities, the threat of violent crime was still a major factor for residents of some peripheral areas, particularly given the lack of basic infrastructure (explored in Chapter 10). Tulu Dimtu residents also highlighted the difficulty in coming back to the neighbourhood late at night due to the lack of street lights, with the darkness increasing the risk of robbery (Tulu Dimtu SD 053 ♀ Diary; Tulu Dimtu G 078 ♂ Interview). In South Africa a different dimension of safety lay in concerns about the poor condition of many minibus taxis as well as overcrowding: 'when we are seated inside we can see the ground downwards and wires through holes in the taxi ... and as students we are required to sit in fours on seats that are supposed to be sat by three people' (Lufhereng 08 ♀ LM Diary, 2017).

Roads and automobile use

Changes to road networks and quality of road provision

Roads appear in our data as being significant in a myriad of ways. These range from the more obvious aspects of their significance for mobility – in the sense that the presence or absence of roads was fundamental to people's capacity to be physically mobile – to more subtle aspects of road provision, such as changes to surfaces that affected different types of users, and the disruption caused by attempts to improve road networks.

The peripheral areas of Addis Ababa studied were sufficiently new that the main problem was a general lack of roads through which to access different parts of the city, and particularly the centre. Reviewing the overall land use changes across the city, Larsen et al. (2019) discovered that the government investment has led to a significant increase in residential land use, while there has been only a very small increase in the area dedicated to transportation infrastructure, in spite of the repeatedly emphasised importance of enhancing connectivity as a way to promote growth in the government's developmental plans. While some residents of Tulu Dimtu were excited about the opportunities that had recently opened up through new roads, there was a clear sense of limited road connectivity beyond a few major, often traffic-choked routes and that the area was 'not comfortably connected to workplaces' (Tulu Dimtu KT 026 ♂ Interview). It is evident that people have to make trade-offs between the length of journeys in distance versus time, comfort and cost. As one Tulu Dimtu resident highlights,

> To go from the city centre of Addis Ababa to our neighbourhood, there are three main routes. Of the three, two go outside of the city; these are much faster and much longer. This makes the area easily accessible by car. The shortest route, however, is the one that goes through the city. This route is old and damaged by a long use so it is now under construction. (Tulu Dimtu KN 59 ♂ Diary)

The lack of shortcuts, for example from the central commercial hub of Bole down to Tulu Dimtu, meant that people had to divide the transport into more stages than should be necessary, as well as travelling longer distances (Tulu Dimtu H 08 ♂ Interview).

Meanwhile, the construction of new roads, engineering works and resurfacing of road networks directly impact on the connectivity of peripheral locations, restructuring time–space relationships and proving to be a source of significant disruption. In Addis Ababa residents attempting to commute into the city centre sometimes encountered roads partially destroyed in the process of construction or where alternative infrastructure was being implemented. Long-settled spaces which are experiencing significant investment, such as the transitioning periphery of Molweni, witness stark 'change' more readily than those areas with shorter histories and where residents have relocated into spaces with basic infrastructure already in place (such as Hammonds Farm or Lufhereng). Residents in Molweni have deep memories of laborious journeys to areas of employment outside of their settlement and celebrate recent improvements:

> My granny told me that she walked many hours if she [was] going to Waterfall to work because she was working there as the domestic worker. She said the criminal has grabbed their money. She carried

the shopping from Waterfall because there was no road at Molweni and it was the mountain. ... Some people experienced the rape because were walking in forest. The government did the great thing for this community because we are safe. (Molweni HM 11 ♀ Diary)

In contrast, in parts of Winterveld which are yet to benefit from upgrading, despite its long history of residence as an inherited peripheral space, the quality of the road network is very poor. Roads which remain unsurfaced are impacted by flooding, becoming unpassable with persistent potholes:

> our roads are not in good condition, and it is a problem for cars to drive in and most drivers complain about the roads, and when children have to go to school their transport does not come to fetch them inside especially during rainy days – the roads are a mess. (Winterveld KM 11 ♀ Diary)

The absence of tarmac surfacing is also a function of settlement expansion, meaning variable conditions persist in particular peripheral spaces, such as Rethabiseng, which contains some well-surfaced and upgraded roads alongside dirt tracks (see Figure 8.4).

Poor road quality justified the consistent or occasional avoidance by taxi drivers of particular streets and areas of peripheral

Figure 8.4 Unsurfaced roads in Rethabiseng (source: Mark Lewis)

locations, reducing residents' accessibility further. Vehicle operators or owners were concerned about potential damage to their vehicles by poor road quality and selected to avoid such areas, leaving residents entirely reliant on walking. In spaces such as Winterveld where distances between housing, shops and services are higher, tied to larger plot sizes and the low density of urbanisation, a dependency on walking is a significant burden for many residents, particularly during the winter months and at night.

In Addis Ababa, road quality was also a major issue in our case study areas. Roads were considered to be ill suited to the challenges of the rainy season in Tulu Dimtu, with this affecting both condominium dwellers and people living in other kinds of settlements in the area (Tulu Dimtu KN 059 ♂ Diary). As well as periodic flooding, it was noted that the area is muddy during wintertime due to poor-quality road construction and the lack of a functional sewage system (Tulu Dimtu S 060 ♂ Diary). These problems were also worsened by trucks involved in construction, which some residents believed were 'destroying the roads with their heavy weights' with the risk that they could become unuseable (Tulu Dimtu ME 011 ♀ Diary). In Yeka Abado it was also noted that during the rains, the road was often 'filled by running water', worsened by the fact there is only one entrance and one exit road to the community (Yeka Abado SG 006 ♀ Diary).

Interestingly, in some parts of our peripheral sites – particularly outside the condominium areas, in farmers' resettlement sites or cooperative housing areas where road construction is more community-driven – the building of roads was cited as one of the activities that helped in fostering community relations (Tulu Dimtu KN 059 ♂ Interview). However, in Tulu Dimtu it was noted that cobblestone roads – a central strategy for labour-intensive urban development in Ethiopia since the 2000s (Mains, 2019) – were problematic for elderly residents because of their uneven surfaces, as well as children accustomed to playing in the street (Tulu Dimtu ME 011 ♀ Diary; Tulu Dimtu MK 025 ♂ Diary). In Molweni the upgrading of a bridge following the drowning of a child has significantly improved the road network: 'We thank the government for building us the bridge in this community of Nogxaza. We cross easily even if it is raining. Before the bridge, no one cross the river to go to work' (Molweni NS 38 ♀ Diary). Associated changes to road networks (resurfacing, speed bumps, signage, managing roadside vegetation and street lighting) are discussed more fully in Chapter 9 as evidence of significant micro-infrastructural interventions.

Traffic and congestion

In the peripheries of Addis Ababa, it is clear that many residents with the financial resources to acquire or share a car shift their commuting patterns towards private car use at the first opportunity. Other research has also shown that middle-class residents elsewhere in the periphery of Addis opt for car use over the light railway, even when they live close to the railway stations and despite the fact that the light rail system was arguably intended for middle-class commuters (Goodfellow and Huang, 2021).

There is an irony in the increased automobile use in the peripheries in the sense that traffic and pollution in the city are sometimes cited as being among the reasons that people sign up to the condominium lottery in the first place. Indeed, the peripheral nature of these settlements is part of the appeal insofar as it means they are removed from the choking congestion of the centre (Tulu Dimtu Y 054 ♀ Diary). There is thus something of a trade-off between transport provision and clean air, with residents of Tulu Dimtu noting that transport provision is poor but also often appreciating the lack of cars around and the relative cleanliness of the air. As another resident noted, 'The air is nice, it's not polluted *yet*' (Tulu Dimtu WD 027 ♂ Interview; emphasis added).

Congestion was so bad in some major junctions that people reported spending around thirty minutes on average just to get through the junction (Tulu Dimtu WD 027 ♂ Diary). Meanwhile, concerns about traffic accidents due to congestion, sometimes combined with poor road quality, were also common. Indeed, for people living in certain areas, such as the part of Tulu Dimtu known as 'Eritrea' that is cut off by the highway, fear of accidents due to speeding cars – and even collisions with the building itself – is ever present (Tulu Dimtu BA 030 ♂ Interview).

In South Africa, congestion on the roads for residents commuting towards larger urban centres didn't dominate as a concern, although this resident notes: 'sometimes I arrive home late because of traffic jams which cause delays' (Lufhereng LM 08 ♀ Diary). South African cities have fairly sophisticated road networks for vehicle travel on arterial routes, which may reduce congestion. Also, with the very high levels of unemployment noted by residents in the peripheries we researched, it is probable that many are not engaging in such commutes with any frequency.

Walking and walkability

Walking is a dominant mode of travel across most of the South African urban periphery cases and evident with Addis Ababa too. Residents walk to access schools, shops, clinics, other modes of transportation as well as employment or livelihood opportunities. Walking is frequently selected due to a lack of any alternative and also as a mechanism to reduce cost and enhance reliability. Walkability (being accessible through a safe and reasonable length of walk) is fundamental to accessing leisure and recreation opportunities as well as to the potential buzz and liveliness of urban living. In much of the urban periphery, walkability is absent. Where it is present, it transforms residents' social and leisure practices and their connectedness. Despite residents within Hammonds Farm identifying various transport challenges (noted above), its relatively good location, and the potential access through walking to leisure sites and shops, was noted by various residents, with one even describing it as the 'promised land' (Hammonds Farm MM 13 ♂ Diary):

> Sometimes when I feel bored ... I went to Moses Mabhida [stadium] to watch the game for soccer with my friends and visit as well Suncoast Casino. We have also the Isibaya casino and we visit there, and it is easy to go there because we are walking not taking the taxi. ... If the weather is hot, I go to Mdloti beach and sit there to get the fresh air. We are lucky because many things are close to us. At the beach there are swimming pool and games; it is easy for us to go there to relax. Sometimes I stay at the beach the whole day. (Hammonds Farm LS 07 ♀ Diary)

Provision for walking is negligible in most peripheral regions, with the distant location of areas and their (sometimes) relatively low density synonymous with a lack of pavements or pedestrian crossings and traffic lights. This contrasts with what is evident in central urban contexts in the cities of Johannesburg, Addis Ababa and eThekwini, but is not dissimilar to what might be found in centrally located informal settlements in these city regions. Auto-constructed areas of the urban periphery have very poor pedestrian provision (see Figures 6.8 and 9.2 of Caneland/Consiton in northern eThekwini).

In consolidated urban peripheries such as Waterloo, formalised curb edges are evident but not necessarily the provision of wider pavements to support pedestrian movement. Investment in pavement construction was evident in the transitioning peripheral space Molweni, supporting the movement of children and pedestrians and reducing traffic accidents. Furthermore, the construction of pavements provided local residents with employment. In vanguard peripheries such as Tulu Dimtu in Addis Ababa, investment in pavements for pedestrians was evident – although streets were still used as play spaces.

Figure 8.5 Pavements in Tulu Dimtu (source: Mark Lewis)

Concluding comments: 'stuckness' and (im)mobility in the peripheries

The relatively poor transport provision across all our sites, combined with the distances, traffic and costs of public transport, cannot be separated from the sense of these areas as being boring and cut off from the benefits of urban life. Boredom in the peripheries is discussed more fully in Chapter 10, while here we consider how the status of transport provision produces experiences of 'stuckness' and (im)mobility. Straughan *et al.* (2020), whose work focuses on the partners of mobile workers, understand stuckness as a particular form of waiting, whereas in our work we use stuckness to reference being 'stuck in place' (Williams *et al.*, 2022: 923). This may include waiting but commonly involves eschewing plans for travel, delaying or queuing for travel, an inability to take up travel options, an absence of travel infrastructure and unaffordability. Williams *et al.* (2022) explore the intersection of immobility in the peripheries with social immobility. Our discussion within this chapter illustrates how immobility points to both the physical challenges of mobility alongside the impacts on residents' social and economic lives. Immobility also produces particular temporalities for peripheral residents, and these residents are often forced to forgo opportunities as a result of poor and expensive transportation. As noted by residents of Tulu Dimtu, meeting one's daily needs and accessing recreational activity can involve travelling long distances that people either deem to be not worthwhile or cannot afford (Tulu Dimtu MK 025 ♂ Diary; Tulu Dimtu KT 026 ♂ Interview). This severely limits the ways in which people can engage with the supposed benefits of urban living. One resident even mentioned that 'Unless I have important matters, I don't even think of going to the inner city for recreation; the distance is unthinkable' (Tulu Dimtu MK 025 ♂ Diary). This could also have effects on family life, with a Yeka Abado resident noting that since living there, 'on the weekends I rarely go to visit family, as it's far to go from here to the city', adding that they would only go 'if there are unescapable social events like a funeral' (Yeka Abado KT 017 ♂ Interview). Immobility and stuckness in the urban peripheries of South Africa was also a dominant theme. As this resident explains, 'Yes, this is the only place that I'm staying – I love to travel, but I don't have money and stuff; I don't go anywhere' (Winterveld 37 VK ♂ Interview).

Intra-urban migration to the urban peripheries of African cities produces a relational experience of stuckness and immobility. In Addis this is commonly the experience of new condominium owners and tenants, paralleling the experiences of some beneficiaries of state housing in South Africa where migration away from work and services was fundamental to securing a house, such as those in Lufhereng. People's sense of attachment to their old neighbourhoods was often pronounced, partly because these are so much more accessible from their workplace, and in some ways this has contributed to the difficulty of accepting life in the peripheries. As one Yeka Abado resident noted, 'most of the time I spend my free time around my old neighbourhood', both because of ongoing social connections there and because traffic is so bad in rush hours that it is easier to just stay in their previous neighbourhood until late in the evening (Yeka Abado TE 071 ♂ Interview). More generally, people often simply find ways to kill time in the city for hours to wait until the traffic has eased, for example surfing the web and looking for places to charge their phone (Yeka Abado M 100 ♀ Interview).

In our South African cases, stuckness is experienced in rather different ways, including by people who haven't necessarily moved from somewhere more central (although historically their parents or grandparents may have) but where the nature of transportation infrastructure and the location of their peripheral settlements produce isolation, dislocation and a sense of immobility. The logics of the peripheries outlined in the Introduction resonate across different explanations for and experiences of stuckness and immobility in both Ethiopia and South Africa. Historic and current (under) investment practices in transport (and housing, work and services) produce particular peripheral realities for residents, which are context-specific, fluid, contested and variably encountered.

9

Producing places: Services, infrastructure and the public realm

Paula Meth, Sarah Charlton and Alison Todes

Viewed from an everyday life perspective, infrastructure in the peripheries of African cities is highly uneven, with different forms of infrastructure having varying significance for residents. In this chapter the five logics of urban peripheries, namely vanguard, speculative, transitioning, auto-constructed and inherited (see the Introduction), are employed to explore their association with distinct infrastructural realities. We find clear intersections, including the extent of access to housing, water and related services. The chapter, however, avoids a simplistic conflation of infrastructural forms and experiences with any one logic, noting instead how a contextualised and complex range of practices and processes account for what are often quite contradictory stories of infrastructure from residents. These contradictions reveal that the methodological approach underpinning these insights, that of everyday/lived experiences, is critical in understanding the important complexities and contingencies associated with how places are produced.

Infrastructure is employed here as a label capturing a range of services and material structures and processes predominantly provided by the state (at multiple scales) or private individuals or companies. The argument here is mindful of important debates (see Silver, 2014) detailing the infrastructural labour and incremental contributions of residents of African cities who perform and produce infrastructure. These practices are evident across all the African cities analysed in this book, captured within but also beyond the auto-constructed peripheries logic detailed in the Introduction, but they are not the central focus here. Instead, the chapter focuses on distinguishing macro or 'big' infrastructure from what we here term 'micro' infrastructure (often state-led) but rejects a binary classification. We recognise varying scales of infrastructure along a continuum (for example, macro, meso and micro) and note the networked, interconnected nature of infrastructure, precluding analysis of 'discrete' infrastructure examples. The significance of micro-infrastructure (particularly from the perspective of residents) is a key finding of this chapter. We emphasise this scale of infrastructure deliberately, noting that an exploration (and recognition) of micro-infrastructure is conceptually (and in empirical and policy terms) significant. This chapter shares the concerns of Nugent (2018) who questions the return to a focus on 'big infrastructure' on the part of African governments, international agencies and corporate investors, particularly in terms of major port and rail projects. Nugent's concerns relate to the potential financial, bureaucratic and political gamble associated with commitments to 'big infrastructure' projects and 'downstream consequences of overreach', arguing that 'resources are diverted away from competing priorities, such as urban water and power generation, which may be more pressing needs' (2018: 80).

Our wider peripheries project set out to understand some of these bigger (macro- or meso-scale) infrastructure interventions (often associated with economic logics) across our different case study areas but quickly discovered that it was often the micro-scale (often associated with the public or household realm) that captured resident attention or produced a locally experienced impact. A focus on sanitation and electricity and related 'priority' infrastructure is evident in wider studies (and detailed here too), but we argue in this chapter that more ordinary micro-infrastructures, such as bus shelters and paving, must also be brought into vision, particularly when elevating how the production of place interconnects with infrastructure. The neglect of the public realm in urban development is a key point raised by Dewar (2008), where attention is rather given to individual housing units, at least in the South African context and arguably applicable too to our Ethiopian cases. He argues that public spaces are key for low-income households, in particular where homes are inevitably likely to be modest. Hence, public investment planning should focus 'on actions which benefit the collective, as opposed to the individual household. Of particular importance is the quality of the public spatial environment, for this has the potential to give dignity to entire settlements and all inhabitants' (Dewar, 2008: 37). We use the concept 'incubator urbanism' or 'incubator infrastructure' (Charlton, 2017: 102) to crystallise the significance of infrastructure for poor households, even in peripheral contexts where locational disadvantages and economic disconnections are prevalent. Charlton, drawing on the work of Amis (2001), illustrates how improvements in basic infrastructure can have important outcomes for precarious residents, improving quality of life, health, etc. The term incubator infrastructure centres the 'potential for people to leverage off infrastructure, to improve life and advance prospects, to offer hope, and ultimately to thrive'. Yet the notion of 'incubator urbanism' can also indicate how this merely sustains life, so residents keep going 'rather than thriving' (Charlton, 2017: 102–3).

Lemanski's concept of 'infrastructural citizenship' is used here to interrogate the relationship between infrastructure and residents' relationships with the state or perceptions of the state (as failing or delivering) and their own subjectivities in view of their infrastructural experiences. Lemanski argues that 'citizenship is embodied in infrastructure for both citizens and the state. For citizens, the state is materially and visibly represented through everyday (in)access to public infrastructure, while the state imagines and plans for citizens through infrastructure provision and maintenance' (2020: 115). The importance of being recognised by the state, and having the state respond to, see and acknowledge residents, is also significant (alongside material gains) (Zack and Charlton, 2003). The emphasis on the state–citizen relationship in relation to infrastructure underscores the importance of governance and regimes of governance in shaping infrastructural decisions and policies. This is especially evident in the cases of Ethiopia and South Africa, where much infrastructure delivery is associated with the state, including remedial, extension and new infrastructure interventions (see Charlton, 2017 in relation to South Africa). In Ethiopia public sources fund most infrastructural interventions, including electricity, water, roads, transport and telecommunications. Infrastructure is closely tied to Ethiopia's poverty alleviation efforts through an integrated urban development approach, and employment creation is a core goal of urban infrastructure development. However, despite the state being the driver of infrastructure provision, the demands of peripheral locations mean standardised, networked technologies are often unsuitable, and decentralised heterogenous alternatives are implemented, including by the state, as evidenced in the provision of sanitation to mass housing estates in Addis Ababa (Cirolia *et al.*, 2021).

The chapter first considers planning, investment and the governance of the peripheries by drawing out the connections between infrastructure and the varying logics of the periphery (identified in the Introduction). It then explores the question of micro- versus large-scale infrastructural interventions, using an everyday lived experience framing through a focus on the public realm, services and key provisions and the online and electronic realm. The chapter concludes with a focus on uneven infrastructural realities. Brief mention of transport infrastructure as a key infrastructural element is made, but detailed analysis of transport is provided in Chapter 8 and not here.

Planning, investment and the governance of infrastructure in the peripheries

Our 'logics' of peripheries highlight some of the differences in experiences of infrastructure and place across our case studies. Several of our residential areas were developed through vanguard logics as state housing schemes in South Africa or state-supported/-initiated housing developments in Ethiopia. These were developed as formal areas with a range of services and facilities. In the South African context, these include the original part of Ekangala 'proper' created as a 'model apartheid town' in 1982 (TRAC, 1985): for instance, respondent DM (Ekangala 05 ♀ Diary) refers to Ekangala as a developed neighbourhood as they have water, electricity, roads, street lights and schools. In the post-apartheid era, so-called RDP (Reconstruction and Development Programme) housing areas developed by the state offer basic services, such as water, electricity and roads. Such service conditions differ sharply from those in informal settlements, as is evident in both our social surveys and in resident diaries and interviews. For instance, residents noted that moving into formal houses in Lufhereng brought 'dignified living' through access to electricity, water, a cleaner environment and a bigger space compared to the Protea South informal settlement, which they often described as a place not suitable to live in, especially with children. 'It is so nice to live in an area with so much development' (Lufhereng AR 11 ♀ Diary). In Lufhereng greater attention was given to the quality of the environment and to housing design: 'Compared to other RDP housing beneficiaries in other places, we are better and should be grateful' (Lufhereng BD 29 ♂ Diary). In Tulu Dimtu, Addis Ababa, residents observed positive changes, including how the brightness of lighting from the new bus station and street lights meant that 'The way the street is lively has made it, unusually, look like Europe' (Tulu Dimtu KN 59 ♂ Diary).

However, such environments do not necessarily provide a full range of social or material facilities: they may be planned but are not yet realised due to the limits of coordination and varying agendas across spheres and departments within government. They may also take several years to materialise, so resident experience is of difficulty in accessing a range of facilities. These delays in 'critical provisions' (discussed further below) can prove 'injurious' and raise questions about 'the politics of medium to long-term disruption associated with relocation' (Meth *et al.*, 2022: 19–21), where disruption is often a feature of vanguard development. In Addis Ababa's Tulu Dimtu condominium settlement, residents complained about incomplete development: 'What the government has provided is not sufficient. The assigned green areas are full of construction waste. After the houses are assigned, there was no change made by the government. Rather, it's the community that is pushing and working for change' (Tulu Dimtu BY 028 ♂ Interview).

The incomplete nature of the neighbourhood was repeatedly remarked on in Lufhereng. Facilities called for in diaries and interviews included halls, schools, clinics, sports fields, a clinic and a police station. In her diary, NB (Lufhereng 03 ♀ Diary) noted among other things that Lufhereng lacks a mall, a concern shared by several residents and discussed further in Chapter 11. NM (Lufhereng 22 ♀ Diary) says that there are not enough schools, parks, sports grounds or trees in Lufhereng – 'The government is not providing the things we always request.' If the children wish to visit a library, they have to cross a 'dangerous bridge' and travel a long distance to Mndeni (Lufhereng CC 18 ♀ Diary; Lufhereng GC 21 ♀ Diary). The paucity of play areas for children, the lack of pavements and the absence of design supporting disabled and elderly people were noted by some residents in Hammonds Farm. A sports facility was being developed in more established Waterloo, and there were some play areas, but absences in this regard and a lack of maintenance were still sources of complaint for some residents there. For instance, MM's diary (Waterloo 12 ♀) noted that a designated open space had become overgrown: 'If the municipality cut the grass and trees, our children will have the place to play.' Some respondents noted that children therefore play in the road, where they are likely to be hit by a car. Poor quality of services was also noted, for instance complaints about long queueing times and limited availability of staff at clinics in several areas, a lack of maintenance of services and facilities and about affordability of services and more, as detailed below.

The condominium housing programme in the peripheries of Addis has produced a particular set of unanticipated relationships between tenants and owners, often evidencing social differentiation (see Chapter 10 and Chapter 4 on governance). The vanguard approach in Addis is more than just the provision of a particular housing form; it also incorporates local-scale governance structures in the form of local committees which are responsible for organising and working locally to improve their living environment. Compulsory development fees are paid by all condominium owners (but not tenants) to fund neighbourhood projects (gardens, fencing, paving). Tenants, who may be wealthier than condo owners, are not always formally integrated into the local residence committee governance structures set up to manage the new condo blocks. Their buying power, and thus their ability to relocate, and exclusion from committees translate into tenants having weak commitment to condominium living and its communal spaces (arguably fundamental to vanguard success in particular, where alternative public spaces and facilities in surrounding neighbourhoods do not exist):

> [M]ost residents in our building are not owners and impact our living situation negatively. ... Since most residents in this building do not own this place, they do care less about the area. They do not collaborate to make our residential area clean and also contribute money for things we need to erect. For instance, when they are asked to come for a meeting, they do not show up. Hence, we are not able to resolve issues related to solid and liquid waste management. (Tulu Dimtu ME 11 ♀ Interview)

Areas produced through a speculative logic of private sector property firms in South Africa such as Protea Glen were more likely to have a fuller range of services than residential areas produced through a vanguard logic. Reasons for this include the often higher levels of household income than in our state-driven housing cases, the need to make these areas marketable and their sometimes longer histories reflecting investment over time. Levels of service and satisfaction are much higher here than in Lufhereng: 'In Protea Glen we have schools, churches, police station, malls' (Protea Glen SM 11 ♂ Diary); 'Everything is there maybe like accessing wi-fi internet, it's almost in every corner; the wi-fi is … for free' (Protea Glen GM 09 ♂ Interview). Commercial facilities such as shops and garages have been established, as well as schools and clinics. However, even these took time to establish, and new extensions lack facilities such as schools and police stations. Further, there are still gaps as private property development focuses on houses. Some complain about the lack of facilities for children (Protea Glen CC 08 ♂ Diary; Protea Glen WM 20 ♂ Diary), so children play in the street and are at risk of being hit by cars (Protea Glen GA 04 ♀ Diary). In an echo of comments made in vanguard Lufhereng, GA (Protea Glen 04 ♀ Diary) says that Protea Glen needs playing grounds, a library, tennis courts and parks in order to keep children off of the streets. In Addis Ababa the Legetafo area in the surrounding Oromia region (see Figure 9.1) just beyond the border of Addis Ababa is an example of a high-end residential area attracting 'well-to-do residents' (Ethiopian Consultant, 2018). A resident living in the Ropack neighbourhood who has two hired helps explained how difficult it was initially settling there (although they are very happy there now): 'there was no social life. There was no electricity meter and there was a big water problem. The roads were not proper like now; it was not so comfortable for living. We lived in this area for five years with such conditions' (Yeka Abado A 095 ♀ Diary). Water access was critical, with supply available once a month for two days. She goes on to explain how the design of the neighbourhood intersected with water shortages:

> [On the] Ropack real estate plan there are many gardens, and water is required to water the plants. However, since there is water shortage and because the water we buy is not enough for ourselves let alone for plants, during the non-rainy season the aesthetics of the area is very much affected. (Yeka Abado A 095 ♀ Diary)

Figure 9.1 Country Club Developers, Legetafo, Addis Ababa
(source: Mark Lewis)

Informal settlements produced through an auto-constructed logic generally had very poor services and conditions, and social facilities were lacking. However, there were variations, with some facilities such as ablution blocks and toilets being provided by the local authority in Coniston and Canelands, informal settlements in eThekwini (see Figure 9.2). These were seen as providing dignity and a great improvement. Nevertheless, some argued that they were only accessible in some sub-areas: SM (Canelands 17 ♀ Diary) claims that the nearest toilets are very far away from their home – 'One has to walk a distance before you get there' – so streams and open spaces were still being used. A logic of auto-construction is evident in the way services and infrastructure are produced by local residents. This is particularly evident in informal settlements but also across other settlement types, overlaying and intersecting with other logics. A particular example is illegal electricity connections, evident in several areas. Coniston and Canelands informal settlements lack a legal electricity connection, and so residents have to use *izinyokanyoka* (illegal connections). This enables access to the service for free but involves serious risks. AM (Coniston 05 ♀ Diary) noted that three people had died so far,

Figure 9.2 State provision of ablution facilities, Canelands and Coniston, northern eThekwini (source: Mark Lewis)

but residents continue to connect illegally. Residents cited cases of the electrocution of children who had been playing with the wires that lie on the ground uncovered. The supply is also unreliable, with the municipality disconnecting illegal connections. Claiming 'infrastructural citizenship' (Lemanski, 2020) in this way is highly contested: residents described protests against municipal disconnection, comprising roadblocks and tyre burning, which were met by the police with tear gas and rubber bullets. ZC (Canelands 07 ♀ Diary) identifies the lack of electricity as a primary challenge that makes living in Canelands difficult. However, even in areas where electricity reticulation is available, illegal connections are made for reasons of affordability. For instance, in Hammonds Farm, residents struggle with the cost of legal access, and some prioritise paying for food from their grants over electricity and so connect illegally. In Addis Ababa, informal housing dominates much of the city and is evident in the urban peripheries too. In Yeka Abado, various informal structures exist alongside the condominium structures. Infrastructural investments by the state to support the condominium housing (roads, power, communication, health services, schools, etc.) are considered to have benefited informal residents alike. However, much previously auto-constructed farmers' housing has been removed from these areas in Addis Ababa; indeed, one key informant (AW) explained: 'this infrastructure development, which is good on its own, has in fact facilitated the displacement of many thousand farmers who were dependent on the land' (Ethiopian Government Official 2, 2018).

The logic of a transitioning periphery is most evident in Molweni, where densification and urbanisation are occurring, and there have been improvements in infrastructure and services over time. According to DM (Molweni 09 ♂ Diary), 'There is no big gap between us and the suburbs.' Similarly, LS (Molweni 03 ♀ Diary) argued that 'A lot of development has taken place in the Molweni area from the tar roads that join into Inanda Road, the petrol stations as well as the shopping centres. We are proud of the development that is still going to take place.' Likewise, MM (Molweni 12 ♀ Diary) said:

> I know my area before any development came in this area or before any changes take place. The first development in this area [was the] building of the RDP houses, good roads, tap water and the flush toilets. All that development provided by the government in front of my eyes ... This area is on the map because of the development happening in this area.

However, others argue that such development is still not enough. Further, it is uneven, with some areas neglected and severe infrastructural and service deficits in some places. For instance, Nogxaza has a gravel road, no pavements, no taxis and people still have to collect water from the communal tap in the street (Molweni OM 19 ♂ Interview). These differences in part reflect the specific history and governance of various parts of Molweni and the current relationships between traditional authorities and councillors in the area (see Chapter 4) shaping differential experiences of service delivery.

Considering the logic of inherited peripheries and its influence on infrastructure and services requires understanding the specific histories shaping these spaces. In the Introduction we referred to 'inherited peripheries' as spaces of obligation, but there is also a broader sense in which histories of particular places shape infrastructure and services in the area. For instance, Canelands library in northern eThekwini is an apartheid-era intervention provided historically for Indian race groups who were predominant in that area, which is now highly significant to broader (poor black) residents' lives in that region as it has densified. This, alongside other investments in housing and schools, have ongoing importance as consolidation occurs.

In the South African context, Winterveld and Ekangala are cases that most closely reflect areas created under apartheid through processes of forced removals and homeland development (see Chapter 6 on housing) which might be seen as places of obligation for the state as a consequence of this history and which are poorly located in relation to economic development and/or have experienced economic decline (see Chapter 1 on visions and Chapter 2 on investment). However, they are also areas with quite different dynamics and histories which continue to shape current conditions. Hence, Ekangala 'proper' was the product of a vanguardist apartheid government, as noted above, its prototype nature resulting in a relatively more complete set of facilities and better infrastructure and services than many other areas at the time. Later developments in Greater Ekangala within the apartheid era were less complete, reflected in resident comments on, for instance, Dark City (the name reflecting the lack of electricity at the time), created in 1991. In this area there have since been some improvements in the residential infrastructure through post-apartheid state investment, although it remains relatively poorly serviced compared to others in Ekangala. From the perspective of economic infrastructure, the creation of Ekandustria as an industrial decentralisation point, its rise and decline and new forms of investment are discussed in the Introduction and Chapters 1, 2 and 3. There are clear impacts for local residents, as noted in Chapter 3, although infrastructural and service conditions in residential areas are to some extent delinked from these processes.

Winterveld is quite a different case where the histories of forced removals and landownership (see Chapter 6 on housing in South Africa) resulted in a very poorly serviced area, complicated also by the presence of 'big men' landowners in some areas such as Madibeng Hills (see Chapter 4). The area benefited from a post-apartheid Presidential Project to improve service delivery in the mid-1990s, and as noted in Chapter 1, there has been substantial investment in service delivery despite it not being a priority area for the municipality. Nevertheless, resident perceptions of services and infrastructure in the area are overwhelmingly negative, although there is acknowledgement by some residents that improvement has occurred. For instance, 'No street lights ... full toilets, no bins, less electricity, pick it up (*Papa-dopa*), no roads – we use gravel roads – no water meters and proper bridges, bridge is incomplete, no RDPs and street names' (Winterveld MT 20 ♀ Diary). With regard to Madibeng Hills, SC (Winterveld 29 ♂ Interview) said 'This place doesn't meet all our needs; we haven't received proper service delivery; we're just doing things on our own', paralleling practices in auto-constructed peripheries.

Respondents report very variable access to water and electricity, though some who do have access are getting it 'for free'. Water supply is a particular issue in Madibeng Hills, with some people still having to walk some distance to fetch water, despite in some cases having paid the local strongman for access, R750 in the case of MM (Winterveld 22 ♀ Interview). There is a similar frustration around how electricity access, payments and disconnections are controlled by 'the founder'/ strongman in Madibeng Hills, while other problems include having to pay households to illegally connect via them and periods of outages, sometimes for two weeks. Some respondents use wood from trees in the area for cooking as an alternative to other energy sources, and many people are still using pit toilets and complain of the lack of decent sanitation, especially in Madibeng Hills. There are problems with waste removal and dumping in Winterveld more generally. Some of our Madibeng Hills respondents report that residents fear making any complaints as there is retaliation such as threats, eviction or destruction of their shelters. Governance dynamics overlay these histories of 'inherited spaces' as tensions surface between party officials and local strongmen.

While there is a sense among many respondents of little delivery or responsiveness by local councillors, some government interventions were mentioned, including some bus transportation and three clinics. Overall, there is a sense that services are very stretched and hospitals are far away. Other initiatives include the RDP houses that were built in Extension 3, the paving of the road at Mboneni and the ongoing construction of a small complex with a South

African Social Security Agency (SASSA), Home Affairs and a library (Winterveld SG 31 ♂ Diary).

Hence, our constructs referred to by the logics of peripheries help to capture and highlight overall realities and differences within areas, but there are variations on or within each theme, and they can play out in various ways in different contexts. Further, as we argue in the Introduction, logics overlap and intersect within areas. In addition there is unevenness and difference within areas of our case studies. Close scrutiny is needed of particular areas, their histories, trajectories and current dynamics to surface these often multifaceted characteristics, but the framing provided by the logics and their conceptual elaborations offer some of the tools to do this. At the same time there can be commonalities: maintenance is a concern across all areas, especially in the South African context, although there are differences in the nature and extent of the problem.

Big infrastructure versus micro-infrastructure: the dominance of micro in terms of residents' experiences

A key finding across most of the seven case study areas was the significance of micro-infrastructure for residents living in these spaces. As noted above, these varying forms of infrastructure are often quite ordinary, less spectacular and in some cases less significant for garnering votes or external funding (see Nugent, 2018, who in contrast notes how big infrastructure often aims to achieve these). This finding stands in contrast to the lesser significance accorded by residents (in relative terms) to the presence and role of big infrastructure in all case study areas. On the whole, residents were aware of the presence or arrival of the 'bigger' infrastructures, and some noted benefits tied to employment or transport access (e.g. to the city centre), but generally residents dismissed these interventions as less significant for their everyday lives or their significance was partial.

Our cases evidence various instances of 'big infrastructure' with key examples including the King Shaka International Airport and associated Dube TradePort (DTP) and the Gateway/Umhlanga economic node in the northern eThekwini case, Ekandustria in the Ekangala case (see Chapter 2 for further analysis), the Addis Light

Rail in the Yeka Abado case and the Industrial Park at Dukem south of the Addis border along the Addis–Adama Expressway in the case of Tulu Dimtu. While some residents in areas surrounding the King Shaka airport did make reference to jobs available there, others argued that such work was mainly accessible to people outside the area or they did not mention it at all (see Chapter 3; Todes and Houghton, 2021). Similar observations can be made about the industrial parks close to Tulu Dimtu (see Chapter 3). Overall, the impact of the airport in terms of employment was far less than might be expected. Often, references to the airport focused on the excitement of watching aeroplanes take off and land (Hammonds Farm LS 07 ♀ Diary) or its role as a spatial reference: 'I love Waterloo because it is in between the city of Durban, international King Shaka airport' (Waterloo MM 12 ♀ Diary). Other smaller but key infrastructural interventions are the Rea Vaya bus extension to Protea Glen, the Protea Glen shopping mall, the Watercrest Mall between Crestholme and Molweni, the Spar supermarket complex between Hammonds Farm and Waterloo and the Mabopane Station near Winterveld. As noted above, residents' dismissal of 'big infrastructure' was by no means blanket, and shopping malls and supermarkets proved to be highly significant to their lives, as is discussed in detail in Chapter 11.

In contrast to the examples of big interventions identified here, when asked about key infrastructure, the majority of residents identified micro-infrastructure changes or challenges which were deemed to have great significance for their lives. The discussion moves now to explore varying forms of micro-infrastructure alongside meso-scale infrastructure. It is divided into three sections, namely infrastructure commonly tied to the public realm, key services and infrastructure and those related to the online realm.

Public realm infrastructures

Linked to various policies and schemes often at the local scale or driven by city administrations, there is significant evidence of concurrent investment in a wide range of public realm infrastructures working to (partially) transform the material basis of urban peripheries. As noted above, the explanation for these investments is commonly tied to wider governance and investment processes typical of particular peripheral logics. What is evident in material terms is the spatial transformation of place, not always wholesale but certainly showing urban change. These changes shape how residents perceive their area: 'this area now looks like a township instead of a rural area' (Molweni NS 04 ♀ Diary). In Yeka Abado and Tulu Dimtu, investment in pavements, surfacing of condominium and retail frontages, and road paving was evident in places (see Figure 8.5), shifting the look and finish of the block, contrasting with the often unfinished nature of other parts of the development.

The introduction of street lights to urban peripheral locations is celebrated in various cases, its significance tied to the potential to reduce or alleviate crime (Ekangala Dark City RN 03 ♂ Interview) but also simply to reduce the reality of darkness and improve the quality of place. The introduction of street lights (Lufhereng TM 27 ♂ Interview) is a core part of why the area is 'so nice ... unlike where we came from' (Lufhereng AR 11 ♀ Diary), which was an informal settlement. In Dark City, Ekangala, residents note that the introduction of street lights in around 2014 means that it is effectively no longer dark (Ekangala Dark City ST 01 ♀ Interview). In Winterveld street lights were implemented near a local school following electrification in 2008.

Bus shelters (see Figure 9.3) and taxi ranks were positively noted in Waterloo and also Molweni for protecting residents from inclement weather (Molweni OM 19 ♂ Interview; Molweni DM 9 ♂ Interview). In Molweni they replaced previously insufficient community-constructed shelters (Molweni HM 10 ♀ Diary). Residents' views were positive despite the minimal nature of the shelters which lacked seating. A Waterloo resident noted how new taxi shelters were cleverly designed to prevent criminals hiding behind them compared to old-style shelters (Waterloo MM 12 ♀ Interview). The construction of pavements was also noted by Molweni and Hammonds Farm residents as improving pedestrian access and enhancing safety (Molweni ZS 30 ♀ Interview; Molweni OM 19 OM ♂ Interview), prompting one resident to explain: 'We are happy because our area is improving' (Hammonds Farm ZN 11 ♀ Diary). In Molweni the formalisation of passageways has improved residents' access to their housing and enhanced their ability to carry groceries (Molweni NS 05 ♀ Diary).

Minor improvements (including street names and speed bumps) and major engineering works on road networks (including the

Producing places

Figure 9.3 Bus shelter in Molweni (source: Mark Lewis)

construction of a new bridge in Molweni) are widely cited across cases as significant. Postal boxes were noted by residents in Waterloo as being introduced in 2012 (Waterloo MM 12 ♀ Diary). In Molweni residents claim that improvements in road quality mean that local taxis are willing to drop passengers closer to their properties (Molweni MC 02 ♀ Interview) and that street-naming facilitates deliveries (Molweni TG 26 ♀ Diary). Residents cite significant reductions in travel times, including walking, where in Molweni they previously crossed 'mountains' to access urban centres but now used direct roads (Molweni HM 11 ♀ Diary). Tarred roads are noted by former residents of informal settlements as a significant gain, for example in Lufhereng (PR 13 ♂ Interview), with one resident explaining: 'it was a very bad road but now it's a hundred per cent' (Lufhereng PD 01 ♀ Interview). Similarly, in Rethabiseng one resident contrasts the new tarred road with what was previously 'just dust' (Rethabiseng MB 11 ♀ Interview). The muddy nature of previous gravel roads is commonly cited across cases. DM in Ekangala uses the introduction of roads as evidence of living in a 'developed neighbourhood' and that they are 'recognised by the government' (Ekangala DM 05 ♀ Diary), echoing Zack and Charlton's framing (2003). Road development occurred alongside storm water improvements reducing blockages along roads (Hammonds Farm

ZN 11 ♀ Diary). Similarly, in Tulu Dimtu, Addis, road improvements were noted, as the condo area of Eritrea is seen to benefit from its proximity to the expressway and the asphalt road linking Goru to the region (Tulu Dimtu KT 026 ♂ Interview).

Improvements in traffic lights were evident in both Lufhereng and Hammonds Farm but in both cases tied to residents' pleas for their provision. In Lufhereng, 'robots' were installed following the death of a child: 'This is when community members raised their voices to say we have had enough of this. Fortunately, after so much struggle, our voices were heard ... Many lives are being spared now because of these robots' (Lufhereng AR 011 ♀ Diary). Between Hammonds Farm and Waterloo, traffic wardens from 'Safer City' were introduced in the mornings to assist children crossing the road to access schools in adjacent Waterloo, necessary despite the introduction of traffic lights (Waterloo FB 24 ♀ Diary).

The introduction of parks, community gardens and sporting and leisure facilities was observed by numerous residents across all cases. A new park, which included a gym (Ekangala Dark City LS 16 ♀ Interview) was noted as evidence of improvements in the area (Ekangala Dark City ST 01 ♀ Diary), and in Ekangala the introduction of play parks by the municipality for children was celebrated (Ekangala Q 08 ♀ Diary): 'They built parks for children with outdoor games like merry-go-around etc.; the toddlers have a safe place to play now instead of the streets where they were subjected to car accidents' (Ekangala Q 08 ♀ Diary). The same resident noted the construction of a football stadium too in Ekangala, key for young people in particular. For residents living in informal Coniston in northern eThekwini, their relative proximity to Verulam, with its sports facilities, was an appealing feature of their location (Coniston LM 03 ♂ Diary). In nearby Waterloo the construction by the municipality of a new sports centre was celebrated by numerous residents. They cite how this development reduces the need to exercise in unsafe spaces such as on the road (Waterloo PZH 05 ♂ Interview) and how it will encourage younger residents to engage in sports (Waterloo NGS 17 ♀ Diary) and assist in diverting youths from involvement in drugs and alcohol (Waterloo NN 03 ♀ Interview; Waterloo PZH 05 ♂ Interview; Waterloo ZD 09 ♂ Interview). In contrast, in Tulu Dimtu and Yeka Abado in Addis Ababa, parks and playgrounds were absent; however, condominium residents worked in community groups to transform semi-public spaces between buildings into gardens: 'Even though it's tiresome, I feel like I have to work towards the common good ... We're working on creating playgrounds for children, constructing fences, planting seedlings and the like to create a better living environment' (Tulu Dimtu KT 026 ♂ Interview).

Key services and infrastructure

In addition to numerous micro-infrastructures identified above, multiple residents detailed the introduction of other key infrastructures, including electricity and sanitation, alongside the arrival of key services and associated buildings/vehicles and staffing, such as clinics, schools, refuse removal and school bus services. Many of these are priority interventions and can be understood as 'incubator infrastructure' (Charlton, 2017), fundamentally impacting residents' lives, transforming the liveability of a location and illustrating the changing nature of urban peripheries.

In Yeka Abado, Addis, the arrival of key services followed the condominium construction, with one resident noting: 'If I would compare it to the area I used to live in, here you find everything. Actually it's more than I expected it' (Yeka Abado SHT 003 ♀ Interview). However, as is discussed below, with many of these services, lags in provision proved very problematic, particularly for early migrants to these areas:

> When we moved first, the living situation was difficult. We had no water supply for a short while. We used to carry water from Gedera by cart or *bajaj* ... There was also no electricity. We used to get power lines from a nearby construction site ... [now] We don't get power outs more often than any part of the city. The same thing with water supply as well. That has also been a huge improvement. (Yeka Abado TA 061 ♂ Interview)

The introduction of priority infrastructure and services was evident also in the relatively informal villages adjacent to the condominium housing areas:

> Yes, there are changes. There was no water and now there is; there was no electricity (at least not a proper one and not widely used) and now there is. The road is also under construction. I am happy with

the changes; I wouldn't have thought such changes will occur here. (Yeka Abado AA 046 ♂ Interview)

As noted above, much of the infrastructural investment followed the construction of the condominiums.

Within Dark City a wide range of services are identified as having improved in the area, including a new school building, shops, parks, free education, weekly dustbin collection and new toilets (Ekangala SM 12 ♂ Diary). Similarly, in Molweni, a transitioning periphery, the introduction of a clinic, school buses, along with electricity were experienced as highly significant by residents. Being able to warm up water, rely on street lights, prepare food and avoid having to collect wood made a remarkable difference to residents' lives (Molweni FM 2 ♂ Diary; Molweni LS 4 ♀ Diary; Molweni VN 28 ♂ Interview; Molweni ZN 34 ♀ Diary; Molweni MS 35 ♀ Diary; Molweni DM 10 ♂ Interview; Molweni NN 37 ♀ Interview; Molweni OM 19 ♀ Interview; Molweni VN 29 ♂ Diary).

For many residents moving from informal housing to state housing (such as AN from Hammonds Farm, AN 10 ♀ Diary), the provision of water, electricity and toilets was noted as a key relative gain. As noted above, the installation of ablution blocks in informal areas in northern eThekwini by the state shaped residents' sense of dignity (see Figure 9.2). These toilets and better access to clean water are commonly identified as the most significant change in the community in Coniston and Hilltop.

The online and electronic realm

Across the South African cases in particular, changes to the online realm are evident, although often quite limited in scope and range. Provision is a mix of state and private sectors. In both Addis cases there was less evidence of a significant, well-bedded online realm, although some partial ICT interventions are evident. Residents living in Protea Glen explicitly contrast their enhanced internet cafes and wi-fi accessibility with their previous informal settlements: 'everything is there maybe like accessing wi-fi … if you are a student is very beneficial to have access to the internet for free to do their research assignments' (Protea Glen GM 09 ♂ Interview). This resident claims that Protea Glen was the first place in Soweto to be given wi-fi. CT (Protea Glen 14 ♀ Diary) explains that the internet cafes also enable residents to compare service prices and decide which providers to use. This, however, has ultimately done very little to alleviate the reality that some residents cannot afford to pay the basic rates for water and electricity (Protea Glen TN 01 ♂ Diary).

In nearby Lufhereng, school pupils have access to the internet via school computers, but broader free access or the presence of internet cafes isn't evident in the area, although one resident notes: 'The first thing that catches my attention is the poles for wi-fi', suggesting a forthcoming or partial investment (Lufhereng NB 03 ♀ Diary and Interview). Wi-fi and its connection with jobseeking is emphasised by residents in Hammonds Farm and Waterloo who state that there is an internet cafe in the settlement, supporting the drafting of CVs locally, precluding travel to nearby Verulam for this service. Residents also liked the ability to browse for jobs online and teach children to use computers (Hammonds Farm MS 14 ♂ Diary; Waterloo MJ 11 ♂ Diary). Internet cafes are mentioned in several areas, including in Molweni: 'We also have an internet cafe, which means that we are developing since we did not have such things in our area' (Molweni TH 24 ♀ Diary). In Ekangala, internet cafes are considered very popular with young people and perceived as having a positive influence on people's lives (Ekangala Q 08 ♀ Interview).

Internet access was also provided by the local state. Libraries played a key role in providing free wi-fi to residents, including those living informally in Coniston (Coniston LM 03 ♂ Diary), and in Molweni, again the library near the Water Crest mall was noted for its free wi-fi (Molweni VN 28 ♂ Diary). In Winterveld, free wi-fi was installed and provided at schools (Winterveld SG 31 ♂ Diary) but was insufficient for small businesses in terms of strength and spatial reach, and they had to rely on their own arrangements (Khumalo, 2018). In Dark City, Ekangala, several residents noted the provision of wi-fi in a local park (Ekangala Dark City EK 07 ♀ Interview), and this location encouraged mixing sport and internet access, although safety problems precluded use at night (Ekangala Dark City FM 13 ♂ Interview).

In Yeka Abado the absence of wi-fi was notable: 'Yeka Abado has a huge problem when it comes to telecommunications' (Yeka Abado EH 063 ♂ Diary), with residents explaining they travel to other areas to make use of it (Yeka Abado BA 072 ♂ Diary) or that introducing wi-fi may prove a viable business opportunity: 'To date there are different businesses in this area. However, activities such as internet shops, mobile repair shops and electronics shops are not widely common, and so we're thinking such businesses might be profitable' (Yeka Abado SHT 003 ♀ Diary). Similarly, in Tulu Dimtu very little discussion of wi-fi access was evident, although one resident noted some improvements: 'There weren't supermarkets, and now they're opening up. We now have commercial places, shops, bakery, there is one internet shop with secretarial service, and these things are developing' (Tulu Dimtu H 008 ♂ Interview).

The introduction of ATMs was noted, particularly in the eThekwini cases, as significant. In Molweni, ATMs removed the requirement to travel to urban centres to access and send money (Molweni SG 21 ♂ Diary; Molweni DM 09 ♂ Interview), and the provision of an ATM in Waterloo was noted as one of 'the best improvement[s] yet' (Waterloo ZD 09 ♂ Diary). In Dark City, residents note that tablets and smart boards have been introduced into classrooms in local schools (Ekangala Dark City NS 06 ♀ Interview).

Uneven and inadequate infrastructural realities

The chapter has thus far outlined the ways in which the varied peripheral logics have shaped infrastructure provision and experience, but it has also demonstrated that relationships between infrastructure provision and peripheral logics are not simple or straightforward; for example, a vanguard development may come with some services, but reliable or equitable supply is not guaranteed, or may take many years to be implemented, and may still decline in the future through lack of maintenance. The chapter has also considered the significance of micro-infrastructures and ICT interventions for residents across the many cases. It has argued that there is evidence of change, of infrastructural investment on the part of the state, the private sector and changes driven by individuals or community groups. Nonetheless, the overwhelming evidence across all seven cases revealed that infrastructure (its absence or its quality, where present) was a fundamental challenge for nearly all residents living in the urban peripheries, no matter their housing situation, although there were clearly inequalities within and across areas too. The dominant challenges are discussed below.

The absence of water and/or electricity and/or sanitation was a common feature of informal settlements, with negligible state intervention, although in other informal contexts (such as Caneland and Consiton), temporary provisions were evident, but these suffered from serious failings such as blockages. In Phumekaya the lack of access to individual water stand pipes and clean water via taps was a serious difficulty, with residents having to wake at 4 a.m. to secure access from communal taps (Phumekaya Ekangala JS 05 ♀ Diary), a situation compounded by high rates of crime. The absence of legal electricity forces the use of unsafe and expensive alternatives, including paraffin, firewood, candlelight and illegal connections, with all the challenges that go along with these. The impact on children's safety and ability to study is strongly noted: children using candlelight must be supervised at all times: 'I can't go to the bathroom or to the bedroom' (Phumekaya Ekangala Focus Group 3).

In areas where electricity is provided, inconsistent and unreliable connections are a serious concern, noted in numerous case study areas. In Tulu Dimtu a resident notes: 'Power and water cut off is what I worry about, especially electricity. I always thought it is going to get better, but it never did. ... Sometimes I feel like I live in a rural area' (Tulu Dimtu KF 012 ♂ Interview). In Waterloo, eThekwini, despite being a relatively consolidated settlement, inconsistent electricity supply was widespread as a problem, with impacts on food wastage a particular issue (Waterloo TN 20 ♀ Diary; Waterloo NG 02 ♀ Diary).

Similarly, water provision in areas where water infrastructure is present but inadequate or uneven poses substantial problems for residents, enforcing frugal usage, sourcing alternative water or using purifiers (Tulu Dimtu ME 011 ♀ Diary), along with sanitation difficulties. Tulu Dimtu is a particular case in point here, with water supplies appearing once a week or less (Tulu Dimtu BG 010 ♀ Diary). Residents fill containers to store water for the week, and water quality is compromised (Tulu Dimtu ME 011 ♀ Diary). People therefore have to purchase bottled water and water purifiers (Tulu Dimtu 011 ♀ Diary), and sewage lines are constantly breaking (Tulu Dimtu HK 008 ♂ Interview). Residents living on upper floors in condominium buildings are particularly disadvantaged as weak water pressure results in low or no water. In Yeka Abado an uneven supply of water afflicts some residents but not others: 'Some are benefiting from water while others are suffering from water provision. The government should know that we buy eight plastic containers of water each day [see Figure 3.1 showing an informal water seller in Yeka Abado]. I ask the government to reach out to us' (Yeka Abado AGT 037 ♂ Diary). In the Ekangala region, inconsistent access was an ongoing concern: 'we are always facing a problem of electricity and water in our community' (Rethabiseng AC 06 ♂ Diary).

Uneven and limited attention to the public realm (see Dewar, 2008) was widely evident, in particular the absence of high-quality public space and play spaces for children – a persistent concern in every case study location. Arising out of a lack of state investment in, as well as poor maintenance of, parks, squares, playgrounds and walkways, many of the locations have an incomplete appearance (see Figure 9.4) or fail to provide safe and comfortable social and leisure spaces. Given the generic small internal dimensions of most of the state-provided and informal housing (in both country contexts), external living environments were key for wellbeing (as

Figure 9.4 Incomplete public space in Tulu Dimtu (source: Mark Lewis)

argued by Dewar, 2008) and nearly always fell short: 'due to the lack of sufficient recreational spaces such as proper playing fields for younger people, they are forced to play football on the vehicle roads which might bring harm to them. There are no playing spaces for little children even within the compounds' (Yeka Abado KA 069 ♂ Interview).

At a broader spatial scale and partly a function of the geographic nature of peripheral urban spaces, the location of services can prove very challenging for residents, particularly where transport options are limited (see Chapter 8) or services are overstretched or poor in quality. In Lufhereng, health services require costly journeys to neighbouring areas, and in Hammonds Farm, easy access to a clinic is not present. This directly affects the elderly and women more specifically as their health needs and childbearing and childcare often require more consistent healthcare access. Nearby Waterloo has access to a clinic, but the quality of service is poor, with insufficient staffing, long queues, poor management and small size.

A further issue experienced by residents is that of excessively long waiting times for the provision of infrastructure alongside broken promises on the part of politicians or service delivery providers, discussed above in relation to Meth *et al.* (2022) as often producing injurious impacts. Much state-subsidised housing in both countries is relatively recently built, often with an associated delay in the provision of wider services in the area, especially social services. This is often a function of how state housing is planned and budgetary constraints shaping delivery of infrastructure beyond bulk services and housing. This delay can be conceptualised as a temporal feature of state housing, which indeed in some cases may never be resolved. Alternatively, local services may not have been planned if the area was deemed to be sufficiently serviced by surrounding areas. In Tulu Dimtu, for example, residents compare the speed of change occurring in the city in contrast to the slow pace of change in their area: 'We spend the day in the city and we can see fast changes. The changes here, even if they do exist, are slow' (Tulu Dimtu BA 030 ♂ Interview; Tulu Dimtu TZ 031 ♀ Interview). In Molweni the elderly were particularly concerned about the delay in the delivery of RDP houses, given that they had been waiting so many years for them (Molweni HM 10 ♀ Diary). In Dark City, residents metaphorically describe waiting a very long time for basic improvements such as road upgrading, noting they have to 'pray and fast before they do it' (Ekangala Dark City BM 05 ♀ Interview). Villagers in areas surrounding the condominium housing in Yeka Abado perceive slower development compared to the condo projects: 'Our needs are not met. Even the toilet we're using is overflowing because services are not provided by the *kebele*. The roads just started getting paved. The government only gives focus to the condominiums and not to the villages like this' (Yeka Abado AA 046 ♂ Interview).

Across particular cases, particularly in South Africa, residents' frustrations with different issues (poor-quality services, political disagreements, failures to deliver on promises, perceptions of corruption, etc.) led to violent protests and riots within which infrastructure was commonly implicated and impacted. These expressions of 'infrastructural citizenship' (Lemanski, 2020) are fairly commonplace in the South African context and illustrate one dimension of how infrastructure and governance are entangled. In Chapter 4 we explore in more detail residents' relationships with the state in South Africa and Ethiopia, but here the key point is the targeting of infrastructure during acts of protest (through destruction, burning, boycotting) and subsequent impacts, and the strength of feeling evoked by poor-quality infrastructure.

Conclusion

The uneven interconnections between our five peripheral logics and infrastructure were the focus of this chapter. Where relevant, the chapter has identified the intersections between particular peripheral logics and related infrastructural realities but has argued that a neat relationship cannot be identified between these. Instead, the chapter recognised how infrastructure is continually evolving (sometimes improving, sometimes collapsing) and transforming at the hands of residents, various private entrepreneurs and the state. Exploring key gains for residents living peripherally as a result of varying governance logics, the chapter traced the significance of micro-infrastructural interventions from an everyday life perspective. In many cases urgent 'incubator infrastructures' transform the liveability of remote locations for residents, and the chapter traced these also in relation to the public and online realms. For many, however, the self-provisioning of infrastructure, which is partially captured by the term auto-construction, is obligatory when state provision is lacking. The chapter argued that the absence of infrastructure and long waiting times, costs, poor quality and variability of service dominate much of the African urban periphery, and that this produces 'infrastructural citizenship' that is sometimes characterised by protest and often by frustration.

10

Social differentiation, boredom and crime in the peripheries

Paula Meth, Metadel Sileshi Belihu and Sibongile Buthelezi

This chapter addresses the social and experiential dynamics constructed in African urban peripheries. Focusing on social differentiation, the relational experiences of boredom and the dominance of crime and violence, the chapter examines how urban change shapes social processes. It considers how these processes are comparatively experienced, overcome and often perpetuated by current and historical trends tied to urban change, and it draws on the voices of residents living in diverse peripheries to unpack the complexities.

The chapter emphasises particular processes and interventions (demolitions, investments, relocations, etc.) and transformations of urban change occurring across multiple scales with generic and individualised impacts, including how communities function and their access to services. Where relevant, it draws on our five logics of urban peripheries (transitioning, speculative, vanguard, inherited and auto-constructed) to crystallise the interconnections between urban change and social differentiation, boredom and crime, revealing a wide mix of urban processes co-constructing social relations and practices in African urban peripheries. The chapter draws on three key concepts to advance its analysis, namely intersectionality, contextualisation and relationality – briefly outlined below.

Recognising that differentiation is evident across multiple axes, the chapter's empirical focus opens with attention on race and ethnicity, tenancy, age, income and gender as axes of differentiation. It then considers how urban change, including patterns of densification often engineered through changes to housing or infrastructure, works to produce new community relations, social mixing and ways of living. Fluid social relations are evident in African urban peripheries. The chapter then turns to the topic of boredom, examining its multiple and relational expressions, and considers how boredom serves as a metaphor for living peripherally and how it ties to residents' explanations of crime. Finally, the chapter focuses on crime and violence in relation to urban transitions and considers their dominance across most of the cases in Ethiopia and South Africa. Fear and anxiety about crime structure residents' everyday lives. Rather than listing an extensive repository of accounts of crime, the discussion considers how crime and the fear thereof shape living peripherally and how urban changes are explicitly interwoven with crime.

Qualitative mixed-methods data from all seven case study areas in the urban peripheries of Addis Ababa, Gauteng and eThekwini is used to illustrate and tease open these social dynamics and experiences. This frames social differences, boredom and crime in the peripheries as lived, contextualised, contingent, interdependent and fluid, rather than fixed or measurable. Our conclusions to the chapter are necessarily partial, but they do signal inequality and the production of uncertainty and marginalisation for some. This finding is key. The politics of difference in the peripheries matters, as does the politics of boredom and crime.

Key concepts for exploring social differentiation, boredom and crime

Three key concepts or principles underpin this examination of social dynamics and experiences in the peripheries, namely intersectionality, (historical) contextualisation and a relational analysis. Although this chapter's structure commences by addressing individual facets of differentiation in turn, for example age and then gender, it is grounded in a recognition of intersectionality (Crenshaw, 1989) and the ways in which peripheral spaces and wider socio-political processes work to produce intersectional outcomes. Intersectionality recognises that certain junctures of difference produce acute experiences of marginalisation, vulnerability to crime and violence and even boredom. This is often witnessed in the intersection between race, gender and class but compounded by a range of other related factors, including living insecurely and remotely and lacking a secure income. As a result personal safety often remains elusive, and achieving meaning in one's life proves unattainable. In this chapter a focus on more acute outcomes may necessitate a narrowing down on particular social differences, recognising that 'often the attribute to be emphasised is that which contributes most significantly to a subject's marginalisation or empowerment and this can and does vary significantly with place, and time' (Watson, 2016: 35). The chapter opens with a focus on race, given its foundational impact on urban lives across the continent.

A (historically) contextualised approach recognises that analysis must be tied to both historical processes as well as an in-depth understanding of context, noting the significance of values, local politics, culture and place. Watson (2016: 37) ties both an appreciation for historical processes – '(capitalism, imperialism, postcolonialism)' – and a contextualised approach to the efforts of Southern theorists to overcome universalising analyses. Drawing on the work of Fincher and Jacobs (1998: 9), Watson also notes how difference is both socially produced and located, rather than something which is pre-given or fixed: 'social distinctions are constituted in specific contexts through multiple and interpenetrating axes of difference' (Fincher and Jacobs, 1998: 9, cited in Watson, 2016: 35). In this chapter the distinct cases under examination demand recognition that the production and experience of difference, boredom and crime are historically and contextually varied and nuanced. In this regard the social processes and experiences analysed in this chapter must be read in conjunction with the analysis of the logics shaping peripheries and case study summaries outlined in the Introduction of this book.

Finally, a relational view of space in the urban peripheries and social processes and experiences is employed. The chapter recognises that space is 'first, composed through inter-relations of near and far, second, as a contemporaneous plurality of co-existing trajectories, and third as always under construction, a "simultaneity of stories-so-far"' (McFarlane, 2020: 318, after Massey, 2005: 9). African peripheries, constantly shifting, are formed in relation to changes in near and far urban cores in relation to global processes and highly localised interventions. Social differences are similarly relationally constructed (e.g. ideas of gender are often shaped by location and in relation to each other), as are residents' experiences of difference. Relationality underpins how residents judge or make sense of place and change, including the construction of difference, through relational accounts of housing conditions before and after moving in, differentiated conditions for us versus them, here versus there and now versus the future, etc. This is particularly relevant to our understanding and analysis of boredom, as well as perceptions of vulnerability and safety tied to crime and violence. The chapter turns now to examining varying axes of social differentiation.

Social differentiation in the peripheries

Race, ethnicity and religion

Race, ethnicity and religion are central axes of identity and differentiation in both South Africa and Ethiopia, tied to distinct histories of widely varying colonial domination and consequent racial subjugation alongside complex ethnic-based governance regimes. In both contexts urban peripheries are key sites of conflict or expressions of racially or ethnically determined inequality or indeed dominance. South Africa's history of racially inscribed apartheid produced legacies of ongoing racial conflict and persistent racial and class-based inequality evident in labour markets, access to housing and quality of life. National agendas around foreign in-migration in the post-apartheid period entrenched rising xenophobia, while historical, regionally inscribed ethnic differences compounded by apartheid's homeland programme (see Figure 6.1 map of apartheid Bantustans) persist in shaping perceptions and practices of difference played out in varied ways across unique urban contexts. Several of the cases are located within or on the borders of former homelands, shaping decades of underinvestment. In Ethiopia, ethnic identity and associated tension and conflict are a dominant feature. With the constitutional adoption of ethnic federalism in the 1990s, rights to land were entrenched in ethnic terms. Rising ethno-nationalism and ethnic tension saw a wave of protests from around 2014 onwards, tied to the politics of borders and landownership and development (Lavers, 2018). Záhořík describes recent tensions associated with the implementation of the 2015 Addis Ababa Integrated Development Master Plan, a key strategy of the developmentalist government of Ethiopia, as the revolt of the periphery against the centre (2017: 258). Addis Ababa and its surrounding urban peripheries where much condominium construction is occurring are located firmly within this site of contestation. Peripheries are hence sites of ethnic contestation but also key places of diversity, as new housing forms facilitate new forms of mixing.

Experiences of racism in South African urban peripheries resemble regional and national trends. However, it is the intersection of racial discrimination alongside limited employment opportunities accentuated by location which shape how it impacts residents. In Canelands informal settlement, where black residents depend on employment in local factories and businesses, allegations of racism at the hands of Indian employers were noted, including iniquitous treatment in the workplace (Canelands NK 11 ♂ Diary), and in nearby Verulam access to work was deemed racially determined: 'There are black people who qualified to do certain job but are not because they employed people according to the race' (Waterloo PZH 05 ♂ Interview). These concerns about unequal access based on race or ethnicity were noted in Addis Ababa too. In one of the informal villages near Yeka Abado, ethnicity shapes a resident's life: 'The neighbourhood is good, but there is racism. ... Since most of the residents here are Oromo, it would have been easier for me if I'm Oromo' (Yeka Abado FG 047 ♀ Interview). She does go on to explain, however, that racism is subsiding in the area more generally:

> During the construction period there was also a problem of racism. The construction workers used to come here in groups based on their ethnic background. The people from Tigray wants Tigrayan music, and the Amhara Amharic and people used to get into huge fights over this. But the people coming from the city are a mix and so you don't see such problems any more. (Yeka Abado FG 047 ♀ Interview)

Residents were also anxious about the potential for further ethnic tension and how new patterns of social mixing found in the urban peripheries would shape resilience: 'Considering the current political situation, if things get worse, I worry about our supporting and protecting capacity to one another. Since we don't know each other and if the problems that will arise are ethnic-based, it might be an issue here' (Tulu Dimtu KT 026 ♂ Interview). Religious cleavages were also evident. In Tulu Dimtu, where associated services were highly circumscribed, an absence of butcheries and places of worship for Muslim residents was identified (Tulu Dimtu MK 025 ♂ Interview). Fellow residents in Tulu Dimtu queried the politics and implications of failed decision-making around the provision of land for a mosque: 'When such decisions are made, one has to think what this will create among the people' (Tulu Dimtu F 073 ♂ Diary). However, religious affiliation was also a critical social bond for residents across all cases, and sites for religious practice were evident, including those more formally and informally provided (see Figure 10.1).

Urban peripheries can also serve as spaces of refuge, beyond the gaze of government, as a safer location for immigrants, particularly those who are illegal. This was particularly evident in Winterveld, where significant numbers of undocumented migrants from Zimbabwe and Mozambique were noted. In Dark City, Ekangala, a Zimbabwean man explained that 'most foreigners here don't have passports; it's safe to be here considering that when you go out, none will stop you to ask about your documents ... [in other places] police officers patrol around to fish out illegal migrants' (Dark City Ekangala Anonymous ♂ Interview). Urban peripheries were attractive to migrants too due to cheaper or free plots of land and services

Figure 10.1 Informal church in Waterworks (source: Mark Lewis)

(Winterveld MD 24 ♂ Interview). Within the Addis peripheries, the cheapest form of condominium housing was also used to house refugees: 'it's common to have Eritreans who have come here due to the difficult conditions in their country ... I feel really sorry for them' (Yeka Abado AT 015 ♂ Interview).

The presence of foreigners and the expression of xenophobic statements were prolific across South African cases. In Winterveld, BM misses the 'tranquillity and togetherness' that they had before the 'influx of foreigners' started arriving in Winterveld (Winterveld BM 06 Diary, Gender Unknown). In Waterloo, MB claims that 'Our children are in love with Nigerians, and those people are stealing cars' (Waterloo MB 22 ♀ Interview), and in Canelands informal settlement, SM's concerns about language are expressed as 'we are not sure if they are gossiping about you or are they talking about stealing you' (Canelands SM 17 ♀ Interview). Much of the xenophobic rhetoric in South Africa pertains to concerns over the loss of work and income generation to foreigners, a sentiment repeated across the urban peripheries in relation to workers from Zimbabwe, Mozambique and Lesotho asking for lower wages and taking jobs. Similarly, South African entrepreneurs complained about the arrival of foreign businesses from Pakistan and China, arguing their presence has damaged their business viability, including in food sales and cheap goods: 'I wish they could place them in another area not here because our business falls down' (Waterloo FB 24 ♀ Diary). These concerns often reflect the capacity of foreign businesses to purchase in bulk and to operate collectively. Economic anxiety is tinged with racism, as the same woman queries migrants' hygiene: 'What we are worried about is that they are [living] in the container; where do they bath?'

Despite such sentiments, various residents celebrated the diversity found in the urban peripheries. In Addis, residents commented: 'There are people with different ethnic backgrounds and religion. We live with each other in love, through the good and bad times' (Yeka Abado 037 AG ♂ Interview), and 'Everyone lives together happily as one, and this is an amazing fact for me and others' (Tulu Dimtu BG 010 ♀ Diary). In Waterloo, South Africa diversity is applauded: 'This area is good because have different people such as Indians, blacks, Sotho, Xhosa and foreigners' (Waterloo LN 06 ♀ Diary), and residents identified their own personal journeys of learning to adapt to difference, concluding: 'Everyone feels at home in this community' (Waterloo ZD 09 ♂ Diary).

Tenancy

Tenancy variations in urban peripheries are a key axis of social differentiation, often produced by unequal tenancy security and attendant power relations. State housing provides eligible beneficiaries the prospect of homeownership. In Addis this varies according to the financing model (ratio of deposit to longer-term mortgage payment) of the condominium structure. In Tulu Dimtu all condominiums were 20/80, whereas in Yeka Abado they varied between 10/90, 20/80 and some 40/60. In South Africa, state housing is free at the point of delivery to those eligible. Homeownership was a significant source of pride, shaping status and a sense of independence and marking out difference through property relations. Residents contrasted prior tenancy relations embedded within informal settlements, communal living or renting with perceptions of new-found security and freedom. 'I'm very happy [with] my life in my home and in this area. Because I have suffered a lot with rental house, it's better to have my own house and my own neighbourhood' (Tulu Dimtu RG 034 ♀ Diary).

Yet homeownership proved unaffordable (or inappropriate) for many in both contexts, producing new differentiation. State housing precludes resale within a set number of years in each country. Yet informal, illegal sales and renting out were occurring because beneficiaries could not afford the costs and were thus forced to exploit their assets. In both Addis Ababa cases, numerous lottery-winning owners struggled to finance mortgage and services payments; 'for this reason most have rented out their houses in this area' (Yeka Abado 015 OR ♂ Interview); 'when we consider the economic capacity of people, the price of getting by is expensive ... On this block there are seventy households, and of these only fifteen residents are owners. The others have chosen to rent the place and pay their debts' (Yeka Abado TB 001 ♂ Interview). As FW in Yeka Abado notes: 'I think a condominium resident can be classified into three groups. And these are: the one who won the house and is living in it, a tenant who is renting and the one who purchased it from a winner and is living in it' (Yeka Abado FW 065 ♀ Diary). In South

Africa, residents struggled with bills associated with state housing, and several resorted to informal and illegal accessing of electricity and water to overcome these issues.

State housing is also not uniform. It is distinguished by building design, for example, Ethiopian condominiums versus South African detached single-storeys. In better-designed Lufhereng (in Gauteng), properties are variously detached or semi-detached. In Hammonds Farm, structures are terraced, operating on two different floors. These architectural differences, including the absence or presence of a yard or space to garden, the presence or absence of communal spaces, etc., shaped social and economic relations. Furthermore, in various areas residents are moving into unfinished housing or sites that resemble construction zones, shaping their sense of safety and neighbourliness.

Peripheries also house those yet to qualify for state housing, are on long waiting lists, are awaiting resettlement or who are ineligible and are commonly living in less secure housing, including informal settlements such as Canelands and Coniston in eThekwini. Living informally can be a key avenue towards independence for young families. Tenancy security varies significantly, depending on local governance mechanisms (see Chapter 4), landownership and their historical legitimacy of claims to housing and plots of land. Included in this are former farm owners in the Addis cases, displaced from condominium sites, residing in villages or informal spaces. Wider urban-planning agendas and the policies of government shape residents' security: 'I think I'm living in an illegal house ... They say we're illegal and that we'll be evicted from the area, but now they are no longer coming to us' (Yeka Abado 037 AG ♂ Interview). Residents living in Waterworks in Gauteng experienced full-scale resettlement (shortly after our project completed) outside of the Gauteng province, as Waterworks was earmarked for commercial development. Residents were living in very strained conditions: 'We are struggling, hey. We are cold. We are very poor. We don't have anything here' (Waterworks R 14 ♀ Interview).

The status and social differentiation of tenants renting housing across all cases varied significantly. In Addis Ababa a common theme was the relative wealth of many tenants occupying or buying condominium apartments belonging to original owners. Across the cases in South Africa, this trend was less glaring, but some evidence pointed to wealthier tenants renting from beneficiaries of state housing. For example, NM in Hammonds Farm described a clear affluence disparity between those living there who'd relocated from informal settlements versus those who rent from owners; she points to car ownership as evidence of their prosperity (Hammonds Farm NM 08 ♀ Interview). Yet numerous renting residents in the Addis cases noted that the steady climb in rentals and the lack of price controls were influencing their decisions to relocate from the area.

The tenancy dimension of social relations in Addis evidences a clear line between owners and tenants. Tenants are mostly excluded from traditional social structures such as Iddir or neighbourhood associations such as the committees. Sometimes this is due to the exclusionary bylaws of such organisations and other times because of the lack of tenant protective policies, including setting a ceiling for rental prices, leading tenants to constantly move from one location to another in search of affordable housing. Either because of the prohibitive conditions or because of not having a long future, tenants often do not participate in social organisations.

Age

Multiple age-related differentiation is evident in African urban peripheries. Age and precarity were evident in Molweni, where numerous HIV/AIDs 'orphan' households were identified with very severe financial struggles because of years of poverty, a lack of social networks tied to having no parents and the disease stigma. Their poverty in contexts of state housing was distinctive. More broadly, children and youths living in peripheral spaces frequently lacked appropriate facilities. This trend was evident whether the area was one shaped by a vanguard logic, auto-constructed by residents or transitioning from a more rural setting to one with commonly attributed 'urban' services. This absence produces a key axis of differentiation, affecting the lives of their parents or carers and children very directly: 'We do not have schools. Our children walk a distance to school, they have to cross a very busy road and cars always hit them. My child, who is in high school, walk from school and back. They have to walk as a group because there are criminals' (Hammonds Farm NM 08 ♀ Interview). Constrained access to schools was echoed in Addis Ababa. For example, in parts of Tulu

Dimtu, residents described an absence of kindergartens, daycare centres or schools: 'I don't like that these things are not found in this area' (Tulu Dimtu MK 025 ♂ Diary). Children had incredibly early starts to access transport to schools elsewhere (Tulu Dimtu KT 026 ♂ Diary). Recreational facilities, particularly for children, are often absent or poorly invested in: 'there is no comfortable playground for children ... There are no recreational facilities for the youth' (Tulu Dimtu AG 056 ♀ Diary), and in Yeka Abado (Yeka Abado 020 ♀ Diary), TG states that children play in open spaces used for garbage disposal and toilets. A very high proportion of residents from South Africa noted that a lack of facilities resulted in excessive drug and alcohol misuse by young people as well as engagement with dangerous activities, including gambling: 'This is their sports' (Waterworks 02 KL ♀ Interview), and 'The situation in our area has become unbearable because our young children are smoking the drug called *Wunga*' (Waterloo BN 14 ♀ Diary). The twin challenges of boredom and crime, endemic to many urban peripheral spaces, often afflicting youths, are discussed in more detail later in this chapter.

Residents used a relational understanding of place, comparing it to their previous location, to determine difficulties associated with children's changed access. CC moved from Chiawelo to Lufhereng:

> in Chiawelo you could be free as a person. Everything, all the facilities were there. There were libraries, you understand? A child doesn't suffer ... [for sports fields] ... they must travel far to Doornkop to play (soccer). ... They must [cross] the street and you know that road is a killer road, hey. (Lufhereng CC 18 ♀ Interview)

Old age, physical limitations and disability emerge as a small but significant axis of difference in African urban peripheries, primarily a function of accessibility. State housing in peripheral urban cases in Addis and eThekwini adopts vertical living as a design choice. In Hammonds Farm, eThekwini, where housing is two-storey and arranged in rows, older and infirm residents struggle with steps and living on two floors (see Figure 6.6). The two bedrooms are located on the upper floor, with the kitchen and dining room as a single space alongside a small bathroom on the ground floor. In Addis all new condo housing is built vertically, with many not including elevators to support ease of movement within buildings (see Figure 5.2). Inflexible housing design which privileges density over form works well for able-bodied, younger residents who can maximise the layout and are less troubled by it. Housing is a blunt instrument where the delivery of a massive programme precludes taking difference into account. 'This house has too many steps; in my yard from the road there are stairs, and how can I climb those when I am old? I even sleep downstairs because I cannot afford to move up and down the stairs all the time' (Hammonds Farm NM 08 ♀ Interview).

UN-Habitat notes in relation to Addis' condominium allocation: 'There are no special provisions for the elderly or disabled, although if their name is drawn in the lottery they have first choice in choosing a ground floor condominium' (UN-Habitat, 2011: 26). However, Yeka Abado residents challenge this: 'the houses are assigned based on a lottery system, but unfortunately most of these elders are allocated a house above the fourth floor' (Yeka Abado TB 001 ♂ Interview), and KT witnessed older people navigating flights of stairs where handrails were missing and wondered 'for how long these elders can live under this condition' (Yeka Abado KT 017 ♂ Diary). However, being older afforded some benefits. In Waterworks, residents identified former older inhabitants (along with orphans) as being prioritised in state housing allocations (Waterworks EN 01 ♀ Diary and Interview). Finally, enhanced vulnerability to crime associated with being older was noted by various respondents, including from Winterveld, where older residents walking home at night are at particular risk of being robbed (Winterveld LM 16 ♂ Diary and Interview).

A final age-related axis of difference evident in the urban peripheries relates to employment opportunities. In South Africa, opportunities are often facilitated by councillors, often specifying age categories for labour allocation. This has severe impacts on those in the middle, too old to be considered for employment and too young to receive state pensions. This preferential allocation of work is also adopted by the private sector. This resident (Molweni PS 42 ♀ Interview) explained that in the developing area of Molweni, the recently constructed mall will only offer employment to work seekers under the age of thirty-five, precluding her as she was forty-two.

This tendency is corroborated by other Molweni residents, as well as in Lufhereng:

> the councillor has said that people over thirty-five cannot apply for certain jobs ... So what about those older? It means they won't work ... it is older women who are breadwinners; there aren't many fathers here. And if you look at that women you'll find she is not working. How must they live? (Lufhereng CC 18 ♀ Interview)

Age restrictions to jobs do not infer that work, when provided, is secure, permanent or well paid. The lack of meaningful employment for young people is discussed in Chapter 3 in this volume.

Income

Differentiation, as well as similarities, across African urban peripheries in terms of income or class were evident, with peripheral urban change fostering new forms of 'class' mobility and consumption, often a result of access to land and housing. In Addis Ababa, geographically segregated class differentiation is much more noticeable in peripheries as compared to central locations. Some renters of condominium housing in Addis Ababa – bonded homeowners in Protea Glen (Gauteng) at one end of the spectrum and homeowners occupying luxury housing in Legetafo (Addis) and Cresthome (eThekwini) at the other – represent a varied but higher-income group compared with most urban poor living in African urban peripheries. In Legetafo's Country Club Developers (CCD) complex, a resident describes her challenge of attracting hired help to this wealthy neighbourhood, who viewed it as a 'rural', hard-to-access area, but she confirmed securing the residence of three 'hired helps' on her property, illustrating wealth and property size (Yeka Abado M 100 ♀ Diary). In Protea Glen, for example, access to work is mixed, but the area's development and mall have provided employment for some, while others commute to Johannesburg's central business district (CBD) or Randberg.

In areas of state housing in both South Africa and Ethiopia, the developmentalist intentions of the housing programmes often precluded the very poor either through the prohibitive conditions and costs of the mortgage required (Addis) or the costs of living in state housing (both countries), as noted above. Residents' employment status and dependency ratios were critical. In Addis, access to housing through a lottery system requires formal employment, with unemployed residents automatically disqualified. Much employment was, however, tied to the construction industry, at first prominent but since in decline, meaning condominium costs were unsustainable. Single-headed households with children and unemployed young adults struggled desperately with new costs for water, electricity, rates and mortgage repayments: 'On the one hand having a house is good, but when you finally get a house but nothing to eat then it's difficult. This is not easily solvable. ... Job activity is weak, but the fact that I've a house I can call my own is a good thing' (Yeka Abado ED 002 ♀ Interview). In South Africa, access to state housing presupposes a lack of regular waged employment, with beneficiaries commonly seeking employment or economically inactive. Noting the prohibitive costs of services, residents questioned who this new housing was really for:

> I do not know [why electricity is so expensive] because I do not have many things that uses electricity; the only thing that is always on is the fridge. I do not know whether it is because these houses were built for nurses, and the nurses did not want these houses because they were too small for them. (Hammonds Farm NM 08 ♀ Interview)

Peripheries are sites of change, sometimes tied to state housing projects or speculative developments, fostering differentiation: A female informal village dweller in Addis Ababa noted: 'Other than the government the ones that are benefiting are those who are economically able to buy and sell land or construct [a] building in the city. The country has become a country for the rich' (Yeka Abado FG 047 ♀ Interview). Rising costs in the urban peripheries, particularly in state housing, was evidenced by survey data, where, for example, 53.8 per cent of residents in Lufhereng and 80 per cent in Rethabiseng note living costs have increased. The provision of public housing inserts residents into a neoliberal state, particularly for those previously living informally confronted with new formal payments for water and electricity, etc. This produces new forms of income inequalities, particularly because residents no longer have the flexibility to practise various livelihoods as they may have done in informal settlements.

Across all informal settlements and farming areas in the urban peripheries, the extent of poverty is palpable and persistent. The lack of accessible and appropriately paid work opportunities, significant costs of living, particularly for transport, electricity, water and food, and partial access to minimal welfare support (in South Africa) explain much of this trend. A northern eThekwini resident notes: 'We are just staying here because there is nothing we can do; we are swimming in poverty' (Canelands SM 17 ♀ Diary). In Winterveld, residents detail reliance on patchy feeding schemes and an inability to survive on existing incomes due to high transportation costs and poor access to services and shops. In Waterworks a young woman describes her inability to complete her education: 'I was supposed to go to school; well that's bad for me because I don't have money to take a taxi or even the train – what a shame. I was supposed to submit an assignment; well I didn't do it on purpose – the situation didn't allow me to' (Waterworks EN 01 ♀ Diary). Generally, residents detail food insecurity, health complications, stress, environmental discomfort (cold and unhealthy living conditions), foregone opportunities, educational curtailment and unrealised dreams. While urban peripheries may be sites of speculation for some, the majority live in dire poverty.

Gender

Gender shapes differentiation in urban peripheries in multiple ways, with variations in gender norms and expectations context-dependent. Both the Ethiopian and South African housing programmes include gender as an important factor in the policy intentions of the programmes. In Addis Ababa the condominium lottery system ensures the first '30 per cent quota is drawn for women, then the remaining 70 per cent for men and women together' (UN-Habitat, 2011: 26), although Planel and Bridonneau note that this was only utilised earlier in the programme (2017: 28), and high levels of female-headed household poverty precludes most from the housing programme (UN-Habitat, 2011: 40). In northern eThekwini around 70 per cent of housing in Hammonds Farm was allocated to women (Meth *et al.*, 2018), explainable in relation to historic inequities in housing allocation and the ownership of land and housing in both racial and gendered terms. Access to housing (state, informal, etc.) can facilitate independence for women, particularly in contexts of relationship breakdown: 'I used to live in [my ex-husband's family's] compound shared by many and with no privacy. And when I compare this to that I really like [this]. ... I'm very happy. I and all the children are happy about this decision. You can live your own life here' (Yeka Abado SHT 003 ♀ Interview). For residents who may lack confidence in maintenance skills, state housing can reduce the demands associated with informal housing, shaping positivity and independence:

> I am happy about the house because in my previous area, since I do not have a man, I used to climb up the roof when it is raining to repair the sail roof, and if the house break down I used to mix mud with water and patch it up. I no longer do that. ... I did everything for myself. (Hammonds Farm NM 08 ♀ Interview)

Experiences of work and (un)employment vary significantly across all the cases, with gendered trends arising in relation to localised labour markets, sensitive to movement and urban change. More generally, work experiences were often ubiquitous. For example, a dominant concern in both Addis Ababa case study areas, for men and women, was the hindrance that distance and lack of affordable transport posed for accessing work. However, urban change in the peripheries produced gendered consequences. In Hammonds Farm, eThekwini, many men have lost employment because of their relocation from Ocean Drive Inn informal settlement, where piecemeal construction work was available. In Lufhereng some women previously living in better-located informal housing, near better-off Lenasia, have lost access to domestic worker jobs as transport is unaffordable, compounded by very low wages. Domestic labour was undertaken by some women living in Waterworks informal settlement, but on very low wages, around ZAR1,200–1,500 per month (Waterworks KL 02 ♀ Interview), and now that this settlement has been eradicated and all residents relocated, it can be assumed this source of work has ended or that their commuting times have risen.

The gendering of construction and manual work shaped local labour markets. For many living in the peripheries of Addis Ababa, the prior availability of construction work privileged the employment of men, although informal work for women (selling food, etc.) was evident. Similarly, in Canelands informal settlement, located near factories, employment was often male-oriented: 'There are jobs the females fail to do ... and many jobs such as construction need the males ... We cannot carry the heavy stuff' (Canelands ZC 07 ♀ Interview). Gendered expectations over roles and responsibilities of domestic versus paid employment were evident in particular peripheral contexts. In Winterveld a young male participant referred to 'the old law' which fostered gender inequality, as women are expected to remain at home looking after the children while men seek work 'in cities'. He notes how this constructs women as 'single parents because males go and look for jobs in cities and do not come back home' (Winterveld VK 37 ♂ Diary). Multiple residents in South African peripheries referred to young women turning to sex work to secure an income or access resources in view of limited alternatives.

Anxiety about crime and violence, and concerns about the safety of residents across all urban peripheries, dominated data collection in many cases. Many of these concerns were gendered, with women expressing significant concerns about the impact of crime and their fear thereof in shaping their wellbeing and mobility and indicating how gendered vulnerability is tied to women's roles and work. At Waterworks informal settlement, numerous residents reported on the rape and murder of women locally and stressed women's vulnerability, including when collecting firewood for cooking in 'the veld' (Waterworks KL 02 ♀ Interview). Elsewhere, similar stories emerge: 'And when it gets dark since there are no street lights we're forced to use our mobile phone lights. It's scary at night; women cannot go out that late – there are gangsters' (Yeka Abado ED 002 ♀ Interview); 'Women living alone are especially vulnerable to being attacked by those smoking nyaope and pash pash' (Winterveld MM 22 ♀ Interview). Women spoke explicitly about their fears of rape and sexual violence, noting how this impeded their ability to access services and employment. In Hammonds Farm, women felt unable to walk to the nearby airport to access work due to safety concerns and a lack of feasible transportation. In Lufhereng, mothers were concerned about the safety of their daughters attempting to access a library as they had to rely on a bridge for access. The bridge was noted as a risk in terms of rape.

Social differentiation

African urban peripheries are sites of protracted and hasty transformation, as well as significant demographic churn alongside relative stability. Migration into and out of the peripheries is significant across all cases, sometimes for purposes of securing land or housing but also tied to jobseeking and livelihood opportunities within and beyond the peripheries. Rapid demographic change, often more organic in nature, has long been a feature of informal housing but is amplified in new areas of state housing. Such transformations shape social relations in varied ways and cut across the varying social differences detailed above.

The desirability or undesirability of these constant and magnified shifts are often expressed in relation to past lived social relations, further shaping future relations. There, the shift from communal to individualised living arrangements, leaving behind customary ways of living together, produced new (often compromised) social relations, often referenced as a disruption of social ties: 'Everyone lives behind closed doors. There is no social life' (Yeka Abado TB 001 ♂ Interview). Loneliness and isolation were dominant themes:

> Our way of life is private to ourselves. For example, there is no culture of inviting and drinking coffee with neighbors and getting close to neighbors ... We Ethiopians have a culture of eating and drinking with other people, and we feel very sad that we don't even have people to talk to us. (Yeka Abado S 099 ♂ Diary)

These sentiments are tied to the politics and practice of housing allocation and new housing design – 'We all come from different places with different backgrounds and characteristics, and so it takes time to adjust to that' (Tulu Dimtu DT 029 ♀ Interview) – and are matched across all the South African cases too, where a similar randomness of residential patterning arises, producing similar concerns. Places of origin and their housing form shaped social relations and othering of residents. In Waterloo a resident declares those who've moved from informal settlements as having 'no goals', contrasting them with those moving there from townships who 'need to move forward' looking for a brighter future where they live in a good house and pay for electricity (Waterloo DN 23 ♂ Interview). In Tulu Dimtu, condominium homeowners express anxiety about the unknowability and hence 'danger' of tenants: 'We don't know what kind of person would move in ... This is the major source of our concern' (Tulu Dimtu H 008 ♂ Interview).

At times these shifts are also seen as opportunities to break away from controlling social structures and norms or as opportunities to build relations and social structures anew. The temporalities of urban peripheries are key here, with many residents noting changes such as improvements over time, including in terms of social bonds, neighbourliness and social relationships.

> Today is Genbot 1, a day celebrated by Orthodox Christians. People celebrate this day with neighbours. I have been celebrating this day with neighbours for three years now (three years since I moved here); and we had warm celebrations. The number of households celebrating this day has increased. (Tulu Dimtu Y 054 ♀ Diary)

> This community is very supportive. They take [care] of you; even when there's a death in one's family they give you donations and help out. (Waterworks EN 001 ♀ Interview)

The narrative of broken social structures versus freedom from these is also related to age group. For most young adults or older children, it means both freedom from social norms but also declining friendships along with a lack of services. For the older generation it is mostly expressed in terms of a lack of social structures due to destroyed social ties. The problems related to insecurity can also be linked to the lack of strong, place-based social relations and accountability. Similarly, social relations are important factors for income generation. Broken social ties and the support that comes with them means the loss of income opportunity or a physical distance from it. Mostly, those affected are the ones coming from central locations, who are at times dependent on the informal sector. In contrast, for others migrating into the city, the less established social relations provide an opportunity to move into a relatively anonymous urban space and potentially enter the job market it has to offer.

Within informal settlements too, histories of location and conflict and migrant status alongside current circumstances shape social relations. The data is replete with accounts of jealousy, scorn, unkindness and mistrust, but also significant dependence, reliance, support and rallying to assist those who are suffering.

Boredom in the peripheries[1]

Linked to the accounts of social isolation detailed above, the description of areas of the periphery as 'boring' was evident, particularly for those whose analysis of the region was tied to their relative experiences of living elsewhere. This label is briefly considered before turning to some reflection on the state of boredom, typifying life for many in the urban peripheries.

Categorisations of particular urban spaces as boring cut across a variety of urban peripheral spaces and logics, including in areas that were vanguard spaces, inherited peripheries and transitioning. The categorisations often rested on the lack of social activity, the absence or limited supply of urban services, the quietness of spaces, the more isolated nature of state-provided housing, which had shifted everyday life indoors compared with previous informal living, and their relative isolation from more vibrant urban centres. In Yeka Abado the failure to provide comprehensive leisure facilities shapes residents experiences: 'There are no recreational areas. Especially my wife is bored of staying at home. We both like going to the cinema, but they are now far' (Yeka Abado TA 040 ♂ Interview). The sense of spatial disconnection characterises peripheral places as boring:

> the GPS does not find our place so it's like we've been forgotten ... there are no tarred roads; the dust from the cars comes into the house. The house is always dusty, it's boring ... we [receive] information late, even the letters from the post, they come [late] ... everything is late. (Winterveld MK 18 ♀ Interview)

In Ekangala the lack of business in the area makes resident EB describe the place as 'boring' (Ekangala EB 01♀ Interview), but being boring can shift over time as areas consolidate and 'improve' in terms of urban qualities. Waterloo in Durban has transformed significantly over time, and this female resident notes how urban changes shape her perception of the place: 'I came here in 2005, and it was a boring area. The houses were not good, and I did not recognise that Waterloo will become beautiful and my real home' (Waterloo MM 12 ♀ Interview). Boring is relational, frequently contrasted with former residences or spaces experienced through travel or work. This resident had moved from Debre Zeyt (a town south of Addis) to a cooperative house in Tulu Dimtu and claimed Tulu Dimtu in contrast was boring: 'Here the neighbourhood is so quiet; we're not yet used to it, and we don't have friends' (Tulu Dimtu HW 055 ♂ Interview).

The relationality of boring as a label was also evident *within* the urban peripheries themselves. Particular parts of the periphery were deemed 'more boring' by residents than others, and this linked both to its material features but also to particular residents' individualised comparable experiences, i.e. which places they put into contrast. Residents also recognised how fluid this perception was: 'Living in Lufhereng can sometimes be boring, but if you are not here for some time, you start to miss this place' (Lufhereng BD 29 ♂ Diary). Being boring was also a function of particular built forms in the periphery. In Addis in Yeka Abado, a resident linked condominium living with being boring, noting: 'When you live in a condominium you don't see many new things. Everything is similar and repetitive' (Yeka Abado TB 001 ♂ Diary).

Boredom was a frequent emotional register for residents living in the urban periphery. Tied to the 'boring' qualities of place outlined above, boredom was produced through a combination of these realities alongside very high levels of unemployment and poverty, reducing what residents could participate in on a daily basis and what they could achieve. Mains (2017: 39) argues in relation to young men in urban Ethiopia that '[b]oredom is not only the sensation of having too much time; it is also the sense that the passage of time and day-to-day experience are not meaningful because they do not conform to expectations of progress'. Mains shows how this can be erased during times of employment or education but that a disjuncture remains between expected futures and 'lived experiences' (Mains, 2017: 39). This argument resonates strongly with findings across urban peripheries in Ethiopia and South Africa too. Winterveld in Gauteng is an example of an inherited periphery produced through apartheid measures and struggling to offer residents any benefits aside from cheap land. It is a space of significant unemployment and spatial dislocation: '[it] is boring, this place, it is just boring; there's nothing, there's no work; you just sit, only you clean, you eat and then you sleep only – it's just boring' (Winterveld LM 15 ♀ Interview).

Reference to the repetitive qualities of the lives of the urban poor means that boredom is a metaphor for poverty in the urban peripheries, but as Mains (2017) notes, it has a particular significance for young people who dream of securing employment and progressing their life ambitions. In her diary, answering what it is like to live there, this young woman from Ekangala ultimately questions herself in view of her experiences of boredom: 'Boring, because I am doing the same thing every day and seeing the same people, telling you same story always; nothing changes, or is it me – I don't know' (Dark City Ekangala ST 01 ♀ Diary). The repetitive nature of everyday life in the urban peripheries linked to being distanced from everything else is expressed several times in the Addis cases. Living within so-called boring spaces can, however, prove restful for some. MK, living in Winterveld, identifies age as shaping place perception: 'Yes it's quiet here, there is no noise because there are no taverns ... but it's not a cool place. It's a place where let me say old people would love to live because they love quiet places' (Winterveld MK 18 ♀ Interview).

The intersection between youth, boredom and unemployment is frequently cited as an explanation for high levels of substance abuse, including drugs and alcohol and youth engagement in crime. This chapter moves now to examine crime in the African urban peripheries.

Crime and violence in the African urban peripheries

Narratives of crime and violence

Significant insecurity shaped the daily lives of residents, and anxiety about a lack of safety dominated many of their diary and interview accounts. It was only in areas of Molweni in western eThekwini where some residents (although not others) claimed crime levels to be relatively low. There, residents suspected this would change rapidly as new transport routes through the settlement meant it was far more accessible to criminals. In Addis Ababa, narratives of crime were less dominant than in South Afican cities and usually referred to petty criminal practices such as theft rather than violent crime (such as rape, murder, assault), as is more common in South Africa. However, residents in Yeka Abado and Tulu Dimtu did express concerns about their lack of safety.

In Yeka Abado the theft of clothing hanging outside was frequently reported as well as theft of vehicle parts: 'Well theft is very common. I have lost my car's side mirror three times' (Yeka Abado TB 001 ♂ Interview). Residents identified the G7 area as specifically vulnerable to crime; however, the region's relative safety was frequently noted: one resident (Yeka Abado AT 021 ♀ Diary) states that she likes her neighbourhood; everything is peaceful there. By contrast Tulu Dimtu appeared to struggle with more crime, and the range of criminal practices is more varied here than Yeka Abado, although once again theft of washing was cited by several residents. Theft of construction materials, firewood, cables, water containers and the vandalism of shops were noted in this area, and robbery from persons was reported to be a problem in the past, when residents first moved to the area (Tulu Dimtu BF 087 ♀ Interview). Of note in Addis Ababa, very few residents living peripherally described a significant fear of crime within their area, and references to reduced mobility as a result of fear were sparse, although the gendered dimensions of this were observed: 'There are no street lights at night, and I get concerned for women not to be attacked going around in the evening' (Tulu Dimtu G 078 ♂ Interview).

In contrast, in South Africa, fear of crime, and fear as a result of crime, impact wellbeing and residents' freedom of movement and confidence. GA from Protea Glen describes how being stabbed in the face by a thief left her traumatised and unable to work: 'I started living in fear and that left me jobless; even now whenever I get a job that knock[s] off at night [I] am scared' (Protea Glen GA 04 ♀ Diary). And in Lufhereng this resident observed that 'It's not safe my child because at night when you sleep you thank God when you wake up because when you wake up you'll hear that they broke into such and such a place' (Lufhereng EM 15 ♀ Interview).

Sexual violence, and the threat thereof, littered residents' accounts within South Africa. In Hammonds Farm, eThekwini, the rape of women and children was cited, with horrendous accounts of violence on the part of men:

> There was an incidence of a child rape and thrown in the forest. They were thinking that girl is dead. One community member found that girl in the forest crying. That girl was staying with the mother and granny. The granny left the child while she was sleeping to visit her neighbour. The man went to her house, and he searched the money in the bag for that granny. Unfortunately he did not get it, and he saw the child who were sleeping in the bed and he raped the child and beat her with the bottle. That child faint, and he took to the forest and leave her because he thought she was dead. When they asked

the child who beat and rape her, she didn't know him. The family didn't find the person who raped the child. (Hammonds Farm NM 04 ♀ Diary)

This same participant and others detailed further stories of rape by a security guard who abused his power and possession of a weapon in Hammonds Farm to enact sexual violence. His case made it to the courts (Hammonds Farm NM 04 ♀ Diary), but residents had to protest when he was granted bail. This protest proved successful, and residents can walk along the road 'without hav[ing] any problem' now (Hammonds Farm ZN 11 ♀ Diary).

Processes shaping crime and violence

Explanations for why crime and violence were prevalent and increasing but also in some cases managed focused on youth boredom and unemployment, excessive drinking and drug use and the weakness and failings of security services alongside reliance on resident-run patrol groups.

Drug abuse was perceived as a core explanation for high levels of crime, particularly in South Africa. Residents detailed the impacts of crime on their neighbourhoods: 'nyaope is destroying Protea Glen' (Protea Glen CC 08 ♂ Diary), and in Winterveld and Ekangala drug abuse was directly associated with high crime rates (Winterveld TN 35 ♀ Interview; Winterveld VK 37 ♂ Diary). Although anxiety about drugs and the impact on insecurity pervaded all South African cases, residents' accounts were often empathetic, recognising the humanity of young drug users but also the risks they posed:

> I am appealing/requesting that the Council eradicates/reduces nyaope (drug abuse only). The nyaope addicts, they are criminals because they steal, they are house breakers and they steal clothes on the washing lines. It's sad because they are still young people/youths. If you try to intervene, and if they find you, you will be killed. (Protea Glen WM 20 ♂ Diary)

The lack of sporting facilities, employment and areas for recreation were all noted as fostering drug use as well as criminal activities. In Hammonds Farm, unemployment and the lack of jobs on offer (Hammonds Farm LS 07 ♀ Interview) and eventual hunger were flagged as the primary drivers of crime in the area. One resident described how his friend was murdered without any explanation other than '*indlala ibanga ulaka*' (hunger causes anger) (Hammonds Farm BR 03 ♂ Diary). Interestingly, he does query this lack of employment given the settlement's relatively good location: 'we stay near Umdloti Beach and Isibaya Casino, but we are not employed' (Hammonds Farm BR 03 ♂ Diary).

Criticisms of the police were abundant, referencing their lack of capacity, distances to the nearest station and their limited effectiveness. Residents complained about lax arrest procedures with criminals bailed rapidly, police corruption and the ease with which police are bribed. In various cases residents turned to informal or local procedures and practices to manage crime. These were at times reminiscent of vigilante gangs managing crime and violence in local neighbourhoods (discussed further below) but also revealed more formalised engagement in Community Policing Forums and also community groups cooperating to respond to crime. For example, in Tulu Dimtu, Addis, through the establishment of a condominium residents' committee, which collected money from each household, the community were organising a security guard service and fencing (Tulu Dimtu HK 008 ♂ Interview). In addition some of the committee groups have specific security groups taking turns to patrol in the evenings. In Lufhereng, residents described the operation of 'night guards' organised by the local political party African National Congress (ANC), who protect the area (Lufhereng BD 29 ♂ Interview).

Peripherality, crime, violence and producing security

Being geographically peripheral is significant for practices and experiences of crime, violence and also the production of (in)security. The scale of settlements and their history and patterns of urbanisation and development are arguably central to crime trends. In Molweni, South Africa, identified as a 'transitioning periphery', crime rates were argued to be relatively low, and residents reported theft and hijacking of vehicles as typical but were less concerned about more violent crimes. The area has a long history of residence, with less rapid in-migration compared with other peripheral sites, particularly those built through the logics of the vanguard or inherited periphery. Informal, vigilante-style responses to crime persist in this context, and residents argue this is a key factor in shaping the lower crime levels. Here, community knowledge generated through longer residence and a familiarity with neighbours supported lower crime rates:

> in my neighbourhood, it is safe and I can walk even at ... midnight. No one will stop me on the road. There is a low crime rate in my area. If I am not mistaken, we had only one thief at KwaNogxaza. If you come home and your stuff is missing, you just go to his home and ask to bring it back. It is easy to get your stuff back. (Molweni VN 29 ♂ Interview)

In contrast, Winterveld and the Greater Ekangala area, both examples of an inherited periphery, are cited as suffering exceptionally high crime levels by residents living there. Some residents refer to Winterveld's history as a site for refugees as an explanation for this, but others cite high levels of drug abuse and unemployment as causes of crime. In Winterveld a significant number of residents live in informal structures acquired relatively easily as land is readily available. Residents living informally were particularly anxious about insecurity, and this reduced their mobility and freedom, particularly at night: 'They [my children] know that this place is not safe because when it's 6 p.m., I need to make sure they're in the house' (Winterveld AD 02 ♀ Interview). In Ekangala the informal area of Phumekaya had mixed stories about vulnerability, with residents using whistles to alert neighbours, and it was in the other areas of Ekangala, Rethabiseng and Dark City where a cacophony of stories and anxieties about very violent crime were articulated. In both Winterveld and Ekangala, rape was mentioned frequently, as was the presence of violent gangs.

The absence of police stations or the long distances required to access one were frequently identified in the South African cases and Addis Ababa. Again, peripheral location and investment in housing rather than other facilities mean services are frequently lacking in the urban peripheries, and costly and lengthy journeys are required. Residents believed this absence of policing services fostered crime: 'Now when you cry and no one comes, he knows that the police will come after a long time. He'll do everything they want to do until they leave' (Lufhereng DM 16 ♀ Interview). Residents in Lufhereng were required to travel if they wanted to officially report a crime: 'They want you to go to Dobsonville yourself and go open a case. They don't take a case from the street; you have to be the one who takes a taxi and goes to open a case for them to take you seriously' (Lufhereng VZ 20 ♀ Interview). Residents there believed that 'this place need[s a] small police station where we can report cases' (Lufhereng BD 29 ♂ Diary).

However, where police stations were installed (again potentially evidence of a transitioning periphery), residents did celebrate this and cited a subsequent reduction in crime; for example, in Molweni, including in the underinvested area of Nogxaza, the opening of a new police station near Dinabakubo High School was noted (Molweni NS 38 ♀ Interview). This was within walking distance of residents' homes, meaning 'Living in this area has become safer' and that the police's support for the elderly and their safety was evident (Molweni NS 5 ♀ Diary) and impacted on crime positively (Molweni NN 37 ♀ Interview). Similarly, in Tulu Dimtu, Addis, the establishment of a police station and the subsequent presence of the police in the area meant 'conditions improved' (Tulu Dimtu BA 032 ♂ Diary).

Infrastructural changes shape security and insecurity and reflect urban changes in vanguard, transitional and speculative peripheries. The introduction of street lights (Tulu Dimtu BA 032 ♂ Diary) improved safety: 'It's only recently that the street lights are on at night; before that when it gets a little dark they would attack people, especially women; this, however, is now better' (Tulu Dimtu BA 030 ♂ Interview). The positive impacts of street lighting are evident in Rethabiseng too. Residents praise their introduction and effects on lowering of crime (Rethabiseng NH 03 ♂ Interview; Rethabiseng MB 11 ♀ Interview). Similarly, the provision of CCTV in the area, and security cameras on tower structures along the main arterial road in Molweni (Inanda Road), have arguably reduced car hijackings (Molweni SG 22 ♂ Diary; Molweni TD 28 ♂ Diary): 'That camera watching the whole Molweni.' Lighting in buildings also enhances security, including shop lights which make residents feel safe when walking around at night (Tulu Dimtu KF 012 ♂ Interview).

The fencing of areas, as plots and boundaries become established and enforced, is used by residents to foster security, with those in Yeka Abado noting that residents worked communally to secure areas as a result of the threat of crime (Yeka Abado TB 001 ♂ Interview).

Conclusions: social differences, boredom and crime

This chapter charts numerous axes of social differentiation within African urban peripheries. Integral to these are the nature and pace of urban change, producing new differentiations and compounding existing inequalities. Peripheral spaces are critical sites of opportunity variously shaped by all peripheral logics outlined in the Introduction, in terms of access to land and housing, but often resting on locational compromise, particularly in terms of supporting meaningful social relations and functions. Here we see differences with inner-city experiences. Geographic peripherality and the sparseness of good-quality, affordable service and infrastructural provision amplify differences tied to age, gender, ethnicity and class. At the same time, boredom as a metaphor for living peripherally is shaped by the frequent absence of urban qualities alongside the persistence of poverty and spatial isolation. Experienced predominantly by youths, the rise in anxiety over drug use and consequent impacts on crime and violence are very real concerns for urban peripheral spaces.

Note

1 We acknowledge the ideas and contributions of Dr Tatenda Mukwedeya to this section on boredom. It was he who identified this as a critical social reality of the urban peripheries.

11

Supermarkets, retail and consumption in peripheral areas

Sarah Charlton and Meseret Kassahun Desta

In what we term 'vanguard' peripheries, state-driven housing dominates in generally large-scale and relatively recently built neighbourhoods. Residents' accounts of life in these areas in their diaries, interviews and photographs were striking in their reflections on the experiential and practical aspects of shops and shopping, both in these peripheral localities and elsewhere. In this chapter we discuss experiences of a seemingly mundane or routine activity which is significant in shaping daily lives and is at times profoundly experienced. We draw mainly on material from the vanguard developments of Yeka Abado and Tulu Dimtu on the edges of Addis Ababa, and in South Africa, Waterloo/Hammonds Farm in eThekwini and Lufereng and Protea Glen in Gauteng, although we also make brief reference to other areas. We set respondents' views against the differing approaches to facilitating neighbourhood retail and commerce reflected in the Ethiopian condominium developments as compared with the South African state-funded housing projects, and in relation to a broad assessment of control of and opportunity for retail activity in each context. While both countries' ambitious, large-scale national housing programmes share government-subsidised, standardised design and an emphasis on homeownership, not only their built form but the inclusion of non-residential land uses such as retail and businesses in the multistorey condominium areas occurs very differently to that in the low-rise developments of individual houses in South African cities. These differences shape residents' experiences in various ways, but there are also similarities in the shared nature of urban-edge localities.

The chapter further discusses how big supermarket chains in South Africa, and large markets in Ethiopia, as well as local neighbourhood stores in the vanguard peripheries in both contexts, impact on experiences and imaginaries. Beyond the issue of needing to buy affordable fresh food conveniently, residents' stories are also about employment, leisure and, in the case of South Africa, welfare services linked to retail outlets, highlighting the significance of shops and shopping in daily lives. In South Africa, 'big shops' (in effect chain supermarkets with financial muscle) are prized by residents and promoted in policy and practice, though significantly critiqued by some analysts. Our data shows the direct material effects of these supermarkets but also their emotional pull. In Ethiopia, residents of condominium developments value the small-scale retail that establishes on the ground floors of strategically located residential buildings, but they also complain of limitations and the need to travel elsewhere for better prices and range. The chapter shows how these diverse situations impact on consumer convenience as well as localised economic opportunity, and how this is heightened by the peripheral locations of our cases where alternative service providers are scarce and the transport options for accessing choice elsewhere are limited, costly and time-consuming. We start by briefly outlining the relevant economic structure of each context.

The retail context in South Africa and Ethiopia

As we show below, our South African respondents privilege access to large supermarkets, but in South Africa there is extensive critique of big stores establishing in poorer neighbourhoods, with arguments that they crowd out small retailers or cap their profits, stifle local entrepreneurial activity and drive up food prices, while also short-changing agricultural producers (Ledger, 2016). However, while the 'supermarket revolution' in the Global South has altered food supply chains and food access, effects are argued to be more complex than initially assumed: these include, for example, predictions that informal food retailers will not disappear but 'compete, complement and coexist' with formal food economies (Crush, 2014: 550). In South Africa, where informal food retailers hardly existed until the collapse of apartheid and thereafter 'grew very much in tandem' with supermarkets (Crush, 2014: 550), indications are that poor people now shop across diverse forms of food suppliers, including supermarkets (Crush *et al.*, 2012, in Crush, 2014).

Since the ending of apartheid, retail-led development – mainly in the form of shopping centres, which are generally dependent on one or two large supermarket tenants – has been advocated as a strategy to aid economically deprived township areas. The impact of these retailers and shopping complexes on neighbourhoods arguably needs specific and contextualised assessment to tease out positive as well as negative aspects (Adatia, 2010). Nevertheless, there is widespread recognition that in South Africa the 'Big Four' supermarket chains dominate 'entire value chains' in the country, providing 'much more than a "basket of goods" at a specific price' but many other services as well and an 'overall shopping experience' (Das Nair, 2018: 315, 318).

Small entrepreneurs struggle to enter this grocery retail space in any significant way, a situation paralleled also in manufacturing, where production underpinned by big capital penetrates every part of the country, reflecting the highly concentrated nature of the economy. Illustrating this economic structure, Philip (2018: 145) makes the point that by the end of apartheid, although South Africa was in some ways a developing country, there was little opportunity for ordinary people to sell home-made goods: 'a highly centralised corporate sector was already mass producing almost every manufactured or agro-processed product that poor people consume, with distribution systems reaching the most remote corners of the country'. Yet at the same time as they shape this highly restrictive entrepreneurial space, which exists alongside massive unemployment, shopping malls – the epitome of retail centralisation – arguably hold a certain allure for many people, including those without the purchasing power to be a consumer in them. Along with attractions such as relative quietness and a pleasant ambient temperature, malls and big shops can represent places of aspiration, an escape from a hard reality (Heer, 2017) and sites of recreation, as also demonstrated elsewhere on the continent (Eduful and Eduful, 2021).

In the ways described above, the structure of the South African economy is notably different to a number of other countries in the Global South, including Ethiopia. Although rapid transformation to a more industrialised economy has been dramatically underway in Ethiopia in recent decades, this overlays a strongly agricultural economy with a small manufacturing sector (Shiferaw, 2017). There is a much more localised and fine-grained set of economic activities, which include small-scale manufacturing and retail, than in South Africa. In particular the structure of the food retail economy differs: there are no multinational supermarkets in the country as this type of foreign investment was prohibited by government under the Ethiopian People's Revolutionary Democratic Front (EPRDF), which instead assisted in the establishment of various forms of cooperatives, some specifically aimed at shielding and aiding the consumer (Aseffa et al., 2016; Gebremariam, 2020).

Cooperatives are 'user owned, user controlled and user benefited organisations' which work to support the economic wellbeing of their members (Meniga, 2015: 351). Existing across a wide range of rural and urban sectors and activities, cooperatives are also to be found in grocery retail. In this sector, in addition to and alongside cooperatives, data from a 2012 study found that in Addis Ababa there is in fact a noticeable growth of privatised shops (Aseffa et al., 2016). This includes 'modern retail outlets' which have self-service, one or more cash tills and a wider variety of products, though without many of the characteristics of the large supermarket chains increasingly found in other developing countries (Woldu et al., 2013). However, the market share of this 'domestic modern private retail sector' is very low (Aseffa et al., 2016: 92). While these shops offer valuable goods, their prices are high relative to cooperatives, where lower food costs reflect the benefits of subsidisation and price controls. But the same study (2012) noted the disadvantages of cooperatives to include unreliability of product supply, rationing and the need to queue for purchases (Aseffa et al., 2016: 92). They were also highly politicised under the EPRDF; for example, the 'Urban Consumers Cooperatives' created in 2008, due to fears about political unrest following steep rises in basic food prices, were effectively controlled by the ruling party. Thus, party loyalty played an increasing role in relation to access to goods in the EPRDF period (Gebremariam, 2020). Alongside these two forms of retail are a variety of other sellers of food, including grain mills and 'informal microsuppliers'. Outdoor food markets are also significant for both fresh and processed food, sometimes acting as both wholesalers supplying shops as well as direct retailers to households (Woldu et al., 2013). Cooperatives tend to dominate in certain grocery supplies and not others, being strong in the areas of wheat, sugar and oil supply for example, whereas fruit and vegetables tend to be sold in small shops (Woldu et al., 2013).

Overall, the food retail environment in Ethiopia is fundamentally different to that of South Africa, with the government heavily present in intervening and supporting food distribution and prices in the former and an extremely strong presence of private capital in a free-market system in the latter. In Ethiopia the 'supermarket revolution' is not yet evident, with consumers 'not able yet to benefit from the one-stop shopping that might reduce consumers' search costs significantly' (Woldu et al., 2013: 12). The Ethiopian Development Research Institute concludes that one of the consequences of the current system includes that the country 'might be missing out on investments by large (potentially multinational) retailers ... [which] ... might be able to increase consumer choice, ensure stability in supply, allow for one-stop shopping, and deliver products at cheaper prices because of the economies of scale of these large retailers' (Assefa et al., 2016: 92). With this as a broad contextual background, we now turn to how retail activity in particular is incorporated in the South African and Ethiopian housing developments that make up selected vanguard peripheries.

Retail activity in South African housing developments

In South Africa the bulk of government-subsidised housing in the late- and post-apartheid eras takes the form of houses for ownership in newly laid out suburbs, with land uses formally planned and administered. These developments, and similar ones in Addis Ababa, are vanguard peripheries in the sense of being led by government planning and investment, at a level of scale, with the ambition of encouraging or driving complementary development (Meth et al., 2021a). For diverse reasons, in South Africa these developments are often on the edges of urban areas (such as our case of Lufhereng on the outer edge of Soweto, Johannesburg; see Chapter 2) or in detached or satellite localities originally motivated by apartheid logics (such as Ekangala in Gauteng – see Chapter 3 – or Waterloo in eThekwini). Within these generally low-rise areas on the peripheries, often consisting of single- or double-storey detached or semi-detached houses along with some walk-up apartment buildings in newer developments, formal retail and business activities are intended to locate on designated sites. Businesses apply to establish on these sites, though there is often a time lag of several years before the area is sufficiently attractive to them, such as occurred even in the peripheral but relatively connected flagship mixed-income development of Cosmo City in Johannesburg (Turok, 2015).

Within this approach, small-scale and home-based businesses on or near residential sites are largely not encouraged or planned for, although some neighbourhoods provide blanket zoning rights for certain low-impact activities provided residential usage remains dominant. This lack of facilitation of small-scale economic activity is a noticeable gap in planning relative to evident needs. However, even if not facilitated or permitted, retail and service activity arises informally in different ways, such as people selling basic foodstuffs and groceries from 'spazas' (micro-shops, sometimes within houses) or from superettes (slightly bigger establishments, often in a separate building and with refrigeration permitting a wider range of products), as well as hair salons, creches, internet cafes and taverns/drinking establishments within residential yards (see Figure 11.1). These businesses can be a response to a lack of alternative shopping opportunities, along with the high cost of transport to travel elsewhere, but their pervasiveness across predominantly low-income

Figure 11.1 Informal micro-retail in Hammonds Farm
(source: Mark Lewis)

neighbourhoods in many different localities (beyond government-subsidised housing developments) points also to income generation efforts in a context of massive unemployment, as well as limited local authority capacity to manage and enforce land use regulations. In state-sponsored housing projects, authorities respond to these businesses, and other modifications such as unauthorised rental rooms, in various ways: often by overlooking them, by investigating particular complaints about land use conflicts or by regularising uncontroversial, de facto situations.

In our South African cases on the urban peripheries, however, it was not these unauthorised businesses that were particularly notable but rather our respondents' largely positive comments on the presence of large supermarkets and malls (or lamenting the absence of these). Later in the chapter we illustrate the extent and texture of their experiences, but first we outline the approach taken to retail activity in the condominium developments of Addis Ababa.

Retail in the condominium developments of Addis Ababa

In the condominiums of Addis Ababa, the establishment of retail and commercial services is encouraged on the ground floor of government-subsidised apartment blocks in key neighbourhood streets. This is mainly explained in terms of the 'mixed use' motto of the government in relation to the housing programmes. Taking the form of relatively small-scale shops, restaurants and other businesses, these premises are sold to non-resident entrepreneurs. This strategy is complemented by the provision of a number of separate sites in the development which are allocated for commercial purposes and made available through long leases. Together, commercial or retail land uses amount to 10 per cent of the land area of the development (UN-Habitat, 2010).

The inclusion of retail is intended to retain expenditure locally, provide accessible shopping without the need for travel, encourage social interaction and promote after-hours activity in the street, while a further financial motivation is to enable a form of subsidy for the housing units (UN-Habitat, 2010). Allocation of both forms of commercial premises (within buildings and on separate plots) is to bidders at auctions, with administration via city authorities (UN-Habitat, 2010). Experiences from the older, more consolidated and

Supermarkets, retail and consumption

now quite desirable condominium development of Jemo, some 13 km from the centre of Addis, show that there are many neighbourhood shopping options available but that these are considered pricey, and with good transport options available to them, people travel elsewhere, including 'the downtown markets', to shop (Planel and Bridonneau, 2017: 31).

The retail and commercial activities provide some offset to the multiple and largely standardised array of apartment blocks, ranging from four to eight storeys, that make up the mass delivery of housing to low- and lower-middle income households in Ethiopia. As explained in Chapter 5, individual homeownership is achieved via a partially subsidised mortgage system (Delz, 2014) shared in defined configurations between household and government, with loans provided by the Commercial Bank of Ethiopia (CBE) (Planel and Bridonneau, 2017). As discussed in Chapter 3, substantial job creation in the construction sector through small-scale contractors was integral to the mass housing programme.

While Delz (2014) is critical of the unproductive leftover space created by how the blocks of flats are configured, there is street-level vitality evident in various mass housing projects, attributable to a considerable extent to the retail activities (see Figure 11.2).

Figure 11.2 Retail space in Yeka Abado (source: Mark Lewis)

However, as might be expected, this vibrancy does not translate into widespread job opportunities. In 2017 UN-Habitat reported that 57 per cent of condominium households in a survey noted they were unable to earn an income in their neighbourhood, and many of those that previously had informal businesses in the central parts of the city were unable to replicate these in the new developments, often because 'a neighbourhood-based clientele network [was] lost in the renewal and relocation process' (UN-Habitat, 2017: 66). Further, apartment living was often not supportive of home-based businesses, with one respondent noting: 'My house is on the fourth floor, there is no place to cook and run my restaurant' (UN-Habitat, 2017: 67). Overall, the report concludes that the condominium housing strategy 'has run its course' given various problems, and that more diverse forms of housing supply are needed (UN-Habitat, 2017: 94). Nevertheless, key informants in our study argued that ongoing infrastructure development had stimulated the emergence of a variety of micro and small enterprises (MSEs) in the vicinity of condominium developments.

We now turn to our participants' views on shopping and retail stores to illustrate the experiential differences between the two peripheral contexts and the significance of these.

Residents' views: Yeka Abado and Tulu Dimtu, Addis Ababa

In Addis Ababa, in both Yeka Abado and Tulu Dimtu our respondents were of the view that shops had been opening in the period shortly before the research was conducted in 2017/18 and that there was a growing choice and diversity of goods and services (Yeka Abado GS 48 ♂ Interview; Yeka Abado 100 M ♀ Interview; Yeka Abado TZ 066 ♀ Interview; Yeka Abado EN 014 ♀ Diary; Yeka Abado HA 023 ♀ Interview). In Yeka Abado these included banks and pharmacies (Yeka Abado M 100 ♀ Interview); in Tulu Dimtu, although some refer to a shortage of pharmacies (Tulu Dimtu HT 089 ♀ Interview), other facilities such as an internet cafe are mentioned. In both areas the increase in supermarkets is specifically referred to along with the convenience they bring: 'These have made life easier' (Yeka Abado HA 023 ♀ Interview), or alternatively, frustration is expressed where supermarkets are not nearby: 'I don't like the fact that there are no big shops and I don't find the things I want easily' (Yeka Abado FB 039 ♀ Interview). In general the increase in retail and other activities is welcomed for the vibrancy it brings. A young person who previously lived in 'a very vibrant neighbourhood, where you find everything you need' comments favourably on the improvements in Tulu Dimtu: 'There weren't many shops; it was a dead area. We used to feel like we moved to a rural area. But now things are becoming more active and shops are opening. There are cafes and recreational spaces now' (Tulu Dimtu KF 12 ♂ Interview). However, there are specific facilities that residents note are not available, such as grain mills and hair salons, and speciality services such as Halaal meat (Tulu Dimtu MK 25 ♂ Interview). Even with the existing shops there is a sense of insufficient range. In particular, fresh produce markets were lacking or in short supply, with people from different subsections of the wider Yeka Abado area feeling they are in competition with others for a very limited amount of fresh goods. In addition, there are complaints that prices are high in the local neighbourhoods (Yeka Abado YG 064 ♀ Diary; Yeka Abado FB 039 ♀ Diary; Yeka Abado AA 068 ♀ Interview). For these reasons respondents in both areas feel the need to travel elsewhere for some purchases, particularly for fresh goods:

> Shops have opened [here], but prices are higher than [in] the city. We do major grocery shopping outside of this area, not only because of the price but also availability of things like vegetables. For a quick solution it's good, we can find things here. But we mostly travel around 5 km away to do some shopping. (Yeka Abado TM 016 ♂ Interview)

> We don't easily find what we need here. We have to bring things from the centre. (Tulu Dimtu WD 27 ♂ Interview, condo owner)

Having to source particular goods elsewhere, outside of the development, requires organisation and purchasing large quantities in advance. Respondent Yeka Abado M 100 (♀ Interview), a working professional, noted that moving to Yeka Abado 'has made me very cautious and organised. There weren't any shops around here when we moved in so we plan and buy groceries in bulk.' Likewise, in Tulu Dimtu: 'We must plan, and we must buy in bulk our foodstuffs. We go to Akaki market to buy these items, which is the only available market close by' (Tulu Dimtu YK 052 ♀ Interview).

In Tulu Dimtu the need to travel elsewhere for certain goods is remarked upon by both condominium residents and those in nearby cooperative housing, but there are also internal variations: for the smaller shops people must often go to the condominium area, which is better served than the cooperative area (Tulu Dimtu HW 55 ♂ Interview). The situation can be exacerbated by inactive local retail spaces. A professional in Yeka Abado commented that some shops are not yet occupied 'because of the high leasing price by the authorities' (Yeka Abado KA 069 ♂ Interview). This is compounded by the relatively high levels of employment (in locations elsewhere in the city) among residents of his neighbourhood (see Chapter 3), with the result that in his perception weekday sales are slow and thus 'many service providers hesitate in opening or expanding business' (Yeka Abado KA 069 ♂ Interview).

Yet among our respondents, there were also those interested in starting a shop but unable to get permission to do so (Yeka Abado GW 048 ♂ Interview; Yeka Abado M 043 ♀ Interview), and indications that unauthorised businesses would be policed and terminated:

> I don't have work; I haven't done anything so far. If they let me I would like to open a little shop here, as my house is next to the road. We have been asking, but they don't give you a permit; we can't just construct something and then they'll stop us. (Yeka Abado GW 48 ♂ Interview)

> There are no job opportunities, and I couldn't open a small shop or sell some vegetable in my own compound; they will say that I'm illegal. (Yeka Abado M 043 ♀ Interview)

Other respondents are scouting for opportunities in the area, within retail and outside of it, identifying gaps in the market such as the need for mobile phone sale and repair shops (Yeka Abado HT 003 ♀ Interview) and running evening classes (Tulu Dimtu H 008 ♂ Interview). Various of our respondents had already managed to take up an opportunity. For some people this has enabled a move from being an employee to being self-employed, with one family in Tulu Dimtu now selling 'pottery, traditional cooking stoves and similar things' (Tulu Dimtu KF 12 ♂ Interview) in a *Gulit* (market) space provided to them 'through the sub-city, as cooperatives': 'business is good and there are enough customers'. A condominium owner notes that as 'having a job in this area is difficult … we rented this shop my wife works in, and we're trying to create a livelihood by ourselves' (Tulu Dimtu MK 025 ♂ Interview).

In addition, despite the controls respondents mentioned earlier, informal businesses appear fairly common, both used by our respondents (because they sell things more cheaply – Yeka Abado SF 045 ♀ Interview) as well as operated by some of them. A young person selling plants in Tulu Dimtu 'just appropriated the space according to my own will' (Tulu Dimtu KF 012 ♂ Interview) and has the view that there are multiple opportunities for work in the area, as quoted in Chapter 3. But there are also some negative impacts from unauthorised businesses, such as noisy machinery (Yeka Abado HT 003 ♀ Interview).

While retail activity in both areas appears to be fairly active and growing, for one respondent it is the mall some distance away that represents leisure and entertainment, but access can be hampered by traffic: 'Even for children's play area the closest is Century mall, and you have to drive at least thirty minutes to get there. Even sometimes when we want to catch a movie we always get there late. The road is unpredictable' (Yeka Abado M 100 ♀ Interview).

Residents' views: Durban and Johannesburg, South Africa

In the South African cases, the emphasis in our respondents' narratives was on supermarkets and shopping complexes, either positively celebrating the presence of these in their areas or commenting negatively on their absence. This is not to say that there are not small shops and businesses within the residential areas, as mentioned earlier in the chapter. In all of our case study sites, these were present, mostly in the form of unauthorised or informal, small home-based forms of retail and generally limited in their range of goods. However, what our respondents chose to remark on in their diaries and interviews, often unprompted, was to do with the large, formal chain stores or centres and the significance of these in their lives (see, for example, Figure 11.3 showing Protea Glen Mall). In various ways their comments reinforce a fairly well-known picture of the concentration of retail services and capital in a few large companies in South Africa, but residents' experiences provide a fine-grained insight into the multiple ways in which their lives are

Figure 11.3 Protea Glen Mall (source: Mark Lewis)

shaped by this context and how its impacts are intensified in particular forms in peripheral areas.

Noteworthy among our South African respondents were the emotions associated with people's comments about supermarkets and big shops. Referring to the Superspar franchise chain store located in our northern eThekwini case, MK chose to write in her diary that 'I am very happy to live here because we have the Spar near to us' (Hammonds Farm MK 02 ♀ Diary), while other remarks were 'it is joyful to have the Spar' (Waterloo MM 12 ♀ Interview) and 'we were thankful to get a Spar' (Waterloo GM 15 ♀ Interview). By contrast, IN, writing in Lufhereng on the edge of Soweto, confided in her diary that 'it would bring me great joy to have a mall close by' (Lufhereng 14 ♀ Diary). It is important to note that the word 'mall' was used at times by our respondents to refer to what might conventionally be termed a mall (i.e. a large-scale retail complex), and in other instances the term was used more interchangeably with 'supermarket', or a cluster of small shops along with a supermarket.

Diverse remarks made about the Waterloo Superspar in our northern eThekwini case shed light on the multiple roles it plays in people's lives. It is positively associated with fresh, unexpired groceries but also with the various financial services it offers, including dispensing state-provided social grants, providing employment to people from the area and also providing a destination for an outing or a meal out.

Crucially, the location of the shop and its associated small complex on the edge of Hammonds Farm across the road from Waterloo meant it was within walking distance for many people in these two neighbourhoods. It is hard to overstate the importance of this. Time after time respondents commented on the cost saving of not having to take transport for shopping and how this enhanced their ability to afford groceries. Both for those who had relatively recently moved to Hammonds Farm from more distant informal settlements and for residents in the consolidated neighbourhood of Waterloo, the establishment of the Spar was a dramatic improvement on previous circumstances:

> Before where we lived the shops were far, and we spend the last money on transport to go to the Verulam for shopping. We are happy to be in this area because we are not paying [for a] taxi, but we just walk to do the shopping at the Spar. (Hammonds Farm ZN 11 ♀ Diary)

Elsewhere in our study localities, managing transport costs for shopping were similarly a concern. Respondents from our Gauteng case study Lufhereng commented repeatedly on the costs of having to use transport to access large shops, such as Protea Glen Mall, their closest big retail centre some 5 km away:

> Another problem is that at Lufhereng there is no mall. We have to use the taxis for everything. When you want to buy meat for R50 at the mall, you must have taxi fare as well and there is no money. (Lufhereng EN 17 ♀ Diary)

> We don't have shopping malls and we rely on small tuckshops that are in people's residential places. If these small spaza shops don't have what we want, we will have to take a taxi and go where shopping malls are. (Lufhereng NM 10 ♀ Diary)

> Many people in this area struggle to get to the mall because the malls are too far. For people to get to the malls, they spend a lot of money for transport. (Lufhereng GC 21 ♀ Diary)

For those able to walk to the Waterloo Superspar in northern eThekwini, the range of services it offered also assisted with time and transport savings. As with many supermarkets, beyond selling food and groceries, it also sells electricity vouchers for the pre-paid systems in houses and mobile phone airtime; it had a facility for sending and receiving money from relatives, for booking long-distance bus tickets, paying bills such as telephone accounts and people were able to withdraw cash from the supermarket or the cash machines outside the shop in the small complex: 'I feel happy because I can go to Spar and withdraw money. I no longer go to Verulam to withdraw money and buy grocery. I go to Spar' (Waterloo MM 021 ♂ Interview). Other conveniences were also appreciated because 'it's open long hours and we have … enough time to do shopping' (Hammonds Farm ZN 011 ♀ Diary).

Feeling safe while shopping was also a key benefit for some of our study participants, as the following diary entry from the Molweni case study reflects, in this case referring to the large enclosed mall that opened several kilometres away in 2015: 'It is safe there to do the shopping at Water Crest Mall, and we walk freely at the mall' (Molweni VN 29 ♀ Diary). As the threat of theft, crime and mugging hangs over many public spaces and activities, having this peace of mind at the mall is significant. The mall also plays a recreation function for respondents, and similarly, the Waterloo Superspar in Hammonds Farm, although a much smaller facility, was for some people in our study a place to go for an outing, to enjoy its in-house facility serving cooked food: 'If it is a weekend, I took out my children to Spar for eating' (Waterloo MM 012 ♀ Interview).

As might be expected, employment opportunities for local people were praised, even if they meant other people from the area were working in the Spar. 'I am happy if I am doing shopping and get help from the person I know who is working at Spar' (Waterloo LN 06 ♀ Diary). For this respondent local employment as well as being able to shop without using transport means 'That development has changed the life of the community' (Waterloo LN 06 ♀ Diary).

A further highly significant aspect to the Spar is that social grant holders can receive their monthly government payments from the supermarket and do not have to incur the cost and crime risk of travelling out of the area to receive their money. Although there is no unemployment benefit in South Africa, the disbursement of social support payments is massive in scale: in 2019 about 18 million people (or 30 per cent of the population) received a state grant of some kind, the main ones being the child support grant, the older person's grant and the disability and war veteran grant (Statista, 2022). The monthly social grant day is hugely important for the retailers, who run special deals and inevitably benefit from expenditure within their stores, particularly if people are accessing their cash from the till points in the store itself (Steyn, 2012). The Waterloo Superspar pays out grants to well over one thousand people every month, managing a long queue and providing complimentary refreshments as well as promoting keenly priced special offers (Senior Management Superspar, 2018).

Overall, it was the combination and diversity of goods, services and other benefits that was noteworthy about convenient and low-cost access to a big supermarket: as LS wrote in her diary, 'we have everything in that Spar', before elaborating on the many different ways she felt she benefited from it (Hammonds Farm LS 07 ♀ Diary). For many of our respondents in the area, the arrival of the supermarket was the most noticeable infrastructural transformation affecting life on the urban periphery. Central to this experience was the difficulty and cost of travelling elsewhere for shopping and other services, as Chapter 8 shows. There were, nevertheless, a few criticisms, notably a sense that goods were cheaper in busier urban centres.

Conclusion

Our respondents in South Africa drew our attention to the significance of retail in their lives and the specific nature of this through their spontaneous and positive commentary on supermarkets and the convenience, quality and diversity of offerings they reflect. Supermarkets are not necessarily present in vanguard peripheries, though, and where they are absent, people experience enhanced disconnection and practical inconvenience. Similarly, our Ethiopian respondents wanted better access to large retail outlets such as fresh produce markets, which they currently have to travel some distance to. However, big-chain supermarkets of the kind found in South Africa are not part of the Ethiopian retail landscape, and the small neighbourhood shopping opportunities that are planned into housing developments are valued, though in some places need a greater concentration of local purchasing power to sustain them.

In our vanguard developments in South Africa, a local big shop with its multifaceted services, convenience and transport cost-saving in an area distant from competing retail offerings brings considerable and diverse practical benefits, and these work also to influence the affective and emotional aspect of the supermarket experience alluded to by our respondents.[1] Where such a shop is absent, residents lament their disconnection. In our Ethiopian cases there are by contrast multiple examples of retail and business activity within peripheral residential developments in the form of small enterprises and cooperatives, but despite this residents still experience the isolation and dislocation of their edge localities, with travel hampered by long distance and traffic congestion.

Vanguard peripheries reflect state vision and ambition, opening up new sites of infrastructure investment and residential accommodation. Intended to be generative, they are conceived as magnets stimulating other forms of spending across various scales, some realised only over a medium to long time horizon (Meth et al., 2021a). This chapter has shown how the manner in which one additional layer is conceptualised within state-led residential development, that of retail, profoundly affects lived experience. In a context dominated by large supermarket chains, the South Africa approach of zoning and designating sites for formal private sector investment reaps dividends when it eventually arrives: residents in the decades-old neighbourhood of Waterloo celebrated the supermarket being made viable – despite very low household incomes – by the added spending power in vanguard Hammonds Farm. But long periods of relative retail isolation and frustration can precede this, including where large projects are incrementally occupied but take years to achieve full habitation. Despite their often bold image or appearance, as even our terminology for them might imply, vanguard peripheries may remain areas thinly resourced for their residents for long periods. In Ethiopia a more fine-grained approach of designing in cooperatives and small enterprises within multistorey developments of relative population density that assist in making them viable avoids some of this dislocation, though convenient access to larger forms of retail is similarly missed.

Note

1 Events of July 2021 in South Africa raised questions about this emotional relationship: several days of widespread looting and arson included malls and large shops as targets, including the Spar in Waterloo/Hammonds Farm, as part of what the President called an 'attempted insurrection'. However, our subsequent interviews showed our respondents' positive views of the supermarket were largely unchanged (Charlton, in progress).

Conclusions

Paula Meth, Sarah Charlton, Tom Goodfellow and Alison Todes

Key conclusions relating to the planning visions, investments, jobs and livelihoods, governance, housing, land, social processes and retail and consumption of African peripheries have been advanced in each chapter of this book. The articulation of key findings in relation to the five logics of urban peripheries are outlined in the introductory chapter, drawn on throughout the book where relevant, to illustrate and extend analytically a variety of arguments. This final chapter presents brief concluding comments in relation to three key elements, namely the value of urban comparison, the book's analytical contributions to core literatures along with reflections on the value and limits of our conceptual framework to the study of urban peripheries more generally and finally some policy implications of the arguments and evidence detailed in the various chapters. We see this book as restarting a conversation about urban peripheries by foregrounding African city-regions and – crucially – the lived experience of people living there, rather than taking structural processes or arbitrary rural–urban distinctions as our main entry point. As such, we offer our approach as one possible road into comprehending these dynamic spaces.

The value of urban comparison

A core aim of this book was to illustrate the value of urban comparison, drawing on Robinson's (2016, 2022) framings of genetic and conceptually generative comparative tactics. We recognise and build on her argument that any understanding of the urban should be underpinned by a 'double multiplicity', in the sense of being 'grounded in a multiplicity of experiences and observations' as well as subject to 'a potential multiplicity of conceptualisations' (2022: 6). While 'genetic' and 'generative' are conceptualised separately by Robinson, they are not so much separate forms of comparative process as 'two *grounds* for comparative urban practice' (2022: 11; emphasis added). As such, a study may be (and ours indeed is) rooted in both genetic and generative framings, tracing the intertwined genesis of peripheral formations while also generating new concepts. Our focus on genetic tactics targeted an understanding of historical processes, drivers of urban change and the multiple everyday experiences of African urban peripheries. We address these three elements in turn.

Historical processes, including the making of these places and key drivers of change, were explicitly detailed within analyses of planning and urban visions within the South African and Ethiopian peripheries (Chapter 1) and interrogations of state and private sector investments therein (Chapter 2), as well as investigations of the histories and current realities of housing in South Africa and Ethiopia (Chapters 5 and 6). We supplemented this with assessments of changes to landownership and markets in Accra, Ghana (Chapter 7), tracing colonial impacts and more recent reductions in the powers of customary authorities. Chapter 4 examined changing governance institutions and practices at varying scales, also important drivers in shaping urban peripheries, using an historical lens to identify critical contestations particularly associated with borders and demarcation. These analyses reveal how the intersections and particularities of political and economic regimes over time have worked to produce urban peripheries, centring temporality as critical in understanding the peripheries, their evolutions and how such spaces are now lived. Robinson defines genetic tactics as 'tracing the interconnected genesis of repeated, related but distinctive, urban outcomes' (2016: 195), which can 'reveal elements of the flows and interactions which make up the process of urbanisation' (2022: 138). Our historical investigations reveal some 'genetically connected' phenomena both within country contexts (e.g. historic investment strategies tied to apartheid policies across different spaces in South Africa) and between countries, for example in terms of the ideas about the catalytic potential of industrial zones and benefits of homeownership that informed peripheral development in both countries. Yet they also evidence significant variation across the urban, both within and between country contexts (South Africa, Ethiopia and Ghana), depending on how history, location, politics and economics collide in specific peripheral contexts.

Genetic comparison was central to our analyses of drivers of urban change. Analyses of distinct governance practices as central drivers of change (including producing decline and contestation), leading vanguard interventions and aiding speculative investments, produce core comparisons throughout the book, as do the absences or failings of governance practices which produce or facilitate auto-construction. Land is a fundamental variable in urban peripheries, explicitly examined through the critical and changing role of land markets as a key driver of change in Accra's peripheries (Chapter 7), but also central in our Ethiopian and South African cases, including with respect to how land is sourced and acquired for major housing and infrastructure cases. The focus on customary authority (in both Accra and South African cases) and rising contestation over land informs our analysis of hybrid governance and also the centrality of land in servicing the powers of 'big men' in various South African cases. It also points to an area ripe for further consideration, that of comparisons of land markets, authority, pricing and changing land use across African peripheries.

Significant comparisons are evident in the book of how places and urban change are produced and experienced in relation to infrastructure (Chapter 9), including through housing programmes (Chapters 5 and 6). Comparison across cases reveals that although big infrastructure is evident, its role in shaping the lived peripheries is varied, and small-scale/micro-infrastructures are key urban elements conditioning everyday life. For example, issues around street lighting or sanitation facilities appear to have more meaning for people living in the peripheries of Addis Ababa than the proximity of major railway investments, which were barely mentioned as drivers of change. Retail and consumption in the peripheries of South Africa and Ethiopia (Chapter 11) constitute a core but comparatively distinct driver of change tied to diverse strategies. Desires for homeownership and affordable housing are dominant drivers of urban change, evident through comparison of cases in Accra, Addis Ababa and the South African cases, where take-up (and at times subsequent rejection) of state housing and investment in property or house-building on the fringes of cities shape movement patterns and the viability and density of settlements.

Genetic comparison here is again a complex and productive tactic. Much of the evidence of 'repeated urban phenomena' occurs where state intervention is partial (such as the co-occurence of experiences of infrastructural limitations of new housing neighbourhoods in Addis Ababa and Lufhereng, South Africa) or where wider processes such as commodification, deindustrialisation, political contestation, rising unaffordability and poor articulation of policy integration work to produce nearly predictable outcomes of marginalisation, suffering and insecurity for many living in peripheral spaces. Governance practices and their unfolding over time and within spaces are less directly comparable across Ghana, South Africa and Ethiopia. Instead, we see quite significant variation in how centralised and powerful regimes interconnect with the politics and practices of citizens, formalised community groups, customary authorities, localised and often powerful actors and newly emerging committee structures. Genetic comparison here fosters insights through difference generated at the national scale, manifested and reshaped locally, but it also poses key questions for how comparison across other African urban contexts is likely to generate further variation but also repetition of phenomena.

Comparing lived experiences across multiple African urban peripheries as a genetic tactic produced a cacophony of insights and often generated the most easily comparable observations across all countries and cases. Here, the art of 'living the peripheries' proved a critical axis of comparison, with residents' embodied, experiential accounts proving highly comparable, although with significant contextual variation. In this book particular chapters really evidence these comparative perspectives through the voices of residents in seven different case study contexts, primarily within Ethiopia and South Africa. Asafo's analysis of the transformations occurring within land markets in peri-urban Accra, Ghana, focuses more on actors engaged in land markets and less on the lived experiences of these (drawing on qualitative accounts), although Asafo's wider publications speak directly to these experiential dimensions (see Asafo, 2020, 2022). The lived experiences of jobs and livelihoods (Chapter 3) in urban peripheries reveal the limits of generating local jobs in peripheral locations. The ongoing reliance on urban centres for employment (with implications for commuting, disposable income and time with family) for some peripherally located residents was evident in Ghana, South Africa and Ethiopia (discussed in Chapters 7 and 8). Here, and surfaced in other chapters, comparisons across cases point to the relative precarity for many living the peripheries of African cities but also that the peripheries are sites of wealth, for the middle classes and the urban rich, who choose edge locations because land and costs often facilitate a high-quality lifestyle or at least an affordable lifestyle.

Peripheries as key spaces for living, migrating and relocating are evident across all cases. In Ghana, intra-urban migration to plots of land purchased in Accra's peripheries facilitates affordable private housing construction, albeit incrementally, while cheap, often unserviced land supports the auto-construction of poorer peripheral settlements sites, evident across South Africa and Ethiopia, supporting housing needs of migrants from various locations. State housing shapes living in the peripheries through the production of home-ownership, access to (often costly) services and new affordability constraints. Immobility, stuckness and extensive travel times are relatively consistent comparative experiences detailed in Chapter 8 but noted also in Accra's peripheral cases. These emphasise the geographic characteristics of urban peripheries privileged in this book, underscoring that location does matter and that despite investments across urban peripheries, cost and the infrequent transportation commonly work to exclude and marginalise peripheral dwellers or entrench a reliance on private vehicle use for wealthier residents. Finally, social trends, including crime and violence, and differentiations across gender and other axes are comparable across cases. Violence underpins some of the land market practices in Accra and is widespread in relation to crime across the South African cases, with particular settlement types (often informal) more vulnerable, as discussed in Chapters 7 and 10. The social differences of African urban peripheries were detailed in Chapter 10, noting how gender, age, ethnicity, tenancy, etc. informed experiences of peripheries, but there is extensive scope here for further comparison across other African cities, presenting an area for future research asking in what ways peripheries are differentiated, by gender for example.

Arguably, many of these genetic comparisons of historical processes, drivers of urban change and the lived experiences of African peripheries are comparable across various other African countries and their urban peripheries. These include the influences of globalisation, state tactics which enable particular forms of investment, alongside capacity constraints, clientelism and absence, ongoing impacts of colonial histories of dispossession shaping current land-ownership, contestation and governance practices and challenges of housing affordability, poor-quality infrastructure, lack of economic opportunity and relative stuckness. In the body of the book, we emphasised case-specific empirical evidence of these processes rather than reporting on (and cross-referencing) evident comparisons across urban Africa more generally, but the introductory chapter does begin the process of explicit comparison beyond our country focus. More broadly, we see this book as contributing to a wider future conversation about comparisons across African urban peripheries.

This book also explicitly employed conceptually generative tactics. Through its choice of cases, where characteristics were partially shared, it sought to 'generate and revise concepts' (Robinson, 2016). Our aim was to work with the complexities and specificities of cases and to draw them into dialogue through which conceptual innovation could be marshalled. In drawing out the key generative aspects of our comparative research, we return now to the five logics of the peripheries and their potential contributions to the wider literature.

Living the peripheries: conceptual contributions and reflections

Our introductory chapter outlined five logics of African urban peripheries, namely speculative, vanguard, transitioning, auto-constructed and inherited. Here, we briefly reflect on the generative contributions of these concepts, exploring their insights and limitations in relation to broader debates. As we showed in the Introduction, there is a rapidly growing literature on the nature of suburbs, peri-urban areas, urban frontiers, extended urbanisation, edge spaces and margins. Indeed, one might ask what room there is for further conceptual generativity and analytical novelty on this topic. Yet the nature of urban peripheries in Africa is even more diverse, and evolving even more quickly, than the literature itself. While the earlier literature on peri-urbanisation was often empirically rooted in specific African contexts (e.g. Gough and Yankson, 2000; Mbiba and Huchzermeyer, 2002; Simon, 2004), much of the recent turn towards a focus on dynamics of extended urbanisation has tended towards high-level 'universalising' discussions about how peripheral growth reconfigures what we understand to be 'urban'.[1] The experience of African urbanisation is still a minority element within these debates. Where it does enter into analysis of peripheral change – as it does in a number of important recent contributions that do examine the dynamism and diversity of African urban peripheries (e.g. Mabin *et al.*, 2013; Sawyer, 2014; Mercer, 2017; Karaman *et al.*, 2020; McGregor and Chatiza, 2019; Sawyer *et al.*, 2020; Bloch, 2015; Bloch *et al.*, 2022) – the focus is largely on the ways these places are *produced* rather than how they are *lived*.

As such, our contribution combines a focus on the logics of peripheral space production, reproduction and transformation with attention on the experience of these logics from a diverse range of residents. We argue that the peripheral logics we present help to characterise and account for the *variety* of conditions we find in our case studies on the edges of city-regions and the contradictions and tensions evident in residents' narratives of their lives. We can, for example, understand why one resident's account of a particular area like Tulu Dimtu might indicate rapid progress and optimism while another suggests stagnation and despair if we consider how the logic of the vanguard periphery also triggers displacement and land value increase that set in train logics of speculation, auto-construction and deepening dependence on the state (i.e. potential future 'inherited peripheries'). The logics thus offer an intellectual platform to manage divergent and contradictory empirical material and bring nuance to an analysis of peripheral conditions through explicit attention to differentiation. Our recognition that logics overlap and are not singular is central to this claim. The relationships between logics and associated characteristics are also necessarily provisional, and our urban comparisons bear witness to this provisionality. Certain developments (vanguard for example) may come or be associated with the promise of services, but this doesn't necessitate their high-quality provision or ongoing maintenance.

It is thus the texture of the qualitative empirical material examined in this book that evidences the generative aspects of our conceptual framing, and at times its limitations. These empirical details are productive in adding substance to the logics, showing how they play out in varying ways (an example being the contrasts in vanguard housing initiatives in Ethiopia versus South Africa). As this book has illustrated, the logics can variously be deployed to identify and account for drivers and forces shaping areas, motivations underlying initiatives and experiential dimensions/life in these areas. However, this needs to be accompanied by contextual analysis and depth of engagement for particular dimensions of the logics to become apparent. This confirms both the utility of our conceptual framing but also the need to populate the concepts in context-specific ways and to recognise the differentiating effects of key drivers of urban change, and how important intersectional realities are for those living the peripheries. Here, the interplay between conceptual logics and the nuances of the 'everyday' work to constantly challenge and test our framings. In this way we also show how different viewpoints on a situation (validating our methodological approach) can surface different logics, or aspects of them. For example, the household experience of a place driven by a vanguard logic may reflect a much more muted/incomplete form of vanguardism, and an inherited periphery for the state (which may be out of kilter with current planning directives) can, for some people living there, reflect a kind of cherished 'personal inheritance' where strong personal histories and social ties shape attachment to place.

The five logics are productive across different scales of analysis, and this is a further advantage empirically and theoretically building on their generative qualities. Their application can stretch across analyses of wider spatial plans, strategies, visions, to investigations within a locality or even a household, and can be used thematically across different cases but also within a particular locality. Questions of geography are central to the logics, and our book argues that size and location really do matter. Distance between a peripheral settlement and areas of opportunity can become so extreme that prospects of stitching in or fostering supporting economies remain unviable. This impacts both individual households and municipalities in terms of the relative location of the burden or the dividend. The book has shown the significance of location in terms of livelihoods and access to a range of services and opportunities. While critics have questioned the importance of location in view of the growing polycentricity of cities, people's mobility across cities (Pieterse, 2019) and the way a broader set of factors affect poverty (Peberdy, 2017), our study of lived experience has underscored that location matters. Our conceptual logics reveal that as a result of different interventions and histories, there are peripheries within the peripheries, both in a geographic sense but also socio-politically. These relational experiences of the peripheries are exacerbated by their overall spatial peripheral location.

The book has also illustrated how different logics can intertwine and fuel or undermine one another. For example, speculation on the periphery can hook in vanguardism (as in the case of Protea Glen and Lufhereng in South Africa), and vanguardism can hang on the coat-tails of speculative logics, where the state stage-manages demand and private sector interests gain further momentum from subsequent vanguard interventions. Infrastructure delivery in an inherited or speculative periphery can attract or consolidate auto-construction, and a vanguard periphery, while predicated and delivered as a particular vision of complete formal housing, can become overlain with households' own adaptations and transformations. This can evidence 'reworked urbanism' or 'adapted urbanism' or reveal how vanguardist logics are challenged by the decisions of individual householders (Charlton, 2018b), evidenced also in condominium residents' choices to rent out their properties to tenants in Addis Ababa. This is an important contribution of our conceptual framing, where compared with wider peripheral urbanisation discussions, we note the ways in which residents adapt or respond after formal state housing delivery, rather than primarily emphasising people's incremental delivery which is then subsequently responded to by the state.

When viewed in conversation with each other, our five logics offer the conceptual flexibility to trace change over time, unpacking the temporal dynamics of peripheral change noted in the previous section. The book includes case studies with long histories of occupation and also spaces with more recent developments, including one experiencing fundamental change through household removals and replacement investment. In older areas households' histories of living there often lead to significant attachment, entrenching desires to remain in place despite the many disadvantages they have experienced in the location. Inherited peripheries can reflect both this personal attachment alongside the burden of living there. Newly created peripheries, sometimes inhabited by urban migrants, may over time build similar household ties. However, being partly composed of residents who have grown used to displacement and mobility, these areas also witness ongoing migration and movement elsewhere, including from one auto-constructed space, vanguard or speculative zone to another, as property values in one place rise beyond what they can afford or their tenuous foothold is overridden by alternative plans or catastrophic events. This kind of 'location-hopping' was especially evident among the tenants in formal housing units in Addis Ababa, where people would sometimes move from one condominium site to a very similar one elsewhere just because of the constantly changing differentials in rent. Entire settlements may also disappear as with two auto-constructed areas within our multinodal South Africa cases, where, subsequent to our research, households were relocated to state housing (or evicted) in one instance, and in the other the area was devastated by flooding.

Looking across all our case studies, we can see how areas produced under a vanguard logic can morph into an inherited periphery or an auto-constructed one, offering cautionary lessons about whether large state-driven peripheral investments will ultimately prove fruitful. Ongoing investment, including individual household investment in the home and state investments in infrastructure, can create dynamism. But forms of positive change can co-exist with stagnation, albeit economic, or maintenance stagnation as facilities are rendered unusable, and can co-exist with decline. This dynamism underscores a potential limitation of our logics, whose analytical value may well be superseded by other logics as changes over time unfold across different African urban peripheries. We argue that this is inevitable, even desirable, and is a key feature of generative comparison.

We recognise here that the book's dominant focus on two countries, with a lesser focus on Ghana, can generate empirical and conceptual concerns about the generalisability of our analysis. Ethiopia and South Africa are certainly quite exceptional countries – albeit in very different ways – in terms of the state's developmental role and its willingness to finance massive amounts of urban housing. Yet although these two states might be seen as unusually interventionist in this respect, by focusing on them we have been able to make a particular contribution to an understanding of vanguardist peripheries, their evolution over time and people's experience of these places from a variety of perspectives. Our focus countries are also ones that have extensive informal settlements, an intense mix of state and private-owned property (particularly in Ethiopia), major foreign as well as diasporic and domestic investment projects and the substantial involvement of traditional authorities in peripheral urban governance (in South Africa, as well as Ghana). As such, between them they contain many of the major features that characterise peripheral urban development across the continent. This book has offered a long view of these places in contexts where poverty and unemployment are major concerns and where the growth of new economic centralities on the periphery may be limited, unstable or offer narrow sets of employment. It has also highlighted how the lack or failure of multisectoral integrated planning or implementation produces incomplete places, affecting the quality of place and access to a range of services and facilities. As economies and cities elsewhere in Africa grow, and with this we see resources channelled into urban peripheries in a range of ways, the experiences of Ethiopia, South Africa and Ghana are sure to resonate – despite important contextual differences.

Policy implications

The research informing this book highlights the dynamism and complexity of urban peripheries and the need for policy to understand and appropriately manage growth and change in these areas, rather than seeing them as residual spaces. Multisectoral frameworks focused on sustainability and inclusion are needed to bring together planning for environment, infrastructure, residential and economic development and to move beyond the divided, fragmented spaces often produced through large speculative and vanguardist projects. Responsiveness to the dynamics and needs of particular areas is also critical.

Much growth is occurring incrementally through logics of auto-constructed and transitioning peripheries – particularly as these are usually less regulated spaces where lower-cost land is available, although as the chapter on Ghana showed, speculative logics are increasingly evident. Managing these areas requires addressing overarching questions of land management, regularisation, finance and governance, and providing appropriate forms and levels of infrastructure and service delivery that can enhance often precarious lives.

While vanguardist and speculative projects may provide a better level of initial infrastructure than incremental development, our studies of existing peripheral settlements produced through a variety of logics show that the provision of infrastructure and services is incomplete and uneven, affecting peoples' experiences. There is a need to improve conditions in existing areas, including in inherited spaces, through, for example, facilitating employment and economic activity accessible to people living there (such as public works schemes) and improving the conditions for everyday life through better physical and social infrastructure (including retail, recreational facilities, schools inter alia), as well as social programmes, all of which tend to be neglected in these areas. The prevalence of 'boredom', and its varied meanings, needs to be addressed, particularly given its consequences for mental and physical wellbeing. The difference that social and physical infrastructure make when well provided is evident in some of our cases. Improvements to transport provision locally – as well as major investment in roads – is also critical. Hence, a re-emphasis on 'micro-infrastructure' affecting everyday life, rather than simply large-scale and grand projects, is warranted. The research also suggests that micro-governance, in terms of how services are negotiated and accessed, needs to be better understood and addressed.

Given the legacy of inherited spaces in South Africa, and the historical and current significance of vanguard investments in both Ethiopia and South Africa, the research speaks particularly to contemporary emphases on creating large new cities and residential estates on the urban edge. The book highlights the interrelationship of structural economic problems and urban spatial inequalities. It shows that urban peripheral location can exacerbate socio-economic inequalities and marginalisation, although there is differentiation across places and social groups. Economic opportunities in several peripheral areas are limited, and in some cases declining, although there are levels of local entrepreneurship. Initial commitments to economic development may not be sustained or realised, or not to the extent anticipated. In areas of speculative private investment, or major state-led economic and infrastructure projects, some forms of employment and economic opportunities are being generated, but these may not be accessible to the poor due to skills mismatches, or they may be temporary. However, even places offering limited jobs may present other kinds of opportunities, such as access to housing and land availability. These dynamics can result in extensive reliance on commuting to access work, necessitating careful consideration of transport to and within urban peripheries. Hence, plans to develop large projects on the urban edge need to be approached with caution and with careful attention to the real prospects for creating local urban economies in specific places. Consideration also needs to be given to what sorts of jobs are created and for whom in these places. It suggests the need for greater attention to these issues in planning, across all scales including at the neighbourhood level, to recognise and enhance how home-based economic and social strategies emerge to help offset deficits in residential-led developments. Of course, local entrepreneurship and new forms of urbanism may emerge as places develop and change over time (Charman *et al.*, 2020; Mosiane and Gotz, 2022). Planning for such areas needs to make space for and enable such economies, which are often informal, contrary to new city imagery. Attempts to stamp out or over-regulate informal economic activity, as seen to some extent in the Addis condominium sites, simply perpetuates the problems of people having to engage in long and expensive commutes to work elsewhere, reducing both the potential customer base and purchasing power within the peripheral sites and thereby stifling their potential economic dynamism.

A particular problem for mega-housing developments is the slow pace of growth in service provision and the long time horizons for investment in transport, facilities and other infrastructure. These delays limit the benefits of new housing developments for many years and raise additional questions about the sustainability and value of this kind of development or the way it is implemented.

Problems related to a lack of effective, integrated planning in new settlements are sharply evident. In the Ethiopian context, the fragmented nature of planning and the failure to consider some of the fundamental impacts of building so much housing in these areas – which were freely admitted by many officials involved – suggest the need for much more coherent and multisectoral planning processes before sites are chosen and housing delivered. South Africa has stronger integrated planning policies, but in practice there is poor intersectoral coordination and often disjunctures between planning and implementation. Further, integrated development is often undermined by the failure to account for service and livelihoods needs and how these are fundamentally changed by being geographically peripheral. These arguments point to the need for broader conversations about planning, investment and the management of urban growth in African cities.

Finally, complex inter-governmental relationships and differences in the way governance occurs across boundaries and scales of government also affect the prospects for sustainable development. Significant variations exist between places on the urban periphery and even within areas located adjacent to each other. Some of these reflect the different 'logics' of periphery we outline. Thus, responses through policy formulation and the implementation of development plans need to be locally contextualised. There is no 'one shoe fits all' policy recommendation or practice guideline for the urban periphery, but it is clear in all cases that peripheral governance requires intensive inter-sectoral and inter-scalar coherence. This will often be resisted by those who benefit from the liminal, contested and blurry existing governance in the peripheries and necessitates concerted efforts on the part of central and regional authorities as well as meaningful inclusion of peripheral residents as active citizens.

Closing words

Our book has centred a lived experience approach to understanding African city peripheries in conversation with an analysis of drivers of urban change employing a genetic and generative comparative strategy. It has advanced five logics to characterise and interpret variation within African peripheries, which we believe hold substantial resonance beyond the cases studied here. We view these logics as potentially overlapping categories to be understood contextually in the light of histories of urban change and contemporary dynamics, cautioning against mechanistic application. Our methodological and conceptual approaches are explicitly intertwined, producing a fresh analytical perspective that has the potential for wider application, inviting further theorisation across other African peripheries and beyond.

In concluding the book we also offer some reflections on the growing enthusiasm for researching urban peripheries around the world and how this might be harnessed to push forward the debates with which this book is concerned. Amid increased interest in the many and varied forms of 'extended urbanisation' that characterise the contemporary global landscape, there lies a risk that a focus on the restless dynamics of capital and its entanglements with state authority obscure a focus on the experiences of peripheral life on the ground. Without denying the importance of the endless efforts to monetise land, and how these intersect with shifting paradigms of planning and a hunger for investment in large-scale infrastructure among many global actors, equally important stories are emerging with respect to the social lives of urban peripheries. As spaces of disconnection, aspiration, boredom and (perhaps above all) hope, these are locations in which the imaginaries of future urban places are being made. The more that we can explore and better understand the experience of everyday life in the urban periphery, and its evolution over time, the more likely that life itself can be centred in the making of urban futures.

Note

1 See Fox and Goodfellow (2022) for a discussion.

Bibliography

Aalen, L., and Tronvoll, K. (2009). 'The end of democracy? Curtailing political and civil rights in Ethiopia.' *Review of African Political Economy* 36(120), 193–207.

Abate, A. G. (2019). 'The Addis Ababa Integrated Master Plan and the Oromo claims to Finfinnee in Ethiopia.' *International Journal on Minority and Group Rights* 26(4), 620–38.

Abebe, G., and Hesselberg, J. (2015). 'Community participation and inner-city slum renewal: Relocated people's perspectives on slum clearance and resettlement in Addis Ababa.' *Development in Practice* 25(4), 551–62.

Adam, A. G. (2014). 'Land tenure in the changing peri-urban areas of Ethiopia: The case of Bahir Dar City.' *International Journal of Urban and Regional Research* 38(6), 1970–84.

Adam, A. G. (2020). 'Understanding competing and conflicting interests for peri-urban land in Ethiopia's era of urbanization.' *Environment & Urbanization* 32(1), 55–68.

Adatia, R. (2010). *Retail Centres and Township Development: A Case Study*. Training for Township Renewal Initiative Case Study Series. https://africanplanningschools.org.za/images/downloads/handbooks-and-guides/SACN-Training-for-Township-Renewal-Initiative-Case-Study-Retail-Centres-and-Township-Development.pdf (accessed 14 September 2021).

Adogla-Bessa, D. (2018). 'Cost of land up by 450% in 13 years.' Citi Newsroom, 23 January. https://citinewsroom.com/2018/01/cost-of-land-up-by-450-in-13-years-infographic/ (accessed 30 January 2018).

Agyeman, E. (2015). *Transportation System as a Climate Mitigation Strategy for the Greater Accra Metropolitan Area (GAMA)*. PhD thesis. Legon: University of Ghana.

Ahmad, P. (2010). 'Inner city nodes and public transportation networks: Location, linkages and dependencies of the urban poor within Johannesburg.' In A. Ayala and E. Geurts (eds), *Urbanising Africa: The City Centre Revisited*. Rotterdam: Institute for Housing and Urban Development Studies, 5–19.

Akaateba, M. A. (2019). 'The politics of customary land rights transformation in peri-urban Ghana: Powers of exclusion in the era of land commodification.' *Land Use Policy* 88, 104197. https://doi.org/10.1016/j.landusepol.2019.104197.

Ali, S. N. (2019). 'Infrastructure and economic transformation in Ethiopia.' In F. Cheru, C. Cramer and A. Oqubay (eds), *The Oxford Handbook of the Ethiopian Economy*. Oxford: Oxford University Press, 191–212.

Amanor, K. (2008). 'The changing face of customary land tenure.' In K. Amanor, J. Ubink and K. S. Amanor (eds), *Contesting Land and Custom in Ghana: Chief, State and the Citizen*. Leiden: Leiden University Press, 55–80.

Amis, P. (2001). 'Rethinking UK aid in urban India: Reflections on an impact assessment study of slum improvement projects.' *Environment & Urbanization* 13(1). https://doi.org/10.1177/095624780101300108.

Anane, G. (2021). *The Relationship between Land Administration Systems and Spatial Change in the Peri-Urban Areas in Ghana: The Case of Kumasi and Sunyani*. PhD thesis. Johannesburg: University of the Witwatersrand.

Andreasen, M., Agergaard, J., and Møller-Jensen, J. (2017). 'Suburbanisation, homeownership aspirations and urban housing: Exploring urban expansion in Dar es Salaam.' *Urban Studies* 54(10), 2342–59.

Angel, S., Blei, A., Parent, J., Lamson-Hall, P., Sanchez, N., Civco, D., Lei, P., and Thom, K. (2016). *Atlas of Urban Expansion: The 2016 Edition*. Vol. 1: *Areas and Densities*. New York: New York University.

Angel, S., with Parent, J., Civco, D., and Blei, A. (2011). *Making Room for a Planet of Cities*. Cambridge, MA: Lincoln Institute of Land Policy.

Anyidoho, N. A., Amanquah, S. T., and Clottey, E. A. (2007). *Chieftaincy Institutions and Land Tenure Security: Challenges, Responses and the Potential for Reform*. Accra: Land Policy Reform in Ghana Project, Institute of Statistical, Social and Economic Research, University of Ghana.

Arko-Adjei, A. (2011). *Adapting Land Administration to the Institutional Framework of Customary Tenure: The Case of Peri-Urban Ghana*. Amsterdam: IOS Press.

Asafo, D. M. (2020). *Peri-Urban Development: Land Conflict and Its Effect on Housing Development in Peri-Urban Accra*. PhD thesis. Sheffield: University of Sheffield.

Asafo, D. M. (2022). 'Fragile and compromised housing: Implications of land conflicts on housing development in peri-urban Accra, Ghana.' *Housing Studies*, 1–24. https://doi.org/10.1080/02673037.2022.2119209.

Assefa, T., Abebe, G., Lamoot, I., and Minten, B. (2016). 'Urban food retailing and food prices in Africa: The case of Addis Ababa, Ethiopia.' *Journal of Agribusiness in Developing and Emerging Economies* 6(2), 90–109.

Ayee, J. R. A., Frempong, A. K. D., Asante, R., and Boafo-Arthur, K. (2008). *The Causes, Dynamics and Policy Implications of Land-Related*

Conflicts in the Greater Accra and Eastern Regions of Ghana (Ghana Report). Leiden: African Studies Centre, University of Leiden.

Ballard, R., Hamman, C., and Mkhize, T. (2021). 'Johannesburg: Repetitions and disruptions of spatial patterns.' In A. Lemon, R. Donaldson and G. Visser (eds), *South African Urban Change Three Decades after Apartheid: Homes Still Apart?* Cham: Springer, 91–109.

Ballard, R., and Rubin, M. (2017). 'A "Marshall Plan" for human settlements: How megaprojects became South Africa's housing policy.' *Transformation* 95, 1–31.

Bank, L. (2011). *Home Spaces, Street Styles: Contesting Power and Identity in a South African City*. Johannesburg: Wits Press.

Bank, L. (2015). 'City slums, rural homesteads: Migrant culture, displaced urbanism and the citizenship of the serviced house.' *Journal of Southern African Studies* 41(5), 1067–81.

Bansah, D. K. (2017). *Governance Challenges in Sub-Saharan Africa: The Case of Land Guards and Land Protection in Ghana*. PhD thesis. Kennesaw, GA: Kennesaw State University. https://digitalcommons.kennesaw.edu/incmdoc_etd/14 (accessed 23 October 2023).

Barry, M., and Danso, E. K. (2014). 'Tenure security, land registration and customary tenure in a peri-urban Accra community.' *Land Use Policy* 39, 358–65.

Bartels, L. E. (2019/2020). 'Peri-urbanization as "quiet encroachment" by the middle class: The case of P&T in Greater Accra.' *Urban Geography* 41(4), 524–49.

Beall, J. (2006). 'Cultural weapons: Traditions, inventions and the transition to democratic governance in metropolitan Durban.' *Urban Studies* 43(2), 457–73.

Beall, J., Parnell, S., and Albertyn, C. (2015). 'Elite compacts in Africa: The role of area-based management in the new governmentality of the Durban city-region.' *International Journal of Urban and Regional Research* 39(2), 390–406.

Bekele, S. (2019). 'Ethiopia's transition from a traditional to a developing economy, 1890s–1960s.' In F. Cheru, C. Cramer and A. Oqubay (eds), *The Oxford Handbook of the Ethiopian Economy*. Oxford: Oxford University Press, 17–32.

Belihu, M. S., Goodfellow, T., and Huang, Z. (2018). 'Life in the urban periphery: Boundaries and mobility in Ethiopia's new housing geographies.' Paper presented at the Royal Geographical Society (with Institute of British Geographers) Conference, Cardiff, UK, 28–31 August.

Benit-Gbaffou, C. (2012). 'Party politics, civil society and local democracy: Reflections from Johannesburg.' *Geoforum* 43, 178–89.

Bhorat, H., Lilenstein, K., Oosthuizen, M., and Thornton, A. (2020). *Structural Transformation, Inequality, and Inclusive Growth in South Africa*. WIDER Working Paper 2020/50. Helsinki: World Institute for Development Economics Research, United Nations University.

Black, A. (ed.) (2016). *Towards Employment-Intensive Growth in South Africa*. Cape Town: Juta Press.

Black Sash (1976). *The Black Sash National Conference: Report on Conditions Prevailing in Winterveld; A Summary of a Series of Articles Prepared for the Pretoria News by Neil Jacobsohn*. www2.lib.uct.ac.za/blacksash/pdfs/rep19760317.026.001.000b.pdf (accessed 24 October 2023).

Bloch, R. (2015). 'Africa's new suburbs.' In P. Hamel and R. Keil (eds), *Suburban Governance: A Global View*. Toronto: University of Toronto Press, 253–77.

Bloch, R., Mabin, A., and Todes, A. (2022). 'Africa's suburban constellations.' In R. Keil and F. Wu. *After Suburbia: Urbanization in the Twenty-First Century*. Toronto: University of Toronto Press, 303–18.

Bräutigam, D., and Tang, X. (2014). '"Going global in groups": Structural transformation and China's special economic zones overseas.' *World Development* 63, 78–91.

Bredenoord, J., Van Lindert, P., and Smets, P. (eds) (2014). *Affordable Housing in the Urban Global South: Seeking Sustainable Solutions*. London: Routledge.

Brenner, N., and Schmid, C. (2015). 'Towards a new epistemology of the urban?' *City* 19(2/3), 151–82.

Buckley, R., Kallergis, A., and Wainer, L. (2016). 'Addressing the housing challenge: Avoiding the Ozymandias syndrome.' *Environment & Urbanization* 28(1), 119–38.

Budlender, J. (2016). *Edged Out: Spatial Mismatch and Spatial Justice in South Africa's Main Urban Eras*. www.escr-net.org/resources/edged-out-spatial-mismatch-and-spatial-justice-south-africas-main-urban-areas (accessed 24 October 2023).

Buire, C. (2014). 'The dream and the ordinary: An ethnographic investigation of suburbanisation in Luanda.' *African Studies* 73(2), 290–312.

Burton, A. (2001). 'Urbanisation in eastern Africa: An historical overview, c. 1750–2000.' *AZANIA: Journal of the British Institute in Eastern Africa* 36(1), 1–28.

Butcher, S. (2016). *Infrastructures of Property and Debt: Making Affordable Housing, Race and Place in Johannesburg*. PhD thesis. Minneapolis, MN: University of Minnesota.

Butler, J., Rotberg, R. I., and Adams, J. (1977). *The Black Homelands of South Africa: The Political and Economic Development of Bophuthtswana and Kwa-Zulu*. Berkeley, CA: University of California Press.

Caldeira, T. (2017). 'Peripheral urbanization: Autoconstruction, transversal logics, and politics in cities of the Global South.' *Environment and Planning D: Society and Space* 35(1), 3–20.

Castells, M. (1983). *The City and the Grassroots: A Cross-Cultural Theory of Urban Social Movements*. Berkeley, CA: University of California Press.

Cervero, R. (1995). 'Planned communities, self-containment and community: A cross-national perspective.' *Urban Studies* 32(7), 1135–61.

Charlton, S. (2009). 'Housing for the nation, the city and the household: Competing rationalities as a constraint to reform?' *Development Southern Africa* 26(2), 301–15.

Charlton, S. (2014). 'Public housing in Johannesburg.' In P. Harrison, G. Gotz, A. Todes and C. Wray (eds), *Changing Space, Changing City: Johannesburg after Apartheid*. Johannesburg: Wits University Press, 176–93.

Charlton, S. (2017). 'Poverty, subsidised housing and Lufhereng as a prototype megaproject in Gauteng.' *Transformation* 95(1), 85–110.

Charlton, S. (2018a). 'Access, opportunity and the peripheral "big shop" in South Africa.' Paper presented at the Royal Geographical Society (with Institute of British Geographers) Conference, Cardiff, UK, 28–31 August.

Charlton, S. (2018b). 'Spanning the spectrum: Infrastructural experiences in South Africa's state housing programme.' *International Development Planning Review* 40(2), 97–120.

Charlton, S. (in progress). 'We have everything in that Spar.' Supermarket encounters in African urban peripheries.

Charlton, S., and Kihato, C. (2006). 'Reaching the poor? An analysis of the influences on the evolution of South Africa's housing programme.' In U. Pillay, R. Tomlinson and J. du Toit (eds), *Democracy and Delivery: Urban Policy in South Africa*. Cape Town: HSRC Press, 252–82.

Charlton, S., and Meth, P. (2017). 'Lived experiences of state housing in South Africa's cities: Johannesburg and Durban.' *Transformation* 93(1), 91–115.

Charman, A., Petersen, L., and Govender, T. (2020). *Township Economy: People, Spaces and Practices*. Cape Town: HSRC Press.

Cheru, F., Cramer, C., and Oqubay, A. (eds) (2019). *The Oxford Handbook of the Ethiopian Economy*. Oxford: Oxford University Press.

Chimhowu, A. (2019). 'The "new" African customary land tenure: Characteristic, features and policy implications of a new paradigm.' *Land Use Policy* 81, 897–903.

Chimhowu, A., and Woodhouse, P. (2006). 'Customary vs private property rights? Dynamics and trajectories of vernacular land markets in sub-Saharan Africa.' *Journal of Agrarian Change* 6, 346–71. https://doi.org/10.1111/j.1471-0366.2006.00125.x.

Cirolia, L. R. (2020). 'Fractured fiscal authority and fragmented infrastructures: Financing sustainable urban development in Sub-Saharan Africa.' *Habitat International* 104, 102233.

Cirolia, L. R., Hailu, T., King, J., Da Cruz, N., and Beall, J. (2021). 'Infrastructure governance in the post-networked city: State-led, high-tech sanitation in Addis Ababa's condominium housing.' *Environment and Planning C: Politics and Space* 39(7), 1606–24.

Cirolia, L. R., and Harber, J. (2022). 'Urban statecraft: The governance of transport infrastructures in African cities.' *Urban Studies* 59(12), 2431–50.

Clapham, C. (2017). *The Horn of Africa: State Formation and Decay.* Oxford: Oxford University Press.
Clapham, C. (2018). 'The Ethiopian developmental state.' *Third World Quarterly* 39(6), 1151–65. https://doi.org/10.1080/01436597.2017.1328982.
COGTA (Department of Cooperative Development and Traditional Affairs) (2016). *Integrated Urban Development Framework.* https://iudf.co.za/pdf_downloads/2016-integrated-urban-development-framework/ (accessed 25 October 2023).
COJ (City of Johannesburg) (2015). 'Lufhereng housing development gathers pace.' www.joburg.org.za/media_/Newsroom/Pages/2016%20&%202015%20Articles/Lufhereng-housing-development-gathers-pace.aspx (accessed 24 October 2023).
COJ (2016). *Spatial Development Framework.* Johannesburg: COJ. https://unhabitat.org/sites/default/files/download-manager-files/SDF%20JOHANNESBURG.pdf (accessed 3 November 2023).
COJ (2021). *Draft Spatial Development Framework 2040 (2020/21 Update).* Johannesburg: COJ. www.joburg.org.za/documents_/Pages/Key%20Documents/Draft-Spatial-Framework-2040.aspx (accessed 25 October 2023).
COT (City of Tshwane) (2013). *Spatial Development Framework for the City in the East.* Pretoria: COT.
COT (2021). *Metropolitan Spatial Development Framework – (MSDF) 2021.* Pretoria: COT. www.tshwane.gov.za/?page_id=40453 (accessed 25 October 2023).
Cote-Roy, L., and Moser, S. (2019). '"Does Africa not deserve new cities?" The power of seductive rhetoric around new cities in Africa.' *Urban Studies* 56(1), 2391–407.
Cox, A. (2009). 'Mashatile wants to create lots more jobs.' IOL News, 17 February. www.iol.co.za/news/south-africa/mashatile-wants-to-create-lots-more-jobs-434812 (accessed 24 October 2023).
Crankshaw, O., and Parnell, S. (1996). 'Housing provision and the need for an urbanisation policy in the new South Africa.' *Urban Forum* 7, 232–7.
Crenshaw, K. (1989). 'Demarginalizing the intersection of race and sex: A black feminist critique of antidiscrimination doctrine, feminist theory, and antiracist politics.' *University of Chicago Legal Forum* 1(Art. 8), 139–67.
Crush, J. (2014). 'Approaching food security in cities of the global south.' In S. Parnell and S. Oldfield (eds), *The Routledge Handbook on Cities of the Global South.* Oxford: Routledge, 543–55.
CSP (City Support Programme) (2016). *Guidance Note for Built Environment Support Programme (BEPP), 2016/7–2018/9.* Pretoria: National Treasury.
CSP (2021a). *City Spatialised Economic Data Metro Level Report: eThekwini.* Pretoria: National Treasury.
CSP (2021b). *City Spatialised Economic Data Metro Level Report: eThekwini.* Pretoria: National Treasury.

Dahl, R. A. (1961). *Who Governs: Democracy and Power in an American City*. New Haven, CT: Yale University Press.

Dardagan, C. (2012). 'Houses contractors built "aren't safe".' Mercury, 12 March. www.pressreader.com/south-africa/the-mercury-south-africa/20120312/281681136820672 (accessed 1 March 2022).

Das Nair, R. (2018). 'The internationalisation of supermarkets and the nature of competitive rivalry in retailing in Southern Africa.' *Development Southern Africa* 35(3), 315–33.

Davies, R. J. (1981). 'The spatial formation of the South African city.' *GeoJournal* 2(Suppl. 2), 59–72.

Dawson, H. J. (2022). 'Living, not just surviving: The politics of refusing low-wage jobs in urban South Africa.' *Economy and Society* 51(3), 375–97.

De Boeck, F., and Plissart, M. (2004). *Kinshasa: Tales of the Invisible City*. Gent: Ludion.

Dechassa, T. T., and Jalata, G. G. (2021). 'Freedom from want and the constitutional right to development in Ethiopia: Urban productive safety net programme –the case of Addis Ababa.' In C. C. Ngang and S. D. Kamga (eds), *Natural Resource Sovereignty and the Right to Development in Africa*. London: Routledge, 212–28.

Delz, S. (2014). *Ethiopia's Low-Cost Housing Program: How Concepts of Individual Home-Ownership and Housing Blocks Still Walk Abroad*. Zurich: ETH Zurich. https://ethz.ch/content/dam/ethz/special-interest/conference-websites-dam/no-cost-housing-dam/documents/Delz_160530_Low-No-Cost%20Housing%20Conference_Paper_Sascha%20Delz.pdf (accessed 6 March 2022).

Demissie, F. (2008). 'Situated neoliberalism and urban crisis in Addis Ababa, Ethiopia.' *African Identities* 6(4), 505–27.

Derso, A., Bizuneh, H., Keleb, A., Ademas, A., and Adane, M. (2021). 'Food insecurity status and determinants among urban productive safety net program beneficiary households in Addis Ababa, Ethiopia.' *PloS One* 16(9), e0256634.

Dewar, D. (2008). 'A critique of South African housing policy and some postulations about planning and policy-making in African cities.' *Town and Regional Planning* 52, 32–7.

Dewar, D., and Uytenbogaardt, R. (1990). *South African Cities: A Manifesto for Change*. Cape Town: Urban Problems Research Unit, University of Cape Town.

Di Nunzio, M. (2014). '"Do not cross the red line": The 2010 general elections, dissent, and political mobilization in urban Ethiopia.' *African Affairs* 113(452), 409–30.

Di Nunzio, M. (2015). 'What is the alternative? Youth, entrepreneurship and the developmental state in urban Ethiopia.' *Development and Change* 46(5), 1179–200.

Di Nunzio, M. (2019). *The Act of Living: Street Life, Marginality, and Development in Urban Ethiopia*. Ithaca, NY: Cornell University Press.

Di Nunzio, M. (2022a). 'Evictions for development: Creative destruction, redistribution and the politics of unequal entitlements in inner-city Addis Ababa (Ethiopia), 2010–2018.' *Political Geography* 98, 102671.

Di Nunzio, M. (2022b). 'Work, development, and refusal in urban Ethiopia.' *American Ethnologist* 49(3), 401–12.

DPME (Department of Planning, Monitoring and Evaluation) (2015). *Summary Report on the Design and Implementation Evaluation of the Urban Settlements Development Grant*. Pretoria: Presidency.

Duminy, J., Parnell, S., and Brown-Luthango, M. (2020). *Supporting City Futures: The Cities Support Programme and the Urban Challenge in South Africa*. Cape Town: African Centre for Cities, University of Cape Town.

Dupuis, A., and Thorns, D. C. (1998). 'Home, home ownership and the search for ontological security.' *Sociological Review* 46(1), 24–47.

Duroyaume, P. (2015). 'Addis Ababa and the urban renewal in Ethiopia.' In G. Prunier and É. Ficquet (eds), *Understanding Contemporary Ethiopia*. London: Hurst, 395–413.

Eduful, A. K., and Eduful, M. (2021). 'Malls, modernity and consumption: Shopping malls as new projectors of modernity in Accra, Ghana.' *Journal of Consumer Culture* 22(4), 949–68.

Ehwi, R. J., and Mawuli, D. A. (2021). '"Landguardism" in Ghana: Examining public perceptions about the driving factors.' *Land Use Policy* 109, 105630.

Ehwi, R. J., Morrison, N., and Tyler, P. (2019). 'Gated communities and land administration challenges in Ghana: Reappraising the reasons why people move into gated communities.' *Housing Studies* 36(3), 307–35.

Ejigu, A. G. (2012). 'Socio-spatial tensions and interactions: An ethnography of the condominium housing of Addis Ababa, Ethiopia.' In M. Robertson (ed.), *Sustainable Cities: Local Solutions in the Global South*. Rugby: Practical Action Publishing, 97–112.

Ekers, M., Hamel, P., and Keil, R. (2012). 'Governing suburbia: Modalities and mechanisms of suburban governance.' *Regional Studies* 46(3), 405–22.

Ellero, J. (2015). *Crumbling Housing and Failed Promises: A Critical Study of Corruption in Low-Cost Housing in the Phoenix Area*. Masters dissertation. Durban: University of KwaZulu Natal. https://researchspace.ukzn.ac.za/bitstream/handle/10413/12474/Ellero_Justin_2015.pdf?sequence=1&isAllowed=y (accessed 1 March 2022).

Endale, A. (2022). 'IPDC, Electric Utility, city admin lock horns over Kilinto, Bole Lemi industrial parks.' *The Reporter*, 22 September. www.thereporterethiopia.com/26458/ (accessed 14 November 2022).

ePropertyNews (2018). 'Ekandustria Industrial Park a boon for Mpumalanga town.' *ePropertyNews*, 26 March. https://eprop.co.za/commercial-property-news/item/21126-ekandustria-industrial-park-a-boon-for-mpumalanga-town (accessed 17 November 2020).

Bibliography

Erasmus, D. (2019). 'Contractor continues to rake in tenders despite "dangerous and substandard" work.' *City Press*, 21 August. www.news24.com/citypress/business/contractor-continues-to-rake-in-tenders-despite-dangerous-and-substandard-work-20190821 (accessed 1 March 2022).

Erasmus, J. (2013). 'How the deals worked, and how the costs spiralled.' *The Witness*, 14 November. www.news24.com/witness/archive/How-the-deals-worked-and-how-the-costs-spiralled-20150430 (accessed 24 October 2023).

eThekwini (2020). *Municipal Spatial Development Framework 2020–2021: Final Report May 2020*. eThekwini: eThekwini Municipality. https://economic.durban.gov.za/storage/Documents/DPEM/Documents%20%20Notices/Strategic%20Spatial%20Planning/SDF/SDF%202020%20-%202021/Report/SDF%202020%20-%202021%20Report.pdf (accessed 5 March 2024).

Etim, E. E., Atser, J., and Akpabio, F. (2007). 'The new social housing scheme in Nigeria: How beneficial for the less privileged?' *Global Journal of Social Sciences* 6(1), 1–6.

Farole, T., and Sharp, M. (2017). *Spatial Industrial Policy, Special Economic Zones, and Cities in South Africa: World Bank Urbanisation Review, Report to National Treasury*. Pretoria: National Treasury.

Fei, D., and Liao, C. (2020). 'Chinese eastern industrial zone in Ethiopia: Unpacking the enclave.' *Third World Quarterly* 41(4), 623–44.

Fincher, R., and Jacobs, J. (1998). *Cities of Difference*. New York: Guilford Press.

Fine, B., and Rustomjee, Z. (1996). *The Political Economy of South Africa: From Minerals-Energy Complex to Industrialisation*. London: Hurst.

Fishman, R. (1989). 'Bourgeois utopias: Visions of suburbia.' In *Bourgeois Utopias: The Rise and Fall of Suburbia*. New York: Basic Books, 21–31.

Follmann, A. (2022). 'Geographies of peri-urbanization in the global south.' *Geography Compass* 16(7), e12650.

Follmann, A., Kennedy, L., Pfeffer, K., and Wu, F. (2022). 'Peri-urban transformation in the Global South: A comparative socio-spatial analytics approach.' *Regional Studies* 57(3), 447–61.

Forrest, R., and Hirayama, Y. (2018). 'Late home ownership and social re-stratification.' *Economy and Society* 47(2), 257–79.

Fox, S., and Goodfellow, T. (2022). 'On the conditions of "late urbanisation".' *Urban Studies* 59(10), 1959–80.

Fraser, A. (2010). 'The craft of scalar practices.' *Environment and Planning A* 42(2), 332–46.

Gaborit, P. (2010). *European New Towns: Image, Identities, and Future Perspectives*. Brussels: Peter Lang.

Gaborit, P. (2013). *New Medinas: Towards Sustainable New Towns? Interconnected Experiences Spanning the North and South Mediterranean*. Brussels: Peter Lang.

Garreau, J. (1991). *Edge City: Life on the Frontier*. New York: Anchor Books.

Gauteng Department of Human Settlements (2022). *Decisive Spatial Transformation of Human Settlements and Urban Development. Issue 5: Summary Report*. Johannesburg: Gauteng Department of Human Settlements.

Gebre-Egziabher, T. (2014). *The Effect of Development Induced Displacement on Relocated Household: The Case of Addis Ababa*. MA in Development Studies. The Hague: International Institute of Social Studies.

Gebre-Egziabher, T., and Yemeru, E. A. (2019). 'Urbanization and industrial development in Ethiopia.' In F. Cheru, C. Cramer and A. Oqubay (eds), *The Oxford Handbook of the Ethiopian Economy*. Oxford: Oxford University Press, 785–803.

Gebremariam, E. B. (2020). *The Politics of Dominating Addis Ababa (2005–2018)*. Effective States and Inclusive Development Working Paper 148. Manchester: University of Manchester.

Geda, A. (2022). *The Challenge of Unemployment and Youth Unemployment amidst Fast Economic Growth in Ethiopia: African Economic Research Consortium Working Paper GSYE-008*. Nairobi: African Economic Research Consortium.

Giannecchini, P., and Taylor, I. (2018). 'The eastern industrial zone in Ethiopia: Catalyst for development?' *Geoforum* 88, 28–35.

Gilbert, A. (2016). 'Rental housing: The international experience.' *Habitat International* 54(3), 173–81.

Gillespie, T. (2020). 'The real estate frontier.' *International Journal of Urban and Regional Research* 44(4), 599–616.

Goldman, M. (2011). 'Speculative urbanism and the making of the next world city.' *International Journal of Urban and Regional Research* 35(3), 555–81.

Gómez-Álvarez, D., Rajack, R. M., López-Moreno, E., and Lanfranchi, G. (eds) (2017). *Steering the Metropolis: Metropolitan Governance for Sustainable Urban Development*. Washington, DC: Inter-American Development Bank.

Goodfellow, T. (2015). *Taxing the Urban Boom: Property Taxation and Land Leasing in Kigali and Addis Ababa*. ICTD Working Paper 38. Brighton: Institute for Development Studies.

Goodfellow, T. (2017a). 'Urban fortunes and skeleton cityscapes: Real estate and late urbanization in Kigali and Addis Ababa.' *International Journal of Urban and Regional Research* 41(5), 786–803.

Goodfellow, T. (2017b). 'Taxing property in a neo-developmental state: The politics of urban land value capture in Rwanda and Ethiopia.' *African Affairs* 116(465), 549–72.

Goodfellow, T. (2022). *Politics and the Urban Frontier: Transformation and Divergence in Late Urbanizing East Africa*. Oxford: Oxford University Press.

Goodfellow, T., and Huang, Z. (2021). 'Contingent infrastructure and the dilution of "Chineseness": Reframing roads and rail in Kampala

and Addis Ababa.' *Environment and Planning A: Economy and Space* 53(4), 655–74.
Goodfellow, T., Huang, Z., and Belihu, M. S. (2018). 'The politics of life in the urban periphery: Territory, mobility and class formation in Addis Ababa.' Paper presented at the Biennial Conference of the African Studies Association of the UK, Birmingham, 11–13 September.
Goodfellow, T., and Mukwaya, P. I. (2021). *The Political Economy of Public Transport in Greater Kampala: Movers, Spoilers and Prospects for Reform*. Kampala: Frederich Ebert Stiftung.
Gough, K. V., and Yankson, P. W. K. (2000). 'Land markets in African cities: The case of peri-urban Accra, Ghana.' *Urban Studies* 37(13), 2485–500.
Gough, K. V., and Yankson, P. W. K. (2006). 'Conflict and cooperation in environmental management in peri-urban Accra, Ghana.' In D. McGregor, D. Simon and D. A. Thompson (eds), *The Peri-Urban Interface: Approaches to Sustainable Natural and Human Resource Use*. London: Earthscan, 196–210.
Güney, K., Keil, R., and Üçoğlu, M. (eds) (2019). *Massive Suburbanization: (Re)building the Global Periphery*. Toronto: University of Toronto Press.
Gyapong, P. (2009). *Assessing Customary Land Tenure Institutions for Land Administration in Ghana: Good Governance Perspective. Case study of Gbawe, Greater Accra, Ghana*. Thesis. Enschede: University of Twente.
Haddis, E. (2019). *Inner-City Redevelopment in an Aspiring Developmental State: The Case of Addis Ababa Ethiopia*. PhD thesis. Manchester: University of Manchester.
Hansmann, R. (2020). *Planning for Airports and Logistics: Case of Dube Trade Port*. PhD thesis. Durban: Durban University of Technology.
Harper, P. (2022). 'Former Tongaat Hulett bosses in court for fraud.' *Mail and Guardian*, 2 February. https://mg.co.za/news/2022-02-11-former-tongaat-hulett-bosses-in-court-for-fraud/ (accessed 28 July 2023).
Harrison, P., and Dinath, Y. (2017). 'Gauteng – on the edge.' In S. Peberdy, P. Harrison and Y. Dinath (eds), *Uneven Spaces: Core and Periphery in the Gauteng City-Region; GCRO Research Report 6*. Johannesburg: GCRO, 208–314.
Harrison, P., and Todes, A. (2015). 'Spatial transformations in a "loosening state": South Africa in a comparative perspective.' *Geoforum* 61, 148–62.
Harrison, P., and Todes, A. (2017). 'Satellite settlement on the spatial periphery: Lessons from international and Gauteng experience.' *Transformation* 95(1), 32–62.
Harrison, P., and Todes, A. (2020). 'Strategic planning and the challenges of spatial transformation in Johannesburg.' In D. Rukama (ed.), *Planning Mega-Cities in the Global South*. London: Routledge, 79–90.
Harrison, P., Todes, A., and Watson, V. (2008). *Planning and Transformation: Lessons from the Post-Apartheid Experience*. London: Routledge.

Hart, P. (2002). *Disabling Globalization: Places of Power in Post-Apartheid South Africa.* Berkeley, CA: University of California Press.

Harvey, D. (1982). *The Limits to Capital.* London: Verso Books.

Heer, B. (2017). 'Shopping malls as social space: New forms of public life in Johannesburg.' In O. Moreillon, A. Muller and L. Stiebel (eds), *Cities in Flux: Metropolitan Spaces in South African Literary and Visual Texts: Festschrift in Honour of Professor Em. Dr. Therese Steffen.* Münster: LIT Verlag, 101–22.

Henderson, V., and Mitra, A. (1996). 'The new urban landscape: Developers and edge cities.' *Regional Science and Urban Economics* 26(6), 613–43.

Himmelreich, J. (2010). 'Suburbing Addis: Marketing an African suburbia.' In M. Angélil and D. Hebel (eds), *Cities of Change Addis Ababa: Transformation Strategies for Urban Territories in the 21st Century.* Basel: Birkahuser, 133–8.

Hindson, D., Byerley, M., and Morris, M. (1994). 'From violence to reconstruction: The making, disintegration and remaking of an apartheid city.' *Antipode* 26(4), 323–50.

Horn, A., Hattingh, P., and Vermaak, J. (1992). 'Winterveld: An urban interface settlement on the Pretoria metropolitan fringe.' In D. Smith (ed.), *The Apartheid City and Beyond: Urbanization and Social Change in South Africa.* London: Routledge, 113–24.

Horn, P. (2022). 'The politics of hyperregulation in La Paz, Bolivia: Speculative peri-urban development in a context of unresolved municipal boundary conflicts.' *Urban Studies* 59(12), 2489–505.

Houghton, J. (2013). 'Entanglement: The negotiation of urban development imperatives in Durban's public–private partnerships.' *Urban Studies* 50(13), 2791–808. https://doi.org/10.1177/0042098013477696.

Houghton, J. (2018). 'Jobs and livelihoods in the periphery of three South African cities.' Paper for the African Centre for Cities Conference, University of Cape Town, 1–3 February.

Houghton, J. (2019). 'International evidence on aligning economic activity with housing policy.' Paper presented at the Centre for Development and Enterprise, Johannesburg.

Houghton, J., and Todes, A. (2019). 'Employment, livelihoods and marginality in two South African urban peripheries.' Paper presented at the European Conference on African Studies, Edinburgh, 12–14 June.

Howe, L. (2022). 'Processes of peripheralisation: Toehold and aspirational urbanisation in the GCR.' *Antipode* 54(6), 1803–28.

Huchzermeyer, M. (2001). 'Housing for the poor? Negotiated housing policy in South Africa.' *Habitat International* 25(3), 303–31.

Industrial Property News (2019). 'Ekandustria Industrial Park receives facelift.' *Industrial Property News*, 15 April. www.bizcommunity.com/Article/196/711/189755.html (accessed 1 November 2020).

Jones, G. A., and Datta, K. (2000). 'Enabling markets to work? Housing policy in the "new" South Africa.' *International Planning Studies* 5(3), 393–416.

Kabale, U. (2020). *Exploring the Tshwane: Kungwini Municipal Amalgamation Process.* Masters research report. Johannesburg: University of the Witwatersrand.

Kanai, J. M., and Schindler, S. (2019). 'Peri-urban promises of connectivity: Linking project-led polycentrism to the infrastructure scramble.' *Environment and Planning A: Economy and Space* 51(2), 302–22.

Kanai, J. M., and Schindler, S. (2022). 'Infrastructure-led development and the peri-urban question: Furthering crossover comparisons.' *Urban Studies* 59(8), 1597–617.

Karaman, O., Sawyer, L., Schmid, C., and Wong, K. P. (2020). 'Plot by plot: Plotting urbanism as an ordinary process of urbanisation.' *Antipode* 52(4), 1122–51.

Kasanga, K., and Kotey, N. A. (2001). *Land Management in Ghana: Building on Tradition and Modernity.* London: International Institute for Environment and Development.

Kassahun, M., and Bishu, S. G. (2018). *The Governance of Addis Ababa City Turn-Around Projects: Addis Ababa Light Rail Transit and Housing.* Nairobi: Partnership for African Social and Governance Research.

Kefale, A. (2011). 'The (un) making of opposition coalitions and the challenge of democratization in Ethiopia, 1991–2011.' *Journal of Eastern African Studies* 5(4), 681–701.

Keil, R. (2018). *Suburban Planet: Making the World Urban from the Outside In.* Cambridge: Polity Press.

Keil, R., Hamel, P., Boudreau, J. A., and Kipfer, S. (eds) (2016). *Governing Cities through Regions: Canadian and European Perspectives.* Waterloo: Wilfrid Laurier University Press.

Keil, R., and Wu, F. (2022). *After Suburbia: Urbanization in the Twenty-First Century.* Toronto: University of Toronto Press.

Keller, E. J., and Mukudi-Omwami, E. (2017). 'Rapid urban expansion and the challenge of pro-poor housing in Addis Ababa, Ethiopia.' *Africa Review* 9, 173–85.

Khumalo, K. (2018). *The Role of Technology on Small Businesses in Peripheral Townships: The Case of Winterveld.* BSc Honours research report. Johannesburg: University of the Witwatersrand.

Kinfu, E., Bombeck, H., Nigussie, A., and Wegayehu, F. (2019). 'The genesis of peri-urban Ethiopia: The case of Hawassa city.' *Journal of Land and Rural Studies* 7(1), 71–95.

Kloosterboer, M. H. (2019). *The "New" Addis Ababa: Shantytown or Global City? An Assessment of Large-Scale Inner-City Renewal, Redevelopment and Displacement for the Construction of a 'New' Addis Ababa.* PhD thesis. Glasgow: University of Glasgow.

Klopp, J. M., Harber, J., and Quarshie, M. (2019). *A Review of BRT as Public Transport Reform in African Cities.* VREF research synthesis project, Governance of Metropolitan Transport.

Kusaana, E. D., and Gerber, N. (2015). 'Institutional synergies in customary land markets: Selected case studies of large-scale land acquisitions (LSLAs) in Ghana.' *Land* 4(3), 842–68.

Lall, S., Henderson, J., and Venables, A. (2017). *Africa's Cities: Opening Doors to the World*. Washington, DC: World Bank.

Lang, R., and Knox, P. K. (2013). 'The new metropolis: Rethinking megalopolis.' In R. Lang and P. K. Knox (eds), *The Futures of the City Region*. London: Routledge, 29–42.

Larbi, W. O. (1996). 'Spatial planning and urban fragmentation in Accra.' *Third World Planning Review* 18(2), 193–214.

Larsen, L., Yeshitela, K., Mulatu, T., Seifu, S., and Desta, H. (2019). 'The impact of rapid urbanization and public housing development on urban form and density in Addis Ababa, Ethiopia.' *Land* 8(4), 66. https://doi.org/10.3390/land8040066.

Lavers, T. (2013). 'Food security and social protection in highland Ethiopia: Linking the productive safety net to the land question.' *Journal of Modern African Studies* 51(3), 459–85.

Lavers, T. (2018). 'Responding to land-based conflict in Ethiopia: The land rights of ethnic minorities under federalism.' *African Affairs* 117(468), 462–84.

Lavers, T. (2019). 'Social protection in an aspiring "developmental state": The political drivers of Ethiopia's PSNP.' *African Affairs* 118(473), 646–71.

Lavers, T. (2023). *Ethiopia's 'Developmental State': Political Order and Distributive Crisis*. Cambridge: Cambridge University Press.

Ledger, T. (2016). *An Empty Plate: Why We Are Losing the Battle for Our Food System, Why it Matters and How We Can Win It Back*. Johannesburg: Jacana Media.

Leduka, R. (2006). 'Chiefs, civil servants and the city council: State–society relations in evolving land delivery processes in Maseru, Lesotho.' *International Development Planning Review* 28(2), 181–208.

Lefort, R. (2007). 'Powers – mengist – and peasants in rural Ethiopia: The May 2005 elections.' *Journal of Modern African Studies* 45(2), 253–73.

Lefort, R. (2015). 'The Ethiopian economy: The developmental state vs the free market.' In G. Prunier and E. Fiquet (eds), *Understanding Contemporary Ethiopia*. London: Hurst, 357–94.

Lemanski, C. (2020). 'Infrastructural citizenship: The everyday citizenships of adapting and/or destroying public infrastructure in Cape Town, South Africa.' *Transactions of the Institute of British Geographers* 45(3), 589–605.

Lemanski, C., Charlton, S., and Meth, P. (2017). 'Living in state housing: Expectations, contradictions and consequences.' *Transformation: Critical Perspectives on Southern Africa* 93(1), 1–12. https://doi.org/10.1353/trn.2017.0000.

Lewis, B. (2012). *A Justice Perspective of Water and Sanitation Service Delivery*. Masters dissertation. Amsterdam: University of Amsterdam.

Lim, G.-C., Follain, J., and Renaud, B. (1980). 'Determinants of home-ownership in a developing economy: The case of Korea.' *Urban Studies* 17(1), 13–23.

Lin, J. Y., Xu, J., and Hager, S. (2019). 'Special economic zones and structural transformation in Ethiopia: A new structural economics perspective.' In F. Cheru, C. Cramer and A. Oqubay (eds), *The Oxford Handbook of the Ethiopian Economy*. Oxford: Oxford University Press, 807–23.

Lin, S.-H. (2001). *The Relations between the Republic of China and the Republic of South Africa, 1948–1998*. PhD thesis. Pretoria: University of Pretoria.

Lloyd-Jones, T., and Brown, A. (2002). 'Spatial planning, access and infrastructure.' In C. Rakodi and T. Lloyd-Jones (eds), *Urban Livelihoods: A People-Centred Approach to Reducing Poverty*. London: Earthscan, 188–204.

Logan, J., and Molotch, H. (1987). *Urban Fortunes*. Berkeley, CA: University of California Press.

Lombard, M. (2016). 'Land conflict in peri-urban areas: Exploring the effects of land reforms on informal settlement in Mexico.' *Urban Studies* 53(13), 2700–20.

Lombard, M., Hernandez-Garcia, J., and Lopez Angulo, A. (2021). 'Informal rental housing in Colombia: An essential option for low-income households.' *International Development Planning Review* 43(2), 257–77.

Lund, C. (2013). 'The past and space: On arguments in Africa land control.' *Africa* 83(1), 14–35.

Mabin, A. (1992). 'Dispossession, exploitation and struggle: An historical overview of South African urbanization.' In D. Smith (ed.), *The Apartheid City and Beyond*. London: Routledge, 13–24.

Mabin, A. (2020). 'A century of South African housing acts 1920–2020.' *Urban Forum* 31, 453–72.

Mabin, A., Butcher, S., and Bloch, R. (2013). 'Peripheries, suburbanisms and change in sub-Saharan African cities.' *Social Dynamics* 39(2), 167–90.

Mabin, A., and Smit, D. (1997). 'Reconstructing South Africa's cities? The making of urban planning 1900–2000.' *Planning Perspectives* 12(2), 193–223.

Mains, D. (2011). *Hope Is Cut: Youth, Unemployment, and the Future in Urban Ethiopia*. Philadelphia: Temple University Press.

Mains, D. (2017). 'Too much time: Changing conceptions of boredom, progress, and the future among young men in urban Ethiopia, 2003–2015.' *Focaal: Journal of Global and Historical Anthropology* 78, 38–51.

Mains, D. (2019). *Under Construction: Technologies of Development in Urban Ethiopia*. Durham, NC: Duke University Press.

Makgetla, N. (2020). 'Inequality in South Africa: An overview.' Trade and Industrial Policy Strategy working paper.

Manyazewal, M. (2019). 'Financing Ethiopia's development.' In F. Cheru, C. Cramer and A. Oqubay, *The Oxford Handbook of the Ethiopian Economy*. Oxford: Oxford University Press, 175–94.

Marais, L., Ntema, J., Cloete, J., Rani, K., and Lenka, M. (2016). 'Reinforcing housing assets in the wrong location? The case of Botshabelo, South Africa.' *Urban Forum* 27(3), 347–62.

Marcuse, P. (2013). 'Housing policy and the myth of the benevolent state.' In J. R. Tighe and E. J. Mueller (eds), *The Affordable Housing Reader*. Oxford: Routledge, 36–43.

Marcuse, P., and Madden, D. (2016). *In Defense of Housing: The Politics of Crisis*. London: Verso.

Markakis, J. (1974). *Ethiopia: Anatomy of a Traditional Polity*. Oxford: Oxford University Press.

Massey, D. (2005). *For Space*. London: Sage.

Matsumoto, T., and Crook, J. (2021). *Sustainable and Inclusive Housing in Ethiopia: A Policy Assessment*. Coalition for Urban Transitions policy brief. https://urbantransitions.global/wp-content/uploads/2021/03/Sustainable-and-Inclusive-Housing-in-Ethiopia_A-policy-assessment_FINAL.pdf (accessed 2 November 2023).

Mbatha, S. (2018). *Informal Transactions of Low-Income Houses in South Africa: A Case Study of eThekwini Municipality*. PhD thesis. Stuttgart: Stuttgart University. https://elib.uni-stuttgart.de/bitstream/11682/9816/1/Sandile_Mbatha%202018.pdf (accessed 1 March 2022).

Mbatha, S., and Mchunu, K. (2016). 'Tracking peri-urban changes in eThekwini Municipality: Beyond the "poor–rich" dichotomy.' *Urban Research and Practice* 9(3), 275–89.

Mbiba, B., and Huchzermeyer, M. (2002). 'Contentious development: Peri-urban studies in sub-Saharan Africa.' *Progress in Development Studies* 2(2), 113–31.

McCarthy, J., and Robinson, P. (2000). *Patterns of Moreland's Urban Development: Impact on Employment and Investment in Infrastructure*. Unpublished report for Moreland, Durban.

McCord, A. (2012). *Public Works and Social Protection in Sub-Saharan Africa: Do Public Works Work for the Poor?* Helsinki: United Nations University Press.

McFarlane, C. (2020). 'De/re-densification.' *City* 24(1–2), 314–24.

McGregor, D. F. M., Adam-Bradford, A., Thompson, D. A., and Simon, D. (2011). 'Resource management and agriculture in the peri-urban interface of Kumasi, Ghana: Problems and prospects.' *Singapore Journal of Tropical Geography* 32(3), 382–98.

McGregor, J., and Chatiza, K. (2019). 'Frontiers of urban control: Lawlessness on the city edge and forms of clientalist statecraft in Zimbabwe.' *Antipode* 51(5), 1554–80.

Megento, T. (2013). 'Inner city housing and urban development-induced displacement: Impact on poor female-headed households in Arada sub city of Addis Ababa, Ethiopia.' *Journal of Sustainable Development in Africa* 15(2), 131–41.

Melo, V. (2017). 'Top-down low-cost housing supply since the mid-1990s in Maputo: Bottom-up responses and spatial consequences.' *Transformation: Critical Perspectives on Southern Africa* 93(1), 41–67.

Meniga, M. (2015). 'Growth and challenges of cooperative sector in Ethiopia.' *International Journal of Scientific Research* 4(3), 351–6.

Mercer, C. (2017). 'Landscapes of extended ruralisation: Postcolonial suburbs in Dar es Salaam, Tanzania.' *Transactions of the Institute of British Geographers* 42(1), 72–83.

Mercer, C. (2020). 'Boundary work: Becoming middle class in suburban Dar es Salaam.' *International Journal of Urban and Regional Research* 44(3), 521–36.

Meth, P. (2013). '"I don't like my children to grow up in this bad area": Parental anxieties about living in informal settlements.' *International Journal of Urban and Regional Research* 37(2), 537–55.

Meth, P., Belihu, M., Buthelezi, S., and Masikane, F. (2022). 'Not entirely displacement: Conceptualising relocation in Ethiopia and South Africa as "disruptive re-placement".' *Urban Geography* 44(5), 824–49.

Meth, P., and Buthelezi, S. (2017). 'New housing/new crime? Changes in safety, governance and everyday incivilities for residents relocated from informal to formal housing at Hammond's Farm, eThekwini.' *Geoforum* 82, 77–86.

Meth, P., Buthelezi, S., and Rajasekhar, S. (2018). 'Gendered il/legalities of housing formalisation in India and South Africa.' *Environment and Planning A: Economy and Space* 51(5), 1068–88.

Meth, P., and Charlton, C. (2016). 'Men's experiences of state sponsored housing in South Africa: Emerging issues and key questions.' *Housing Studies* 32(4), 470–90.

Meth, P., Goodfellow, T., Todes, A., and Charlton, S. (2021a). 'Conceptualizing African urban peripheries.' *International Journal of Urban and Regional Research* 45, 985–1007.

Meth, P., Todes, A., Charlton, S., Mukwedeya, T., Houghton, J., Goodfellow, T., Belihu, M. S., Huang, Z., Asafo, D., Buthelezi, S., and Masikane, F. (2021b). 'At the city edge: Situating peripheries research in South Africa and Ethiopia.' In M. Keith and A. de Souza Santos (eds), *African Cities and Collaborative Futures: Urban Platforms and Metropolitan Logistics*. Manchester: Manchester University Press, 30–52.

Ministry of Federal Affairs (2003). *Low Cost Housing Technical Manual, Volume I*. Addis Ababa: Ministry of Federal Affairs.

Ministry of Works and Urban Development (2008). 'Integrated housing development programme of the Federal Democratic Republic of Ethiopia.' Paper presented at the African Ministerial Conference on Housing and Urban Development (AMCHUD), Abuja, Nigeria.

Mireku, K. O., Kuusaana, E. D., and Kidido, J. K. (2016). 'Legal implications of allocation papers in land transactions in Ghana – a case study of the Kumasi traditional area.' *Land Use Policy* 50, 148–55.

MoFED (Ministry of Finance and Economic Development) (2006). *Plan for Accelerated and Sustained Development to End Poverty (PASDEP)*. Addis Ababa: MoFED.

Mohamed, A., Worku, H., and Lika, T. (2020). 'Urban and regional planning approaches for sustainable governance: The case of Addis Ababa and the surrounding area changing landscape.' *City and Environment Interactions* 8 (Art. 100050), 1–11. https://doi.org/10.1016/j.cacint.2020.100050.

Moseki, B. (1979). 'The Winterveld squatter area.' *Reality* 11(6), 8–9. https://web.archive.org/web/20200907144349/www.disa.ukzn.ac.za/renov794 (accessed 24 October 2023).

Mosiane, N., and Gotz, G. (2022). *Displaced Urbanisation or Displaced Urbanism? Rethinking Development in the Peripheries of the Gauteng City-Region*. Gauteng City Region Observatory Provocation 8. https://doi.org/10.36634/SVRW2580.

Mosoetsa, S. (2011). *Eating from One Pot: The Dynamics of Survival in Poor South African Households*. Johannesburg: Wits University Press.

MoUDHC (Ministry of Urban Development, Housing and Construction) (2014). *National Report on Housing and Sustainable Urban Development*. Addis Ababa: MoUDHC.

Mukhija, V. (2001). 'Enabling slum redevelopment in Mumbai: Policy paradox in practice.' *Housing Studies* 16(6), 791–806.

Mukwedeya, T. (2018). 'Boredom and the construction of peripherality in Gauteng and eThekwini.' Paper presented at the Royal Geographical Society (with Institute of British Geographers) Conference, Cardiff, UK, 28–31 August.

Myers, R., and Hansen, C. P. (2020). 'Revisiting a theory of access: A review.' *Society and Natural Resources* 33(2), 146–66.

National Department of Human Settlements (2014). *Celebrating 20 Years of Human Settlements: Bringing the Freedom Charter to Life*. Pretoria: National Department of Human Settlements.

National Treasury (2013). *Identification of the Urban Hub: Document 1: Methodology Development*. Pretoria: National Treasury.

National Treasury (2019). *Labour Market Macro Monitor*. Pretoria: National Treasury.

Ntema, J., and Van Rooyen, D. (2016). 'Redressing spatial inequalities in a former R293 town.' *Journal of Public Administration* 51(1), 136–53.

Nugent, P. (2018). 'Africa's re-enchantment with big infrastructure: White elephants dancing in virtuous circles?' In J. Schubert, U. Engel and E. Macamo (eds), *Extractive Industries and Changing State Dynamics in Africa beyond the Resource Curse*. Oxford: Routledge, 22–40.

Obala, L. M. (2011). *The Relationship between Urban Land Conflicts and Inequity: The Case of Nairobi*. PhD thesis. Johannesburg: University of the Witwatersrand.

Obeng-Odoom, F. (2016). 'Understanding land reform in Ghana: A critical postcolonial institutional approach.' *Review of Radical Political Economics* 48(4), 661–80.

Ogu, V. I., and Ogbuozobe, J. E. (2001). 'Housing policy in Nigeria: Towards enablement of private housing development.' *Habitat International* 25(4), 473–92.

Olayiwola, L. M., Adeleye, O., and Ogunshakin, L. (2005). 'Public housing delivery in Nigeria: Problems and challenges.' Paper delivered to the IAHS World Congress on Housing, Pretoria, South Africa.

Oldfield, S., and Greyling, S. (2015). 'Waiting for the state: A politics of housing in South Africa.' *Environment and Planning A* 47(5), 1100–12.

Oqubay, A. (2015). *Made in Africa: Industrial Policy in Ethiopia*. Oxford: Oxford University Press.

Oqubay, A. (2019). 'Industrial policy and late industrialization in Ethiopia.' In F. Cheru, C. Cramer and A. Oqubay (eds), *The Oxford Handbook of the Ethiopian Economy*. Oxford: Oxford University Press, 605–29.

Oranje, M., and Merrifield, A. (2010). 'National spatial development planning in South Africa 1930–2010: An introductory comparative analysis.' *Town and Regional Planning* 56, 29–45.

Ortalo-Magné, F., and Prat, A. (2014). 'On the political economy of urban growth: Homeownership versus affordability.' *American Economic Journal: Microeconomics* 6(1), 154–81.

Oteng-Ababio, M., Melara Arguello, J. E., and Gabbay, O. (2013). 'Solid waste management in African cities: Sorting the facts from the fads in Accra, Ghana.' *Habitat International* 39, 96–104.

Pankhurst, R. (1961). 'Menelik and the foundation of Addis Ababa.' *Journal of African History* 2(1), 103–17.

Parnell, S. (1992). 'State intervention in housing provision in the 1980s.' In D. Smith (ed.), *The Apartheid City and Beyond: Urbanization and Social Change in South Africa*. London: Routledge, 53–65.

Parnell, S., and Mabin, A. (1995). 'Rethinking urban South Africa.' *Journal of Southern African Studies* 21(1), 39–61.

Peberdy, S. (2017). 'Uneven development: Core and periphery in Gauteng.' In S. Peberdy, P. Harrison, and Y. Dinath, *Core and Periphery: Uneven Spaces in the Gauteng City-Region*. Gauteng City Region Observatory Report 6. Johannesburg: GCRO.

Pellerin, C. L. (2018). *The Politics of Public Silence: Civil Society–State Relations under the EPRDF Regime*. Doctoral dissertation. London: London School of Economics and Political Science.

Philip, K. (2018). *Markets on the Margins: Mineworkers, Job Creation and Enterprise Development*. Woodbridge: James Currey.

Philip, K., Tsedu, M., and Zwane, M. (2014). *The Impacts of Social and Economic Inequality on Economic Development in South Africa*. New York: United Nations Development Programme.

Pieterse, M. (2019). 'Where is the periphery even? Capturing urban marginality in South African human rights law.' *Urban Studies* 56(6), 1182–97.

Planel, S., and Bridonneau, M. (2017). '(Re)making politics in a new urban Ethiopia: An empirical reading of the right to the city in Addis Ababa's condominiums.' *Journal of Eastern African Studies* 11(1), 24–45.

Pryor, R. J. (1968). 'Defining the rural–urban fringe.' *Social Forces* 47(2), 202–15.

Pugh, C. (1994). 'Housing policy development in developing countries: The World Bank and internationalization, 1972–1993.' *Cities* 11(3), 159–80.

Rahmato, D. (1994). *Land Tenure and Land Policy in Ethiopia after the Derg*. Addis Ababa: Land Tenure Project, Institute of Development Research, Addis Ababa University.

Rakodi, C. (2006). 'Social agency and state authority in land delivery processes in African cities: Compliance, conflict and cooperation.' *International Development Planning Review* 28(2), 263–85.

Rakodi, C., and Leduka, R. C. (2004). *Informal Land Delivery Processes and Access to Land for the Poor: A Comparative Study of Six African Cities*. Policy Brief 6. Birmingham: University of Birmingham.

Rasmussen, B., and Lund, C. (2017). 'Reconfiguring frontier spaces: The territorialization of resource control.' *World Development* 101, 388–99.

Ren, X. (2021). 'Suburbs and urban peripheries in a global perspective, city and community.' *City and Community* 20(1), 38–47.

Ribot, J. C., and Peluso, N. L. (2003). 'A theory of access.' *Rural Sociology* 68(2), 153–81.

Robbins, G. (2015). 'The Dube Trade Port, King Shaka International Airport mega-project: Exploring impacts in the context of multi-scalar governance processes.' *Habitat International* 45(3), 196–204.

Robinson, J. (2016). 'Thinking cities through elsewhere: Comparative tactics for a more global urban studies.' *Progress in Human Geography* 40(1), 3–29.

Robinson, J. (2022). *Comparative Urbanism: Tactics for Global Urban Studies*. Oxford: Wiley-Blackwell.

Rode, P., Terrefe, B., and Da Cruz, N. F. (2020). 'Cities and the governance of transport interfaces: Ethiopia's new rail systems.' *Transport Policy* 91, 76–94.

Rohe, W. M., Van Zandt, S., and McCarthy, G. (2013). 'The social benefits and costs of homeownership: A critical assessment of the research.' In R. Tighe and E. Mueller, *The Affordable Housing Reader*. Oxford: Routledge, 196–213.

Ross, F. (2010). *Raw Life, New Hope: Decency, Housing and Everyday Life in a Post-Apartheid Community*. Cape Town: UCT Press.

RSA (Republic of South Africa) (2011). *National Development Plan, South Africa*. Pretoria: National Planning Commission.

RSA (2022). *National Spatial Development Framework*. Pretoria: Department of Rural Development and Land Reform and Department of National Planning and Evaluation.

Sackeyfio, N. (2012). 'The politics of land and urban space in colonial Accra.' *History in Africa* 39, 293–329.

SACN (South African Cities Network) (2015). *Winterveld(t): Despite Being a Once Forgotten Folk with Existing Challenges … People Are Coming Back Home!* SACN CDS Programme, Hidden Urbanities. Research Report, Draft 2. Johannesburg: SACN.

SACN (2016). *Hidden Urbanities: South Africa's Displaced Settlements 30 Years after the Abolition of Influx Control.* Johannesburg: SACN.

SASSA (South African Social Security Agency) (2021). *Annual Report 2020/21.* Pretoria: SASSA. www.sassa.gov.za/statistical-reports/Documents/Annual%20Report%20-%202021.pdf (accessed 24 October 2023).

Sawyer, L. (2014). 'Piecemeal urbanisation at the peripheries of Lagos.' *African Studies* 73(2), 271–89.

Sawyer. L., Schmid, C., Streule, M., and Kallenberger, P. (2021). 'Bypass urbanism: Re-ordering center-periphery relations in Kolkata, Lagos, and Mexico City.' *Environment and Planning A* 53(4), 675–703.

Schaefer, F., and Oya, C. (2019). *Employment Patterns and Conditions in Construction and Manufacturing in Ethiopia: A Comparative Analysis of the Road Building and Light Manufacturing Sectors.* IDCEA Research Report. London: SOAS, University of London.

Scheba, A., and Turok, I. (2020). 'Informal rental housing in the South: Dynamic but neglected.' *Environment & Urbanization* 32(1), 109–32.

Schindler, S., and Kanai, J. M. (2021). 'Getting the territory right: Infrastructure-led development and the re-emergence of spatial planning strategies.' *Regional Studies* 55(1), 40–51.

Schmid, C., Karaman, O., Hanakata, N. C., Kallenberger, P., Kockelkorn, A., Sawyer, L., Streule, M., and Wong, K. P. (2018). 'Towards a new vocabulary of urbanisation processes: A comparative approach.' *Urban Studies* 55(1), 19–52.

Schnore, L. F. (1957). 'Satellites and suburbs.' *Social Forces* 36(2), 121–7.

Sen, A. (1981). *Poverty and Famines: An Essay on Entitlement and Deprivation.* Oxford: Clarendon Press.

Shatkin, G. (2016). 'The real estate turn in policy and planning: Land monetization and the political economy of peri-urbanization in Asia.' *Cities* 53, 141–9.

Shiferaw, A. (2017). 'Productive capacity and economic growth in Ethiopia.' CDP Background Paper 34. New York: Committee for Development Policy, United Nations Department of Economic and Social Affairs.

Shiferaw, D. (1998). 'Self-initiated transformations of public-provided dwellings in Addis Ababa, Ethiopia.' *Cities* 15(6), 437–48.

Silver, J. (2014). 'Incremental infrastructures: Material improvisation and social collaboration across post-colonial Accra.' *Urban Geography* 35(6), 788–804.

Sim, V., Oelfose, C., and Scott, D. (2016). 'Urban edge challenges in eThekwini Municipality.' *South African Geographical Journal* 98(1), 37–60.

Sim, V., Sutherland, C., Buthelezi, S., and Khumalo, D. (2018). 'Possibilities for a hybrid approach to planning and governance at the interface of the administrative and traditional authority systems in Durban.' *Urban Forum* 29(3), 351–68.

Simon, D. (2004). 'The changing urban-rural interface of African cities: Definitional issues and an application to Kumasi, Ghana.' *Environment & Urbanization* 16(2), 235–48.

Simon, D. (2020). 'Peri-urbanization.' In *The Palgrave Encyclopedia of Urban and Regional Futures*. Cham: Palgrave Macmillan, 1–5.

Simone, A. (2004). 'The invisible: Winterveld, South Africa.' In *For the City yet to Come: Changing African Life in Four Cities*. Durham, NC: Duke University Press, 63–91.

Simone, A. (2011). 'The urbanity of movement: Dynamic frontiers in contemporary Africa.' *Journal of Education and Planning Research* 31(4), 379–91.

SLB Consulting (n.d.). *Company Profile: Consulting Engineers, Project Managers and Implementing Agents.* https://web.archive.org/web/20190801220357/http://stabiroad.com/UserFiles/4%20Documents/1%20Catalogs/Cat%208%20SLB%20Consulting/Corporateprofile2015.pdf (accessed 24 October 2023).

Smith, D. (ed.) (1992). *Apartheid City and Beyond: Urbanization and Social Change in South Africa*. London: Routledge.

Statista (2022). 'Population that received social grants, relief assistance or social relief in South Africa in 2019, by province.' www.statista.com/statistics/1116081/population-receiving-social-grants-in-south-africa-by-province/ (accessed 24 October 2024).

Statistics South Africa (StatsSA) (2021). *Selected Building Statistics of the Private Sector as Reported by Local Government Institutions, 2021*. Statistical Release P5041.3. www.statssa.gov.za/?page_id=1854&PPN=P5041.3&SCH=73148 (accessed 24 October 2023).

StatsSA (2023). *Quarterly Labour Force Survey Quarter 1, 2023*. Statistical Release P0211. www.statssa.gov.za/publications/P0211/P02111stQuarter2023.pdf (accessed 5 March 2024).

Stavrou, S., and Crouch, A. (1989). 'Molweni: Violence on the periphery.' *Indicator SA* 6(3), 46–50.

Steyn, L. (2012). 'Stores score on pension payday.' *Mail and Guardian*, 3 February. https://mg.co.za/article/2012-02-03-stores-score-on-pension-payday/ (accessed 24 October 2023).

Stone, C. (1989). *Regime Politics: Governing Atlanta 1946–1988*. Lawrence, KS: University Press of Kansas.

Straughan, E., Bissell, D., and Gorman-Murray, A. (2020). 'The politics of stuckness: Waiting lives in mobile worlds.' *Environment and Planning C: Politics and Space* 38, 636–55.

Stren, R. E. (1990). 'Urban housing in Africa: The changing role of government policy.' In P. Amis and P. C. Lloyd (eds), *Housing Africa's Urban Poor*. Manchester: Manchester University Press, 35–54.

Bibliography 335

Sutherland, C., and Buthelezi, S. (2013). 'Settlement case 2: Ocean Drive in an informal settlement.' In E. Braathen (coordinator), *Addressing Sub-Standard Settlements WP3 Settlement Fieldwork Report*, 75–80. www.chance2sustain.eu/fileadmin/Website/Dokumente/Dokumente/Publications/pub_2013/C2S_FR_No02_WP3__Addressing_Sub-Standard_Settlements.pdf (accessed 19 January 2016).

Swilling, M., Bhorat, H., Buthelezi, M., Chipkin, I., Duma, S., Mondi, M., Peter, C., Qobo, M., and Friedenstein, H. (2017). *Betrayal of Promise: How South Africa Is Being Stolen*. State Capacity Research Project. Stellenbosch: Centre for Complex Systems in Transition.

Terrefe, B. (2020). 'Urban layers of political rupture: The "new" politics of Addis Ababa's megaprojects.' *Journal of Eastern African Studies* 14, 375–95.

Tesfaye, A. (2007). 'Problems and prospects of housing development in Ethiopia.' *Property Management* 25(1), 27–53.

Tiruneh, A. (1993). *The Ethiopian Revolution 1974–1987: A Transformation from an Aristocratic to a Totalitarian Autocracy*. Cambridge: Cambridge University Press.

Todes, A. (1997). *Restructuring, Migration and Regional Policy in South Africa: The Case of Newcastle*. PhD thesis. Durban: University of Natal.

Todes, A. (2000). 'Reintegrating the apartheid city? Urban policy and urban restructuring in Durban.' In S. Watson and G. Bridges (eds), *A Companion to the City*. London: Blackwell, 617–30.

Todes, A. (2003). 'Housing, integrated urban development and the compact city debate.' In P. Harrison, M. Huchzermeyer and M. Mayekiso (eds), *Confronting Fragmentation: Housing and Urban Development in a Democratising Society*. Cape Town: University of Cape Town Press, 109–21.

Todes, A. (2012). 'New forms of spatial planning? Linking spatial planning and infrastructure.' *Journal of Planning Education and Research* 32(4), 400–14.

Todes, A. (2014a). 'New African suburbanisation? Exploring the growth of the northern corridor of eThekwini/KwaDukuza.' *African Studies* 73(2), 245–70.

Todes, A. (2014b). 'The impact of policy and strategic spatial planning.' In P. Harrison, G. Gotz, A. Todes and C. Wray (eds), *Changing Space, Changing City: Johannesburg after Apartheid*. Johannesburg: Wits University Press, 83–100.

Todes, A. (2017). 'Shaping peripheral growth: Strategic spatial planning in a South African city-region.' *Habitat International* 67, 129–36.

Todes, A., and Houghton, J. (2021). 'Economies and employment in growing and declining urban peripheries in South Africa.' *Local Economy* 36(5), 391–410.

Todes, A., and Turok, I. (2018). 'Spatial inequalities and policies in South Africa: Place-based or people-centred?' *Progress in Planning* 123, 1–31.

Township Realtors Land Developers (n.d.). *History of Protea Glen.* http://townshiprealtors.com/about-us/history-of-protea-glen/ (accessed 1 June 2019).

TRAC (Transvaal Rural Housing Action Committee) (1985). Newsletter 9, September. Ekangala, Johannesburg: Black Sash.

Truneh, F. M. (2013). *Institutional Interfaces and Actors' Behavior in Transitional Real Estate Markets of Addis Ababa.* PhD thesis. Rotterdam: Erasmus University Rotterdam.

Turok, I. (2015). 'What will housing megaprojects do to our cities?' Econ 3x3, 10 November. www.econ3x3.org/article/what-will-housing-megaprojects-do-our-cities (accessed 24 October 2023).

Ubink, J. (2008). *In the Land of the Chiefs: Customary Law, Land Conflicts, and the Role of the State in Peri-Urban Ghana.* PhD thesis. Leiden: Leiden University.

UDIDI (Environmental Planning and Development Consultants) (2012). *Final Draft Comprehensive Report: Molweni Nodal Functional Area Plan.* eThekwini: eThekwini Municipality.

UN-Habitat (United Nations Human Settlements Programme) (2009). *Global Report on Human Settlements: Planning Sustainable Cities.* London: Earthscan.

UN-Habitat (2010). *The Ethiopia Case of Condominium Housing: The Integrated Housing Development Programme.* Nairobi: UN-Habitat.

UN-Habitat (2011). *Condominium Housing in Ethiopia: The Integrated Housing Development Programme.* Nairobi: UN-Habitat.

UN-Habitat (2016). *Urbanization and Development: Emerging Futures. World Cities Report 2016.* Nairobi: UN-Habitat.

UN-Habitat (2017). *The State of Addis Ababa 2017: The Addis Ababa We Want*, at UN-Habitat. Nairobi: UN-Habitat. https://unhabitat.org/the-state-of-addis-ababa-2017-the-addis-ababa-we-want (accessed 3 February 2019).

Urban Dynamics (n.d.a). 'Lufhereng (Doornkoop) inclusionary housing project.' www.urbandynamics.co.za/news/39-lufhereng-doornkopinclusionary-housing-project.html (accessed 24 October 2023).

Urban Dynamics (n.d.b). 'Lufhereng (Doornkop).' www.urbandynamics.co.za/projects/31-programme-management/94-lufhereng-doornkop.html (accessed 24 October 2023).

Urban Econ Development Economists (2014). *Updated Lufhereng Economic Development Plan.* Unpublished report produced for the Lufhereng Development Company.

Urban Landmark (2010). 'Incrementally securing tenure: An approach for informal settlement upgrading in South Africa.' www.urbanlandmark.org.za/research/x31.php (accessed 12 December 2017).

Van Gylswyk, A. (1981). *Report on Winterveld as at 1981–02–20.* Pretoria: Black Sash. www2.lib.uct.ac.za/blacksash/pdfs/cnf19810314.026.001.000.pdf (accessed 24 October 2023).

Van Noorloos, F., and Kloosterboer, M. (2018). 'Africa's new cities: The contested future of urbanization.' *Urban Studies* 55(6), 1223–41.

Vaughan, S., and Gebremichael, M. (2011). *Rethinking Business and Politics in Ethiopia*. Africa Power and Politics Research Report 2. London: UK Aid.
Visagie, J., and Turok, I. (2020). 'The economic landscape of South African cities: Diversity across space, sector and skills.' SA Cities Network, Urban Economies Papers, 5–26.
Watson, V. (2016). 'Shifting approaches to planning theory: Global North and South.' *Urban Planning* 1(4), 32–41.
Wehrmann, B. (2008). *Land Conflicts: A Practical Guide to Dealing with Land Disputes*. Eschborn: Deutsche Gesellschaft für Internationale Zusammenarbeit.
Weldegebriel, A., Assefa, E., Janusz, K., Tekalign, M., and Van Rompaey, A. (2021). 'Spatial analysis of intra-urban land use dynamics in sub-saharan Africa: The case of Addis Ababa (Ethiopia).' *Urban Science* 5(3), 57.
Weldeghebrael, E. H. (2022). 'The framing of inner-city slum redevelopment by an aspiring developmental state: The case of Addis Ababa, Ethiopia.' *Cities* 125, 102807.
William, S. (2013). *Beyond Rights: Developing a Conceptual Framework for Understanding Access to Coastal Resources at Ebenhaeser and Covie, Western Cape, South Africa*. PhD thesis. Cape Town: University of Cape Town.
Williams, G., Charlton, S., Coelho, K., Mahadevia, D., and Meth, P. (2022). '(Im)mobility at the margins: Low-income households' experiences of peri-urbanisation in India and South Africa.' *Housing Studies* 37(6), 910–31.
Woldu, T., Abebe, G., Lamoot, I., and Minten, B. (2013). 'Urban food retail in Africa: The case of Addis Ababa, Ethiopia.' Ethiopia Strategy Support Programme II Working Paper 50.
Work in Progress (1979). 'Winterveld.' 10 November. www.sahistory.org.za/sites/default/files/archive-files3/WpNov79.1608.2036.000.010.Nov1979.pdf (accessed 24 October 2023).
World Bank (2015a). *Ethiopia's Great Run: The Growth Acceleration and How to Pace It*. Washington, DC: World Bank.
World Bank (2015b). *Rising through Cities in Ghana: Urbanization Review-Overview Report*. Washington, DC: World Bank.
World Bank (2021). *Towards an Inclusive and Empowered Ethiopia: Improving Social Safety Nets to Reduce Urban Poverty*. Washington, DC: World Bank. www.worldbank.org/en/results/2021/01/14/towards-an-inclusive-and-empowered-ethiopia-improving-social-safety-nets-to-reduce-urban-poverty (accessed 25 November 2022).
Wu, F., and Keil, R. (2022). 'Beyond suburban stereotypes: Urban peripheries in the twenty-first century.' In R. Keil and F. Wu (eds), *After Suburbia: Urbanization in the Twenty-First Century*. Toronto: Toronto University Press, 3–36.
Xu, L. (2019). 'Factory, family, and industrial frontier: A socioeconomic study of Chinese clothing firms in Newcastle, South Africa.' *Economic History of Developing Regions* 34(3), 300–18.

Yusuf, B., Tefera, S., and Zerihun, A. (2009). *Land Lease Policy in Addis Ababa*. Addis Ababa: Chamber of Commerce and Sectoral Association.

Zack, T., and Charlton, S. (2003). *A Somewhat Better Life: Beneficiaries Perceptions of the Government's Housing Subsidy Scheme*. Johannesburg: Housing Finance Resource Programme.

Záhořík, J. (2017). 'Reconsidering Ethiopia's ethnic politics in the light of the Addis Ababa Master Plan and anti-governmental protests.' *Journal of the Middle East and Africa* 8(3), 257–72.

Zewde, B. (1991). *A History of Modern Ethiopia 1855–1991*. Oxford: James Currey.

Zewde, B. (2005). 'The city centre: A shifting concept in the history of Addis Ababa.' In A. Simone and A. Abouhani (eds), *Urban Africa: Changing Contours of Survival in the City*. London: Bloomsbury, 122–3.

Zewdie, M., Worku, H., and Bantider, A. (2018). 'Temporal dynamics of the driving factors of urban landscape change of Addis Ababa during the past three decades.' *Environmental Management* 61, 132–46.

Zhang, Y. F., Alemayehu, A., Walley, S. C., Wood, D. T., Rajashekar, A. V., Venkatanarayan, A., and ICF International Ltd. (2019). *Unlocking Ethiopia's Urban Land and Housing Markets: Synthesis Report*. Washington, DC: World Bank Group. https://documents.worldbank.org/en/publication/documents-reports/documentdetail/549221572382742218/unlocking-ethiopias-urban-land-and-housing-markets-synthesis-report (accessed 24 October 2023).

Index

Page numbers in *italics* refer to tables and photographs.
The number after the *n* is the footnote number, e.g. 111n2 means page 111 footnote 2.
The term *passim* means scattered references across a number of pages e.g. 39–46 *passim*

ablution blocks 233, *234*, 244
Abokobi
   Accra settlement 14
   landguard selling land 198
   land ownership 193
   price of land *195*
   upgrade of 196
access theory 191, 205
Accra
   case studies 13, 14
   customary landowner authority 38
   drivers of transition 192–3
   land delivery 197–201
   landguards 29
   land management 188–91
   land transition practices 195–201
   peri-urban communities 187–8
   peri-urban land market 188–91, 195–7
   price modalities 195–7
   self-building of houses 34
   see also Ghana
Achiaman
   Accra settlement 14
   land ownership 193
   low cost land 196
   price of land *195*

Addis Ababa
   access to work 103–4
   case studies 15–16, 20–1
   condominium committee structures 37
   condominium resales 29–30
   condominiums on city edge 31–2
   development 77–80
   financing condominiums 31
   housing crisis and affordability 139–44
   housing development and administrative agency 116–17
   housing lived experience 145–51
   housing policy evolution 134–9
   housing policy, programmes and lived experience 133–4
   housing transformation 139
   housing units produced 136
   infrastructure and job creation 61–2
   Integrated Housing Development Programme (IHDP) 137–8
   investment in condominiums 32–3

Addis Ababa (*continued*)
  investment in urban development 77–80
  key governance structures 116–18
  land nationalisation 79
  life in condos 145–9
  life outside condos 149–51
  multiple modes of livelihood 107
  woreda administrations and sub-cities 116, 117
  see also Ethiopia
Addis Ababa City Administration (AACA) 116, 141
Addis Ababa–Djibouti railway 78
Addis Ababa Grand Housing Programme (AAGHP) 140
Addis Ababa Integrated Master Plan 62
Addis Ababa University Technology Campus 81
Addis–Adama Expressway 239
Addis Light Rail 238–9
African National Congress (ANC) 53, 90–1, 119–20, 276
age 253, 261–4
Agricultural Development-Led Industrialisation (ADLI) 77
Ahmed, Abiy 62
Akaki Kaliti Sub-City 117–18
alcohol
  abuse by youth 242, 262
  involvement in crime 273
  related to youth unemployment 275
Alexandra 53
ANC *see* African National Congress
apartheid
  black townships 47
  displaced urbanisation 48
  homeownership 171–4
  housing 155–6, 171–4
  racial segregation 47
  spatial segregation 46, 56, 63
  white areas 55
  see also post-apartheid

ATMs 246
auto-constructed periphery
  see logics
auto-constructed settlements 35, 73, 75
automobile use 217–21

backyard housing 104, 105, 152, 167, 175, 179
Bantustans 71, 157
  see also homelands
'Big Four' supermarket chains (South Africa) 282
borders
  and boundaries 124–8
  ownership protests and 255
  vanguard practices and 32
boredom
  and crime 253–5
  in the peripheries 270–3
  social differences and crime 279
boundaries
  access to land 119
  administrative 114, 116
  borders and 124–8
  metropolitan areas 11
  and profit opportunities 28
Built Environment Programme Plans (BEPPs) 49
bundles of power 191, 198
buses *see* transport
bus shelters 36, 227, 240, *241*

Canelands
  ablution blocks 233, *234*
  employment 256
  housing history 181–3
  service infrastructure 34
capital accumulation 113, 114, 115
case study summaries *14–16*
Checkers 15, 18
child support grant 111n2
  see also disability grant, grants; social grants; war veteran grant

cities
  compaction and integration 47
  development of new 9
  expansion 113
  smart new 50, 54
City Centres and Corridors Development Corporation 60
City of Johannesburg *see* Johannesburg
City of Tshwane *see* Tshwane
city peripheries 7–8
class
  geographic segregation, Addis Ababa 264
  income differences 88
  infrastructural provision 279
  see also middle class
class-based inequality 255
collaborative comparisons 25
Commercial Bank of Ethiopia (CBE) 136
comparisons *see* generative comparisons; genetic comparisons
Concerned Residents of the Ekangala group 121
Condominium House Owners' Association 116–17, 129
condominiums *see* Addis Ababa; Tulu Dimtu
Coniston 34, 181–3, 233, *234*
Cooperativa Muratori Cementisti (CMC) 57
Cooperative Housing Programme 134, 135, 137
cooperative housing settlement 95–6
cooperatives 82, 105, 136, 283–4, 296
'Corridors' project 53
cost
  condominium housing 141–2, 146, 265
  electricity and water connections 179
  food 283
  Hammonds Farm development 177–8
  increase in service 126
  infrastructure, Durban 54–5
  of living 146, 151, 162, 184, 266
  loan repayments 142
  low-cost residential units 74
  mortgage required 264
  rent 146, 150, 151, 177, 190, 202, 259
  services 265
  state housing 265
  see also land; transport
Country Club Developers' (CCD) gated community 83
Crestholme 15, 18, 20
crime
  and absence of transport 216
  access to communal taps 247
  African urban peripheries 273–8
  boredom and 253–5
  elderly persons 263
  fear of 274
  narratives of 273–5
  processes shaping 275–6
  Protea Glen 173
  and security 276–8
  social differences, boredom and 279
  social differentiation, boredom and 252–5
  South African cities 217
  street lights to reduce 240
  Winterveld settlement 38, 162
  Yeka Abado 129
customary institutions 188–9
customary land
  Accra, Ghana 188–91, 193
  commodification of 5
  delivery channels and legitimacy *203*
  residential estates on 7
Customary Land Secretariate (CLS) 190
customary tenure 186–7

DA *see* Democratic Alliance
Dar es Salaam 192–3
Dark City 15, 18, 244, 249–50
data collection methods 21–3
deindustrialisation 39, 301
Democratic Alliance (DA) 52, 53, 90–1, 119–20
Department of Cooperative Housing 136
Derg regime 57, 58, 76, 78, 135
developers *see* private developers
disabled persons 148, 230–1, 263
disability grant 295
  see also child grant; grants; social grant; war veteran grant
displaced urbanisation 18, 47, 48
displaced urbanisation study 50
drugs
  abuse by youth 242, 262
  involvement in crime 273, 275, 277, 279
  reason to move away 168–9, 173
  Wunga 262
  youth unemployment 275
Dube TradePort (DTP) 238
Durban 54–6, 69, 157, 181, 291–5

Eastern Industrial Zone 80
economic decentralisation 50
economic development
  eThekwini municipality 29, 54
  eThekwini north 69
  homeownership 144
  Lufhereng 75–6
  Revitalisation of Industrial Parks Programme 50
  satellite cities 87
  Tshwane east 52
economic growth 42, 66, 69, 76, 77, 123, 138
Ekandustria
  access to work 101
  decline 71–3
  establishment 70
  industrial decentralisation point 18, 52
  low-paid work 100
  management 71
Ekangala
  apartheid development 236
  'big men' controlling 29
  deindustrialisation impact 39
  employment 100, 102
  establishment and development 70–3
  forced relocation 236
  Gauteng settlement 15, 18
  housing history 164–9
  incorporation into Tshwane municipality 106
  integration zone 52
  lack of businesses 271
  unemployment levels 97
  ward councillors 119
elderly persons 148, 230–1, 263
electricity
  access to 29, 34
  Canelands 234
  cost of 179, 265
  cuts in 148
  Ekangala 168, 229
  illegal use 131, 182, 233–4, 247, 260
  informal settlements 247
  investments in 38
  Kilinto and Bole Lemi 81
  Madibeng Hills 237
  Molweni 244
  prepaid meters 126, 294
  provision and maintenance 121
  public funding, Ethiopia 228
  Rethabiseng 168
  variable access 237
electronic realm 244–6
employment *see* jobs
EPRDF *see* Ethiopian People's Revolutionary Democratic Front
eThekwini
  case studies 15, *19*
  decline in municipality 69

government structures and
    peripheries 118–21
job access 90, 100
local business promotion 109
migrant entrepreneurs 105
private sector property
    investment 66–7
public–private partnership 123
ward councillors 119
eThekwini north 67–70
Ethiopia
    Abiy Ahmed regime 62
    after EPRDF period 59
    city regions study 2–3
    civil strife and disputes 81
    communist revolution 57
    Derg period 57–8, 76, 135
    economic policy under
        EPRDF 77
    EPRDF period 133–7 *passim*
    Haile Selassie period 56–7, 76
    imperial rule 76
    investment 76, 77
    Italian occupation 76, 78
    job creation 91
    see also Addis Ababa
Ethiopian People's Revolutionary
    Democratic Front (EPRDF)
    57–8, 75–6, 79, 133–7
    passim
ethnic federalism 56, 63, 255
ethnic homelands 47, 70
    see also homelands
ethnicity
    and apartheid 159
    and inequality 255
    race, religion and 255–9
    service and infrastructure
        based on 279
    unequal access based
        on 256
    see also race
ethnic tension 255, 256
ethno-nationalism 255
Expanded Public Works
    Programme (EPWP) 90

farmers
    categories of displaced 99
    displaced, Addis Ababa 35, 61,
        81, 98–9, 107, 260
    displaced, Tulu Dimtu 98
    displaced, Yeka Abado
        84–5, 98
    small-scale 105
farmland
    conversion to
        condominiums 107
    housing settlements on
        18, 20, 21
    rising price 151
    Tulu Dimtu area 81
    varied use of 27–8
food
    cost of 283
    and energy project, Ekangala 52
    government role in 284
    insecure households 91, 92
    insecurity 266
    locally produced 105
    market benefiting farmers 107
    outdoor markets 283
    programme, Ethiopia
        91–2
    retail, Ethiopia 284
    security 91
    structure of retail economy 283
    subsidised distribution 61
    supermarket prices 281–2
    wastage 247
forced relocation 18, 38, 156
foreign businesses 258
foreign migrants *see* migrants

GAMA *see* Greater Accra
    Metropolitan Area
Gauteng
    case studies 14–15, *17*
    government structures and
        peripheries 118–21
    job access 90
    social marginality 6
    spatial transformation 75

gender
  differentiation 252, 302
  employment 88, 108, 267
  inequality 268
  power and violence 12
  race, class and 253
  social differentiation and 266–8
  work dynamics 108
generative comparisons 22, 25
genetic comparisons 22
geographic peripherality 6, 7, 9, 18, 36, 124, 279
  see also peripherality
German Technical Cooperation (GTZ) 140, 141
Ghana
  city regions study 2, 3
  customary tenure 5
  land markets and (in)security 186–204
  landownership and state interventions 22–3
  state and traditional leader relations 5
  see also Accra
Global Suburbanisms project 7, 10
governance
  borders and boundaries 124–8
  changing 37
  hybrid 121–2
  key structures 115–24
  private 113, 115, 122
  and private sector investment 123–4
  speculative peripheries 28
  state–citizen relationships 128–31
  state involvement 113, 114
  suburban 113, 114
  theorising 112–15
  weak institutions 40
governance structures
  Addis Ababa 116–18
  Gauteng and eThekwini 118–21
grants
  for displaced farmers 99
  paid by Waterloo Superspar 295
  as source of income 111n2
  for urban structure development 49
  see also child support grant; disability grant; social grants; war veteran grant
Greater Accra Metropolitan Area (GAMA) 190, 192
growth see economic growth
Growth and Transformation Plan (GTP) 77

Hammonds Farm 18, 32, 102–3, 175–9, 267, 293
Hillcrest economic node 67
HIV/AIDS 'orphan' households 261
homelands 63, 154, 156–71
  see also Bantustans; ethnic homelands
homeownership 73, 143–6 passim, 155, 171–4, 259, 280, 287, 300, 302
housing
  community-based 135
  construction of cooperative 136–7
  cooperative system 136
  crisis, affordability and rationales 139–44
  Ekangala 164–9
  elderly and disabled 263
  government subsidised 134–5
  Hammonds Farm 175–9
  homelands and urban peripheries 156–7
  informal rental 135
  low-income 31, 47, 53, 67, 68, 87, 88, 137, 142, 227, 285–6
  low-middle-income 68
  Lufhereng 179–81
  middle-income 5, 16, 31, 35, 52, 83, 135–6, 177
  mixed-income 37, 60, 68, 73, 179

Molweni 169–71
Protea Glen 172–4
publicly owned, Addis Ababa 139
residential estates 7
South Africa early apartheid 155–6
South Africa early twentieth century 155
South Africa late apartheid 171–4
state-led programme 133–4
state-owned public 135
state-sponsored, Southern Africa 8
through lottery system 129, 142, 263, 265, 266
transformation, Addis Ababa 139
units produced, Ethiopia 136
Waterloo 175–9
Waterworks 181–3
Winterveld 157–64
see also informal housing; informal settlements; RDP housing; state housing
Housing Construction Corporation 136
housing deficits
Ethiopia 140–4
Greater Accra Metropolitan Area 190
hybrid governance 121–2

income
employment schemes 89–90
female-headed families 171
illegal land sales 29
location-related 34
loss through relocation 137
low-paying work 103
social differentiation and 264–6
income-generating activities 104–6
incubator infrastructure 228, 243, 250
see also infrastructure

incubator urbanism 228
industrial areas 67, 80, 96
Industrial Development Strategy 77
industrial parks 18, 21, 60, 80, 96, 239
Industrial Parks Development Corporation 81
inequality
apartheid and post-apartheid 66
ethnically determined 255
gender 268
new forms, Addis Ababa 152
property ownership 57
race and gender based 256
redressing 118
South African spatial policy 46
informal food retailers 281–2
informal housing 15, 20–1, 29, 139, 165, 234, 244, 267, 269
see also housing; RDP housing; state housing
informal settlements 233
Addis Ababa 79
auto-constructed logic 233
Canelands/Coniston 18, 34, 106, 233
densification 174–5
for displaced farmers 152
on land of traditional authorities 47
northern eThekweni 93–4
post-apartheid peripheries 181–3
poverty 265–6
proximity to manufacturing 101
service conditions 229, 247
Tulu Dimtu and Yeka Abado 149
see also housing; RDP housing; state housing
infrastructural citizenship 115, 228, 234, 250, 251
infrastructural realities 246–50
infrastructural transitions 36

infrastructure
  auto-construction logic 233
  big vs micro 238–46
  condominium developments 231
  delays in delivery 249, 250
  Dukem Industrial Park 239
  Ekangala 229
  governance 229–38
  inadequate 246–50
  key services and 243–4
  Lufhereng 229–30
  maintenance 70, 91, 228, 246, 248
  national funding programmes 48
  pavements 230–1
  planning, investment and governance 229–38
  poor access to 34
  resident perceptions 236–7
  smaller developments 239
  street lights, Tulu Dimtu 230
  uneven 246–50
  see also incubator infrastructure; macro-infrastructure; meso-infrastructure; micro-infrastructure
infrastructure development
  Addis Ababa 78
  Ekandustria 71–2
  eThekwini 68
  Ethiopia 77
  Lufhereng 73, 75
  Tulu Dimtu 80
  Yeka Abado 82–3
infrastructure investment
  facilitating new markets 107
  in industry 110
  in integration zones 49
  linked to jobs 87
  Plan for Accelerated and Sustained Development to End Poverty (PASDEP) 77
  South African cases 93
  Tulu Dimtu 80, 99

vanguard peripheries 296
Yeka Abado 234–5
infrastructure-led development 9
Ingonyama Trust 121
inherited periphery see logics
in-migrants see migrants
insecurity 109, 191, 270, 273, 275, 277, 278
Integrated Housing Development Programme (IHDP)
  condominium construction 59–60, 116
  housing crisis, affordability and rationales 139–44
  housing policy and programming 134, 137–8
  public investment 80
  vanguard investment 133
Integrated Rapid Transport Network 55
Integrated Urban Development Framework 49
integration zones 49, 51, 53
interest rates 136, 141, 142
international policy 40, 46
internet access 245
internet cafes 244, 245, 285, 288
intersectionality 252, 253
interviews see study methods
investment
  Addis Ababa condominiums 32
  generating power 28
  and governance of infrastructure 229–38
  Hammonds Farm 32
  infrastructure and housing 59
  pavements 223, 240
  private and state developers 27
  private sector and governance 123–4
  road and transport 36
  services and infrastructure 170
  speculation and 27
  by state 30, 31
  transport 225

Index

job creation
   Ethiopia 94–7
   inherited, transitioning and auto-constructed periphery 97–9
   programmes in urban peripheries 89–92
   recycling as means of 105
   South Africa 89–90, 92–4
   through construction 90, 93–6 *passim*
   unsustainable 93
   vanguard and speculative periphery 92–7
joblessness 109–10
jobs
   access challenges 99–103
   access to 101–4, 107–8, 110
   after construction, Addis Ababa
   age-related opportunities 263–4
   gender dynamics 108
   limited opportunities 256
   loss through relocation 267
   low-income people 88
   narrow and vulnerable opportunities 39
   refusal of 89
   unfair allocation 90–1
   see also livelihoods
Johannesburg 52–4, 66–7, 291–5

Kilinto Industrial Park 80–1
King Shaka airport 68, 93, 238, 239
Klipspruit water system 74
Koye Feche condominiums 81

land
   Accra vs eThekwini 193
   changes in use 35, 36
   collectively owned 188–9
   cost 151, 192, 195–7, 198
   development for profit 27–8
   growing demand, Accra 28, 201–2
   lower cost and availability 47

non-demarcated 202
permit system 58
price variations, Accra 195–6
subdivision 8
uneven power relations 191
Land Administration Programme 190
land delivery channels 197–201, *203*
   see also secondary land delivery channels
landguardism 34, 190–1, 193, 203
landguards 27, 29, 43, 187, 197, 198, 203–4
land-leasing system 58
land management 188–91, 309
land markets
   change and (in)security 186–8
   changes in peri-urban 191–2
   changing role, Accra 300
   methodology to examine 13
   Molweni 193
   ownership conflicts 190
   transformation, Accra 301
landownership
   customary 13
   EPRDF and 58
   Ghana 189, 197
   informal transactions 151
   multiple systems of 36
   protests of 2014 255–6
   and state interventions 22
   Winterveld 236–7
land reforms 57, 197
land sales advertising *200*
land transactions
   altering existing 187
   fraudulent 199
   peri-urban Accra 195–201
   state regulations 190
   and tenure (in)security 188
land transfers
   based on leasehold 189
   contested 186
   by multiple agencies 197–8

land transformation
  customary land 186–7
  outcomes of 188
  and tenure (in)securities 201–4
land transition practices 195–201
Lanseria 50, 52, 54
leasehold system 79, 189
Legetafo 15, 16, 20, 21, 28, 83, 232, 264
  Country Club Developers (CCD) 264
Lenasia 103, 182, 216, 267
Lesotho 258
lived experience
  comparative urban approach 12–23
  housing in Addis Ababa 145–51
  through case studies 13–21
  livelihoods 104–8, 109, 155
  see also jobs
Living the Peripheries project 13
logics
  auto-constructed periphery 33–5, 42, 97–9, 181, 233
  inherited periphery 38–40, 50
  speculative periphery 27–30, 92–7, 232
  transitioning periphery 35–8, 121–2, 187, 193
  vanguard periphery 30–3, 68, 92–7, 229, 231
'loosening state' 122
lower-middle-income persons 15, 16, 31, 287
Lufhereng
  boredom in 272
  Gauteng settlement 14
  housing designs 260
  housing history 179–81
  jobs 100
  location 53–4
  mixed-income project 16, 74
  relocated households 102–3
  speculative private property development 67

state housing planning 31
vanguard state-sponsored development 73

macro-infrastructure 226, 227
Madibeng Hills 15, 18, 121
market-vending (*gulit*) 107
Mayibuye Business Association 109
medical benefit access 101–2
Menelik, Emperor 78
meso-infrastructure 227, 239
methodologies 12–24
Metsweding municipality 51
Micro and Small Enterprise Strategy 92
micro-infrastructure 110, 238–46
  see also infrastructure; macro-infrastructure
middle class 5, 6, 8, 20, 35, 55, 57, 58, 78, 102, 167, 172, 221
middle-income see housing
migrants
  housing needs 302
  illegal 257
  in less regulated spaces 5, 123
  low wages 89
  undocumented 257
  see also refugees
migration 52, 124, 159, 165–6, 169, 255, 268, 276, 302, 307
minibus taxis see transport
mining industry 75
mobility 207, 208, 217, 224–5
  see also transport
Molweni
  elderly and RDP housing 249
  eThekwini settlement 15, 18
  housing history 169–71
  hybrid governance 121–2
  infrastructure investment 38
  job creation 98
  shopping developments 36
  traditional authorities and council relations 235

transitional periphery logic 235
unemployment levels 97
Mooikloof 52
mortgage housing 73, 74, 175, 179
mortgage repayments 142, 259, 265
Mozambique 187, 257, 258
Mpumulanga Economic Development Agency (MEGA) 72
municipal planning
   City of Johannesburg 52–4
   City of Tshwane 51–2
   eThekwini municipality 54–6

Naledi train station 208
National Development Plan 48–9
national funding programmes 48
national policies 50, 58, 63
national policy discourse 46
National Spatial Development Framework 48–9
National Spatial Development Perspective 48
National Treasury's City Support Programme 49, 50
NDPP *see* Neighbourhood Development Partnership Programme
negotiated payments 199
Neighbourhood Development Partnership Programme (NDPP) 48
Nigeria 187, 258
NIMBYism 27, 73

old-age pension 111n2
online realm 44, 244–6
Oromia region 56, 60–1, 107, 117
Oromia Special Zone Integrated Master Plan 32–3
OR Tambo airport 69
Oshiyie 14, 193, *195*, 196, 202
Oyibi 14, 193, *195*, 197, 202

party politics 119–21
peripherality 6, 122, 123, 276–8
   see also geographic peripherality
peri-urbanisation 5, 6, 7, 8, 10
peri-urban land market
   Accra 198, 202, 204
   changes in 191–2
   land management and 188–91
   non-interference of state, Ghana 197
peri-urban spaces 186–8
Phumekaya 121, 181–3
'piecemeal urbanisation' 8
'planetary urbanisation' concept 10
Plan for Accelerated and Sustained Development to End Poverty (PASDEP) 59, 77
play spaces 231, 232, 242, 248–9
plots 8, 27, 36, 58, 159, 170, 171
'plotting urbanism' 8, 10, 36, 113
police
   absence of stations 277–8
   community policing 117
   corruption 276
   criticism of 276
   Dinabakubo High School station 278
   and illegal migrants 257
   negative perceptions of 163–4
   presence in poor areas 181
polycentric compact city model 53
'popular urbanisation' 33
post-apartheid
   housing 174–81
   informal settlements 181–3
   peripheral experience 174–81
   planning 54
   policies 47–51
   state investment 67
   see also apartheid
post-apartheid Presidential Project 236–7

poverty
  access to infrastructure and services 34
  alleviation 50, 52, 288
  boredom, unemployment and 272, 279
  crime rate, Winterveld 38
  Gauteng cities 6
  geographic peripherality 6
  HIV/AIDs 'orphan' households 261
  social grants 88
  Tulu Dimtu 39–40
  unemployment, Molweni 171
price modalities, changing 195–7
Prime Investment Corridor 55
private authoritarianism 113
private developers 9, 27, 49, 63
private sector
  and governance 123–4
  job creation 87–8, 152
  online development 244–6
  preferential work allocation 263
  property firms in Protea Glen 232
  railway extension plans 209
  relationship with state 85
  role of 41
  vanguard interventions 306
private sector development 16, 68, 76
private sector investment 73, 80, 94, 123–4, 296
profit generation 27, 29
Protea Glen
  development and change 73–5
  Gauteng settlement 14–15
  housing history 172–4
  lower- to middle-income 16
  private sector development 16, 76
  property firms 232
  retail complexes 173
  shopping malls 16, 74, 173, 239
protests
  Addis Ababa 126

anti-government (2014) 56, 255
election process, Addis Ababa 59
infrastructure 250
municipal disconnection 234
Oromia 61, 83–4
services 165
sexual violence 275
slow delivery 131
public realm 44, 114, 226–39, 239–43
public spaces 227, 248, 294
public transport see transport
public works programmes 41, 91
public works schemes 89, 90, 98, 109, 110

qualitative data 23
quantitative data 23

race
  axis of differentiation 252
  and cultural differences 156
  ethnicity and religion 255–9
  intersection of gender, class and 253
  see also ethnicity
racial conflict 255
racial discrimination 256
racial inequality 255
racial segregation 47, 63
racism 256, 258
RDP housing 18, 47, 48, 230, 249
  see also housing, informal settlements; state housing
RDP (Reconstruction and Development Programme) 47, 86n1, 102–3, 130, 185n3, 229
Rea Vaya bus transport 74, 173, 208, 239
refugees 258, 277
  see also migrants
relationality 24, 252, 254–5, 272
relational spaces 24
relative geographic peripherality 18

religion
 and land, Abokobi 193
 landownership and 13
 race, ethnicity and 255–9
 relations and affiliations 145
 sites for practicing 257
rent
 changing differentials 307
 cost of 151, 190, 204
 freezing of 57
 permit system 58
 Tulu Dimtu 96, 146
rentier economy 78
retail
 Addis Ababa condominiums 31, 37, 286–8
 auto-constructed periphery 34
 complexes, Protea Glen 173
 eThekwini, Johannesburg and Tshwane 66–7
 South Africa and Ethiopia 281–4
 South African housing developments 284–6
 state-led housing developments 44
 supermarkets and consumption 280–8
 transitional periphery 35, 36
 vanguard developments 45
 welfare services linked to 281
Rethabiseng 15, 18
Revitalisation of Industrial Parks Programme 50, 52
Revolving Youth Fund 92
roads
 and automobile use 217–21
 community-driven construction 220
 construction of new 218–19
 improvement, Molweni 241
 investment in 36
 lack of, Addis Ababa 217–18
 poor quality 219–20
Ropack real estate 232
rural zone 55
Rwanda 187

sanitation 12, 29, 80, 93, 170, 174, 227, 229, 243, 247, 300
satellite cities 65, 87, 110
school access 32, 159, 210, 216, 261–2
school transport 210, 213, 215, 262
 see also transport
secondary land delivery channels 197, 198, 199, 202
 see also land delivery channels
Selassie, Haile 56, 76, 78
services
 access to 24
 infrastructure and 243–4
 levels, Lufhereng 232
 location of 249
 maintenance 231
 national funding programmes 48
 resident perceptions 236–7
sexual violence 268, 274, 275
shopping centres see shopping malls
shopping malls
 Crestholme 20
 Molweni and Waterloo 36
 Protea Glen 16, 74, 173, 239
 retail development 282
 see also retail; supermarkets
social differentiation
 African urban peripheries 268–70
 and age 261–4
 boredom and crime 253–5, 279
 and gender 266–8
 and income 264–6
 race, ethnicity and religion 255–9
 and tenancy 259–61
social grants 66, 88, 89, 109, 293, 294, 295
 see also child support grant; disability grant; grants; war veteran grant

South Africa
  City of Johannesburg 52–4
  City of Tshwane 51–2
  economic growth post-apartheid 66–7
  eThekwini municipality 54–6
  governing peripheral spaces 122–3
  income-generating activities 104–106
  middle- and upper-income areas 88
  municipalities 118–119
  party politics 119–121
  state–citizen relationships 130–131
  study of city regions 2–3
  urban compaction policies 46, 47, 49, 50, 51
  urban peripheries 118–119
  see also under housing
South African National Civics Organisation (SANCO) 120
Soweto 53–54, 73, 74, 172, 173, 182, 284
Spar 292, 294, 295
spatial marginalisation 39
Spatial Planning and Land Use Management Act, 2013 49
spaza shops 105
special economic zones (SEZ) 50, 68
Special Presidential Lead Projects 48
speculation 27–30 passim, 106, 114, 137, 187, 304, 306
speculative periphery see under logics
'speculative urbanism' 27
state
  control in urban peripheries 9
  and customary institutions 188–189
  intervention 22–23
  land control, Ghana 197
  and traditional leaders 5

state agendas 11
state–citizen relationships 128–131
state governance 113
state housing 12, 31, 37, 259, 260, 262, 264,
  see also housing; informal settlements
state investment 2, 31
state policies 50
state spatial visions 46
street lights 163, 217, 229, 230, 240, 244, 268, 274, 278
'strongmen' 35, 40, 123
study methods
  diaries 21, 22
  fieldwork, Ghana 193
  interviews 21–22, 193
  observations 21, 193
  qualitative approach 193
  surveys 22
sub-cities 116, 126
sub-Saharan Africa (SSA) 114, 186–188
suburb 8, 11, 113, 173
suburban space transformation 7
suburban zone 55
supermarkets
  in low-density areas 105
  retail and consumption 280–288
  South Africa and Ethiopia 44
  see also retail; shopping malls
surveys see under study methods

Taiwanese firms 71
taxi ranks 209, 240
taxis see under transport
tenancy 259–261
tenancy security 260
tenure
  customary forms of 5
  land transactions and 188
  and legal rules 115
  'new' African customary 186–7
  and ownership patterns 121
tenure (in)securities 201–4

tenure security 189, 197, 199, 201–4
tenure uncertainties 201
territorial dimensions 6
Tongaat-Hulett 54, 67–8, 69, 123
Township Realtors 73, 172
townships 47–51 *passim*, 53, 104, 122, 171–2
traditional authorities
   development on land of 63
   eThekwini municipality 38
   houses built in agreement with 55
   land alongside post-apartheid structures 121
   townships on land of 47
traffic 218, 221–2, 225, 291
traffic lights 223, 242
traffic wardens 242
transformation zone 53
transformative state 122–3
transitional dimensions 6
transitioning periphery *see* logics
transitions 36, 37, 43, 192, 205, 253
transit-oriented development 51
transport
   accessibility and choice of 214–16
   access to 24
   buses 208–10 *passim*, 211
   cost of 100, 101–4, 213, 214–16, 285, 293, 295
   lack of public 212, 213
   minibus taxis 208, 209, 211–12, 213
   mobility in peripheries 224–5
   planning in condominiums 210–11
   poor and expensive 210
   provision of public 207–17
   safety and security 216–17
   taxi/bus violence 209
   taxi costs 180, 208, 211–12
   see also mobility; school transport
transport infrastructure

Lufhereng 75
Tulu Dimtu 81
transport modes
   Ethiopia 210–14
   South Africa 207–10
Tshwane 18, 47, 51–2, 66–7, 106, 118, 120–1, 125, 159, 165, 181
Tulu Dimtu
   Addis Ababa settlement 16, 21
   Akaki Kaliti Sub-City integration 117–18
   Chinese investment 80
   condominium locations 31
   Cooperative Housing Programme 134
   dangerous tenants 269
   development 81–2
   financial scheme of IHDP condos 143–4
   housing 143–4
   investment and infrastructure 39–40
   joblessness 109–10
   job opportunities 95–6, 99
   location 80
   residents' views 290–1
   state–citizen relationships 128–9
   transport infrastructure investment 81
   transport, lack of 32

unauthorised businesses 286, 290, 291
unauthorised development 33
unemployment
   and drug abuse 277
   Ekangala 97, 111n2
   Ethiopia 88–9
   female-headed families 171
   informal settlements 93–4
   Molweni 97–8
   rates of 111n3
   South Africa 66, 88–9
   Winterveld 111n2
   and youth boredom 275–6

urban change 3, 12–13, 21, 22, 25, 28, 29, 44, 240, 252, 267, 279, 299, 300
urban compaction 46, 51
urban compaction policies 46, 47, 49, 50
urban comparison 3, 13, 21–3, 206, 298–303
urban development 8, 28, 55, 115, 123, 133, 138, 220, 227, 228
urban farming 105
urban growth 6, 114, 126, 311
urban network approach 48, 49
urban policy experimentation 30–1
Urban Productive Safety Net and Jobs Project (UPSNJP) 92
Urban Productive Safety Net programme 91
Urban Renewal Programme (URP) 48
urban spatial policies 46, 64
urban zone 55

vanguard development
    disruption as feature of 230
    eThekwini north 68
    Lufhereng 73
    Protea Glen 74
    retail opportunities 45
    South Africa 296
    Tulu Dimtu 81
vanguard investment 30, 81, 92–3, 98
vanguard periphery *see* logics
vigilantism
    gangs 276
    and landguardism 190
    response to crime 276–7
violence
    in African urban peripheries 273–8
    narratives of 273–5
    processes shaping 275–6
    and security 276–8
volunteerism 90–1

walking 222–3
ward councillors 118–19
war veteran grant 295
    see also child support grant; disability grant; social grants; grants
water
    communal taps 247
    inadequate provision 247–8
    Madibeng Hills 237
    provision of 148, 170
    Ropack neighbourhood 232
Waterfall 67, 98, 219–20
Waterloo
    African township 68
    economic change 36
    housing estate transition 37
    housing history 175–9
    job opportunities 93
    sports facilities 231
    transformation 271
Waterloo Superspar 292, 293, 294, 295
Waterworks
    Gauteng settlement 15
    housing history 181–3
    rehousing of residents 34–5
    relocation to neighbouring municipality 16
    resettlement 260
'white only' urban settlements 18
wi-fi 74, 173, 232, 244–6
Winterveld
    'big men' controlling 29
    feeding schemes 266
    forced relocation 38, 236
    Gauteng settlement 15, 18
    housing history 157–64
    location 39
    prioritisation zone changes 52
    unemployment levels 97
woreda administrations 116, 128
work *see* jobs
working conditions 99, 101
work scheme programmes 90
Wunga drug 262

xenophobia 255, 258

Yeka Abado
  Addis Ababa settlement 15–16, 20
  condominiums 83
  financial scheme of IHDP condos 143–4
  housing 143–4
  investment 82–4
  job creation 96–7
  joblessness 109–10
  job opportunities 99, 108
  leisure facilities 271
  population increase 128
  residents' views 288–9
  retail space 287
  state–citizen relationships 128–9
  transport congestion 104

Zambia 187
Zimbabwe 124, 187, 257, 258

Printed in the USA
CPSIA information can be obtained
at www.ICGtesting.com
LVHW011827041124
795688LV00004B/390